KV-370-724

Microsoft Works 3.0
for

Timothy J. O'Leary
Linda I. O'Leary

7 8 9 0 BAN BAN 9 0 9 8 7 6

ISBN 0-07-049009-0

Library of Congress Catalog Card Number 94-75715

Information has been obtained by McGraw-Hill from sources believed to be reliable. However, because of the possibility of human or mechanical error by our sources, McGraw-Hill, or others, McGraw-Hill does not guarantee the accuracy, adequacy, or completeness of any information and is not responsible for any errors or omissions or the results obtained from use of such information.

CONTENTS

Introduction to the Works 3.0 for Windows Labs

The labs are designed to provide you with practical skills in using the Works 3.0 for Windows software program. Each lab requires about one hour to complete.

Works is an integrated software program. It contains the following tools:

- Word processor
- Spreadsheet with charting
- Database with reporting
- Electronic communications
- Microsoft Draw

The labs demonstrate the use of all of these tools. The labs describe not only the most important commands and concepts, but also explain why and under what circumstances you will use them. By presenting an ongoing case study—The Sports Company, which is based on input from actual sporting goods store managers—we show how Works is used in a real business setting.

Organization of the Labs

The Labs Are Organized in the Following Categories: Overview, Competencies, Case Study, Lab Activities, Key Terms, Command Summary, Lab Review, Glossary, and Functional Summary of Commands.

Overview   The overview appears at the beginning of each of the sections on the three main tools: word processor, spreadsheet, and database. It describes (1) what the tool can do for you, (2) what the tool is, (3) the generic terms that this and all similar programs use (for example, all word processing programs, regardless of brand name), and (4) the details of the case study to be presented in the series of labs using the tool.

Competencies   The competencies list the concepts and procedures you will learn in that particular lab.

Case Study   The case study introduces the specific case covered by the particular lab—the general problems that the software activities will help you solve.

Lab Activities   The lab activities consist of detailed, step-by-step directions for you to follow in order to solve the problems of the case. Display screens show how a command or procedure is supposed to look. The labs should be followed in the sequence in which they appear in the book, because each succeeding lab builds on those preceding it. In addition, screen displays and directions become less specific as you work through the labs. This feature allows you to think about what you have learned, avoids simple rote learning, and reinforces earlier concepts and commands, helping you to gain confidence.

Key Terms   Terms that appear in **boldface (dark)** type in the labs are listed at the end of each lab in the order in which they appear.

Command Summary   All commands that are introduced in the lab and the action they perform are listed at the end of each lab in the order they were introduced.

Lab Review   Each lab concludes with a series of problems designed to reinforce concepts and commands learned in the lab. The review material may include matching and fill-in questions that do not require the use of the computer. Hands-on practice exercises are also included that require the use of a microcomputer. The practice exercises are arranged in order from easy, step-by-step problems to more difficult and less-directed problems.

Glossary of Key Terms   The glossary, which appears at the end of the book, defines all the key terms that appeared in boldface throughout the labs.

Summary of Commands   The book also concludes with a quick-reference source for selected commands for all tools. The commands are listed in the order they appear in the menu.

How the Case Study Explains Software

The Sports Company Ongoing Case Study Shows How to Solve Real-World Business Problems Using the Word Processor, Spreadsheet, Database, and Communications Tools.

The ongoing case study of The Sports Company, a chain of discount sporting goods stores located in large metropolitan areas throughout the United States, was written with the help of experience contributed by actual store managers. In our scenario The Sports Company has experienced recent growth and is trying to update its facility and management procedures using the newly purchased software program Works 3.0 for Windows.

As a recent college graduate, you have accepted your first job as a management trainee for The Sports Company. The program emphasis is on computer applications in the area of retail management and requires that you work in several areas of the company.

Section I: An Introduction to Works for Windows—Lab 1   This section first describes what the Works program is and the three main tools covered in the labs. It then shows you how to use the program to access the tools, how to use the menus and Help system, and how the tools are used together.

Section II: Word Processing—Labs 2–4   The word processing tool is used to show how a letter welcoming new Sports Company credit card customers is edited, formatted, saved, and printed. In addition you learn how to add footnotes and text and graphic art to a document.

Section III: Spreadsheet—Labs 5–8   Use of the spreadsheet tool is shown by depicting how the operating budget for one of the retail stores is created and modified. Sales data over five years is charted.

Section IV: Database—Labs 9–11   This section explains how to create, modify, update, sort, and query a database of employee information. It also includes procedures to create a professional report from the information in a database.

Section V: Integrating Works Tools—Lab 12   This lab demonstrates how the three tools can be used together. Specifically the student learns how to combine a word processing document with a spreadsheet and chart. It also demonstrates how to create a form letter using the WorksWizard, how to use the communications tool, and how to create a custom template.

Directions and Commands

Commands and Directions Are Expressed Through Certain Standard Conventions.

We have followed certain conventions in the labs for indicating keys, key combinations, commands, command sequences, and other directions.

Keys   Computer keys are expressed in abbreviated form, as follows:

Computer Keys	Display in Text
Alt (Alternate)	Alt
← or Bksp (Backspace)	←Backspace
Caps Lock (Capital Lock)	Caps Lock
Ctrl (Control)	Ctrl
Del or Delete	Delete
End	End
←Enter (Enter/Return)	←Enter
ESC (Escape)	Esc
Home	Home
Ins or Insert	Insert
Num Lock (Number Lock)	Num Lock
Pg Dn (Page Down)	Page Down or Pg Dn
Pg Up (Page Up)	Page Up or Pg Up
Prt Sc or Print Screen	Print Screen
Scroll Lock	Scroll Lock
⇧ Shift	⇧Shift
⇆ or Tab	Tab ⇆

Function Keys
F1 through F12   F1 through F12

Cursor Movement Keys
↑ (up)   ↑
↓ (down)   ↓
← (left)   ←
→ (right)   →

Key Combinations Many programs require that you use a combination of keys for a particular command (for example, the pair of keys Ctrl and F4). You should press them in the order in which they appear, from left to right, holding down the first key while pressing the second. In the labs, commands that are used in this manner are separated by a plus—for example, Ctrl + F4 .

Directions The principal directions in the labs are "Press," "Move to," "Type," "Select," "Choose," and "Click." These directions appear on a separate line beginning at the left margin, as follows:

■ *Press:* This means you should strike a key. Usually a command key will follow the direction (such as Delete for "Delete"). For example:

   Press: Delete

■ *Move to:* This means you should move the insertion point or highlight to the location indicated. For example, the direction to move to cell A5 would appear as:

   Move to: A5

■ *Type:* This means you should type or key in certain letters or numbers, just as you would on a typewriter keyboard. Whatever is to be typed will appear in bright blue type. For example:

   Type: **January**

■ *Choose and Select:* A sequence of selections from a menu or dialog box is often required to complete a command. In the beginning these commands are introduced separately. The command sequences will follow the word "Choose." If a letter of a command appears with an underline and in **boldface**, you can select that command by typing the letter. The command sequence that is to be typed will appear in bright blue.

   "Select" is used to indicate selecting or marking an item from a list of available options. "Select" does not begin an action as "Choose" does. Selecting may be part of a command sequence and will usually appear when procedures are initially introduced. For example:

   Choose: **F**ile
   Choose: **O**pen Existing File
   Select: MEMBERS.WKS
   Choose: OK

Later, as you become more familiar with the program, the commands are combined on a single line. Each command may be separated by a >. For example, the command to open a file will appear as:

   Choose: **F**ile>**O**pen Existing File>MEMBERS.WKS>OK

This means you should type the letter "F" to select File, type the letter "O" to select Open Existing File, select MEMBERS.WKS from a list of files, and then select OK to execute the command.

Additional directions may appear as bright blue text embedded within the main text. They appear like this only after the procedure to perform the directions is very familiar to the student. Follow the directions using the appropriate procedure.

Keyboard and Mouse Directions   In many cases the procedure to perform a command can be completed using either the mouse or the keyboard. The instructions are marked with the mouse or keyboard icon as shown below:

   Introduces a procedure to be followed if you are using a mouse.

   Introduces a procedure to be followed if you are using the keyboard.

Additionally, if a command procedure has a keyboard or mouse shortcut, the shortcut appears below the command sequence. The keyboard shortcut is preceded with the ➢ symbol, and the mouse shortcut is preceded with the word "Click." The keyboard and mouse procedures are separated with the word "*or*." For example:

Choose: Format>Bold
   ➢   Ctrl + B
or
Click: B

Marginal Notes   Throughout the labs notes will appear in the margins. These notes may be reminders of how to perform a procedure, clarifications or alternate methods, or brief side notes that expand upon a concept.

General System Requirements

The Works 3.0 for Windows Program Requires Certain Kinds of Equipment.

Hardware Requirements   To complete the labs, you must have the Works 3.0 for Windows software program installed on your computer system. Works requires the following system specifications:

- A personal computer using a 386SX or higher microprocessor.
- A minimum of 4 megabytes (MB) of memory.
- Microsoft Windows version 3.1 or later and Microsoft MS-DOS version 3.1 or later.
- One or more floppy disk drives at 3.5-inch high density (1.44 MB or 720K) or 5¼-inch low density (1.2 MB).
- A Video Graphics Array (VGA) display or better.
- A printer if you want to print.
- A Microsoft mouse or compatible mouse is recommended but optional.

The directions in the book assume the use of an IBM or IBM-compatible computer system with a hard-disk drive and at least one floppy-disk drive. If you are using a system that is networked, your instructor will provide you with alternate directions.

User Data Disk   The files needed to perform the labs and to complete the practice exercises are included on a separate disk that is supplied by your instructor.

To the Instructor:

The following program assumptions have been made:

- All figures in the manual reflect the use of a standard VGA display monitor and an Epson FX850 printer. If another monitor type is used, there may be more lines of text displayed in the windows than in the figures. This setting can be changed using Windows Setup. The selected printer also affects how text appears onscreen. If possible, select a printer whose display matches the figures in the manual.

- The Welcome Screen is not displayed when Works is first loaded.

- The standard preset toolbars are displayed automatically.

- The horizontal and vertical scroll bars are displayed automatically.

- The Helpful mouse pointers are on.

- The Cue Cards are off (default is on).

All other program settings are assumed to be the default Works settings. Any exceptions will be noted in the Before You Begin section at the end of each Overview.

In addition, these labs assume the student is already familiar with how to use DOS and Windows 3.0 or 3.1.

1 Exploring Works 3.0 for Windows

CASE STUDY

The Sports Company has just purchased the Microsoft Works 3.0 for Windows software program. They plan to use Works for Windows to produce letters, memos, a newsletter, financial and budget reports, and to maintain employee records.

In this lab you will explore the different areas of Works. You will take a quick look at several files the company uses in each of these areas, and will learn how to move around the window and use the menus and commands.

Understanding Works

Works is an **integrated program** consisting of a collection of productivity **tools**. Each tool is a complete application that can be used independently or with the other tools.

The tools are the Word Processor, Spreadsheet, Database, Communications, and Microsoft Draw. The **Word Processor tool** is used to write, edit, and present text. The **Spreadsheet tool** is used to enter, calculate, present, and chart numerical data. The **Database tool** is used to store, access, and organize lists of information and produce reports. The **Communications tool** lets you send and receive information from one computer to another if you have a modem. **Microsoft Draw** is a drawing tool that is used to create and modify pictures.

Because Works for Windows is an integrated program, information can be easily exchanged among tools. For example, you can easily incorporate data or a chart from a spreadsheet file into a word processing file.

Loading the Works for Windows Program

Start Windows. (If you need help, refer to Lab 1 in your Windows 3.1 lab manual or consult your instructor for details.)

Put your data disk in drive A (or the appropriate drive for your system).

The Windows Program Manager should display the Microsoft Works for Windows program group icon.

Note: If your system is set up differently, your instructor will provide alternative instructions.

Open the Microsoft Works for Windows program group.

The Microsoft Works for Windows program window contains three program icons: Microsoft Works, Works Troubleshooting, and Microsoft Works Setup.

Choose the Microsoft Works application icon.

A licensing window is briefly displayed while the computer loads the Works for Windows program into memory. Then Works displays the Works application window and the Startup **dialog box**. As in Windows, a dialog box displays options for you to select to tell the program what to do.

Your screen should be similar to Figure 1-1.

If the Welcome To Microsoft Works window is displayed, press ←Enter to close the window and the Startup dialog box will appear.

Startup dialog box

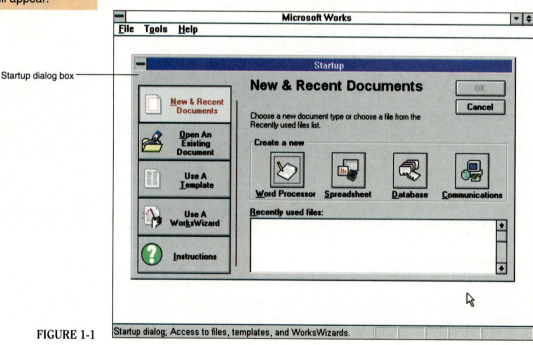

FIGURE 1-1

The Works Startup dialog box is displayed every time you load the program. It allows you to quickly access the different Works tools. You will learn about using the Startup dialog box shortly. For now, to clear the dialog box,

Press: Esc

Your screen should be similar to Figure 1-2.

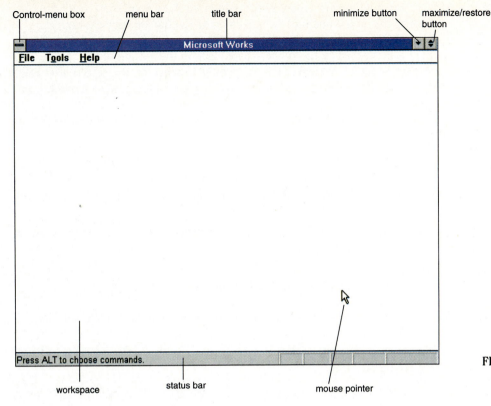

Control-menu box   menu bar   title bar   minimize button   maximize/restore button

Microsoft Works

<u>F</u>ile   T<u>o</u>ols   <u>H</u>elp

Press ALT to choose commands.

workspace   status bar   mouse pointer

FIGURE 1-2

Exploring the Works Application Window

The Works application window consists of several basic parts: the title bar, menu bar, workspace, and status bar. The **title bar**, as in all application windows, displays the control-menu box, the program name, and the **maximize/restore buttons** and the **minimize button**. The second line of the window displays the **menu bar**. It currently displays the names of the three menus, File, Tools, and Help, that can be used in the application window. The menu bar displays different menus depending upon which tool is in use.

Directly below the menu bar is the **workspace**. It is the area of the application window that will display documents as they are opened.

The bottom line of the application window displays the **status bar**. The status bar displays program prompts, descriptions, or instructions. The message currently displayed tells you how to activate the menu.

Using a Mouse

If your computer is connected to a mouse, an arrow appears on your screen. This is the **mouse pointer**. The mouse is a hand-held device that controls the mouse pointer. You move the pointer in the window by moving the mouse over a flat surface such as the mouse pad or the desktop. The pointer moves in the direction you move the mouse. On the top of the mouse are two or three buttons that are used to make selections.

If you do not have a mouse or are already familiar with how to use the mouse, skip to the next section, Using the Menus.

Practice moving the mouse in all directions (up, down, left, and right) in the workspace and note the movement of the pointer on the screen.

Pick up the mouse and move it to a different location on your desktop.

The mouse pointer does not move on the screen. This is because the pointer movement is controlled by the rubber-coated ball on the bottom of the mouse. This ball must move within its socket for the pointer to move on the screen. The ball's movement is translated into signals that tell the computer how to move the on-screen pointer.

You use the following mouse actions to select commands or enter instructions in Works:

Point	To move the mouse until the pointer rests on what you want to point to on the screen
Click	To press and release the mouse button without moving the mouse
Double-click	To press the mouse button twice in rapid succession without moving the mouse
Drag	To press and hold down the mouse button while moving the mouse pointer to a new location on the screen

Unless otherwise directed, the left mouse button is always used to make selections.

> Trackball mice and optical mice operate differently.

Using the Menus

As in other Windows applications, you communicate with Works by choosing a menu from the menu bar. When choosen the selected menu displays a drop-down menu of commands. Generally, when you first load Works, you will want to either create a new file or use an existing file. The File menu contains commands that are used to create and open files.

Since Works is a Windows program, the procedure to activate the menu bar, open a menu, and select and choose commands is the same as in other Windows programs. Commands can be chosen by clicking on the menu title or command with the mouse. If you are using the keyboard, you must first activate the menu bar by pressing [Alt] or [F10]. Then a menu or command can be chosen by typing the underlined letter or by moving the highlight to the command with the directional keys and pressing [←Enter].

> Although you can type the command letter in lowercase or uppercase, it is fastest to use lowercase.

Note: If you are using the directional keys on the numeric keypad, make sure the [Num Lock] (number lock) key is not on. If it is on, "NUM" will be displayed in the status bar and the highlight will not move in the menu. If "NUM" appears in the status bar, press [Num Lock] to turn it off.

To open the File menu,

Click: File

or

Press: [Alt]

Type: F

Your screen should be similar to Figure 1-3.

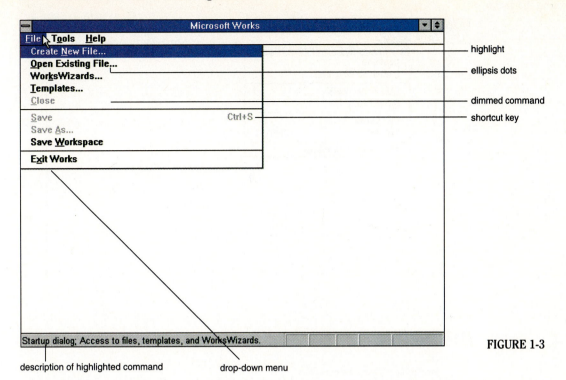

description of highlighted command   drop-down menu

FIGURE 1-3

The File drop-down menu of nine commands is displayed. A highlight bar appears over the first command in the drop-down menu and in the menu bar over the chosen menu title. This identifies the currently selected menu and command. The status bar displays a brief description of the Create New File command, the command the highlight is on in the drop-down menu.

Many of the features in the drop-down menu should be familiar to you. The ellipsis dots (...) indicate that a dialog box will be displayed for you to specify additional information needed to carry out the command. If a shortcut key is available, it is displayed to the right of the command. In this menu, the only shortcut key is Ctrl + S for the Save command. A dimmed command, such as Close, indicates the command is not available for selection until certain other conditions are met.

To preview the commands associated with the other two menus,

Choose: Tools

This menu has one command, Options, that allows you to change the default window settings such as color.

Open the Help menu.

> At the bottom of the File menu, a list of recently used files may be displayed. If they are not displayed, your school has turned this feature off.

> The → and ← keys move the highlight along the menu bar.

Your screen should be similar to Figure 1-4.

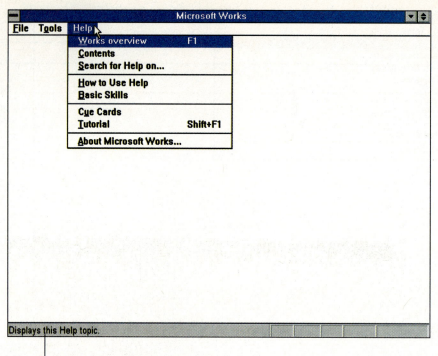

FIGURE 1-4

description of highlighted command

The Help drop-down menu of eight commands is displayed. Every tool in Works has a Help menu. The Help menu provides onscreen information about commands and procedures appropriate to the tool you are using. Since none of the tools is open yet, the Help commands provide introductory information about using the Works program.

You will use the Help menu to review how to choose a command and to find out about the Help system. A command is selected from a menu by clicking the command, typing the underlined letter of the command, or by moving the highlight to the command with the directional keys and pressing ←Enter. Moving the highlight to the command lets you see a description of the command in the status bar before it is executed.

Press: ↓

The second command, Contents, is highlighted and the status bar tells you it will display a Help table of contents. The command you want to use is How to Use Help. You could choose this command by moving the highlight to it and pressing ←Enter. However, if you are sure the command is the command you want to use, you can simply click on the command or type the underlined letter (in this case H).

Click: How to Use Help

or

Type: H

Your screen should be similar to Figure 1-5.

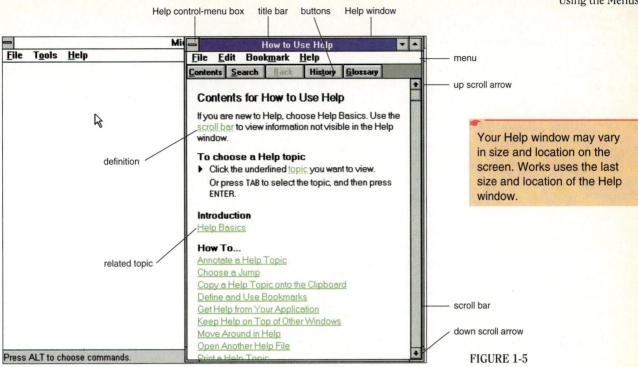

Help control-menu box   title bar   buttons   Help window

menu

up scroll arrow

Your Help window may vary in size and location on the screen. Works uses the last size and location of the Help window.

scroll bar

down scroll arrow

FIGURE 1-5

You have executed the command, and the workspace displays a Help window of information on how to use Help. This window should look familiar to you since it has the same features as Help does in Windows, such as a menu and Help buttons, and operates in the same manner.

As in Windows you can bring other information into view in a window by scrolling. The scroll bar on the right border of the window operates just like the scroll bar in Windows. The ↑ and ↓ scroll arrows in the vertical scroll bar will scroll the document window vertically. Just as in Windows, to scroll continuously, hold down the mouse button while pointing to a scroll arrow. You can also use the ⬆ and ⬇ to scroll the text in the window.

Read the information on this screen.

Terms with a dotted underline will display a definition when selected.

Read the definition for scroll bar.

Scroll the Help window until the end of this Help topic is displayed.

Terms with a solid underline will display related Help information on the topic.

Scroll back up and choose the Help Basics topic. Read the Help information on this topic.

You will be learning more about using Help for information throughout the series of labs. To close the Help window, choose Exit from the Help File menu, choose Close from the Help control menu (the shortcut is Alt + F4), or double-click on the Help control-menu box.

Close Help.

You are returned to the Works application window. However, the Help menu is closed and the menu bar is not active. You can tell that the menu bar is not active because there is no highlight over a menu title. Also, the status bar no longer describes a command, but instead directs you to press Alt to choose commands.

To display a definition or related topic, click on the term or move the highlight to the term by pressing Tab⇆ and then press ←Enter. Clear the definition by clicking anywhere or pressing ←Enter again.

Use the scroll bar or the directional keys to scroll the text in the window.

Alt + Spacebar opens the Help control menu.

Opening a File

You are now ready to open a file that has already been created for you and is on your data disk.

Note: Command instructions will follow the word "Choose:." The letter to type will appear bold and underlined. If you are using the keyboard, first press Alt to activate the menu, then choose the command by either typing the letter or moving the highlight to the menu or command and pressing ←Enter. If you have a mouse, click on the menu to both activate the menu bar and choose the menu. Then click on the appropriate command.

The command to open a file is Open Existing File on the File menu.

Choose: File
Choose: Open Existing File

Your screen should be similar to Figure 1-6.

FIGURE 1-6

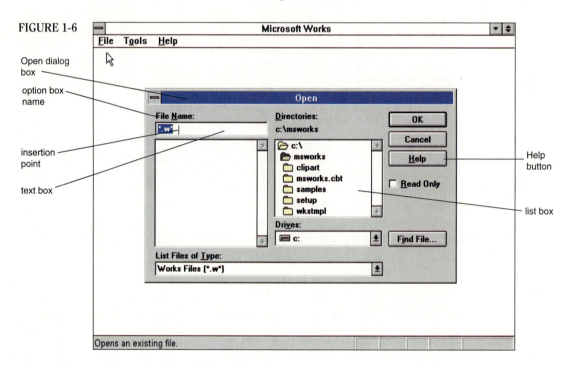

Note: The files and directories displayed on your screen may be different than those in Figure 1-6.

The Open dialog box is displayed. It contains the same dialog box features as dialog boxes in Windows applications, such as a text box, list boxes, and command buttons.

In this dialog box, you need to enter the path and file name of the file you want to open. Before selecting the file name, you will use Help for information about opening a file. Since you are in the middle of a command, you cannot choose Help from the menu. Instead the Help button in the dialog box is used to access the Help system. Pressing the F1 key is the same as choosing this button.

Click: Help

or

Press: F1

Your screen should be similar to Figure 1-7.

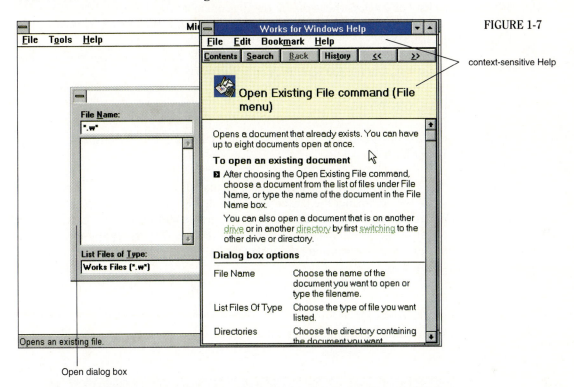

FIGURE 1-7

context-sensitive Help

Open dialog box

Help displays information on whatever command is in use. This is called **context-sensitive** Help. This window tells you how the Open Existing File command works.

Read the information about this command. Read the definitions for drive and directories. When you have read the Help information, close the Help window.

Now you are ready to choose the name of the file to open. As in Windows, you can type the path (drive and directory location) and name of the file in the text box or you can choose the path and file name from the list boxes. Selecting the file name from the File Name list box lets you see all the file names and choose the name you want, which avoids typing errors.

First you need to change the drive to the drive containing your data disk. The line above the Directories list box tells you the drive and directory Works is using to access files (most likely C:\MSWORKS). You change the drive by selecting the appropriate drive from the Drives drop-down list box.

To select from the dialog box, if you have a mouse, simply click on the area you want to use, or if the option you want to select is visible, double-click directly on it to select it. To move from one area to another using the keyboard, press Alt and the underlined letter of the option box name or press Tab ⇆ until the area you want to use is selected. Then select the option from the list by using the directional keys to move the highlight and press ←Enter to choose it.

To change the drive to the drive containing your data disk,

Choose: Drives
Select: a: (or the appropriate drive)

Now the selected drive is displayed above the Directories list box, and the directories, if any, are displayed in the Directories list box. Works will use this drive to open and save files until you change it again or exit Works. This is the **current drive**. The File Name list box displays the names of the files in alphabetical order on the disk in the current drive. If you selected the wrong drive, choose the correct drive from the Drives list box.

Next you need to select the name of the file you want to use from the File Name list box. The file you want to open is GROWTH.WPS.

Select: GROWTH.WPS

Note: If the file name GROWTH.WPS is not displayed in the Files list box, ask your instructor for help.

The file name should be highlighted and displayed in the File Name text box. To complete the command, the OK button is used. OK tells the program to carry out the instructions in the dialog box. It is the preset button and can be chosen by pressing ⎆Enter or by clicking on it with the mouse. The Cancel button closes the dialog box without performing the instructions. The Esc key is the same as choosing this button.

Choose: OK

Your screen should be similar to Figure 1-8.

> If you are using the keyboard, press ⬇ to display the drop-down list of drives.

> If the message "Cannot read drive" appears, make sure your disk is fully inserted in the drive and, if necessary, that the drive door is closed. Then choose Retry.

> If necessary, use the scroll bar or the directional keys to scroll the File Name list box until the file name is displayed.

> You can double-click on the file name to open the file.

> If a Cue Card window is displayed, press ⇧Shift + F3 to close it.

> The text on your screen may end at different points on the line. This is a function of the printer that is selected on your computer.

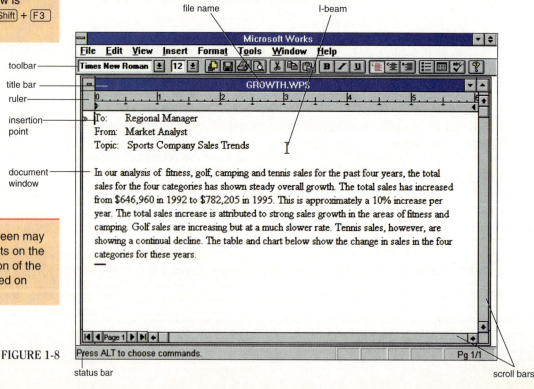

FIGURE 1-8

A copy of the contents of the GROWTH.WPS file is loaded into memory and displayed in the application window workspace. The original file remains on the disk. This file contains a memo created using the Word Processing tool about the Sports Company growth in sales.

Exploring the Word Processing Tool

A word processor is used to create and edit text documents such as letters, memos, and reports. The contents of the file are displayed in the Works word processor **document window**. The document window is where you enter and change text. The workspace can display up to eight document windows of different types at the same time.

You will be learning about this tool in detail in Labs 2 through 4.

At the top of the document window, a title bar displays a control-menu box, the file name, and the minimize and maximize buttons. Below the title bar, a **ruler** is displayed. The ruler shows document margin and tab settings. The right and bottom borders of the document window display scroll bars.

Because the Works application window workspace displays a word processing window, the menu bar displays eight menus that can be used in the Word Processing tool. In addition a **toolbar** of buttons that are mouse shortcuts for many menu commands is displayed below the menu bar. The status bar tells you what action to take, in this case, how to activate the menu bar, and will also display information specific to the word processor as features are used.

The **insertion point**, the blinking vertical bar, shows your location in the window. The mouse or the arrow keys are used to move the insertion point around the window.

In the word processor document window, the mouse pointer can appear as an I-beam or an arrow. To move the insertion point, move the mouse pointer to the location in the window where you want the insertion point positioned and click the left mouse button.

Move to: first "a" in "analysis" (third word in first line)

Follow the directions in *either* the Mouse or Keyboard sections.

To move to the beginning of the fifth line,

Press: ⬇ (4 times)

The insertion point has moved down four lines and is positioned before the "I" in "In."

Press: ➡ (7 times)

The insertion point has moved to the right seven spaces and should be to the left of the letter "a" in "analysis."

Your screen should be similar to Figure 1-9.

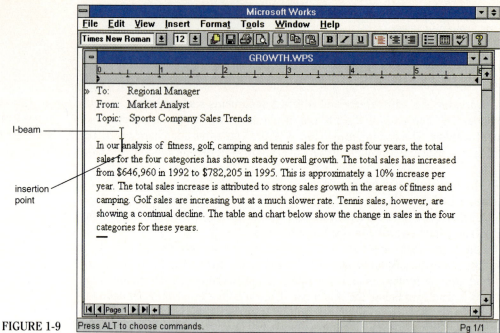

I-beam

insertion
point

FIGURE 1-9

Do not be concerned if the insertion point is not in the same location as in Figure 1-9. You will learn more about moving around the word processing document window in Lab 2. Many of the same commands are available for selection as in the application window File menu.

To see the commands in the File menu,

> Press (Alt) + F or click File.

Choose: File

The menu bar displays the File, Tools, and Help menus as well as several other menus.

Choose: Edit

The Edit menu lists commands that are used to make changes to your word processing document.

Open each of the remaining menus to quickly look at the commands. Leave the File menu open.

Next you want to see the table of data mentioned in the memo. This table was created using the Spreadsheet tool and saved in a file named SALESDTA. You will first close the word processing file and then open the spreadsheet file.

To close this file before opening another file,

> Use (→) to move from one menu to another or click on each menu title.

> If you changed anything in the document, a Save Changes dialog box will appear. Choose No from this dialog box.

Choose: Close

The file GROWTH.WPS is no longer in the computer's memory, and the word processing document window is closed.

> You will learn more about the toolbar, ruler, and status bar in Lab 2.

Your screen should be similar to Figure 1-10.

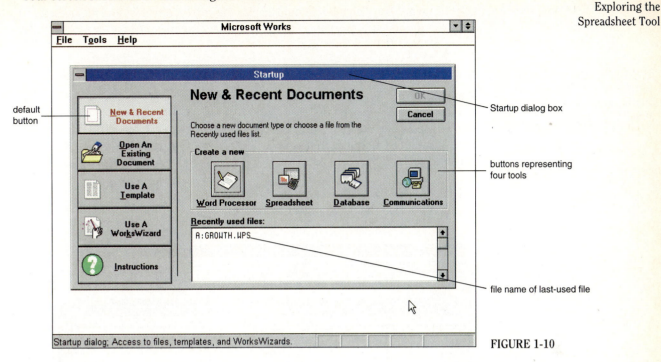

default button —

Startup dialog box

buttons representing four tools

file name of last-used file

Startup dialog; Access to files, templates, and WorksWizards.

FIGURE 1-10

Exploring the Spreadsheet Tool

The workspace displays the Startup dialog box again. The application window displays the original set of menus in the menu bar and the word processing toolbar is closed. You will use the Startup dialog box to open the spreadsheet file of sales growth, SALESDTA.WKS.

The Startup dialog box is used to access the different features of Works. The five buttons on the left side of the box are used to do the following:

Button	Action
New & Recent Documents	Creates new files
Open An Existing Document	Loads an existing file
Use A Template	Opens a preformatted file
Use A WorksWizard	Uses the step-by-step guide called a WorksWizard to create a document
Instructions	Displays instructions on how to use Startup dialog box

The central area of the dialog box displays four buttons that represent the four main Works tools: Word Processor, Spreadsheet, Database, and Communications. When selected these buttons will create a new document in that particular tool. Below these options is the Recently Used Files list box. The file you just used, GROWTH.WPS, should be displayed at the top of this list.

You want to open an existing file. The New & Recent Documents option is the default or preselected button. To change the selection,

> The list of files in the Recently Used Files list box will show the files that were most recently used in Works on your computer.

Choose: **O**pen An Existing Document

The Open dialog box is displayed, just as if you had selected Open Existing File from the File menu. The dialog box should display the correct directory and file names.

Scroll the list of file names in the File Name list box until the spreadsheet file name SALESDTA.WKS is displayed.

> Press ⎣←Enter⎦ to choose OK. Mouse users can double-click on the file name to both select it and choose OK.

Select: SALESDTA.WKS
Choose: OK

Note: Throughout the remaining labs, instructions to select (highlight) an option from a dialog box and then choose OK will appear on a single line following the word "Choose:" and will be separated by > (for example, Choose: SALESDTA.WKS>OK).

The file SALESDTA.WKS is loaded into memory.
Your screen should be similar to Figure 1-11.

FIGURE 1-11

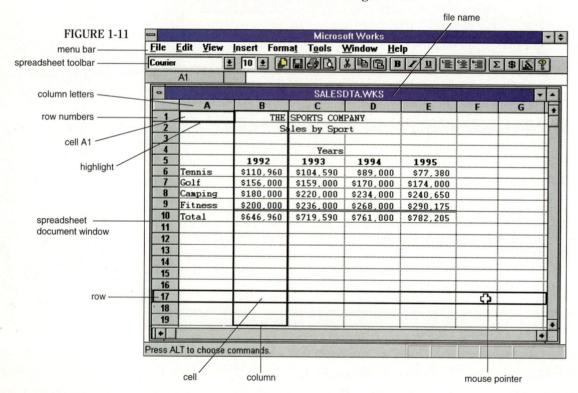

> You will learn more about the spreadsheet tool in Labs 5 through 8.

A spreadsheet is similar to an accountant's ledger and is used to prepare, analyze, and present budgets, cost estimates, and other types of financial or statistical information.

The spreadsheet document window is displayed in the application window workspace. The menu bar displays eight menus that can be used in the spreadsheet tool. They are the same as in the word processing menu, but they contain some different options. The tools on the toolbar are mouse shortcuts for many spreadsheet menu commands. The status bar displays information on command usage and new information specific to the spreadsheet.

The spreadsheet document window displays the data in the SALESDTA.WKS file. The file name of the open file is displayed in the title bar of the document window. The document window displays scroll bars along the right and bottom edges of the window. A row of letters borders the top of the window and a column of numbers borders the left edge of the window. The numbers identify the **rows** in a spreadsheet and the letters identify the **columns**. The intersection of a row and a column creates a **cell**.

The insertion point is now a dark cell border called the **highlight**, which shows you which cell you are currently on. The highlight is currently on the first cell in the spreadsheet. This cell is in column A of row 1. Therefore this cell is called cell A1.

Like the insertion point in the word processing tool, the highlight can be moved from one cell to another using the directional keys or by clicking on the cell with the mouse. The mouse pointer appears as a cross ⬦ in the spreadsheet document window. To move the highlight to cell A6,

Click: cell containing the word "Tennis"

or

Press: ⬇ (5 times)

The highlight should be on the cell containing the entry "Tennis," the cell at the intersection of column A and row 6. To move to the right one cell, to cell B6,

Click: cell B6

or

Press: ➡

Your screen should be similar to Figure 1-12.

FIGURE 1-12

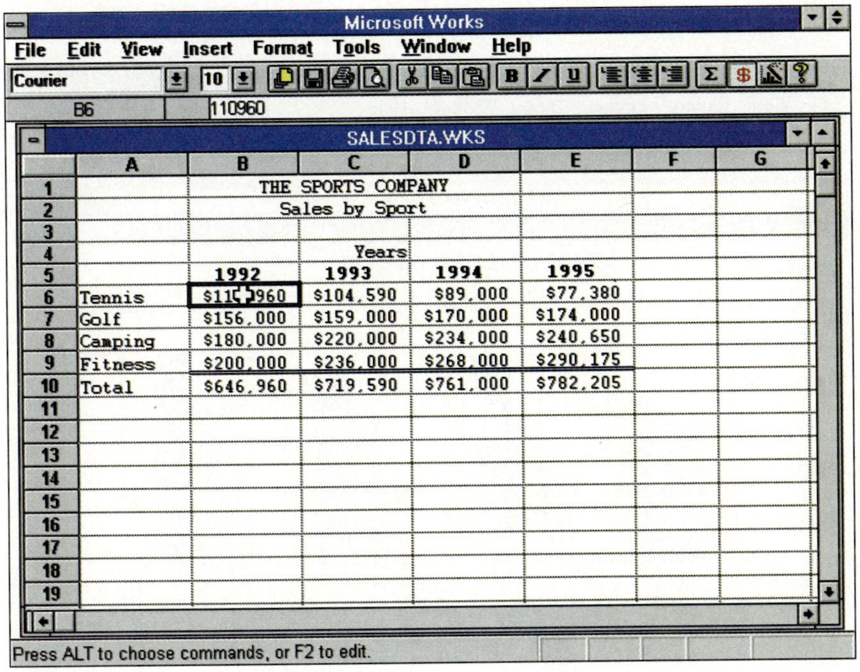

The cell containing the number $110,960 should be highlighted.

Press [Alt] + F or click File.

Press [→] or click Edit.

To browse some of the spreadsheet menus,

Choose: File

Notice that the File commands are the same as in the Word Processing tool.

Choose: Edit

Many of the commands on the Edit menu are also the same as in the word processing Edit menu, but some are different. You will find as you explore and use the menus that many commands will be the same from tool to tool. Others will be different and specific to the tool you are using.

Within the Spreadsheet tool is a feature that lets you create and view charts or graphs of the data in the spreadsheet. To see a chart of this data that has already been created,

Choose: View
Choose: Chart

The Charts dialog box is used to select the name of the chart you want to view. This chart has been stored in the spreadsheet file as GROWTH. Since there is only one chart and it is already selected, to view it,

Choose: OK

Your screen should be similar to Figure 1-13.

FIGURE 1-13

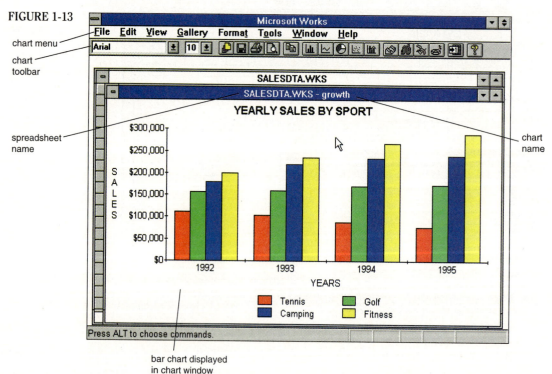

A bar chart of the data is displayed in another window in the workspace.

Notice that the menu bar now displays eight menus associated with the chart window. The toolbar buttons have changed as well to correspond to charting functions. The chart window title bar displays the spreadsheet file name and the chart name. Whenever you create and view a chart, Works changes from Spreadsheet view to Chart view. The commands in Chart view are used to create and modify charts. To return to the Spreadsheet view and menu,

Choose: View>Spreadsheet

To close the spreadsheet file,

Choose: File>Close

You will learn more about charting data in Lab 8.

If you changed anything in this file, a Save Changes dialog box will appear. Choose No from this dialog box.

Exploring the Database Tool

The last tool you will look at is the Database tool. A database is like a filing system. It helps you keep track of and organize records that contain common information. The Sports Company has several database files. One contains information about preferred customers. Another contains information about each employee. The company frequently uses the information in the database files to create mailing labels and reports.

To take a look at the employee database file, from the Startup dialog box,

Choose: Open An Existing Document>EMPLOY.WDB>OK

Your screen should be similar to Figure 1-14.

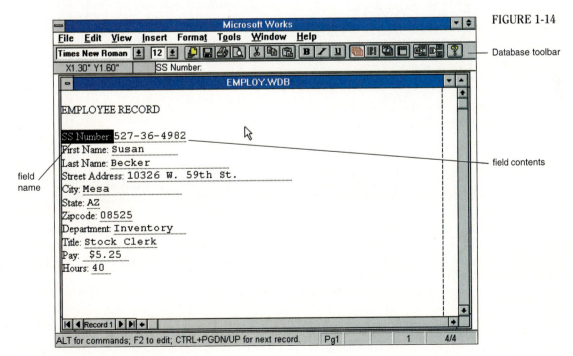

FIGURE 1-14

Database toolbar

field contents

field name

The workspace displays the database document window containing the database file. The window is again similar to the other tools. There are eight menus available in the menu bar. They are the same as in the Word Processor and Spreadsheet tools. The status bar displays information on command usage and database creation.

The database file on employees includes information such as the employee's name, address, pay, and hours worked. The information for the employee Susan Becker is displayed. Each line of information is called a **field**. The highlight is over "SS Number:." SS Number is a **field name**. The field name describes the information displayed to the right of the colon, in this case the social security number.

Press: →

The highlight is over "527-36-4982." This is the **field contents** of the social security number field. To see information on the next employee in the database,

Press: Ctrl + Page Down

Your screen should be similar to Figure 1-15.

FIGURE 1-15

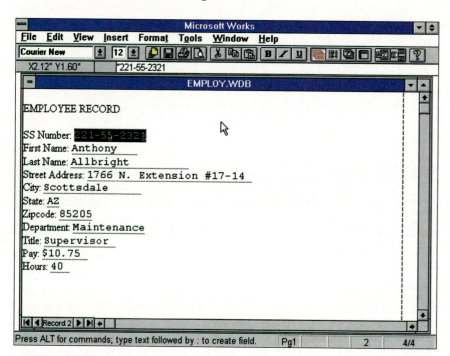

You will learn how to create a database, enter data, and use the database tool in Labs 9 through 11.

The information on the second employee in the database is displayed. It contains the same types of information as for the first employee. The information on each employee is called a **record**.

To see the commands in the File menu,

Choose: File

The File commands are again the same as in the spreadsheet and word processing File menus.

Choose: Edit

Many of the Edit menu commands are the same as in the word processing and spreadsheet Edit menus, but some are different.
 You have looked at the three main tools in Works. To close this file,

Choose: File>Close

If a dialog box reminds you that you have not saved the file before exiting, respond No to saving the file.

Exploring Tool Integration

Works is an integrated program. This allows you to add information to a Works word processor document or a database document and create a link, or a means of communication, between the files. To see a file that is linked to another,

Choose: Open An Existing Document>INTEGRAT.WPS>OK

The file INTEGRAT is a word processing file that also contains the spreadsheet and chart from the file SALESDTA. A message box with the message "Update links when opening document?" is displayed. To update the links,

You will learn about links in Lab 12.

Choose: Yes

The memo is displayed. To see the table and chart below the memo,

Press: ⬇ (until the chart comes into full view)

The data table and chart add emphasis to the memo.
 This is the advantage of Works' integration. It allows you to easily combine information from files created using different tools.

You will learn more about combining or integrating information between tools in Lab 12.

Choose: File>Close

You will learn more about each of these tools throughout the series of labs.

Exiting Works for Windows

The application window with the Startup dialog box open is displayed. To close the dialog box and exit the program,

Choose: Cancel
Choose: File>Exit Works

Press Esc to choose Cancel.

The Windows Program Manager window should be displayed.
 If necessary, exit Windows.

Key Terms

integrated program (7)	menu bar (9)	ruler (17)
tool (7)	workspace (9)	toolbar (17)
Word Processor tool (7)	status bar (9)	insertion point (17)
Spreadsheet tool (7)	mouse pointer (9)	row (21)
Database tool (7)	point (10)	column (21)
Communications tool (7)	click (10)	cell (21)
Microsoft Draw (7)	double-click (10)	highlight (21)
dialog box (8)	drag (10)	field (24)
title bar (9)	context-sensitive (15)	field name (24)
maximize/restore buttons (9)	current drive (16)	field contents (24)
minimize button (9)	document window (17)	record (24)

Command Summary

Command	Action
[Alt]	Activates menu bar
File>**O**pen Existing File	Opens a file
File>**E**dit	Opens Edit menu
File>**C**lose	Closes file
Open An Existing Document	Opens an existing document from Startup dialog box
View>**C**hart	Displays a chart
View>**S**preadsheet	Returns to Spreadsheet view from Chart view
File>E**x**it Works	Exits the Works program

LAB REVIEW

Matching

1. menu bar _____ **a.** blinking vertical line that shows your location in a word processing document

2. insertion point _____ **b.** intersection of a row and column

3. [Esc] _____ **c.** an organized collection of data

4. [Alt] _____ **d.** a bar of buttons that are mouse shortcuts for common menu commands

5. status bar _____ **e.** lists available menus

6. [Alt] + F _____ **f.** used to cancel a command

7. toolbar _____ **g.** line at bottom of application window that displays program conditions

8. database _____ **h.** activates menu

9. cell _____ **i.** displayed whenever program needs more information to complete a command

10. dialog box _____ **j.** opens File menu

1. Identify the parts of the window.

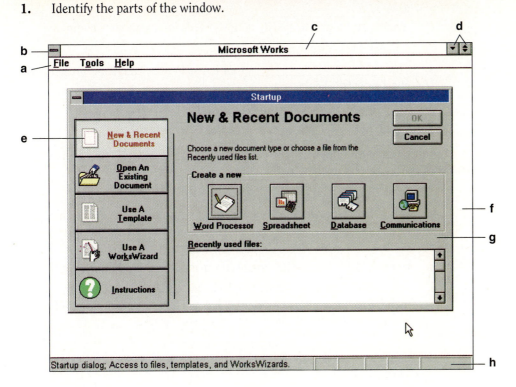

a. _____   e. _____

b. _____   f. _____

c. _____   g. _____

d. _____   h. _____

2. Complete the following statements by filling in the blanks with the correct term.

a. The _____ occupies the largest area of the Works application window.

b. The _____ is located at the bottom of the application window.

c. Name the three ways you can enter a command: _____, _____, _____.

d. The five tools in the Works program are: _____, _____, _____, _____, and _____.

e. _____ allows you to add information to a word processing or database document from another tool and create a link between the files.

f. The word processing tool is used to create and edit _____ documents.

g. A(n) _____ helps you keep track of the current command settings and to specify options needed to complete a command.

h. An open file is displayed in a(n) _____ _____ .

i. The _____ tool is used enter, calculate, present, and chart numerical data.

j. The tool that displays information as records is the _____ tool.

3. In this problem you will use the word processing file GROWTH.WPS to explore the Word Processor tool further.

   a. Load Works. Open the GROWTH.WPS file.

   b. Using the keyboard, move the insertion point to the "4" in the third line of text in the body of the memo. What were the keystrokes you used to move to this position?

   c. Open the Edit menu. How many commands are there in this menu?

   d. Select the Find command. Use Help for information about this command. From the information provided by Help, complete this statement: When you search in the word processor, Works _____ _____.

   e. Exit Help. Cancel the Find dialog box. Close the file. If necessary, exit Works.

4. In this problem you will use the spreadsheet file SALESDTA.WKS to explore the Spreadsheet tool further.

   a. Load Works. Open the SALESDTA.WKS file.

   b. Using the keyboard, move the highlight to the cell containing the entry $234,000. What were the keystrokes you used to move to this cell?

   c. Open the Edit menu. How many commands are there in this menu?

   d. Select the Fill Series command. Use Help for information about this command. From the information provided by Help, answer this question: What are the first two steps under "To fill a series"?

   1. _____

   2. _____

   e. Exit Help. Cancel the Fill Series dialog box. Close the file. If necessary, exit Works.

5. In this problem you will use the database file EMPLOY.WDB to explore the Database tool further.

    a. Load Works. Open the EMPLOY.WDB file.

    b. Using the keyboard, move the highlight to the field containing the entry 08525. What were the keystrokes you used to move to this field?

    c. Open the Edit menu. How many commands are there in this menu?

    d. Select the Go To command. Use Help for information about this command. Read the definition of a record and complete this statement: A record is composed of _____.

    e. Exit Help. Cancel the Go To dialog box. Close the file. If necessary, exit Works.

Word Processing

One of the most widely used applications software programs is a word processor. To put your thoughts in writing, from the simplest note to the most complex book, is a time-consuming process. Even more time-consuming is the task of editing and retyping the document to make it perfect. There was a time when perfection in written communication was difficult, if not impossible, to achieve. With the introduction of word processing, errors should be nearly nonexistent—not because they are not made, but because they are easy to correct. Word processors let you throw away the correction fluid, scissors, paste, and erasers. Now, with a few keystrokes, you can correct errors, move paragraphs, and reprint your document easily.

Definition of Word Processing

Word processing applications software is a program that helps you create any type of written communication via a keyboard. A word processor can be used to manipulate text data to produce a letter, a report, a memo, or any other type of written correspondence. Text data is any letter, number, or symbol that you can type on a keyboard. The grouping of the text data to form words, sentences, paragraphs, and pages of text results in the creation of a document. Through a word processor you can create, modify, store, retrieve, and print part or all of a document.

Advantages of Using a Word Processor

The speed of entering text data into the computer depends on the skill of the user. If you cannot type fast, a word processor will not improve your typing speed. However, a word processor will make it easier to correct and change your document. Consequently your completed document will take less time to create.

Another time saver is a feature called wordwrap. As you enter text, you do not need to decide where to end each line as you do on a typewriter. When a line is full, the program automatically wraps the text down to the next line.

Where a word processor excels is in its ability to change or edit a document. Editing involves correcting spelling, grammar, and sentence-structure errors. As you enter characters using the keyboard, they are displayed on the screen and stored electronically in the computer's main memory. As you find errors, you can electronically delete and correct them. Once the document is the way you want it to appear, it can be permanently saved on a disk and printed on paper. Good-bye, correction fluid!

In addition to editing a document, you can easily revise or update it by inserting or deleting text. For example, a document that lists prices can easily be updated to reflect new prices. A document that details procedures can be revised by deleting old procedures and inserting new ones. This is especially helpful when a document is used repeatedly. Rather than recreating the whole document, you change only the parts that need to be revised.

Revision also includes the rearrangement of pieces or blocks of text. For example, while writing a report, you may decide to change the location of a single word or several paragraphs or pages of text. You can do it easily by cutting or removing selected text from one location, then pasting or placing the selected text in another location. Blocks of text can also be copied from one area of the document to another. This is a real advantage when the text includes many recurring phrases or words.

Combining text in another file with text in your document is another advantage of word processors. An example of this is a group term paper in which each person is responsible for writing a section of the paper. Before printing the document, all the sections, which are stored in different files, are combined to create the complete paper. The opposite is also true. Text that may not be appropriate in your document can easily be put in another file for later use.

Many word processors include additional support features to further help you produce a perfect document. A spelling checker checks the spelling in a document by comparing each word to words in a dictionary stored in memory. If an error is found, the program suggests the correct spelling. A syntax checker electronically checks grammar, phrasing, capitalization, and other types of syntax errors in a document. A thesaurus displays alternative words that have a meaning similar or opposite to the word you entered.

You can also easily control the appearance or format of the document. Formatting includes such operations as changing the line spacing and margin widths, adding page numbers, and displaying page headers and footers. You can also quickly change how your text is aligned with the left or right margin. For example, text can be centered between the margins, or justified—evenly aligned on both the left and right margins. Perhaps the most noticeable formatting feature is the ability to apply different fonts (type styles and sizes) and text appearance changes such as bold and italics to all or selected portions of the document. Some word processing programs also have the ability to produce and display graphic lines and boxes. Graphic boxes can then be used to hold text or graphic images that you place into the document.

Many word processing programs also include the WYSIWYG ("what you see is what you get") feature. This feature allows you to see on the screen exactly (or as close as possible) how your document will appear when printed. This means that the effects of your format changes are immediately displayed on the screen.

If, after reading the printed copy, you find other errors or want to revise or reformat the document, it is easy to do. Simply reload the document file, make your changes, and reprint the text. Now that saves time!

Word Processing Terminology

The following list of terms and definitions are generic in nature and are associated with most word processing programs.

Bold: Produces dark or heavy print.

Center: To align a line of text evenly between the margins.

Copy: To duplicate selected text in another location in the document.

Cut: To remove or delete selected text from an area in the document.

Document: Text-based output created by a word processing program.

Edit: To change or modify the content of the document.

Font: Type style and size.

Format: Defines how the printed document will appear; includes settings for underline, boldface, print size, margin settings, line spacing, and so on.

Insert: To enter new text into a document between existing text.

Justified: Text that is evenly aligned on both the left and right margins.

Paste: To place selected text in another location in the document.

Selection: Any group of characters, words, lines, paragraphs, or pages of text.

Spelling checker: A support feature that checks words or the entire document for correct spelling.

Text data: Any number, letter, or symbol you can type on a keyboard.

Thesaurus: A support feature that displays synonyms and antonyms for words in the document.

Wordwrap: The automatic adjustment of the number of characters or words on a line; eliminates the need to press [←Return] or [←Enter] at the end of each line.

WYSIWYG: The feature that displays a document onscreen as close as possible to how it will appear when printed.

Case Study for Labs 2–4

As a recent college graduate, you have accepted your first job as a management trainee for the Sports Company. The Sports Company is a chain of discount sporting goods shops located in large metropolitan areas throughout the United States. The program emphasis is on computer applications in the area of retail management and requires that you work in several areas of the company.

You are working in the Southwest Regional office and are responsible for setting up the credit card enrollment program and for assisting with the monthly newsletter.

In Labs 2 and 3, you will create a letter to be sent to all new credit card recipients. You will learn how to use the word processing program to edit and format the letter.

In Lab 4 the regional office has decided to send a monthly newsletter to credit card customers. You have been asked to design and prepare several articles for inclusion in the newsletter.

Before You Begin

The following assumptions about the Word Processor tool have been made:

- Times New Roman, 12 pt is the preset font.
- The ruler is displayed.
- The display screen view is Normal.
- The default alignment is Left.
- The left and right margins are at the default setting of 1.25 inches.
- The Wrap for Windows feature is off.
- Always Suggest in the Spelling Checker is not on.

2

Editing and Creating Documents

CASE STUDY

The Sports Company is a chain of sporting goods shops located in large metropolitan areas across the United States. The stores are warehouse oriented, discounting the retail price of most items 15 percent. They stock sporting goods products for the major sports: team sports, racquet sports, aerobics, golf, winter sports, and so on.

As a recent college graduate, you have accepted a job in a management training program for The Sports Company. The training program emphasis is on computer applications in the area of retail management. The program requires that you work in several areas of the company. You have been assigned to work in the Southwest Regional office. You will be responsible for getting the credit card program set up and for assisting with the monthly newsletter.

During the next three labs you will be using Works 3.0 for Windows to create a letter to be sent to the new credit card recipients, and you will design and prepare articles to be included in the monthly newsletter.

Competencies

After completing this lab, you will know how to:

1. Move around a document window.
2. Scroll a document.
3. Use the Go To command.
4. Delete and insert text.
5. Use Insert and Overtype.
6. Insert and delete blank lines.
7. Display special characters.
8. Select text.
9. Use Undo.
10. Save a document file.
11. Print a document.
12. Create a new document.
13. Preview a document.
14. Change line spacing.

Exploring the Word Processor Window

Turn on your computer and, if necessary, respond to the date and time prompts. The DOS prompt should be displayed.

Put your data disk in drive A (or the appropriate drive for your system). Load Windows. Load the Works 3.0 for Windows program.

The Works Startup dialog box is displayed in the Works application window workspace.

The first draft of the credit card letter has already been created for you and saved on your data disk in a document file named LETTER. To open the file LETTER,

Choose: Open An Existing Document

From the Drives drop-down list box of the Open dialog box,

Select: a: (or the appropriate drive for your system)

From the File Name list box,

Select: LETTER.WPS
Choose: OK

> Reminder: If you are using the keyboard, use [Tab↹] to move the highlight within a dialog box or [Alt] + letter to select an option.

> Remember, you can press [←Enter] to choose OK or double-click on the file name.

Note: If you get a system error message, check that your disk is properly inserted in the drive and, if necessary, that the disk drive door is completely closed. Reenter the command.

Your screen should be similar to Figure 2-1.

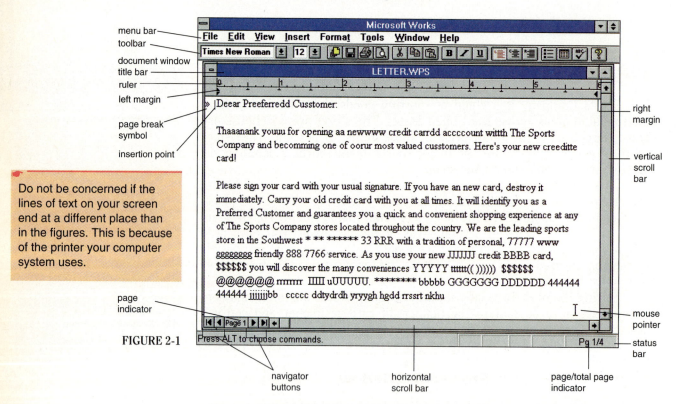

FIGURE 2-1

> Do not be concerned if the lines of text on your screen end at a different place than in the figures. This is because of the printer your computer system uses.

The file is loaded and displayed in the word processing document window. This file contains a first draft of the letter to new credit card customers. As you can see, it contains many errors. You will learn how to correct these errors in this lab.

The menu bar displays the eight menus that can be used in the Word Processor tool. The toolbar contains drop-down list boxes and buttons that are mouse shortcuts for commonly used word processing commands.

The document window title bar displays the name of the file you are viewing. It also contains the control-menu box and maximize and minimize buttons for the document window. It forms the top border of the document window.

Just below the title bar is the ruler. The ruler displays the line length in inches. The size of the right and left **margins**, the blank space between the edge of the page and the text, and the paper size determine the line length. The **default** or initial program settings for the right and left margins are 1.25 inches, and the default paper size setting is 8.5 by 11 inches. This leaves 6 inches of line space on the page for the text.

The zero position on the ruler indicates the location of the left margin. Below the zero position are two triangles that indicate margin and indent settings. The ◄ symbol on the right end of the ruler line at the 6-inch position marks the right margin.

You will learn about margin and indent settings in Lab 3.

If the mouse pointer is positioned in the document window workspace, it appears as an I-beam. As you move the mouse pointer around the window, it changes to different shapes corresponding to its location and the function it can perform. The different shapes and functions of the mouse pointer are shown below.

Mouse Pointer Shape	Meaning
I	Move the insertion point, or select text
↖	Select menus and commands; select toolbar buttons and use the scroll bar
⧗	Wait while Works finishes performing a task
↖ DRAG	Move a current selection by dragging
↖ COPY	Copy a current selection by dragging

The first few paragraphs of the rough draft of the credit card letter are displayed in the document window. The >> symbol on the first line of the document is the automatic **page break symbol**. It identifies the beginning of a page. The blinking vertical line in the upper left corner is the insertion point. It shows you where the next character you type will appear. The vertical scroll bar is located on the right side of the document window and the horizontal scroll bar is located on the bottom of the document window. The left end of the horizontal scroll bar displays four **navigator buttons** and a **page indicator**. The buttons are used to move through the document. The page indicator tells you the page of the document the insertion point is positioned on (page 1).

The status bar at the bottom of the Works window displays descriptions of menu commands, key conditions, and information about your location in the document. Currently the status bar tells you how to activate the menu and displays another page indicator, which tells you that the insertion point is positioned on page 1 of a total of four pages in this document ("Pg 1/4").

Examining the Toolbar

The toolbar provides mouse users with shortcuts to many of the most commonly used menu commands. Even if you do not have a mouse, the toolbar displays information about many of the settings in your document.

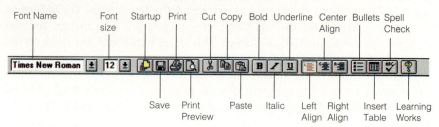

The toolbar consists of 19 buttons. The first two buttons are drop-down list buttons. These display the current setting in the text box and a ⬛ to the right of the box. Clicking on the ⬛ opens a drop-down list of options from which you can select. The two drop-down list buttons in the word processing toolbar are the Font Name and Font Size buttons. The Font Name text box displays the default **font** or typeface, Times New Roman. The Font Size text box displays the default font size of 12.

> You will learn more about
> fonts and type sizes in Lab 4.

To the right of the drop-down list buttons are 17 graphic icon buttons that represent the feature that they perform when selected. To find out what each button does, you can display the name and a description of the button using the mouse.

Note: If you do not have a mouse, skip to the next section, Moving Around the Word Processor Document Window.

Point to the Font Name drop-down list button. Hold it there for a short time.
Your screen should be similar to Figure 2-2.

FIGURE 2-2

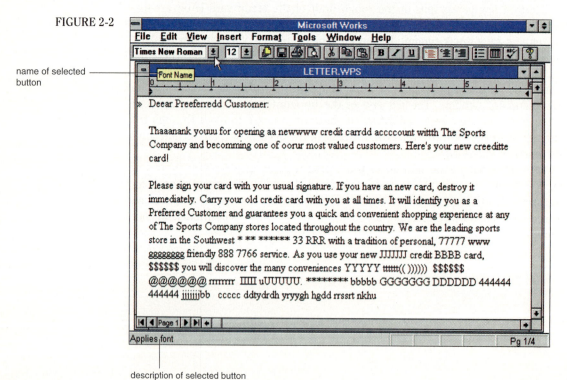

The button name, Font Name, appears below the button in a yellow box. In addition a brief description of the button is displayed in the status bar.

To see the description for the Font Size button, point to the button.

The button name and description are displayed.

To display the name and description for the remaining buttons, point to each button and pause until the name appears in the yellow box and the description appears in the status bar.

Moving Around the Word Processor Document Window

The mouse or the keyboard can be used to move the insertion point in the document window. Depending upon what you are doing, the mouse is not always the quickest means of moving; therefore, if you are using the mouse, you will learn how to move through the document using both methods.

The insertion point can be moved around the screen using the arrow keys. The arrow keys move the insertion point one character space at a time in the direction indicated by the arrow.

Note: To ensure that your screens look like those in the text, use the keys specified as you are following the directions in this section.

Press: → (6 times)

Your screen should be similar to Figure 2-3.

If you are using the directional keys on the numeric keypad, make sure the Num Lock (number lock) key is not on. ("NUM" is displayed in the status bar when it is on.) If it is on, press Num Lock to turn it off.

WORD PROCESSING

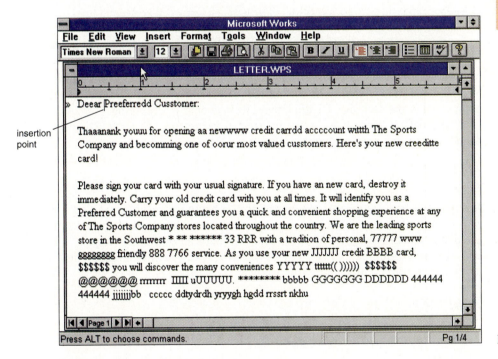

insertion
point

FIGURE 2-3

The insertion point moved six character spaces to the right and should be positioned to the left of the "P" in "Preeferredd." When the insertion point is to the left of a character, the character or space to the right is selected.

Press: ⊡↓

The insertion point moved down one line. Since this is a blank line, the insertion point moved back to the left margin on the line.

Press: ⊡↓

The insertion point moved down to the next line and to the fourth "a" in "Thaaanank." It moved to this position because it was last located in a line containing text at that position ("P" in "Preeferredd"). The insertion point will attempt to maintain its position in a line of text as you move up or down through the document.

When you hold down either ⊡← or ⊡→, the insertion point will move quickly character by character along the line.

To see how this works, hold down ⊡→ until the insertion point is positioned to the left of the "a" in the word "accccount" in the first sentence.

If you moved too far to the right along the line of text, use ⊡← to move back to the correct position.

This saves multiple presses of the arrow key. Many of the Works insertion point movement keys can be held down to execute multiple moves.

Using the arrow keys,

Move to: the third "e" in "creeditte" (last letter of last word on second line)

Note: Throughout the Works word processing labs, you will be instructed to "Move to" specific locations in the text as in the directions above. This means to move the insertion point to the left of the character. To confirm the insertion point position, a brief description of where the text is located follows in parentheses. If your insertion point is not at the described location, move it there before continuing.

The default right margin setting is at 6 inches on the ruler. To see what happens when the insertion point reaches the right margin,

Press: ⊡→ (2 times)

The insertion point automatically moved to the beginning of the next line. Unlike with a typewriter, you did not need to press the carriage return to move from the end of one line to the beginning of the next. It is done automatically for you.

The insertion point can also move word by word in either direction on a line using ⊡Ctrl in combination with ⊡→ or ⊡←.

Press: ⊡↑
Press: ⊡Ctrl + ⊡→ (5 times)

The insertion point moved five words to the right along the line. It should be positioned on the first "o" in the word "oorur." To move back to the first word in this line,

Press: ⊡Ctrl + ⊡← (5 times)

The [Home] and [End] keys can be used to quickly move the insertion point to the beginning or end of a line of text, respectively. To move to the end of this line,

Press: [End]

To move back to the beginning of the line,

Press: [Home]

The insertion point should be back on the "C" of "Company."

If you have a mouse, you can move the insertion point to a specific location in a document by positioning the I-beam at the location and clicking the left mouse button.

Point to: "y" of "youuu" (first line of first paragraph)

Notice that the insertion point has not moved.

Click: left mouse button

The insertion point should now be positioned to the left of the "y." If it is positioned to the right of the "y," this is because the I-beam was positioned too far to the right side of the character when the mouse button was pressed.

Practice using the mouse to move the insertion point by moving it to the following locations on the screen:

Move to: "I" in "If" (second sentence of second paragraph)
Move to: "S" in "Southwest" (fifth line of second paragraph)
Move to: "C" in "Company" (first word, second line of first paragraph)

If the insertion point appears as a wide bar, reposition the I-beam and click without moving the mouse.

When moving to the first character on a line, make sure the mouse pointer is an I-beam, not an arrow. If all the text on a line appears highlighted, reposition the pointer again and click.

Scrolling the Document Window

The document window space is not large enough to display the entire document. You can maximize the document window to allow more text to be displayed in the window.

Choose: Maximize from the document window control-menu box
or
Click: Maximize button (in the document window title bar)

Press [Alt] + - (hyphen) to open the document window control menu.

WORD PROCESSING

Your screen should be similar to Figure 2-4.

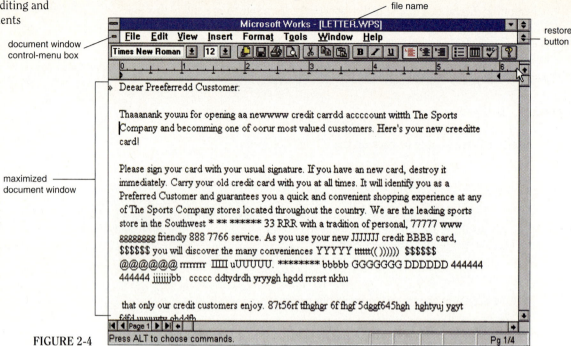

file name

restore
button

document window
control-menu box

maximized
document window

FIGURE 2-4

The document window is the full size of the workspace and it no longer displays a title bar. Consequently more text can now be displayed in the window. The document window control-menu box is now located on the left end of the menu bar, and the restore button is located on the right end. The file name is now in brackets after the program name in the application window title bar.

The insertion point can be moved quickly to the bottom line of the window by pressing [Ctrl] + [Page Down] or to the top line by pressing [Ctrl] + [Page Up]. To move to the bottom line of the window,

Press: [Ctrl] + [Page Down]

To bring additional text into view in the window, you can scroll the text using either the mouse or the keyboard. As you move line by line up or down through the document, the lines at the top or bottom of the window move out of view to allow more text to be displayed.

Press: [↓] (3 times)

> The maximize and minimize buttons change to the restore button when the window is maximized.

Your screen should be similar to Figure 2-5.

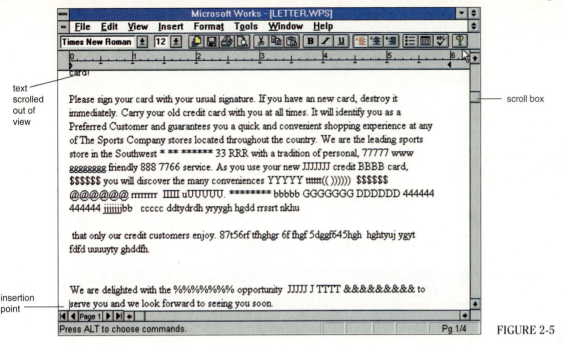

text scrolled out of view

scroll box

insertion point

FIGURE 2-5

Three new lines of text have appeared at the bottom of the window and three lines have scrolled off the top of the window. The insertion point should be at the beginning of the word "serve."

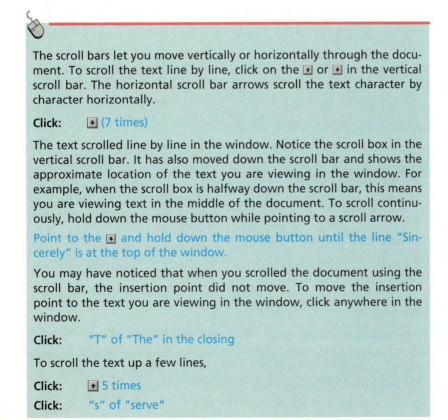

The scroll bars let you move vertically or horizontally through the document. To scroll the text line by line, click on the ⊡ or ⊡ in the vertical scroll bar. The horizontal scroll bar arrows scroll the text character by character horizontally.

Click: ⊡ (7 times)

The text scrolled line by line in the window. Notice the scroll box in the vertical scroll bar. It has also moved down the scroll bar and shows the approximate location of the text you are viewing in the window. For example, when the scroll box is halfway down the scroll bar, this means you are viewing text in the middle of the document. To scroll continuously, hold down the mouse button while pointing to a scroll arrow.

Point to the ⊡ and hold down the mouse button until the line "Sincerely" is at the top of the window.

You may have noticed that when you scrolled the document using the scroll bar, the insertion point did not move. To move the insertion point to the text you are viewing in the window, click anywhere in the window.

Click: "T" of "The" in the closing

To scroll the text up a few lines,

Click: ⊡ 5 times

Click: "s" of "serve"

WORD PROCESSING

You can also move in large jumps quickly through the text in a document by moving a window or a page at a time, moving to a specific page, or moving to the end or beginning of the document.

To move up or down a full window in the document, use the Page Up or Page Down keys.

Press: Page Up

The insertion point moved to the top line of text on the previous full window. To move down three full windows,

Press: Page Down (3 times)

The insertion point is positioned on the first line of the third full window on the document.

Your screen should be similar to Figure 2-6.

> You can click above or below the scroll box on the vertical scroll bar to move a window at a time on the document.

FIGURE 2-6

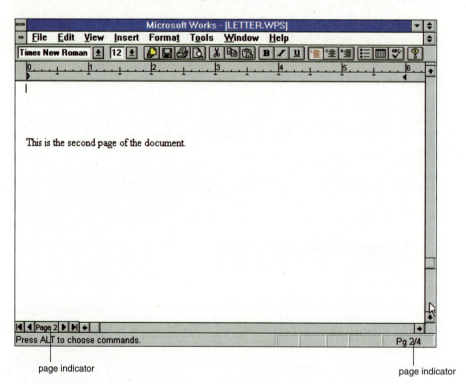

page indicator

page indicator

The page indicators show that the insertion point is on Page 2 of a total of four pages.

Using the Go To Command

To move through several pages of the document at once, you could press Page Down or Page Up multiple times, or you can use the Go To command in the Edit menu. Using this command allows you to move directly to a specific location in the document without scrolling text you do not want to see.

To move directly to page 3 of this document,

Choose: Edit

Notice to the right of the Go To command, the **shortcut key** "F5" is displayed. Many of Work's most frequently used commands have shortcut keys that allow you to initiate the command without using the menu. Instead of choosing Go To from the Edit menu, you can simply press [F5]. Because the menu is already open, however, you need to select the command from the menu.

> Remember, if you are using the keyboard, press [Alt] to activate the menu.

Choose: Go To

Your screen should be similar to Figure 2-7.

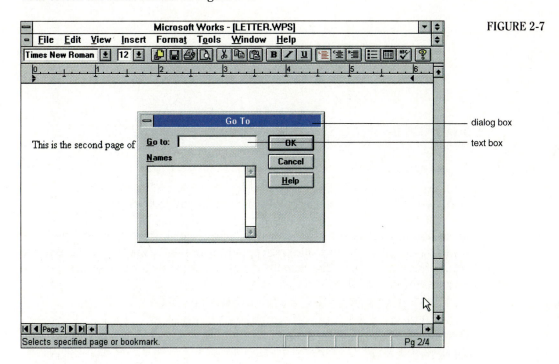

FIGURE 2-7

The Go To dialog box is displayed. In the Go To text box, you need to enter the page number you want to move to. The insertion point is positioned in the text box waiting for you to make an entry. To move to the third page,

Type: 3

To complete the command,

Choose: OK

> Press [←Enter] to choose OK.

WORD PROCESSING

Your screen should be similar to Figure 2-8.

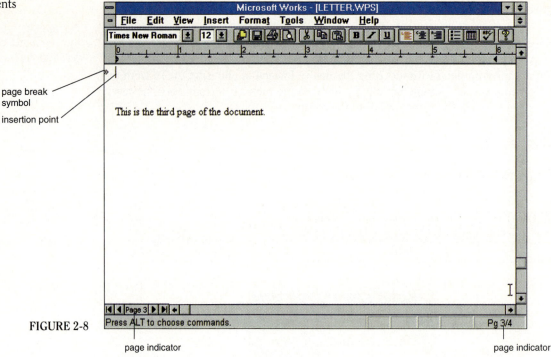

page break
symbol

insertion point

FIGURE 2-8

page indicator   page indicator

The insertion point is positioned on the first line of page 3 of the document file. You can confirm the insertion point location by checking the page indicators. To show where one page ends and another begins, a page break symbol (>>) is displayed. Works inserts an automatic page break to tell the printer where to end one page and begin printing the next. The automatic page break symbol appears whenever you have entered enough text to fill a page.

To use the Go To shortcut key this time to move to page 1,

Press: F5 GOTO
Type: 1
Choose: OK

The insertion point is positioned at the top of page 1 of the document.

Note: Throughout the Works labs, command sequences will appear following the word "Choose." The keyboard shortcut will appear below the command sequence following a ➤. You can use either the menu or the shortcut to enter the command.

The biggest jump the insertion point can make is to move to the beginning or end of a document. To do this Ctrl is used in combination with Home or End. To move to the end of this document,

Press: Ctrl + End

Your screen should be similar to Figure 2-9.

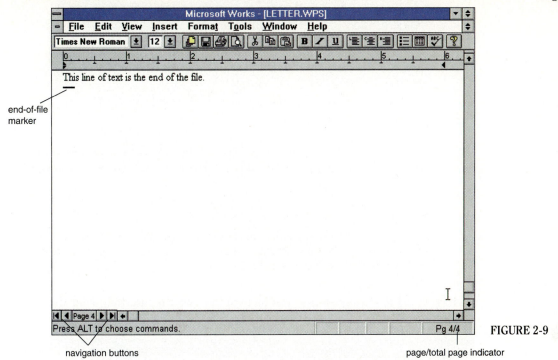

FIGURE 2-9

The insertion point should be positioned on a line of text marking the end of the document. This is the last line in the file. The page indicators show the insertion point location is page 4 of a total of four pages. The solid line below the last line of text is the **end-of-file mark**. You cannot move the insertion point below this line.

To move quickly back to the first line of text in the document,

Press: Ctrl + Home

The insertion point should be positioned on the first line of page 1 of the document.

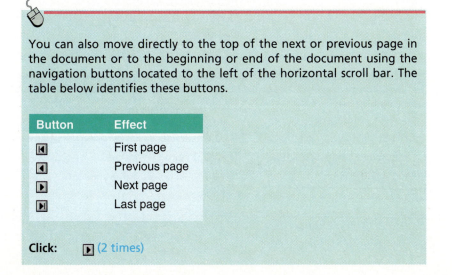

You can also move directly to the top of the next or previous page in the document or to the beginning or end of the document using the navigation buttons located to the left of the horizontal scroll bar. The table below identifies these buttons.

Button	Effect
◄	First page
◄	Previous page
►	Next page
►	Last page

Click: ► (2 times)

The insertion point is positioned at the top of page 3. To move quickly back to the first page of the document,

Click: ◄|

You can also drag the scroll box to move to an approximate location in the file. To drag, hold down the left mouse button while moving the mouse.

Point to the scroll box on the vertical scroll bar. Drag the scroll box downward on the scroll bar. Release the mouse button when the box is near the bottom of the scroll bar. Click anywhere on the window.

The text near the bottom of the document should be displayed in the window. You can check the page indicator to see your actual page location.

Drag the scroll box to the top of the scroll bar. Click on the "D" in "Deear."

The same procedure is followed using the horizontal scroll bar box to scroll text horizontally. The scroll bar feature operates the same way in all Works tools and dialog boxes.

To review, the following features can be used to move the insertion point through the document:

Key	Action
→	One character or space to right
←	One character or space to left
↑	One line up
↓	One line down
Ctrl + →	One word to right
Ctrl + ←	One word to left
Home	Beginning of line
End	Right end of line
Page Up	Top of previous full window
Page Down	Top of next full window
Ctrl + Page Up	Top line of window
Ctrl + Page Down	Bottom line of window
Ctrl + Home	Beginning of document
Ctrl + End	End of document
Edit>Go To or F5	To location specified in Go To dialog box

Mouse	Action
Point to location and click left button	Positions insertion point
Click scroll arrow	Scrolls text line by line in direction of arrow
Click above/below scroll box	Scrolls document window by window
Drag scroll box	Moves multiple windows up/down
◄|	First page
|►	Last page
►	Next page
◄	Previous page

Deleting Characters

Now that you have learned how to move the insertion point around the word processor document, you are ready to learn how to **edit**, or revise and correct errors, in a document.

The first errors you see are in the salutation, which contains several extra characters. These can be removed using the Delete key. The Delete key removes the character to the right of the insertion point. The first extra character is in the word "Deear." The extra "e" needs to be deleted.

Move to: first "e" in "Deear"

Press: Delete

The selected character, in this case the "e," is deleted. The text to the right moved left one space to fill in the space where the deleted character had been.

Continue to correct the salutation using the Delete key. It should read, "Dear Preferred Customer:".

The first paragraph in this letter also contains many errors.

Press: ↓ (2 times)

The first two words on this line should be "Thank you." The insertion point is positioned to the right of these words. A second way to delete a character is with the Backspace key. This key removes the character to the left of the insertion point, therefore it is particularly useful when you are moving from right to left (backward) along a line of text. You will correct these words using the Backspace key.

Using ←,

Move to: end of word "youuu"

Press: Backspace (2 times)

The extra characters are erased.

To correct the first word, using ←,

Move to: last "a" of "Thaaanank"

As you erase text on a line, Works examines the line to see whether the word beginning on the next line can be moved up to fill in the extra space without exceeding the margin setting. Watch the end of this line carefully as you remove the extra characters "aaan" using the Backspace key.

Press: Backspace (4 times)

Either the Delete key on an enhanced keyboard or the Delete key on the numeric keypad can be used.

The Backspace key is located above the ←Enter key. It may also appear as ←.

WORD PROCESSING

Your screen should be similar to Figure 2-10.

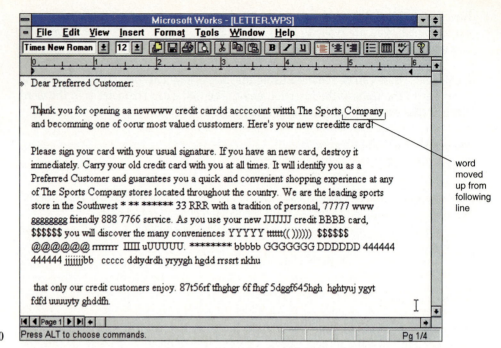

word
moved
up from
following
line

FIGURE 2-10

The characters to the left of the insertion point were removed, and the remaining text moved over to fill in the blank space. Additionally, because there was enough space on the line, the first word on the second line, "Company," moved up to the end of the first line.

Practice using the [Delete] and [Backspace] keys to correct the errors in the first paragraph. (Do not be concerned if you accidentally delete the wrong character.)

When you are done, your screen should be similar to Figure 2-11.

FIGURE 2-11

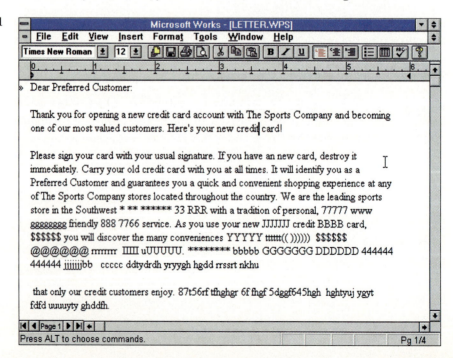

Inserting and Overtyping Text

The next change you need to make is in the first sentence of the second paragraph. It should read: "Please sign your new card in ink with your usual signature." The sentence is missing three words, "new," "in," and "ink." These words can be easily entered into the sentence without retyping it.

Text can be entered into a document using either the Insert or Overtype options. The default setting for Works is Insert. As you type using Insert, new characters are inserted into the existing text. The existing text moves to the right to make space for the new characters, and the text on the line is adjusted as necessary.

To enter the word "new" before the word "card" in the first sentence,

Move to: "c" in "card"

Type: new

Press: [Spacebar]

The word "new" has been entered into the sentence by moving everything to the right to make space as each letter is typed.

Continue to correct the sentence by entering the words "in ink" before the word "with."

In the second sentence, you notice that the word "new" should be "old."

Move to: "n" of "new"

You could delete this word and type in the correct word, or you can use the Overtype method of entering text in a document. With Overtype, new text types over the existing characters. Pressing the *I* key changes Insert to Overtype.

Press: [Insert]

To tell you that Overtype is on, the indicator "OVR" is displayed in the status bar.

To replace the word "new" with "old,"

Type: old

Either the [Insert] key on the enhanced keyboard or the [Ins] key on the numeric keypad can be used.

WORD PROCESSING

Your screen should be similar to Figure 2-12.

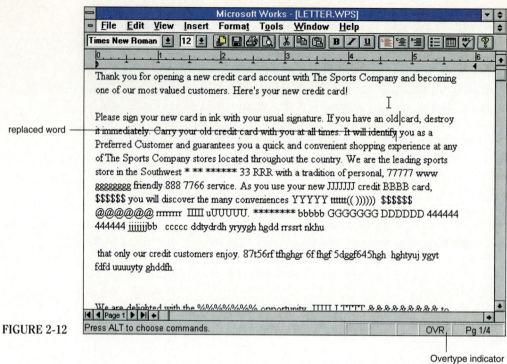

replaced word

FIGURE 2-12

Overtype indicator

As each new character was typed, it replaced the character (or space) at the insertion point.

Next you need to replace the word "old" in the third sentence of this paragraph with "new."

Move to: "o" of "old"

Type: new

To switch back to Insert,

Press: [Insert]

"OVR" is no longer displayed in the status bar.

Use Insert and Overtype to correct any errors you may have accidentally made in the first paragraph.

Inserting Blank Lines

As you continue to proof the letter, you decide the second paragraph is too long and should be two separate paragraphs. The new third paragraph should begin with the sentence "We are..."

Move to: "W" in "We" (fifth sentence of second paragraph)

The ⟨←Enter⟩ key is used to insert a blank line into text or to end a paragraph. This is the same as if you pressed Return on a typewriter. When ⟨←Enter⟩ is pressed in the middle of a line of text, all text to the right of the insertion point moves to the beginning of the next line. To end the paragraph,

Press: ⟨←Enter⟩

Each time ⟨←Enter⟩ is pressed, Works automatically enters a special character called a **paragraph mark** at that location in the document. You cannot see this mark because it is hidden to prevent the screen from becoming cluttered. You will learn how to display these special characters in the next section.

To remove the paragraph mark,

Press: ⟨Backspace⟩

The paragraph mark you just entered is deleted and the text returns to its original location. To reinsert the mark,

Press: ⟨←Enter⟩

To separate this paragraph from the previous paragraph, you want to enter a blank line. When ⟨←Enter⟩ is pressed at the beginning of a line, a blank line is inserted into the document.

Press: ⟨←Enter⟩

Your screen should be similar to Figure 2-13.

FIGURE 2-13

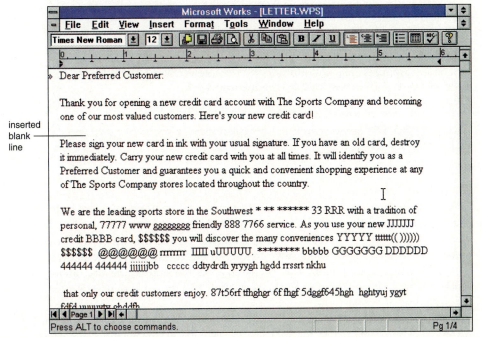

inserted blank line

A blank line is inserted into the text, forcing the line the insertion point is on to move down one line.

Displaying Special Characters

Every time you press the ⏎Enter key, Works inserts a new paragraph mark character into the file. Other special character marks are entered by the program also. Works does not display these special characters because they clutter the screen. However, there are times when you need to delete a special character and need to find out where it is located. The All Characters command in the View menu is used to display these characters.

Choose: View>All Characters

Your screen should be similar to Figure 2-14.

FIGURE 2-14

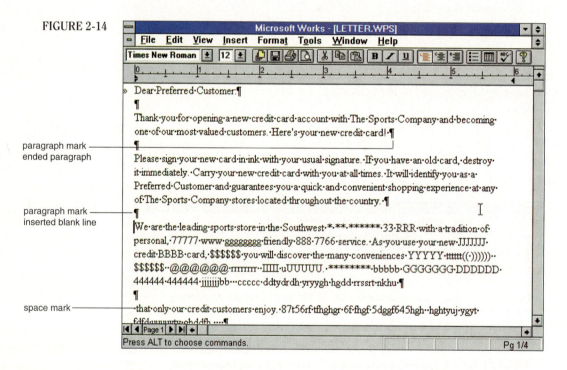

paragraph mark
ended paragraph

paragraph mark
inserted blank line

space mark

The document now displays the special characters. A paragraph mark character ¶ is displayed wherever the ⏎Enter key was pressed. Between each word a dot shows where the Spacebar was pressed. The ¶ character on the line above the insertion point represents ⏎Enter, which was pressed to create the blank line between the second and third paragraphs. The ¶ character at the end of the line above that represents the ⏎Enter that ended the paragraph and moved the insertion point to the beginning of the next line.

To delete a special character, position the insertion point on the character using either the keyboard or the mouse and press Delete, or position the insertion

You can use Works with or without the special characters displayed. It does not affect how the program operates and the characters do not print.

point to the right of the character and press $\boxed{\text{Backspace}}$. This is the same as if you were deleting text in the document. To delete the ¶ that you just inserted,

Press: $\boxed{\uparrow}$
Press: $\boxed{\text{Delete}}$

The blank line is removed. To remove the ¶ character at the end of the previous line,

Press: $\boxed{\text{Backspace}}$

The text moves up to fill in the blank space at the end of the previous line and returns to a single paragraph. To end the paragraph and reenter the blank line,

Press: $\boxed{\leftarrow\text{Enter}}$ (2 times)

Two paragraph mark characters are inserted and the text moves down appropriately.

For normal entry of text, you will probably not want the special characters displayed. To hide the special characters,

Select: View

Notice the ✔ symbol next to the command. This indicates that the feature is in use. To turn the feature off,

Choose: All Characters

The screen returns to normal display. Now that you know how to turn this feature on and off, you can use it whenever you want when entering and editing text.

To review, the following editing keys have been covered:

Key	Action
$\boxed{\text{Backspace}}$	Deletes character to left of insertion point
$\boxed{\text{Delete}}$	Deletes character to right of insertion point
$\boxed{\text{Insert}}$ on	Inserts character into existing text
$\boxed{\text{Insert}}$ off	Replaces existing text by typing over characters
$\boxed{\leftarrow\text{Enter}}$	Ends a paragraph or inserts a blank line

Selecting Text

As you continue proofreading the letter, you see that the third paragraph contains several large areas of "junk" text. To remove these unnecessary characters, you could use $\boxed{\text{Delete}}$ and $\boxed{\text{Backspace}}$ to delete each character individually. However, this is very slow.

To speed up many tasks, you can select the text you want to change by **highlighting** it. When you highlight text, the insertion point expands to a highlight and covers the selected text. The selection can be any group of characters, words, phrases, sentences, paragraphs, or the entire file. Once text is highlighted, you can choose from many different commands to change it, such as moving, copying, or deleting.

To select text by highlighting it, first move the insertion point to the beginning or end of the text to be selected.

The first group of junk characters to be removed (* ** ****** 33 RRR) follows the word "Southwest" in the first line of the third paragraph. To position the insertion point on the first character of the text to be selected,

Move to: "*" (first sentence of third paragraph)

Then select the text by expanding the highlight using the keyboard or the mouse.

To highlight text, point to the first character of text to be selected and drag the mouse to expand the highlight to cover the entire area of text you want to select.

You can drag in any direction in the document to extend the highlight, or drag in the opposite direction to deselect text. You can also drag diagonally across text to extend the highlight from the character the insertion point is on to the last character in the selection.

Drag the mouse until the junk text is highlighted (including the space before the word "with").

Notice as you drag the mouse, the highlight seems to jump by increments of groups of text or words. This is because the default setting is to automatically highlight by words.

Text can be highlighted with the keyboard using several different methods. One way is to hold down ⇧Shift while pressing a directional key or any of the keys used to move the insertion point through the text (refer to the table on page 48).

To extend the highlight,

Press: ⇧Shift + → (5 times)

The highlight extended five characters, including blank spaces, to the right. To quickly select word by word,

Press: ⇧Shift + Ctrl + → (3 times)

> To cancel a selection, simply click anywhere in the window.

> The mouse pointer appears as ⇧DRAG when it is positioned on highlighted text. You will learn about this feature in the next lab.

> To cancel a selection, press any directional key without using ⇧Shift.

> A "word" is any group of characters preceded and followed by a space.

Your screen should be similar to Figure 2-15.

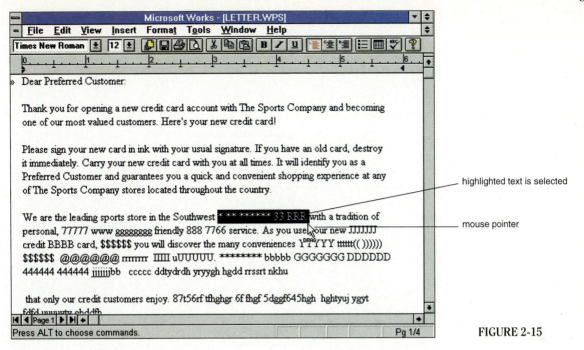

highlighted text is selected

mouse pointer

FIGURE 2-15

The highlight covers the junk text on the line. Whenever text is highlighted, it indicates it is selected. Text that is selected can then be modified using many different Works features. In this case, you want to remove the selected text. To do this,

Press: `Delete`

In a similar manner, select and delete the rest of the junk characters in this sentence.

The rest of this paragraph includes several areas of junk text. Follow the procedure in the appropriate section that follows to clean up this paragraph.

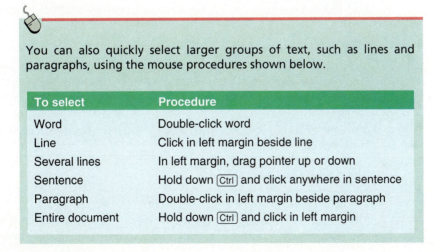

You can also quickly select larger groups of text, such as lines and paragraphs, using the mouse procedures shown below.

To select	Procedure
Word	Double-click word
Line	Click in left margin beside line
Several lines	In left margin, drag pointer up or down
Sentence	Hold down `Ctrl` and click anywhere in sentence
Paragraph	Double-click in left margin beside paragraph
Entire document	Hold down `Ctrl` and click in left margin

WORD PROCESSING

To select the first "word" of junk characters,

Double-click: "JJJJJJJ"

Then to remove the selection,

Press: [Delete]

In the same manner, select and delete the two other "words" of junk characters ("BBBB" and "$$$$$$") in this sentence.

The next two lines of text are made up entirely of junk characters. To select and delete these lines and the blank line below them,

Position the mouse pointer in the left margin of this paragraph.

The mouse pointer shape changes to an arrow ⬈. This indicates the mouse is ready to highlight text.

Click in the left margin next to the first full line of junk text.

The entire line is selected.

Then to select the next two lines, drag down two lines in the left margin.

To show how easy it is to expand the highlight to an entire paragraph or the entire document,

Double-click in the left margin.

All the text between paragraph marks is highlighted. Finally, to expand the selection to the entire document,

Hold down [Ctrl] while clicking in the left margin.

This is more text than you need highlighted. To shrink the highlight to cover the two lines only,

Point in the left margin next to the first full line of junk text and drag down two lines in the left margin. Delete the two selected lines.

Finally, the last line in the paragraph contains a sentence of junk characters that needs to be removed.

Hold down [Ctrl] and click on the sentence.

The entire sentence (text between periods) is selected.

Delete the sentence.

If a period is encountered that is part of an abbreviation, such as Mr., Works interprets the period as the end of a sentence.

Another way to extend the highlight is by using the [F8] key. This feature allows you to highlight text using the directional keys without holding down [⇧ Shift].

The next sentence contains three junk character "words" that need to be removed.

Move to: beginning of "JJJJJJJ"

Press: [F8]

The status bar displays the message "EXT" (for "extend"). This is to show you that the program is in the process of extending the highlight.

Now you can use the directional keys to extend the highlight without holding down ⇧Shift.

Press: → (2 times)

The highlight extended two characters to the right. To highlight the word,

Press: Ctrl + →

The entire word is selected, just as if you had held down ⇧Shift while pressing the directional key combination.

To remove the word,

Press: Delete

"EXT" is no longer displayed in the status bar, indicating the feature is no longer active.

The next "word" of junk characters to be removed is "BBBB."

Move to: anywhere in "BBBB"

Press: F8

You can press F8 repeatedly to quickly extend the highlight in increments, such as a word or a sentence, as shown below:

To select	Press F8
Word	2 times
Sentence	3 times
Paragraph	4 times
Entire file	5 times

Press: F8

The entire word is highlighted including the space following the word. To remove the selection,

Press: Delete

Select and delete the word "$$$$$$."

The next two lines contain junk text only. To select and remove these lines and the blank line below them,

Move to: "Y" at beginning of line

Press: F8

Press: ↓ (3 times)

Press: Delete

Finally, the last line in the paragraph contains a complete sentence of junk characters. To highlight the entire sentence,

Move to: anywhere in last sentence

Press: F8 (3 times)

If at any point you want to cancel the extend feature, press Esc. Then move the insertion point to clear the highlight.

The insertion point can be anywhere in the piece of text to be selected.

WORD PROCESSING

All the text between periods is highlighted. Before deleting it, to show how easy it is to select a paragraph or the entire document,

Press: F8

All the text between the paragraph marks is highlighted. To select the entire file,

Press: F8

This is more text than you need highlighted. To shrink the highlight, press ⇧Shift + F8 . In this case to shrink the highlight to cover the sentence only,

Press: ⇧Shift + F8 (2 times)

Now only the sentence is selected. To remove it,

Press: Delete

Using any of the methods you have learned to highlight text, select and erase the remaining junk characters in the letter.

When you are done, your screen should be similar to Figure 2-16.

FIGURE 2-16

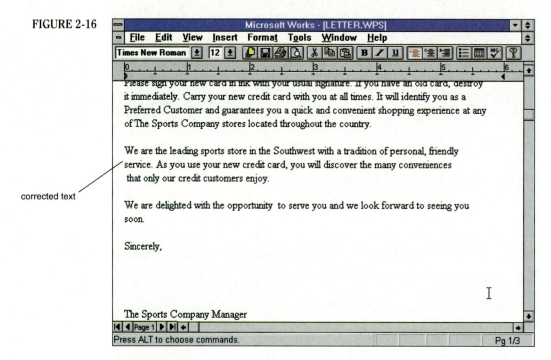

corrected text

Using Undo

Finally, you are not too pleased with the last sentence of the letter and are considering removing it.

Select and delete the last sentence of the letter.

After thinking about this change, you decide the last sentence may not be so bad after all. The Undo Editing command on the Edit menu restores your last

The shortcut for Undo Editing is Ctrl + Z.

deletion to its original location in the text regardless of the current insertion point location. To restore the deleted text,

Choose: **E**dit>**U**ndo Editing
➤   Ctrl + Z

The sentence is restored. Undo Editing reverses the most recent editing or formatting change. It will reverse any typing, deleting, or formatting action.

After you Undo an action, the Undo Editing command changes to the Redo Editing command. This allows you to restore your original revision.

Undo Editing must be used immediately after the editing you want to reverse.

Choose: **E**dit>**R**edo Editing
➤   Ctrl + Z

The sentence is removed again. To restore the sentence,

Move to: any location in window
Choose: **E**dit>**U**ndo Editing
➤   Ctrl + Z

The sentence is restored to its original location in the document regardless of the insertion point's location.

Another use of the Undo Editing command is to delete characters entered since the last command was used or since you last moved the insertion point. To demonstrate this,

Move to: blank line below last sentence
Type: **The Undo feature can save you much time.**

To undo this typing, using the shortcut,

Press: Ctrl + Z

The line of text you just typed is removed. Now the letter should be correct.

Enter your name in the closing one line above "The Sports Company Manager."

Saving an Existing File

Now that you have corrected the letter, you need to save the corrections to the file on your data disk. If you do not save your changes, the changes will be lost when you exit Works.

Two commands on the File menu can be used to save a file, Save and Save As. The Save command saves the current document using the same path and file name by replacing the contents of the existing disk file with the changes you have made. For example, the file you opened and edited in this lab is named LETTER.WPS. Using the Save command would permanently replace the original contents of the LETTER.WPS file with the changes you have made that are currently in memory only.

The Ctrl + S key or 🖫 Save button are the shortcuts for the Save command.

The Save As command saves the current document to the disk by prompting you for a new file name. This command lets you save both the original version of the document and the revised document as two separate files. For example, you could save the changes you have made to the LETTER.WPS file as a new file with a new file name. The original file LETTER.WPS would remain unchanged on your disk, and the new file with the changes you have made would be saved to the disk under a different file name.

Since you may want to redo this lab and use the LETTER.WPS file again, you will save your edited version using a new file name.

Choose: File>Save As

The Save As dialog box displays the file name of the current file, LETTER.WPS, in the File Name text box. The File Name list box displays the names of all Works files in alphabetical order. Notice that the files have several different file extensions. Works automatically adds a file extension to all files created using the program. The file extension that is used varies with the tool, as shown below:

Extension	Tool
WPS	Word Processor
WKS	Spreadsheet
WDB	Database
WCM	Communications

The line above the Directories list box shows the current path. This should be the path where you want Works to save the new file to.

If this path is not correct, select the appropriate drive and path for your system as you do when opening a file.

The new file name can be entered in either upper- or lowercase letters. In the File Name text box, the current file name is highlighted, indicating it is selected, and the insertion point appears at the end of the file name. As soon as you begin typing, the existing file name will be erased. To clear the highlight so you can edit the existing name rather than retype the entire name again,

> A Works file name follows the same rules as DOS file names.

Press: ⬅ 4 times

The highlight is cleared and the insertion point is positioned at the end of the file name. To edit the file name,

Type: EV
Choose: OK

A question dialog box appears asking if you will be saving the file to a different floppy disk.

Choose: No

The new file name is displayed in the title bar. The original file, LETTER.WPS, has remained unchanged on the disk, and the new file, LETTEREV.WPS, has been created on the disk. It contains the edited copy of the LETTER.WPS file.

Printing a Document

Finally, you want to print a copy of the credit card letter to give to the Regional Manager. If you have printer capability, you can print a copy of the document.

First, if necessary, turn the printer on and if you are using a dot matrix printer, adjust the paper so that the perforation is just above the printer scale.

The Print command is an option on the File menu.

Note: Please consult your instructor for printing procedures that may differ from the directions below.

Choose: <u>F</u>ile><u>P</u>rint

➤   Ctrl + P

The shortcut key for the Print command is Ctrl + P.

Your screen should be similar to Figure 2-17.

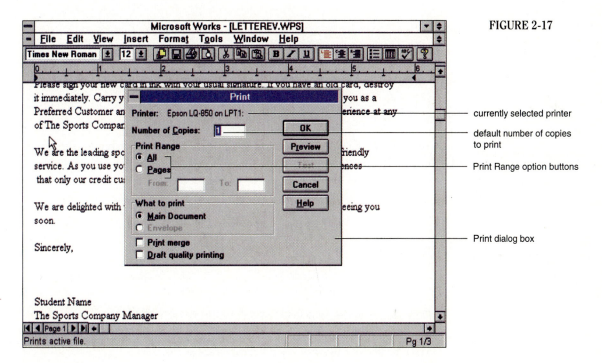

FIGURE 2-17

— currently selected printer

— default number of copies to print

— Print Range option buttons

— Print dialog box

WORD PROCESSING

The Print dialog box is used to specify the settings you want Works to use to print the document. The currently selected printer is displayed in the Printer line.

Note: If the printer in the Print dialog box is not the appropriate printer, you will need to select another printer. To do this choose Cancel to close the Print dialog box. Then choose File>Printer Setup. From the Printer list box, select the name of the printer you want to use to print this document and choose OK. Then choose File>Print again.

The Number of Copies text box shows 1 as the default number of copies that will be printed. The Print Range area is used to specify how much of the document you want printed. The round Print Range buttons are called **option buttons**. A dot

An option is selected by clicking on the option or by pressing [Alt] + underlined letter of the option.

marks the selected option. Only one option button can be selected in a group. The All option prints the entire document file, while the Pages option prints the pages that you specify. The All option is the default selection.

You want to print the first page of the document only. This is the page that contains the letter. To select the Pages option,

Choose: Pages

The From and To text boxes are now active, so you can enter the page numbers to print. In the From text box,

Type: 1

In the To box, you enter the page number of the last page you want printed. In this case it is also page 1.

Select: To
Type: 1

Now you are ready to instruct Works to print the letter.

Choose: OK

Your printer should be printing out the document. The printed copy of the credit card letter should be similar to Figure 2-18.

FIGURE 2-18

Dear Preferred Customer:

Thank you for opening a new credit card account with The Sports Company and becoming one of our most valued customers. Here's your new credit card!

Please sign your card with your usual signature. If you have an old card, destroy it immediately. Carry your new credit card with you at all times. It will identify you as a Preferred Customer and guarantees you a quick and convenient shopping experience at any of The Sports Company stores located throughout the country.

We are the leading sports store in the Southwest with a tradition of personal, friendly service. As you use your new credit card, you will discover the many conveniences that only our credit customers enjoy.

We are delighted with the opportunity to serve you and we look forward to seeing you soon.

Sincerely,

Student Name
The Sports Company Manager

Note: Your letter may not match exactly if the printer you selected prints using a different font size than the one used to print the document in the text. The font size of the selected printer controls the number of words that can be printed on a line. The display of the document on the screen also reflects this change in font size.

Creating a New Document

You also want to include a brief cover memo to the Regional Manager with the credit card letter. To create this memo, you need to open a new document file.

Before opening a new file, you will close the current file using the Close command in the File menu.

Choose: File>Close

The file is no longer in memory. If you had not already saved the file, you would be prompted to save your changes before the file was closed.

You are returned to the Works window, and the Startup dialog box is automatically displayed. To open a new word processing document window,

Choose: Word Processor

A blank word processing window is displayed. The insertion point is on the first space of the first line of the document window. The end-of-document marker is immediately below the insertion point. Notice the file name "Word1" in the title bar. This is the default file name assigned to new word processing files by Works. When you save this file, you will change the file name to a name that is more descriptive of the contents of the file.

A blank document window is like a blank piece of paper. To create a new document, simply begin typing the text. When the insertion point reaches the end of a full line, do not press ⎵Enter. Works will automatically decide when to move text to the next line based on the margin settings. This feature is called **wordwrap**. The only time you need to press ⎵Enter is at the end of a paragraph, to insert blank lines, or to create a short line such as a title.

As you type the memo shown below, do not press ⎵Enter until you are directed. While entering this memo, you will use Tab↹ to align the text following the colon in the memo heading. Pressing Tab↹ moves all text to the right of the insertion point on the line to the next tab stop. The default tab stops are set at every .5 inch and are displayed on the ruler as ⊥ .

One or two spaces may follow a period at the end of a sentence. Traditionally two spaces are used, but with the introduction of word processors and different fonts, one space is more commonly used. Use whichever you prefer in this memo. If you make typing errors as you enter the text, use the editing features you learned to correct your errors.

Enter the memo shown below beginning on the first line of the document.

Type: **TO:**

Press: Tab ↹ **(2 times)**

Type: **James Kennedy**

Press: ←Enter

Type: **FROM:**

Press: Tab ↹

Type: **[your name]**

Press: ←Enter

Type: **DATE:**

Press: Tab ↹ **(2 times)**

Type: **[enter current date]**

Press: ←Enter

Type: **SUBJECT:**

Press: Tab ↹

Type: **Credit Card Letter**

Press: ←Enter (3 times)

Type: **Attached is a copy of the letter I revised to be sent to all new
Sports Company credit card holders. I created the letter using the
Works for Windows program. I can easily make any changes and
additions you may like.**

Press: ←Enter

Your screen should be similar to Figure 2-19.

FIGURE 2-19

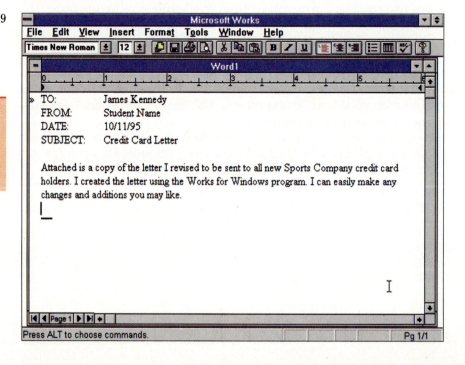

The text on your screen may
wrap at different locations
than the text in Figure 2-19.
The selected printer controls
the default font and type size.

As you can see, the automatic wordwrap feature makes entering text in a document much faster than typing. This is because a carriage return does not need to be pressed at the end of every line.

Proofread the memo to check that you have entered it correctly. If you find any errors, correct them using the editing features you learned in this lab.

Previewing the Document

Before printing, it is helpful to preview how a document will look when it is printed. To do this,

Choose: File>Print Preview

or

Click: 🔍 Print Preview

Your screen should be similar to Figure 2-20.

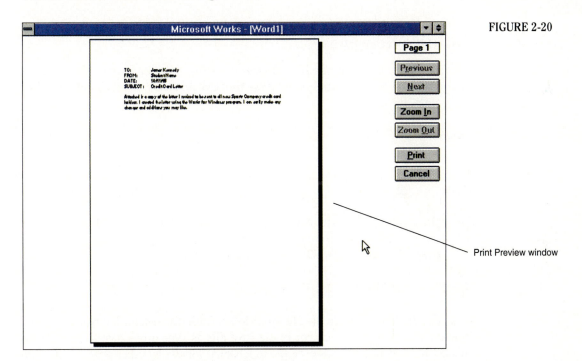

FIGURE 2-20

The Print Preview window displays a reduced view of how the current page will appear when printed. This view allows you to check your page layout before printing. You feel that because the memo is short, it would look better double-spaced. To close the Print Preview window,

Choose: Cancel

You could also select the
entire document by pressing
F8 five times or by holding
down Ctrl and clicking in the
left margin.

You will be learning about
many of the formatting
features in the next lab.

You can use [icon] to print a
document using the default
print settings.

Changing Line Spacing

Works creates word processing documents using single spacing by default. To change to double spacing, select the area of text to change and then use the command. You want the entire document double-spaced. To quickly select the entire document,

Choose: Edit>Select All

The Format menu contains commands that affect the layout of your document, including line spacing. However, to quickly change the line spacing, you will use the shortcut Ctrl + 2.

Press: Ctrl + 2

The selected text appears double-spaced.

Print the memo as you did the letter except use the default Print Range setting All to print the entire document.

Saving a New File

The first time you save a new file, you can use either the File Save or the File Save As command. Both commands will access the Save As dialog box and prompt you to enter a new file name.

Choose: File>Save

   ➢   Ctrl + S

or

Click: [icon] Save

The path should still be the correct path for your system. If it is not, specify the appropriate drive and directory path.

Next, to enter the new file name in the File Name text box,

Type: CRDTMEMO

It is not necessary to enter the file extension because the default file type is set to a Works word processor document in the Save File as Type drop-down list box. From this list box you can also save the file in a format for use by other products. You do not need to change this setting. To complete the command,

Choose: OK

After a few moments, the document is saved on the disk. The file name is displayed in the title bar.

Now you are ready to quit the Works program.

Choose: File>Exit Works

You can also exit the program
by choosing Close from the
Application control menu (Ctrl
+ F4), or double-clicking the
control-menu box.

When you exit the program, if any open documents had not been saved, you would be prompted to save them before the program is exited. This is a safety precaution to help prevent the loss of data.

Always exit the Works program using the File>Exit Works command. Never turn off your computer until you exit properly, or you may lose data.

Works is no longer running and the Windows Program Manager is displayed again.

Key Terms

margin (37)
default (37)
page break symbol (37)
navigator buttons (37)
page indicator (37)
font (38)
shortcut key (45)

end-of-file mark (47)
edit (49)
paragraph mark (53)
highlighting (55)
option buttons (63)
wordwrap (65)

Command Summary

Command	Shortcut	Button	Action
Edit>**G**o To	F5		Moves to specified location
View>**A**ll Characters			Displays special characters
Edit>**Un**do Editing	Ctrl + Z		Reverses most recent editing or formatting change
Edit>**R**edo Editing	Ctrl + Z		Reverses Undo
File>Save **A**s			Saves file using new file name
File>**P**rint	Ctrl + P	🖨	Prints file using selected printer
File>Print Pre**v**iew		🔍	Displays document as it will be printed
Edit>Select **A**ll	F8 (5 times)		Highlights all text
File>**S**ave	Ctrl + S	💾	Saves document using same file name

LAB REVIEW

Matching

1. status bar   _____ a. new text writes over existing text
2. End   _____ b. deletes character to right of insertion point
3. Overtype   _____ c. moves insertion point one word to right
4. Ctrl + Home   _____ d. inserts blank line or ends paragraph
5. Delete   _____ e. moves to end of line
6. F5   _____ f. line of information below document window
7. Ctrl + →   _____ g. special character that shows where ←Enter was pressed
8. Backspace   _____ h. deletes letter to left of insertion point
9. ←Enter   _____ i. moves to beginning of document
10. ¶   _____ j. shortcut for Edit>Go To command

Fill-In Questions

1.   In the following Works 3.0 for Windows screen, several items are identified by letters. Enter the correct term for each item in the space provided.

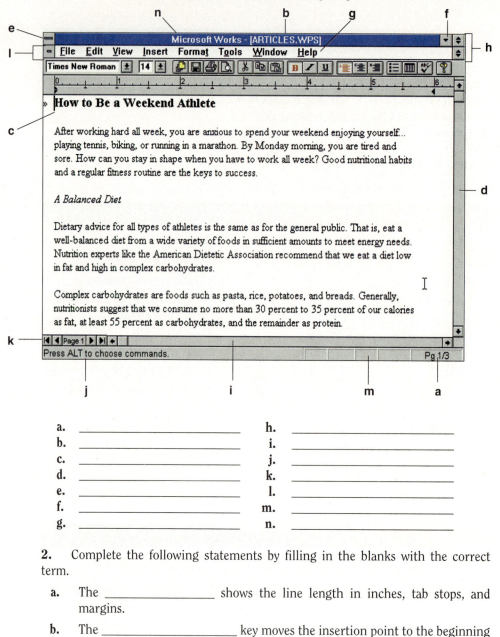

a. _____		h. _____
b. _____		i. _____
c. _____		j. _____
d. _____		k. _____
e. _____		l. _____
f. _____		m. _____
g. _____		n. _____

2.   Complete the following statements by filling in the blanks with the correct term.

a.   The _____ shows the line length in inches, tab stops, and margins.

b.   The _____ key moves the insertion point to the beginning of a line.

c.   Name three ways you can highlight text: _____, _____, and _____.

d.   Text can be entered in a document by using either the _____ or _____ method.

e.   The _____ key erases the character to the left of the insertion point.

f.   The automatic adjustment of words on a line is called _____.

g.   A(n) _____ or a(n) _____ can be used to initiate many commands without using the menu.

h.   The _____ _____ command reverses the most recent editing or formatting change.

i.   A Works word processing document includes _____ that control the display of text.

j.   The _____ key combination will change the selected text to double spaced.

Practice Exercises

1.   Open the file QUOTE.WPS. This file consists of a series of quotes that contain many typing errors. Follow the directions in the file to correct the sentences. Save the edited version of the file as QUOTE1. Print a copy of the edited document.

2.   Open the file BUSCOMM.WPS. This file contains information related to professional communications. Follow the directions above the paragraphs to correct the text in this file. Save the edited file as BUSCOMM1. Print the edited document.

3.   Open the file SPEAKING.WPS. This file is about why many people are afraid of public speaking. Edit the document using the commands you learned in this lab. Save the edited file as SPEAK1. Print a copy of the edited document.

4.   Open the file INTRVIEW.WPS. This document explains how to prepare yourself for an interview. Correct the text in this file using the commands you have learned in this lab. Save the corrected version of the file as INTRVW1. Print the edited document.

5.   You work in the public relations office for the local zoo. You are writing an article about several new additions to the zoo for the monthly newsletter.

a.   Enter the following text into a new Works word processing document. Enter two blank lines below the heading and one blank line between paragraphs.

It Happened at the Zoo

The first anteater ever born at the zoo arrived on February 10, 1994. The sex of the baby has not yet been determined because it clings tightly to its mother's fur. There it will stay until it is almost half her size.

More than one hundred visitors and zoo employees witnessed the birth of Frisco, an African Giraffe. Because the birth took place in an area partially hidden, one question went unanswered: was the calf male or female? After receiving a kick in the shins, the Curator of Mammals announced the new calf was female.

    b. Enter your name and the current date on a blank line at the end of the article. Preview and print the article.

    c. Save the file as ZOO.

You will continue to work on the article in a Practice Exercise in Lab 3.

6. As editor of the children's section of the local newspaper, you have received several short stories on animals that you would like to include in the next special edition.

    a. Enter the text below into a new Works word processing document. Enter two blank lines below the heading and one blank line between paragraphs.

The Sumatran Tiger

The tiger is a big, strong, orange cat with black stripes. It is the largest member of the cat family. Adult tigers are powerful, but a baby is helpless at birth.

The Sumatran tiger is an endangered species. There are fewer than 600 left in the wild.

Gorillas

To most people, gorillas are scary. But this is unfair. Once you get to know them, gorillas are actually gentle giants.

Gorillas are plant-eaters. They eat juicy stems, leaves, and tree bark. They use their large canine teeth to rip the bark right off the trees.

    b. Enter your name and the current date on a blank line at the end of the article. Preview and print the article.

    c. Save the file as STORIES.

You will continue to work on the article in a Practice Exercise in Lab 3.

3 Formatting a Document

CASE STUDY

After editing the rough draft of the credit card letter, you showed it to the Sports Company Regional Manager. The manager would like the letter to include information about The Sports Company newsletter and a discount on the first purchase made with the new credit card. You will copy the new information provided by the manager into the credit card letter document, and then add some finishing touches to the letter.

Start Windows and load the Microsoft Works for Windows Application. Put your data disk in drive A (or the appropriate drive for your system).

Checking Spelling

The Sports Company Regional manager hastily entered the two new paragraphs for the letter into a new file.

To see the paragraphs, open the word processing document NEWPARA.WPS. Maximize the document window.

The two paragraphs are displayed in a document window. As you are reading the document you notice a typing error on the first line: "Sprots" should be "Sports." To help you locate spelling errors quickly, Works 3.0 includes a dictionary and Spelling Checker tool. To use the Spelling Checker to locate spelling errors,

Choose: Tools>Spelling

or

Click: 🔤 Spelling

Your screen should be similar to Figure 3-1.

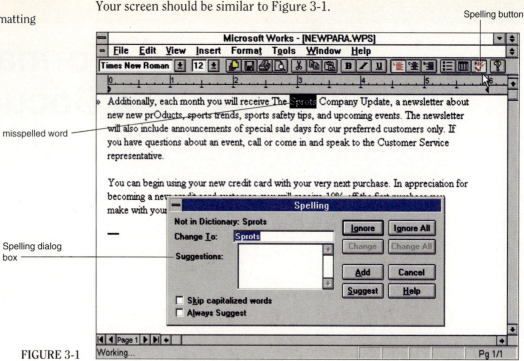

misspelled word

Spelling dialog
box

Spelling button

FIGURE 3-1

The Spelling Checker has encountered the first word that may be misspelled, "Sprots," and highlights it in the document window. The word is also displayed in the Change To text box of the Spelling dialog box.

Spelling Checker locates words that are spelled, capitalized, or hyphenated incorrectly by checking each word in the document to see if the word is listed in its dictionaries. Spelling Checker uses two types of dictionaries, the Houghton Mifflin dictionary containing 113,640 words and a **personal dictionary**. Personal dictionaries are ones you create to hold words you use commonly but that are not included in the Houghton Mifflin dictionary supplied with the program.

To tell Spelling Checker what to do, you need to choose from the following options:

You can also install and check spelling using other dictionaries such as a legal dictionary.

If an option is dim, it is not available for use.

Ignore	Accepts highlighted word as correct for this occurrence only
Ignore All	Accepts highlighted word as correct throughout the spell-check of this document
Change	Enters word displayed in Change To text box in place of the highlighted word
Change All	Enters word displayed in Change To text box in place of the highlighted word throughout the spell-check of this document
Add	Adds word to personal dictionary (Spelling Checker will always accept added word as correct)
Cancel	Exits Spelling Checker
Suggest	Suggests replacement words if Always Suggest check box is turned off
Help	Displays context-sensitive Help

To display a list of suggestions for the highlighted word,

Choose: Suggest

The Suggestions box lists possible replacements. Sometimes the Spelling Checker does not display any suggested replacements. This is because it cannot locate any words in its dictionary that are similar in spelling. The Change To text box now displays the word that is highlighted in the Suggestions list box. If none of the suggested replacements is acceptable, you could edit the word yourself by typing the correction in the Change To text box.

   To change the spelling of the word to one of the suggested spellings, highlight the correct word in the list and then choose Change. Since "Sports" is already highlighted and is the correct replacement,

Choose: Change

The Spelling Checker replaces the misspelled word with the selected suggested replacement and moves on to locate the next error.

   Your screen should be similar to Figure 3-2.

If the Spelling Checker automatically lists suggested replacements, the Always Suggest option is checked.

You can press ←Enter to choose Change or double-click the replacement word to select it and choose Change.

FIGURE 3-2

WORD PROCESSING

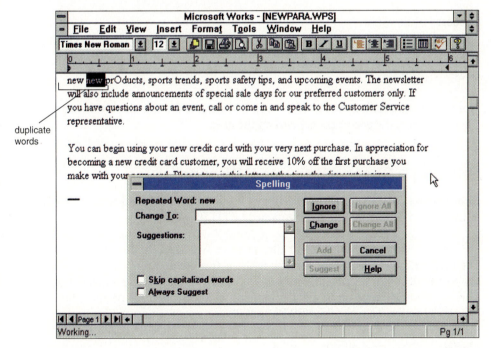

duplicate words

This time Works has located the duplicate words "new new." To remove the second duplicate word,

Choose: Change

The next error the Spelling Checker locates is a capitalization error. Works locates words that contain capital letters within lowercase letters as possible errors. To have the Spelling Checker suggest a correct capitalization,

Choose: Suggest

To accept the first choice to change the word to all lowercase characters,

Choose: Change

The word "products" is corrected. There should be no other misspelled words. However, if the Spelling Checker encounters others in your file, correct them as needed. When no others are located, the Spelling Checker will display a message box telling you that the spelling check is finished. To close the message box,

Choose: OK

You want to save and replace the original two paragraphs with the newly corrected text. To do this,

Choose: File>Save
➤   Ctrl + S
or
Click: 📁 Save

Works does not prompt you for a file name because the file was already named. After a few moments, the document is saved on the disk.

Opening a Second Document Window

Next you will open the credit card letter. A copy of the credit card letter you edited in Lab 2 is on your data disk in a file named LETTER2.WPS.

Open the word processing file LETTER2.WPS.

You now have two document files open in two separate document windows. The LETTER2.WPS document window is the **active window** and completely covers the NEWPARA.WPS document window. The active window is the window you can work in. You can have up to eight document windows open at one time, but only one can be active. To make the NEWPARA.WPS document window active,

The available memory of your computer may limit the number of documents you can have open.

Choose: Window>1 NEWPARA.WPS

The window containing the NEWPARA.WPS file is now the active window and covers the LETTER2.WPS window. From the Window menu, you can select a specific document window that you want to make active. You can also press Ctrl + F6 to cycle forward through all open documents, or Ctrl + ⇧Shift + F6 to cycle backward. When there are only two windows open, Ctrl + F6 will switch from one document window to the other. To make the LETTER2.WPS document window active again,

Press: Ctrl + F6

Using the Thesaurus

After reading the letter again, you are still not happy with how the last line reads. You would like to use the Works **Thesaurus** to see if you can find a better word for "happy." The Thesaurus will display words that are synonyms (have a similar meaning) for the word the insertion point is on.

Move to: "happy" (fourth paragraph)

To use the Thesaurus,

Choose: Tools>Thesaurus

Your screen should be similar to Figure 3-3.

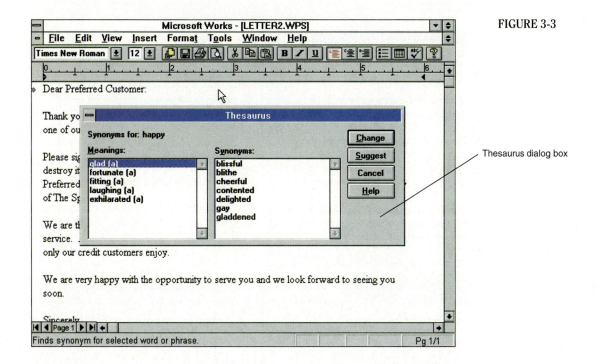

FIGURE 3-3

Thesaurus dialog box

The Thesaurus dialog box is displayed. From the Meanings list box you can select the most appropriate meaning for the word. The highlighted word "glad" is the appropriate meaning for the word "happy" in this sentence. "Glad" is followed by (a) for adjective. Words may also be followed by (n) for noun, (v) for verb, and (o) for other. The Synonyms list box displays synonyms for the word "glad." The best choice from this list is "delighted."

Select: delighted
Choose: Change

The word "happy" is replaced with "delighted" in the paragraph.
    Remove the word "very" from the sentence.

Copying Text Between Documents

After looking at the letter, you decide you want the two new paragraphs from the NEWPARA file to be entered following the second paragraph of the credit card letter.

Just like in the Windows Write and Cardfile applications, you can copy text from one file to another easily by selecting the text, copying it to the Clipboard, and then pasting the text from the Clipboard into another document file.

To make it easier to view the document windows, you can tile them.

Choose: Window>Tile

Your screen should be similar to Figure 3-4.

> You can also size document windows individually by dragging the window borders.

FIGURE 3-4

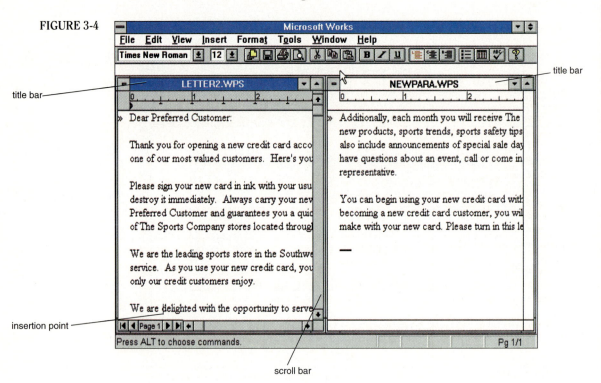

title bar

title bar

insertion point

scroll bar

The workspace now displays two document windows side-by-side. The active document window is LETTER2.WPS, on the left side of the screen. You can tell it is the active window because the title bar is a different color or highlighted, it contains the insertion point, and the scroll bar is displayed. Any text you type or commands you choose affect the document in the active window only. The status bar provides information for the active document window.

Make the NEWPARA document window active.

Now you are ready to copy the two paragraphs from the NEWPARA file.

Select the entire document.

> Use the Window menu or click anywhere on a visible document window to make it active.

> Reminder: Use Edit>Select All, or press F8 five times, or hold down Ctrl and click in the left margin.

Once text is selected, the Edit menu can be used to Cut or Copy the selection to the Clipboard. The options have the following meanings:

Option	Shortcut	Button	Action
Cut	Ctrl + X	✂	Removes selected text from document and copies it to Clipboard
Copy	Ctrl + C	📋	Leaves selected text in document and places a copy in Clipboard

To copy the selected text,

Choose: Edit>Copy
   ➤   Ctrl + C
or
Click: 📋 Copy

The Clipboard is a temporary storage area.

Next you want to copy the information from the Clipboard into the letter.
   Make the LETTER2.WPS window active.

Move to: blank line separating second and third paragraphs

Then, to insert or paste the text stored in the Clipboard into the active document,

Choose: Edit>Paste
   ➤   Ctrl + V
or
Click: 📋 Paste

The two paragraphs from the NEWPARA file have been inserted into the LETTER2 file at the location of the insertion point. You no longer need to view both document windows.
   To make it easier to work with the LETTER2 document window, maximize the window.
   The spacing between the second and third paragraphs needs to be adjusted. To separate the paragraphs with a blank line,

Click on the Maximize button or choose Maximize from the document control menu.

Press: ←Enter

Your screen should be similar to Figure 3-5.

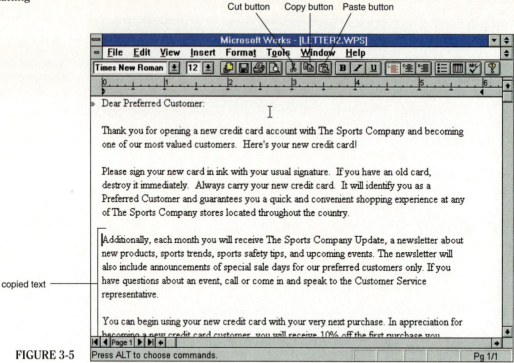

copied text ⸺

FIGURE 3-5

Scroll the window to view the entire letter. When you finish viewing the letter, move to the top of the letter.

Moving Text

After looking over the credit card letter, you decide to change the order of the paragraphs in the letter. You want the paragraph about the 10 percent discount (fourth paragraph) to follow the second paragraph.

Move to: fourth paragraph

Select the paragraph, including the blank line after the paragraph.
   The entire paragraph plus the blank line should be highlighted.
   The Cut command will remove the selected text and store it in the Clipboard. The contents of the Clipboard can then be pasted into a new location in another document or the same document. To cut the selected text,

Choose: Edit>Cut
   ➢   Ctrl + X
or
Click: ✂ Cut

The selected paragraph is removed from the document and stored in the Clipboard, replacing the previous Clipboard contents.

Next you need to move the insertion point to the location where you want the Clipboard contents to be entered.

Move to: "A" in "Additionally" (beginning of third paragraph)

To paste the text into the document from the Clipboard,

Choose: Edit>Paste
   ➤   Ctrl + V
or
Click: 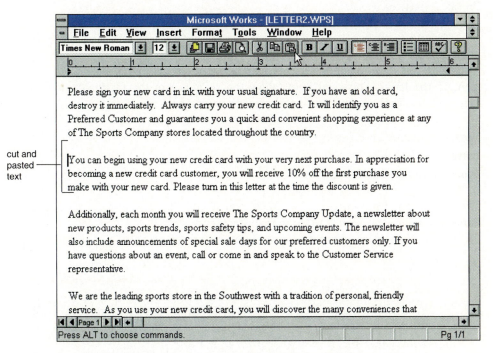 Paste

Your screen should be similar to Figure 3-6.

FIGURE 3-6

cut and
pasted
text

The paragraph is reentered into the document beginning at the insertion point location. That was a lot quicker than retyping the whole paragraph!

Replacing Selected Text

Text can be selected for reasons other than cutting and copying. You can also select text to be deleted and replaced with new text you type.

You would like to reword the last sentence of the second paragraph. Instead of "It will identify you as a..." you would like it to say, "Your new credit card identifies you as a..." Since the part you want to replace is shorter than the new text, Overtype will cut off some of the text you want to keep. By selecting the text you want to remove and then typing in the new text, the part you want to keep will not be affected.

Move to: "I" in "It" (fourth sentence, second paragraph)
Select: "It will identify" (include the space following the last word)
Type: Y

The "Y" is entered on the line, and the selected text has been deleted. You could also press [Delete] before typing the new text. However, as you just saw, this is unnecessary if you want to enter new text at the current location.

To continue entering the new text,

Type: our new card identifies
Press: [Spacebar]

The new text is inserted into the sentence and the text following has been reformatted.

Next you want to add the telephone number of the Customer Service Department to the letter. You want it to follow the reference to the Customer Service representative in the last sentence of the fourth paragraph.

Move to: before period of last sentence of fourth paragraph
Press: [Spacebar]
Type: (1-800-555-9838)

After looking at the sentence, you decide you would like to move the telephone number to follow the word "call" in the same sentence.

Select the telephone number, excluding the parentheses.

Works for Windows includes a **drag-and-drop** feature that you can use instead of selecting Cut and Paste or Copy and Paste from the menu.

To use the drag-and-drop feature to cut and paste the selected text, move the I-beam to the selected text. When it changes to an arrow with the word "DRAG" displayed below it, drag the pointer to the location where you want text inserted. The word "MOVE" appears at the bottom of the arrow, and an insertion point appears where the arrow is pointing to show you where the text will be placed. When correctly positioned, release the mouse button.

Drag the telephone number to the space after "call" in the same sentence.

To use the drag-and-drop feature to copy and paste selected text, follow the same procedure except hold down [Ctrl] while dragging.

Drag-and-drop can only be used within a document because it does not copy text to the Clipboard.

As you learned earlier, cut the selected text and then paste the telephone number after the word "call" in the same sentence.

Delete the parentheses and correct the spacing in the sentence as necessary.

Your screen should be similar to Figure 3-7.

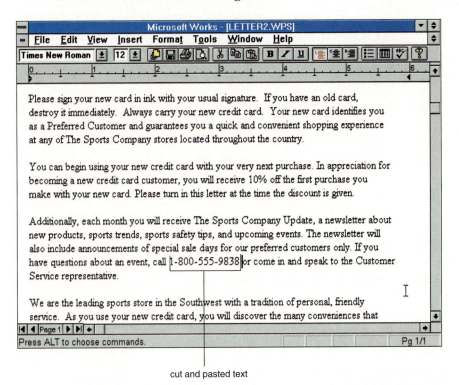

FIGURE 3-7

cut and pasted text

After looking over the letter, you decide you want to make the following changes:

- Enter the current date above the salutation
- Decrease the margin width
- Change the text alignment to full justification
- Indent the paragraphs
- Divide up the first paragraph by indenting the text
- Replace the words "new credit card" with "new Sports Company credit card"

You will make these changes to the credit card letter.

Entering a Date Placeholder

You want the date to be entered on the first line of the letter, four lines above the salutation.

Move to the beginning of the salutation at the top of the letter.

To insert four blank lines and move to the first blank line,

Press: ←Enter (4 times)
Press: Page Up

The insertion point should be at the top of the letter where the date will be entered. Rather than typing the date, you will use a command to automatically enter the current date for you.

Choose: Insert>Special Character

The three date options in the Special Character dialog box are:

Print date	Inserts the *date* **placeholder**, or marker in the document, which instructs Works to print the current date in the format 11/10/96 whenever the document is printed
Print long date	Inserts the placeholder *longdate* so the current date in the format November 10, 1996 is printed
Current date	Inserts the current date as text in the format 11/10/96 into the document. This date is not updated when printed.

Because the credit card letter will be mailed to new credit card customers as they enroll, you want the current long date to be entered whenever the letter is printed. To do this, the Print Long Date option is used.

Choose: Print long date>OK

Your screen should be similar to Figure 3-8.

FIGURE 3-8

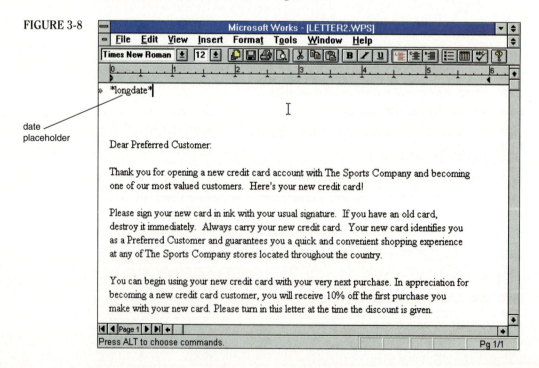

date placeholder

The *longdate* placeholder is entered into the letter at the location of the insertion point. Whenever this file is printed, Works will print the current system date using this format.

Setting Margins

Next you would like to change the right and left margin widths from the default setting of 1.25 inches to 1 inch. To change the left and right margin widths of a document, the Page Setup command on the File menu is used. If you change the margins after entering text into a document, the entire document must be selected for the margin settings to affect the entire document.

> Highlight the entire document.

Choose: File>Page Setup

The Page Setup **tab dialog box** is displayed. A tab dialog box contains tabs across the top of the dialog box and a folder of options for each tab. The names of the tabs indicate the different categories of folders.

The Page Setup dialog box contains three tabs. The tab name of the active tab is displayed in bold. The options displayed in the folder are the available options for the active tab. To choose a tab and open a folder, click on the tab with a mouse or press [Alt] + the underlined letter in the tab name. The Margins folder contains the options to change the margins for the document.

> If necessary choose the Margins tab.

The Margins folder displays the six margin settings that can be changed: Top, Bottom, Left, Right, Header, and Footer. The default margin settings are currently displayed in the text boxes. The Sample layout box shows how the current margin settings will appear on a page.

Choose: Left margin

When an entry in a text box is highlighted (selected), typing new information will replace the existing text.

| If you are using a mouse, click on the Left Margin text box and drag to highlight the text in the text box. |

Type: 1

| You do not need to type the inches (") symbol. |

To move to the Right Margin text box,

Press: [Tab ⇆]

| Be careful not to press [←Enter] after completing information in a text box. Pressing [←Enter] is the same as choosing OK, and completes the command. |

Your screen should be similar to Figure 3-9.

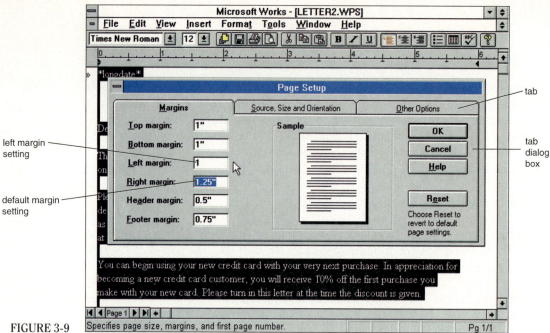

FIGURE 3-9

The highlight moved to the Right Margin text box, and the Sample box has changed to reflect the smaller left margin width.

In a similar manner, change the right margin setting to 1.

To close the dialog box,

Choose: OK

The letter has been reformatted to fit within the new margin settings. Because the margins are smaller, more text fits on a line. The zero position on the ruler still indicates the left margin setting. The right margin marker is positioned at the 6.5-inch position on the ruler and is currently not visible.

Setting Paragraph Alignment

On the screen and when printed, the lines in the credit card letter have an even left margin and an uneven or ragged right margin. This is the default paragraph **alignment** setting for a standard document. Alignment is how text is positioned on a line between the margins. The four possible paragraph alignment settings, their short-cuts, and effects are shown on the next page:

Alignment	Shortcut	Button	Effect
Left	Ctrl + L	📄	Aligns text against left margin, leaving right margin ragged
Center	Ctrl + E	📄	Centers each line of text between left and right margins
Right	Ctrl + R	📄	Aligns text against right margin, leaving left margin ragged
Justified	Ctrl + J		Aligns text evenly against left and right margins by inserting spaces in line

You want the entire credit card letter to have even left and right margins.

If necessary select the entire document.

To change the alignment,

Choose: Format>Paragraph

The Paragraph tab dialog box contains three folders. All options in these folders affect the paragraph the insertion point is on or all highlighted paragraphs.

Choose: Indents and Alignment

To change the alignment to have even left and right margins,

Choose: Justified>OK

Clear the highlight by pressing ⬆ or clicking anywhere in the window.

Scroll the window horizontally to see the alignment change.

Your screen should be similar to Figure 3-10.

> Move to a full line of text and press End or use the horizontal scroll bar.

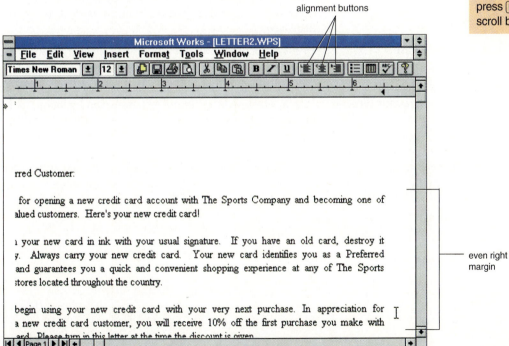

FIGURE 3-10

Notice that the letter no longer has even spaces between words. This is because Works inserts extra spaces so that the text aligns evenly with both the left and the right margins. These are called **soft spaces** and are adjusted automatically whenever additions and deletions are made to the text.

Press: Home

Changing the View

As you have noticed, with the margins set at 1 inch and the text alignment set to justified, the line length is too long to be fully displayed in the window. To see text at the ends of the lines you scrolled the screen horizontally. Rather than do this, you can change how the document is displayed on the screen.

Choose: View

The View menu contains several options that change how the document is displayed on the screen. The options and how they are used are:

Zoom	Enlarges or reduces size of characters onscreen.
Normal	Displays text as it will appear when printed, including formatting, tab stops, alignment, and page breaks. Does not display document features such as headers and footers. This is the default view and is the most convenient view for most of your work.
Page Layout	Displays complete document including features such as headers, footers, and columns. Because a complete document is displayed, this view is slightly slower to work in because all the extra features require more time to be displayed.
Draft	Displays document in one font and size, regardless of settings you may have specified. This view is faster and is especially useful when you need to scroll a large document.
Wrap for Window	Displays text so lines do not extend beyond window. This option can be used in combination with Normal or Draft view.

Except for the long line length, Normal view is the best view for this document. To leave the view as Normal and change only the wrapping of text on the screen,

Choose: Wrap for Window

Your screen should be similar to Figure 3-11.

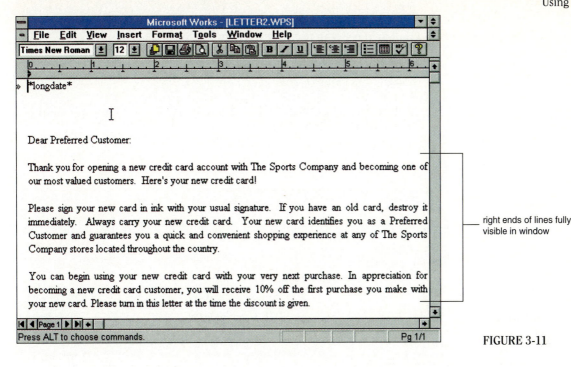

right ends of lines fully
visible in window

FIGURE 3-11

The right ends of the lines are now visible in the window, eliminating the need to scroll the window horizontally. Works accomplishes this by compressing space between characters or by adjusting the wordwrap on a line. In this case, simply compressing the spaces accomplished the task.

> If your text did not adjust, move to the next line.

This setting affects only the onscreen display of the document. It does not affect how the document will appear when printed. You can now see the effect of setting the paragraph alignment to justified—the lines end evenly at the left and right margins.

Using and Setting Tabs

Next you want to change the letter style from block to indented. To do this you will indent the first line of each paragraph and the closing. You could use the preset tab stops to tab along the line, or you can set your own tab stops. By default, tabs are set at every half-inch. These tab settings are indicated on the ruler by the ⊥ mark below the ruler.

You want only two tab stops, at 0.5 and 3.25 inches from the left margin. Just as with the margin settings, the entire document must be selected or the new tab settings will affect only the current paragraph.

Select the entire document.

The default tab settings can be changed by inserting custom tab stops using the mouse or the Tabs command on the Format menu. When you insert custom tab stops, all preset tab stops to the left of the custom tab stops are deleted.

To insert a custom tab stop, point to the location on the ruler where you want the tab inserted and click the left mouse button. To set a tab at 3.25 inches,

Click: 3.25-inch position on ruler

A ↑ tab marker is displayed on the ruler. All default tabs to the left of the new tab setting are cleared.

Add a second tab at position 0.5 inch.

To set custom tab stops,

Choose: Format>Tabs

Your screen should be similar to Figure 3-12.

FIGURE 3-12

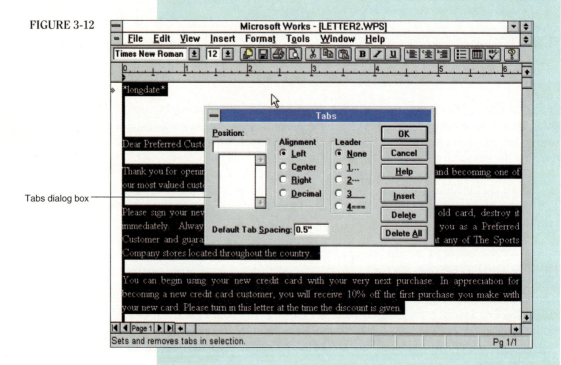

Tabs dialog box

The Tabs dialog box is displayed. In the Position text box, you need to enter the position where you want the first tab stop. To enter .5 inch,

Type: .5

You do not need to type the inches symbol (").

The Insert command button lets you confirm the tab as specified in the text box.

Choose: Insert

The Position list box now displays the tab setting at .5 inch. The dialog box continues to be displayed to let you set other tab stops. The insertion point is in the Position text box waiting for you to enter another position value. To enter a left tab at 3.25 inches,

Type: 3.25

Choose: Insert

To exit the dialog box,

Choose: OK

The Custom tab stops are marked on the ruler with the ↑ tab mark. Notice that the settings to the right of the 3.25" tab stop remain in effect at every .5 inch.

Now you want to indent the first line of the first paragraph one tab stop.

Move to: "T" in "Thank" (first sentence, first paragraph)
Press: Tab ⇆

Your screen should be similar to Figure 3-13.

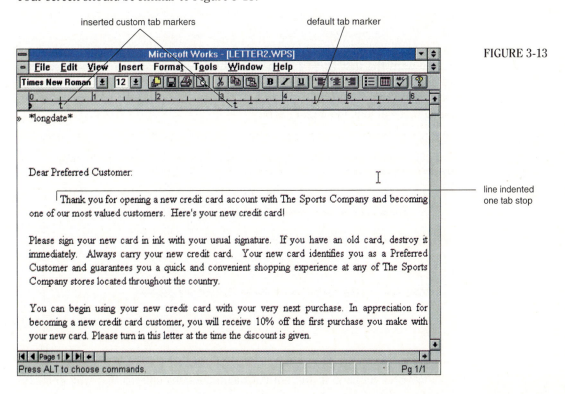

FIGURE 3-13

Pressing Tab ⇆ indents the first line of text a half inch. The text in the paragraph is reformatted as needed. The text on the following line begins at the left margin.

In a similar manner, indent the first line of the other five paragraphs.

To indent the closing lines,

Move to: "S" in "Sincerely"
Press: Tab ⇆ (2 times)

The closing line has moved two tab stops to the right and begins at the 3.25"
position.

Move to: "T" of "The"
Press: Tab ⇆ (2 times)

Move to the top of the document.

Creating a Bulleted List

The next change you want to make to the letter is to add a new sentence to the end
of the first paragraph and to itemize the first three sentences in the next paragraph.
To add the new sentence,

Move to: after space following "card!" at end of first paragraph
Type: Using your new credit card is as easy as 1-2-3.

Next you want the first three sentences in the second paragraph to be on separate
lines preceded with **bullets**. A bullet is a large dot or other symbol that is placed
before text to call attention to the text. When you complete the adjustment of the
paragraph, it will look like Figure 3-14.

FIGURE 3-14

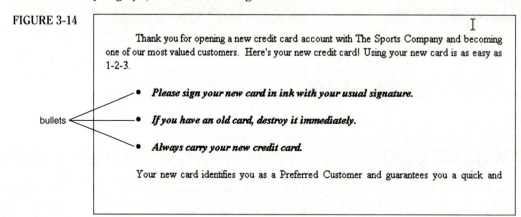

The Paragraph command in the Format menu contains options that will automatically add a bullet to the first line of a paragraph. The feature will also indent the text

Works considers a paragraph
to be any text that ends with a
paragraph mark where ←Enter
was pressed.

following the bullet. To make the first sentence a separate paragraph and remove the tab at the beginning of the paragraph,

Move to:	"P" of "Please"
Press:	Backspace
Move to:	"I" of "If" (second sentence, second paragraph)
Press:	←Enter (2 times)

In a similar manner, place the next sentence on a separate line separated with a blank line.

Make the last sentence beginning with "Your new…" a new paragraph. (Remember to use Tab⇥ to indent the first line of the paragraph.)

You should now have a list of three items, each separated by a blank line. Next you will add a bullet before each of the items. To select the first item and use the bullet feature,

Move to:	"P" of "Please"
Choose:	Format>Paragraph

The Quick Formats folder contains options that provide the most commonly used settings for many of the Paragraph options. You will use the Quick Formats folder to add a bullet to the selected paragraph.

Choose:	Quick Formats>Bulleted

The two options in the Apply Relative To options box let you choose whether to indent the text from the left margin or from the paragraph's current indent. To indent from the left margin,

Choose:	Left Margin

If the Quick Formats tab is already open, you do not need to choose it.

To complete the command,

Choose:	OK

If the Left Margin option is already marked, you do not need to choose it.

WORD PROCESSING

Your screen should be similar to Figure 3-15.

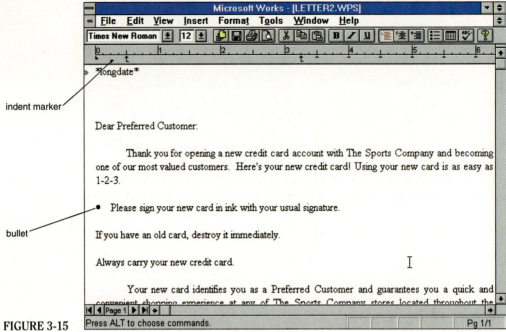

indent marker

bullet

FIGURE 3-15

The Quick Format Bullet option inserts a bullet at the beginning of the line at the left margin and indents the text following the bullet .25 inch. The indent marker ▸ on the ruler moves to the .25-inch position to show the new indent setting for the selected paragraph. If the paragraph was longer than a single line, all subsequent lines would be aligned with the text in the first line.

A bullet is a special Works character that cannot be deleted like normal text. The only way to remove a bullet is to reformat the paragraph to normal format using the Normal option in the Quick Formats folder.

Next you will select the remaining two items and then apply the bullet format to both at once.

Highlight the next two items.

Because each item is a separate paragraph, the command will apply the bullet format to both items.

Choose: Format>Paragraph>Bulleted>OK
or
Click: 📋 Bullets

Clear the highlight.

Your screen should be similar to Figure 3-16.

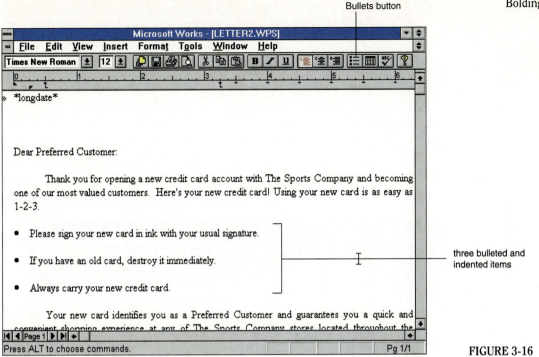

FIGURE 3-16

The items are bulleted and indented.

Finally, you would like to change the indent for the three items so that the bullet aligns with the .5-inch position and the text is indented at the .75-inch position.

    Highlight the three items.

Choose: Format>Paragraph>Indents and Alignment

The Indents and Alignment folder allows you to apply customized settings to the same features as in the Quick Formats folder. To customize the bullets so that the text will be indented at the .75-inch position rather than the default of .25 inch, in the Left Indents text box,

Type: .75

Choose: OK

The entire selection including the bullets has moved to the right to align the text following the bullet at the .75-inch position on the line.

Bolding and Italicizing Text

You would like to make the three items stand out more in the document. One way to do this is to change the text appearance to **bold** and **italics**. The three items should still be selected. If they are not, highlight them.

You will learn more about the
Format menu's Font and
Style commands in Lab 4.

The Font and Style command on the Format menu is used to change the appearance of selected text. The shortcuts for bold and italics are Ctrl + B and Ctrl + I or **B** and **I**. To change the itemized text to bold and italics using the shortcuts,

Press: Ctrl + B
Press: Ctrl + I
or
Click: **B** Bold
Click: **I** Italics

Clear the highlight.

Your screen should be similar to Figure 3-17.

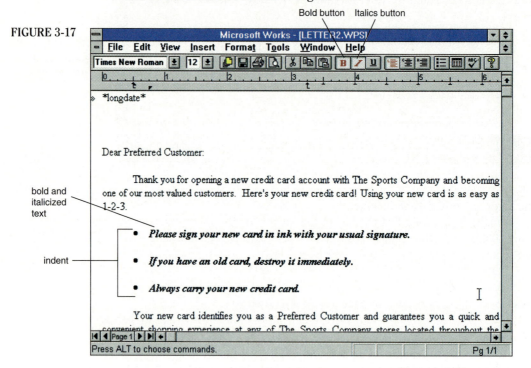

FIGURE 3-17

The three items appear in bold and italics.

Searching and Replacing Text

Next you want to find all occurrences of the words "new credit card" in the letter and change them to "new Sports Company credit card" where appropriate.

The Replace command on the Edit menu will help do this quickly. Works will begin the search for all occurrences of words beginning at the insertion point. If the search does not begin at the top of the document, Works asks if you want to continue searching at the beginning of the document when it reaches the end of the document. You can also highlight text to restrict the search to the selection.

To start the search at the beginning of the letter,

Press: Ctrl + Home
Choose: Edit

The Edit menu contains two commands that can be used to search through text for matching text:

Find   Moves to specified text in document

Replace   Locates specified text and replaces it with specified replacement text

Since you want to find and replace text,

Choose: Replace

The Replace dialog box is displayed. In the Find What text box you enter the text you want to locate. In the Replace With text box you enter the replacement text. When searching for the text to find, Works is not case-sensitive. This means that if you enter lowercase letters in the text box, Works will locate both upper- and lowercase letters in the text. To enter the text to find,

Type: **new credit card** (do not press ⏎Enter)

Your screen should be similar to Figure 3-18.

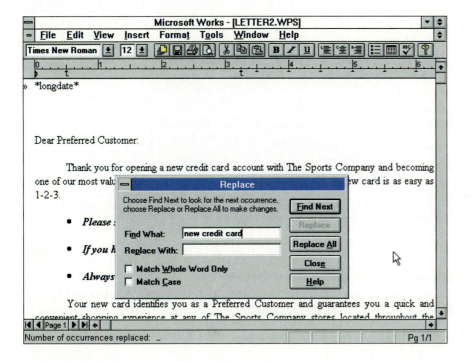

FIGURE 3-18

You want to replace "new credit card" with "new Sports Company credit card." The replacement text must be entered exactly as you want it to appear in your document. To enter the replacement text,

Press: Tab ⇄

Type: **new Sports Company credit card**

The Replace With text box is too small to display the entire entry. You can press
[Home] to see the first characters and [End] to see the last characters.

The Match Whole Word Only option will restrict the search so that only matches
that are complete words, not matches that are part of a longer word, are located. For
example, if the search text is the word "or", the word "for" would not be located.
Generally you want to locate whole words only and would use this option. The Match
Case option will restrict the search to find matches that have the same capitalization
as the search text. In this case, however, you do not need to turn on either option.

To begin the search,

Choose: Find Next

Your screen should be similar to Figure 3-19.

FIGURE 3-19

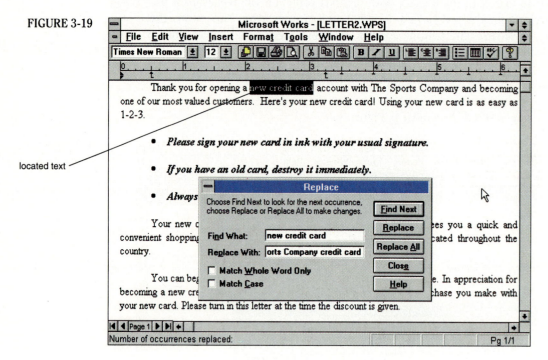

located text

Immediately Works locates and highlights the first occurrence of the search text.
You do not, however, want to replace this text. To tell the program to continue the
search without replacing the highlighted text,

Choose: Find Next

Works continues searching and locates a second occurrence of the search text. This
time you do want to replace the highlighted text with the replacement text. To do
this,

Choose: Replace

The highlighted text has been replaced, and the third occurrence of matching text is located. You want to replace this and all other occurrences of the search text. To do this,

Choose: Replace **A**ll

Using Replace All is much faster than confirming each match separately.

When Works has completed the search, the message "Number of occurrences replaced: 5" is displayed in the status bar and there are no matches highlighted in the document.

Close the Replace dialog box.

Now the letter is complete. To restore the view to wrap text to the right margin setting rather than the window,

Choose: **V**iew>**Wra**p for Window

The text extends beyond the right edge of the window again.

Be careful when using Replace All, because the search text you specified might be part of another word and you may accidentally replace text you did not intend.

Zooming the Document

Another way to see more of the document in the window is to reduce the size of the text displayed on the screen. To do this,

Choose: **V**iew>**Z**oom

The Zoom command lets you magnify or shrink the display of text on the screen. The default display, 100%, shows the characters the same size as they will be when printed. You can increase the character size up to four times normal display (400%) and reduce the character size to half (50%).

To reduce the character size to 75% so you can see the right margin,

Choose: **7**5>OK

WORD PROCESSING

Your screen should be similar to Figure 3-20.

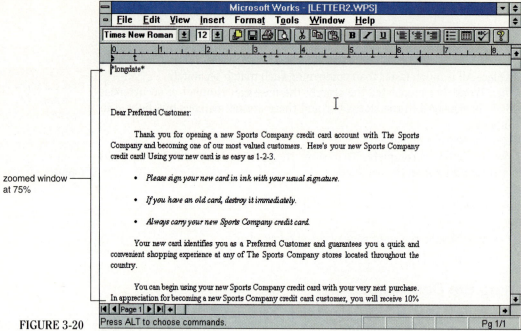

zoomed window
at 75%

FIGURE 3-20

The character size is 25 percent smaller than normal, allowing more text to be displayed in the window. When the text is zoomed, you can still edit the document as usual. Additionally, when the character size is smaller, and therefore more text is displayed in the window, you do not need to scroll the window as frequently.

Scroll to the bottom of the letter.

After looking over the letter, you decide the date would look better if it was tabbed to the same position as the closing.

Move to before the date placeholder at the top of the letter.

To tab the date placeholder to the 3.25-inch position,

Press: Tab ⇥ (2 times)

Set the Zoom back to normal (100%).

You would like to save the edited version of the credit card letter in a new file named LETTER3. This will allow the original file, LETTER2, to remain unchanged on the disk in case you would like to repeat the lab for practice.

Select: File>Save As

In the File Name text box,

Type: LETTER3
Choose: OK

In response to the message dialog box to save to a different floppy disk,

Choose: No

> When the Zoom command decreases the character size, it does not display certain formatting features such as bold and justification.

The revised letter has been saved on the disk as LETTER3.WPS.

Now you are ready to print a copy of the credit card letter.

If necessary, select the appropriate printer for your computer system (File>Printer Setup) and prepare your printer for printing as you did in Lab 2.

Choose: File>Print

➢   Ctrl + P

The Print dialog box is displayed.

Finally, before printing the letter, it is always a good idea to preview the letter.

Choose: Preview

Your screen should be similar to Figure 3-21.

> Remember to press Alt + R to choose Preview using the keyboard.

FIGURE 3-21

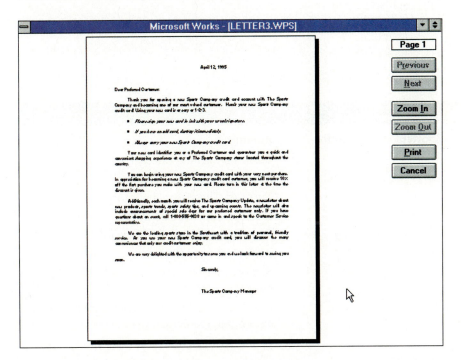

Notice that the date placeholder has been replaced with the current date, as maintained by your computer, in the long date format.

If you see errors, return to the document and correct them. Then preview the document again. If you do not see any errors, you can print the letter directly from the Print Preview window.

> You cannot edit the document in Print Preview, you can only view the document.

Choose: Print

You are returned to the Print dialog box. To start printing,

Choose: OK

WORD PROCESSING

Your letter should be printing out. If you selected a different printer, the letter has been reformatted to the printer settings associated with the printer.

If you are ready to exit the Works program,

Choose: File>Exit Works

If save prompt boxes are displayed,

Choose: Yes

Key Terms

personal dictionary (74)   alignment (86)
active window (76)   soft space (88)
Thesaurus (77)   bullet (92)
drag-and-drop (82)   bold (95)
placeholder (84)   italics (95)
tab dialog box (85)

Command Summary

Command	Shortcut	Button	Action
T**o**ols>**S**pelling			Turns on Spelling Checker application
Window>**#**<file name>	Ctrl + F6		Makes selected window active
T**o**ols>**T**hesaurus			Turns on Thesaurus application
Window>**T**ile			Displays windows side-by-side
Edit>**C**opy	Ctrl + C		Copies selected text to Clipboard
Edit>**P**aste	Ctrl + V		Pastes text from Clipboard
Edit>Cu**t**	Ctrl + X		Removes selected text and places it in Clipboard
Insert>**S**pecial Character>Print lo**ng** date			Inserts placeholder for current date maintained by computer system
File>Page Setup>**M**argins			Changes left, right, top, and bottom margins
Forma**t**>**P**aragraph>**I**ndents and Alignment			Changes indents and alignment of text
>Left	Ctrl + L		Left-aligns selection
>Center	Ctrl + E		Center-aligns selection
>Right	Ctrl + R		Right-aligns selection
>Justified	Ctrl + J		Aligns selection evenly with both left and right margins
View>Wra**p** for Window			Displays text onscreen so lines do not extend beyond window
Forma**t**>**T**abs			Specifies alignment and position of tab stops
Forma**t**>**P**aragraph>**Q**uick Formats>**B**ulleted			Inserts bullets into document
Forma**t**>**F**ont and Style>**B**old	Ctrl + B		Changes selected text to bold
Forma**t**>**F**ont and Style>**I**talics	Ctrl + I		Changes selected text to italics
Edit>Re**p**la**c**e			Locates and replaces specified text
View>**Z**oom			Magnifies or shrinks display of text onscreen

Matching

1.	Thesaurus	_____ **a.**	places text from Clipboard into document
2.	View>Zoom	_____ **b.**	makes next open document active
3.	Ctrl + F6	_____ **c.**	shortcut for bold command
4.	margins	_____ **d.**	displays two windows side-by-side
5.	Ctrl + B	_____ **e.**	magnifies or shrinks display of text onscreen
6.	soft spaces	_____ **f.**	blank area around printed text
7.	Window>Tile	_____ **g.**	removes text from document and stores it in Clipboard
8.	Edit>Paste	_____ **h.**	quickly locates specified text
9.	Ctrl + X or ✂	_____ **i.**	extra spaces added to push text to fit margins
10.	Find	_____ **j.**	displays synonyms for selected word

Practice Exercises

1. To complete this exercise, you must first have completed Practice Exercise 5 in Lab 2. Open the file ZOO.WPS. You have continued to work on your article for the zoo newsletter and have saved your work in another file called ZOO2.WPS.

a. Open the file ZOO2.WPS in another document window. Tile the windows if desired.

b. Copy the text in the file ZOO2 into the end of your file ZOO (before your name). Adjust the spacing accordingly. Close the ZOO2 file. If necessary, maximize the ZOO document window.

c. Rearrange the paragraphs so the first paragraph is about the tiger, the second paragraph is about the tapir, the third paragraph is about the giraffe, the fourth paragraph is about the anteater, and the fifth is about the birds. Adjust the spacing as needed.

d. Set alignment to justified for the entire document. Bold the proper names of all animals. Bold the article heading. Center the heading line.

e. Search the document for the word "zoo" and replace it with "Zoo."

f. Spell-check the file.

g. Replace the word "delicacy" in the first paragraph with a synonym using the Thesaurus.

h. Replace the old date on the last line of the document using the long date placeholder.

i. Save the file as ZOO3. Preview and print the document.

2. To complete this exercise, you must first have completed Practice Exercise 6 in Lab 2. Open the file STORIES.WPS. You have continued to receive several short stories on animals to be included in the next special edition of the children's section of the local newspaper, and have saved these in a file called STORIES2.WPS.

    a. Open the file STORIES2.WPS in a second document window. Tile the windows. Copy the text in STORIES2 into the end of the STORIES file (before your name).

    b. Close the STORIES2 file. Maximize the STORIES document window.

    c. Spell-check the file.

    d. Reduce the document zoom to 75%. Rearrange the document so the first topic is about the gorillas, the second is about the tiger, the third is about the spider, and the fourth is about the wren. Return to normal zoom (100%).

    e. Set the alignment to justified for the entire document. Change the right and left margins to one inch.

    f. Bold and italicize each article heading. Separate all headings from the text above and below it with two blank lines.

    g. Replace the old date with the current date on the last line of the document using the long date placeholder.

    h. Save the document as STORIES3. Preview and print the document.

3.   As Vice President of the Careers Club, you invited several professionals to present information to club members about preparing employment resumes. In this problem you will create and format a letter to thank the guests.

    a. In a new word processing window, set the left and the right margins to 1.5 inches. Enter custom tab settings at .5 inch and 3.0 inches.

    b. Enter the current date on the top line of the page using the long date placeholder.

    c. Enter the following letter:

Ms. Elizabeth Ramage
Human Resources Manager
JBS Services
34 West University Drive
Tempe, AZ 85257

Dear Ms. Ramage:

Thank you for taking the time to speak with the Careers Club at our school last week. The information you presented on how to write resumes and other employment related documents was very helpful.

In addition, the personal attention you gave to many of the club members by reviewing resumes they had prepared was greatly appreciated.

I have received many very favorable comments from the members about this presentation and plan to arrange a similar presentation again next year. I hope you will consider participating again at that time.

Sincerely,

(your name)

d. Tab the date to the 3.0-inch position. Indent each paragraph .5 inch. Tab the closing to the 3.0-inch tab position.

e. Spell-check the document.

f. Save the letter as THANKS. Preview and print the letter.

4. As Assistant Editor of the *Travel Arizona* magazine, you are responsible for researching out-of-the-way places to visit in the state. You send the Managing Editor a quarterly memo describing the places you like best.

a. Enter the memo below using left and right margin settings of 1.5 inches and only one tab setting of 2.2 inches.

To: Tab ⇆ **Jane Walker, Managing Editor**

From: Tab ⇆ **(your name), Assistant Editor**

Date: Tab ⇆ **(enter current date using date placeholder)**

After reviewing the many interesting places we could write about, I have chosen the following three:

Snowflake, the "Home of the Pioneers," was founded in 1878. It is located 27 miles south of Holbrook in Navajo County. This town has an array of old houses, a school house built in 1891, and a library that contains 36,500 books. Snowflake was founded in 1878 and is named for two Mormon pioneers, Erastus Snow and William J. Flake.

Ramsey Canyon is known as "Where you are Nature's guest!" It was established as a preserve in 1975. Fifteen species of hummingbirds, flycatchers, warblers, wrens, and woodpeckers, to name a few, are the birds that can be seen in the canyon. Birds and nature get highest priority in the Mile Hi/Ramsey Canyon Preserve.

Williams, the "Gateway to the Grand Canyon," is named for William Sherley Williams, a colorful mountaineer, trapper, and guide who died in 1849. According to the memorial, a bronze statue displayed in the city park, Williams first visited the area in 1826.

b. Delete the last sentence in the second paragraph ("Snowflake was founded…") using the Cut command.

c. Switch the order of the third and fourth sentences in the Ramsey Canyon paragraph.

d. Set the alignment for the entire document to full justified.

e. Spell-check the document.

f. Save the document as TRAVEL. Preview and print the document.

5. You work for a large pet shop and are working on an article for the company newsletter on feeding wild birds. You want to make several changes to the article. Open the file BIRDS.WPS.

a. Spell-check the document.

b. Bullet the four items under "Equipment."

c. Center the title at the top of the article. Bold the title. Italicize the headings.

d. Under the Feeders subhead, switch the third and fourth paragraphs.

e. Search for the word "bird" and replace it with "wild bird" where appropriate.

f. Enter your name and the current date on the last line of the document.

g. Save the document as BIRDS2. Preview and print the document.

6. Create a cover letter that could be included with your resume. Set the margins so the letter is on one page and is balanced on the page. Spell-check the letter. Save the file as COVERLTR. Preview and print the letter.

4 Creating a Report and a Newsletter

CASE STUDY

The Southwest Regional Manager is very pleased with your work so far and has asked you to help with the design and development of the first monthly newsletter. Specifically you have been asked to develop several topics to be used as articles in the newsletter, and to propose a sample newsletter design.

Inserting a Manual Page Break

Load Windows and the Works program. Put your data disk in the appropriate drive for your system.

You have already researched several topics for the newsletter and would like to present the information to the manager before creating final copy to use in the newsletter.

Open the word processing file RESEARCH.WPS. If necessary, maximize the document window.

The first page of the document begins with a memo you have started to the manager.

Enter your name following "FROM:" beginning at the 1-inch position.

To enter the current date,

Move to: 1-inch position following "DATE:"

Choose: Insert>Special Character>Current date>OK

The date is entered using the current system date as a text entry, not as a place-holder. Unlike the *longdate* placeholder, the date will not change if you open or print the file on a later day.

Competencies

After completing this lab, you will know how to:

1. Insert manual page breaks.
2. Change fonts.
3. Create hanging indents.
4. Enter and edit footnotes.
5. Use Page Layout view.
6. Enter headers and footers.
7. Keep text together.
8. Use WordArt.
9. Create borders.
10. Create columns.
11. Hyphenate text.
12. Add drawings.

The text for the first article begins on the same page, below the text for the memo. You want the memo to be on a page by itself. To begin page 2 with the first line of the article text,

Move to: "H" in "HEALTH AND FITNESS"

Choose: **I**nsert>Page **B**reak

➤   Ctrl + ←Enter

Your screen should be similar to Figure 4-1.

FIGURE 4-1

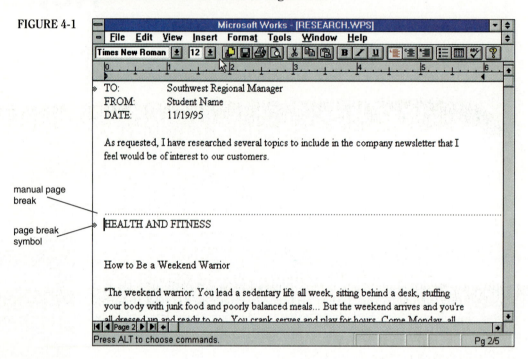

To remove a manual page break, move to the beginning of the line that follows the page break and press Backspace.

A dotted line appears on the line above the insertion point, and the page break symbol (>>) appears in the left margin. The dotted line indicates where you have entered a **manual page break**. A manual page break instructs Works to begin a new page at that location regardless of the amount of text on the previous page. All automatic page breaks following the insertion of a manual page break are immediately adjusted.

Changing Fonts

The text for the articles begins with a category heading followed by the title for the article. The category for the first article is "HEALTH AND FITNESS." The article title, "How to Be a Weekend Warrior," is displayed below the category heading.

To make the heading stand out from the article text, you want to change the character font and size. As you learned in Lab 2, a font, also commonly referred to as a typeface, is a set of characters with a specific design. Each font has a name, such as Roman or Courier, and one or more sizes. Size refers to the height of the characters and is commonly measured in **points**, abbreviated pt. One point equals about $\frac{1}{72}$ inch. Some typefaces are measured in **cpi** (characters per inch). For example, Roman 10cpi means there are 10 characters per inch. Fonts that are measured in cpi are **monospaced**. This means that each character will take up the same amount of space. Fonts that are measured in points are **proportional**, that is, a letter such as m or w takes up more space than an i or t.

Some fonts are **scalable**, which means they can be printed in almost any point size depending upon the capabilities of the printer. Non-scalable fonts are assigned a single point size. In addition, as you learned earlier, you can apply different **styles**, such as bold and italics, to the font to enhance the appearance of the characters. Several common fonts are shown below.

Regular text is usually 10pt or 12pt.

Font	Type Size (12pt)/(18 pt)	Type Style (Bold)
Arial	This is 12 pt./This is 18 pt.	Bold 18 pt.
Courier New	This is 12 pt./This is 18 pt.	Bold 18 pt.
Times Roman New	This is 12 pt./This is 18 pt.	Bold 18 pt.

To change the font, type size, or style, the Font and Style command on the Format menu is used. If you use the command before typing the text, all text you type will appear in the specified font setting until another font setting is selected. To change a font setting for existing text, highlight the text and then use the command. Only the selected text appears in the new font setting.

You would like the heading to be in a different font and a larger type size than the paragraph text.

Select the category heading "HEALTH AND FITNESS."

Choose: Format>Font and Style

WORD PROCESSING

Changing Fonts

Your screen should be similar to Figure 4-2.

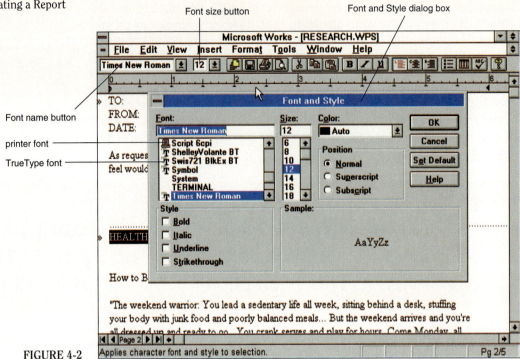

FIGURE 4-2

The Font list box in the Font and Style dialog box lists the fonts supported by your active printer. The symbols next to the names identify TrueType fonts and printer fonts. TrueType fonts are scalable fonts that are provided with Windows version 3.1. Printer fonts are built-in fonts that come with the printer. The Works default font, Times New Roman, is the currently selected font. To change the font to Arial, from the Font list box,

Choose: TT Arial

The Sample area displays an example of the selected font. Then to enlarge the type size to 14 points, from the Size list box,

Choose: 14

Again the Sample area is updated to show the selected size. Finally, you want to bold the selection.

Choose: Bold>OK

The selected text is displayed in the Arial font with a type size of 14 and bold. The toolbar buttons display the current font and size setting for the text at the location of the insertion point.

Next you want to change the article title to 14 points and bold.

Select the article title, "How to Be a Weekend Warrior."

Choose: Forma**t**>**F**ont and Style>14>**B**old>OK

or

Click: `12` Font Size

Select: 14

Click: `B` Bold

> If you have a mouse, you can use the Font Name button to change the font and the Font Size button to change the type size.

In the same manner, change the font of the other category heading and the titles for the other articles shown below:

Location	Text	Font and Style
Page 3	What Fluids Are Best	14pt, bold
Page 4	EQUIPMENT UPDATE	Arial, 14pt, bold
Page 4	Stationary Bikes	14pt, bold

Creating Hanging Indents

As you scrolled the document, you noticed that the four guidelines on fluids at the end of the article would stand out more if the text were indented. The four guidelines are immediately above the category heading "EQUIPMENT UPDATE."

Display the four guidelines in the window. Highlight the four guidelines.
Your screen should be similar to Figure 4-3.

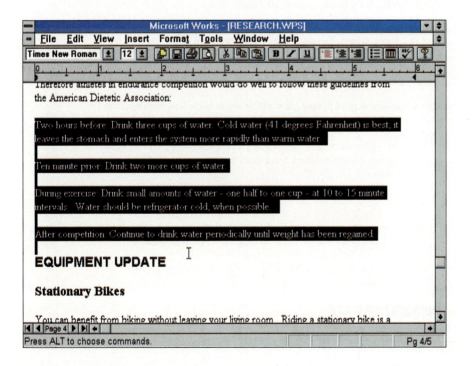

FIGURE 4-3

To indent the text,

Choose: Forma**t**>**P**aragraph

WORD PROCESSING

If necessary choose the Quick Formats tab.

The Quick Formats Hanging Indent option will indent all lines of a paragraph except the first line .5 inch from the left margin.

Choose: Hanging Indent

The Sample area of the dialog box shows how the paragraphs will be indented. The first line of each paragraph is still even with the left margin while the text on subsequent lines of the paragraph is indented. To create a hanging indent, Works sets the left indent at .5 inch for all text except the first line. You want the left indent setting to be 1 inch. To change the indent settings,

Choose: Indents and Alignments

To change the left indent setting to 1 inch, in the Left text box,

Type: 1

Notice the First Line option setting is −.5". This setting makes the first line of the paragraph .5-inch less than the current indent. To see the effect on the selected paragraphs,

Choose: OK

Clear the highlight.

Your screen should be similar to Figure 4-4.

FIGURE 4-4

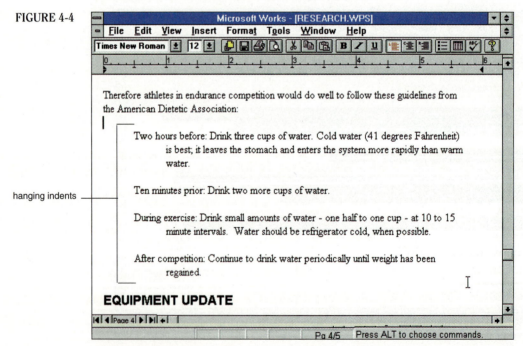

The four guidelines are indented to the 1-inch position except the first line, which is indented to the .5-inch position. The indent markers on the ruler reflect the paragraph and line indent settings whenever the insertion point is positioned in that area.

In the same manner, create hanging indents for the four numbered items on page 3.

113
Adding Footnotes

Adding Footnotes

Next you need to add several **footnotes** (source references placed at the bottom of the page) to the document. The Footnote command on the Insert menu will automatically number and place footnotes properly at the bottom of the page. The first reference that needs to be footnoted is on page 2.

Move to: top of page 2

The first paragraph of the article consists of a quotation whose source needs to be documented in a footnote. Before using the Footnote command, the insertion point must be positioned in the text where the footnote number is to be inserted.

Move to: end of quote (after quotation marks)
Choose: Insert>Footnote

In the Footnote dialog box you specify the type of marker you want to appear in the document: a numbered marker or a special character marker. A special character marker can be any non-numeric character, such as an asterisk. You want the footnotes to be numbered, which is the default option. To number the footnotes,

Choose: OK

Your screen should be similar to Figure 4-5.

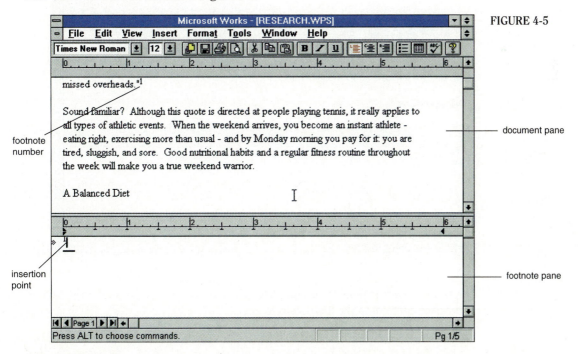

FIGURE 4-5

The window is split into two **panes**. The upper pane is the document pane. It displays the document with the footnote number 1 in superscript at the end of the quote.

The lower pane is the footnote pane. This is where you enter the text for the footnote. The footnote pane also displays the footnote number 1 in superscript. The insertion point is positioned following the number, waiting for you to enter the text for the footnote. To enter a space after the number and before the text of the footnote,

Press: Spacebar

When entering the footnote text, you use the same commands and features as in the normal document window. Any commands that are not available are dimmed. In the footnote you will be entering, you will italicize the magazine title "Tennis." You can use the Italic option in the Font and Style dialog box or the shortcuts Ctrl + I or ⟦I⟧. Whichever you use, turn the feature on before typing "Tennis" and then turn it off by clearing the option in the dialog box, or by pressing Ctrl + I or clicking ⟦I⟧ before typing the comma.

> You can also highlight text in the footnote pane and then add the italic style.

Type: Julie Anthony, "Are You a Nutrition Flunkie?" *Tennis,* May 1992, p. 89. (do not press ⟦←Enter⟧)

Your screen should be similar to Figure 4-6.

Italic button

FIGURE 4-6

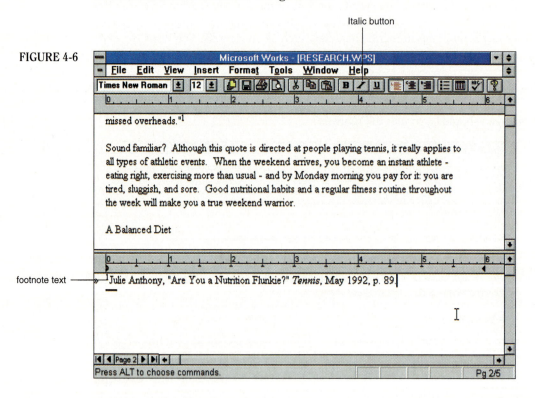

footnote text →

The text for the first footnote is complete. The footnote will be printed at the bottom of the page containing the footnote reference.

The next footnote reference is on page 3. To move to the document pane to position the insertion point,

Press: F6

or

Click: anywhere in the document pane

The insertion point is positioned back in the document pane. The second footnote will provide the source for a quote located on page 3.

Move to: end of quote ("maximum") in second paragraph on page 3

Choose: Insert>Footnote>OK

The footnote number 2 is entered in the document and in the footnote pane. The insertion point is again positioned in the footnote pane so you can enter the text for the second footnote.

Press: Spacebar

Type: Covert Bailey, *The New Fit or Fat,* Houghton Mifflin Company, Boston, p. 161.

This footnote will be printed on the same page as the reference. Each time you add a footnote, Works adjusts the text in the document to allow space at the bottom of the page for the footnote.

Now you notice that you forgot to enter a footnote earlier in the text, on page 2.

Press: F6

Move to: end of third paragraph on page 2

The insertion point should be positioned following the period after the word "protein" on the last line of the third paragraph.

Choose: Insert>Footnote>OK

Notice that the new footnote is number 2, and a blank line has been inserted in the footnote pane where the footnote text will be entered. Works automatically adjusted the footnote numbers to allow you to insert a new footnote.

Press: Spacebar

Type: Doug Henderson, "Nutrition and the Athlete," *FDA Consumer,* May 1987, p. 18.

WORD PROCESSING

To delete a footnote, highlight the footnote number in the document and press Delete. The number and associated footnote text are removed and the following footnotes are renumbered.

To move a footnote, highlight the footnote number and cut the selection to the Clipboard. The number and related footnote text are copied. Then paste the footnote in the new location. All footnote numbers are adjusted appropriately.

Your screen should be similar to Figure 4-7.

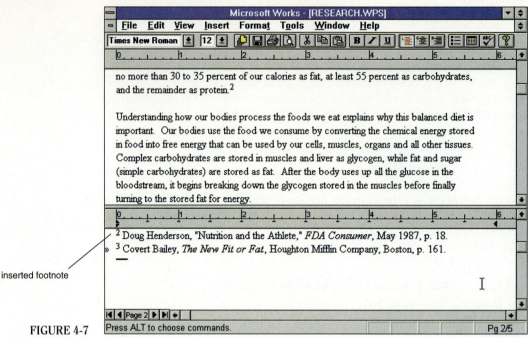

inserted footnote

FIGURE 4-7

Now you are finished entering footnotes. To see all three footnotes in the footnote pane,

Press: Page Up

All the footnotes are displayed in the footnote pane.
> If you see any errors, correct them.
> When you are done, to close the footnote pane,

Choose: View>Footnotes

You can hide and display the footnote pane any time using the Footnotes command on the View menu.

Viewing the Page Layout

To see how the footnotes will appear when printed at the bottom of the page, you can change the view to Page Layout. This view displays all the document elements, including footnotes, as they will appear on the printed page.

Choose: View>Page Layout

The document appears in the window as it would appear on the printed page. However, because the text size is normal, it is difficult to see the page layout without scrolling vertically and horizontally. To see more text in the window, you will reduce the onscreen character size using the Zoom option.

Choose: View>Zoom

The default character zoom size is 100 percent. You can enter any whole number between 25 and 1000 in the text box. To enter a custom size, in the Custom text box,

Type: 65
Choose: OK

Your screen should be similar to Figure 4-8.

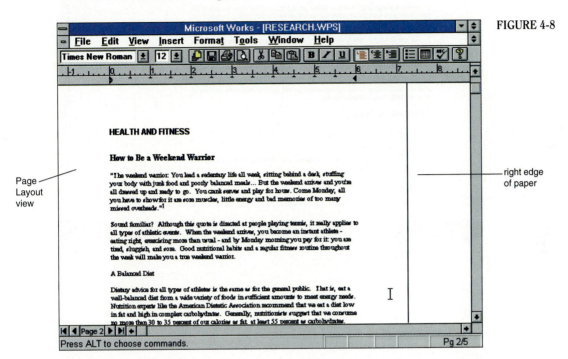

Page Layout view

right edge of paper

FIGURE 4-8

The line along the right side of the window shows the right edge of the page.
To see the footnotes,

Press: Page Down (2 times)

The footnotes are displayed at the bottom of the page, separated from the text by a solid line. The bottom margin is 1 inch. Footnotes are placed immediately above the bottom margin. You can also see the line showing the bottom of the page.
Move to the bottom of the next page to see the third footnote.
While looking at the footnote, you see that you forgot to enter the publication date. While in Page Layout view, you can edit and format the text just as in normal document view. To add the date before the page number of the footnote,

Move to: "p" of "p."
Type: 1991,
Press: Spacebar

> Mouse users can use the scroll bar to see the left edge of the page by scrolling to the left.

> You may also need to scroll the window to see the bottom of the page.

Your screen should be similar to Figure 4-9.

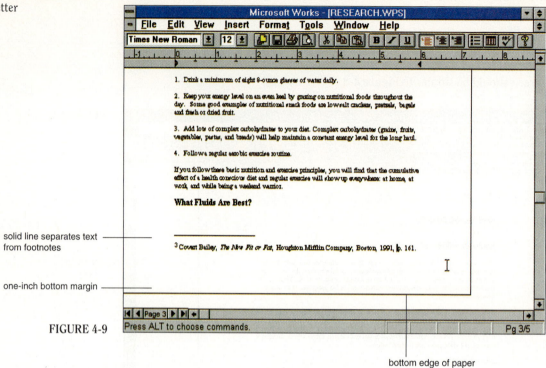

solid line separates text
from footnotes

one-inch bottom margin

FIGURE 4-9

bottom edge of paper

Adding Headers and Footers

Next you want to add page numbers to the document. Although page numbers are displayed in the status line, they do not automatically appear on the printed document.

Page numbers are added to a document in a **header** or **footer**. A header is a line of text that is printed at the top of each page above the top margin. A footer is a line of text at the bottom of each page below the bottom margin. To create headers and footers,

Choose: View>Headers and Footers

The Headers and Footers dialog box is displayed. You would like the page numbers displayed on a footer.

Choose: Footer

You can enter the text you want displayed in the footer in the text box. In addition you can type special codes that control the display of the text in the footer or enter specific information such as the file name or date. The codes and their effects are shown below.

Code	Effect
&l	Left-aligns characters that follow
&r	Right-aligns characters that follow
&c	Centers characters (including spaces) that follow
&p	Prints page number
&f	Prints file name
&d	Prints date
&n	Prints date in long format
&t	Prints time

You would like the page number centered in a footer following the word "Page." To enter the text and codes,

Type: **&cPage &p**

Your screen should be similar to Figure 4-10.

> Enter a space before the page number code to separate the page text from the number.

FIGURE 4-10

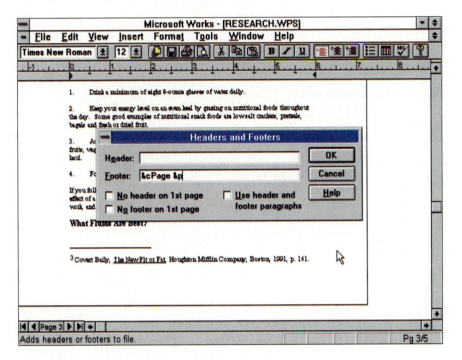

You do not want the page number to be printed on the first page of the document, which contains the memo. To prevent the footer from printing on the first page, the No Footer on 1st Page option is used. This command does not alter the page numbering sequence of the document.

Choose: No footer on 1st page>OK

The page number and text are now displayed as footers at the bottom center of each page. The current page displays the footer "Page 3."

Keeping Text Together

Generally when you print a document, you want section heads and titles to be together on the same page when printed. For example, notice that the section heading "What Fluids Are Best?" is displayed at the bottom of page 3, while the text of the article begins at the top of page 4. In addition there may be certain paragraphs or text that you do not want split between pages.

Text that should remain together on one page, such as a table or a long quote, is often divided over two pages because Works automatically calculates the length of each page and inserts an automatic page break when needed without discrimination as to the text. To control where a page ends, you could simply enter a manual page break to make Works begin a new page. However, if you continue to edit the document by adding and deleting text that affects the length of the document, the location of the manual page break may no longer be appropriate. Then you would need to delete the manual page break and reenter it at the new location.

To keep the fluids article and title together on a page without inserting a page break,

Select: "What Fluids Are Best?" and the blank line below it.
Choose: Format>Paragraph>Breaks and Spacing

There are two options that can be used to keep text together:

Don't break paragraph   Prevents page break within highlighted paragraph

Keep paragraph with next   Prevents page break between highlighted paragraph and following paragraph

To keep the selection together on a page,

Choose: Keep paragraph with next>OK

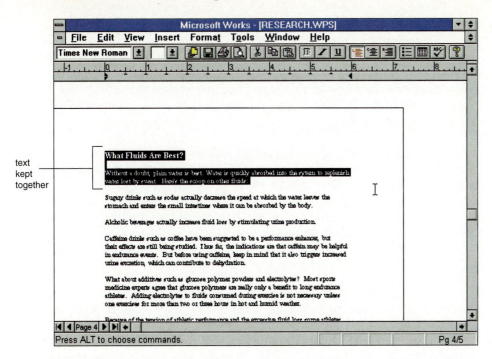

text
kept
together

FIGURE 4-11

WORD PROCESSING

Works moved the title from the bottom of page 3 to the top of page 4 to keep the text together.

As you continue to check the document, you see another problem at the bottom of page 4.

Move to: bottom of page 4

You want to keep the heading "EQUIPMENT UPDATE" and the article title "Stationary Bikes" together on a page with the first paragraph of the article.

Select the text beginning with "EQUIPMENT UPDATE" through the blank line after "Stationary Bikes." Use the Keep Paragraph With Next command to keep the selection together on a page. Clear the highlight.

Save the edited document as REPORT. Set the View back to Normal and the Zoom back to 100%.

You are now ready to print the document.

If necessary select the appropriate printer for your computer system and prepare your printer for printing.

Your text will be reformatted to the capabilities of your printer. Works will pick the closest available font to the one selected in the document.

Before printing you would like to preview the document.

Choose: File>Print Preview

The first page of the document is displayed. Notice that the footer is not displayed at the bottom of page 1 as you specified. To see the second page of the document,

Choose: Next

The second page is displayed in the Print Preview window.

Continue to choose Next to preview the rest of the document. Then print the report. Close the file.

You presented your suggested articles to your manager, who found the topics interesting. The manager suggested, however, that several of the articles were too long and that it would be better not to include any information that requires footnotes. Following your manager's suggestions, you revised the articles and saved them in a file called ARTICLES. Now you are ready to create a sample newsletter using the revised articles.

Open the file ARTICLES.WPS.

Following your manager's suggestions, you shortened several of the articles, removed the footer, and removed any quotations that required footnotes. You also added a brief article on how to train for an upcoming biking event and a list of several upcoming event dates.

Scroll through the text to view the contents of the articles. When you are done, return to the top of the document.

Using WordArt

The first thing you want to do is to enter the title for the newsletter at the top of a new document.

You will create the newsletter title in a new file so that it can be saved and printed on special paper for any newsletter. To display a new blank document window,

Choose: File>Create New File

or

Click: 🖳 Startup Dialog

The Startup dialog box is displayed.

Choose: Word Processor

The title will display the name of the newsletter, "The Sports Company Update," and issue information such as the date of publication and volume number. The completed title is shown below.

**The Sports Company
UPDATE**

A Publication for Customers of The Sports Company

FALL 1995   VOLUME I

The newsletter title will be bold and centered on the page. It will also be in a different font and larger type size. Before typing the title, you will select these settings. First, to center the text,

Choose: Forma**t**>**Pa**ragraph>**I**ndents and Alignment>**C**enter>OK
or
Click: 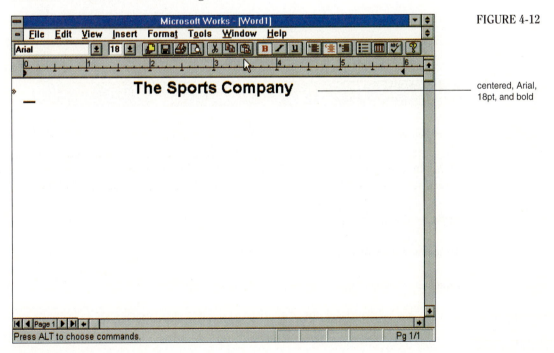 Center Align

The insertion point is positioned in the center of the line.
   Next you want to change the font to a different typeface, a larger size, and bold.

Choose: Forma**t**>**F**ont and Style>**F**ont>TT Arial>**S**ize>18>**B**old>OK
or
Click: `Times New Roman` Font Name
Select: TT Arial
Click: `12` Font Size
Select: 18
Click: `B` Bold

The size of the insertion point has increased to 18pt. To enter the first line of the newsletter title,

Type: The Sports Company

Your screen should be similar to Figure 4-12.

FIGURE 4-12

centered, Arial, 18pt, and bold

The text is centered on the line and is displayed in the font, size, and style you selected. The rest of the newsletter name, UPDATE, will be on the next line.

Press: ⟵Enter

You would like to use the Works WordArt feature for the next line of the newsletter title. WordArt allows you to apply special effects to text, such as arching, rotation, and shadows. To use WordArt,

Choose: Insert>WordArt

Your screen should be similar to Figure 4-13.

editing box   WordArt dialog box

FIGURE 4-13

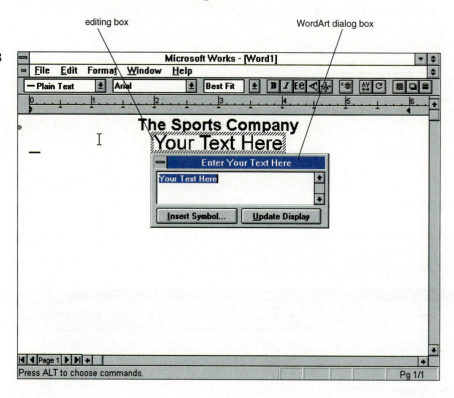

The Enter Your Text Here dialog box is displayed. The words "Your Text Here" are highlighted in the text box and also appear in the document in a box called an editing box at the location of the insertion point. To change the text to "UPDATE,"

Type: **UPDATE**

To see how the word will look in the document,

Choose: Update Display

Now the document displays the word you entered in the editing box.
    Close the dialog box.

Double-click the control-menu box or press Esc or Alt + F4 .

Your WordArt should be similar to Figure 4-15.

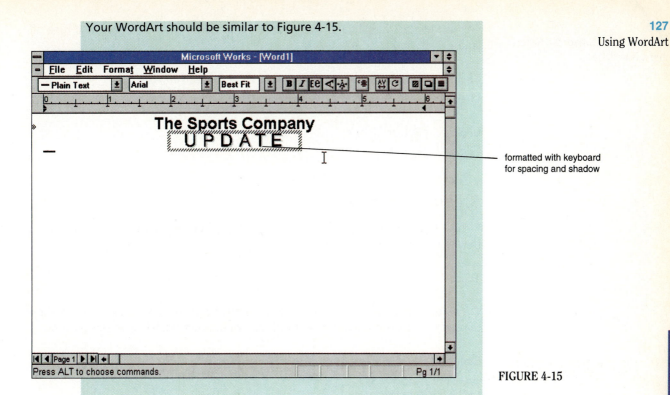

formatted with keyboard
for spacing and shadow

FIGURE 4-15

To deselect the WordArt and return to Works,

Click: anywhere outside the WordArt
or
Press: Esc

The Word Processor menu and toolbar are displayed again, and the WordArt is no longer selected.

If necessary move the insertion point to the right of the WordArt.

The next line in the newsletter title will be in a smaller type size, three lines below the main title. You will change the font size before entering the blank lines so that the blank lines will not be sized for 18pt characters. To change the font and size,

Choose: Format>Fonts and Styles>Times New Roman>Size>12>OK
or
Click: Times New Roman ± Font Name
Choose: TT Times New Roman
Click: 12 Font Size
Choose: 12

To enter the blank lines and the next line of text for the title,

Press: ←Enter (3 times)
Type: A Publication for Customers of The Sports Company
Press: ←Enter (2 times)

WORD PROCESSING

The text appears in bold and centered. To return the alignment to Left and turn off bold,

Choose: Format>Paragraph>Indents and Alignment>Left>OK
Choose: Format>Font and Style>Bold>OK
or
Click: [icon] Left Align
Click: [B] Bold

Creating Borders

Finally, the issue information needs to be entered. The newsletter date is entered on the left margin of the line.

Type: FALL 1995

The volume information will be displayed on the right end of the same line. To align the text with the right margin, you will set a right-aligned tab stop at this position.

Choose: Format>Tabs

In the Position text box,

Type: 6

The Alignment option box lets you specify how text is aligned with the tab. The four alignment options and their effects are:

Tab Alignment	Effect	Example
Left	Left-aligns text on tab	left
Center	Aligns text centered on tab	center
Right	Right-aligns text on tab	right
Decimal	Aligns text on decimal point	350.78
		62.16

> The tab alignment can be changed only with the Format>Tabs menu command, not with the mouse.

Choose: Right>OK

The ⌐ symbol on the ruler indicates a right tab stop is set at the 6-inch position.
    To enter the volume information,

Press: [Tab]

Now, as you type, the characters will align to the left of the right tab stop.

Type: VOLUME I
Press: [←Enter] (2 times)

You want the issue information to have a solid top and bottom border.

Highlight the entire issue line.

Choose: Forma**t**>**B**order>**T**op>Botto**m**>Bold>OK

Clear the highlight.

Your screen should be similar to Figure 4-16.

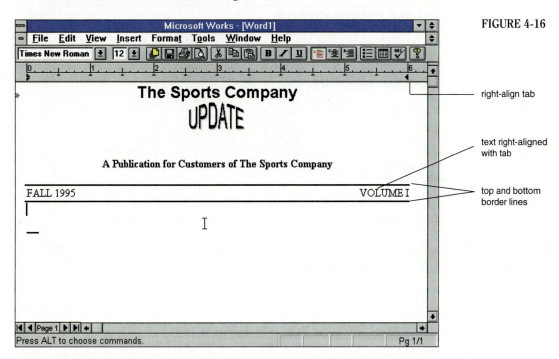

FIGURE 4-16

right-align tab

text right-aligned with tab

top and bottom border lines

A heavy horizontal line appears above and below the issue text. The newsletter title is now complete and can be used with any newsletter.

Save the newsletter title as NSLTITLE. Make the ARTICLES.WPS window active.

The insertion point should be at the beginning of this document. If it is not, move it there.

> Press Ctrl + F6 or use the Window menu.

Creating Columns

Next, you want to change the layout of the articles in the newsletter to be displayed in column format. The Columns command on the Format menu lets you easily set the text format of a document to columns.

Choose: Forma**t**>**C**olumns

Your screen should be similar to Figure 4-17.

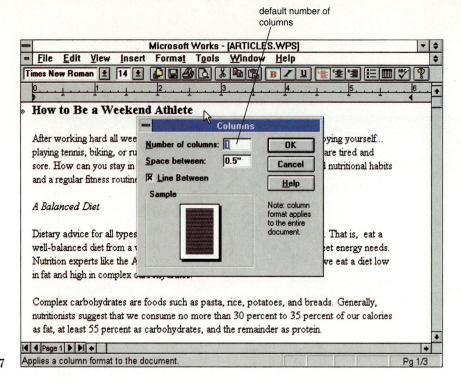

FIGURE 4-17

The Columns dialog box is displayed. To create columns, you specify the number of columns and the spacing between columns. The default number of columns is one. To specify two columns,

Type: 2
Press: Tab

The Sample area shows how text will appear on the page in two-column format. The Space Between option is used to specify how much space you want between the columns. The default setting of .5 inch is appropriate. The Line Between option is on by default. It prints a vertical line between the columns as shown in the Sample area. To turn off the line,

Choose: Line Between>OK

A message box recommends that you switch to Page Layout view. To follow this recommendation and change to Page Layout view,

Choose: Yes

Your screen should be similar to Figure 4-18.

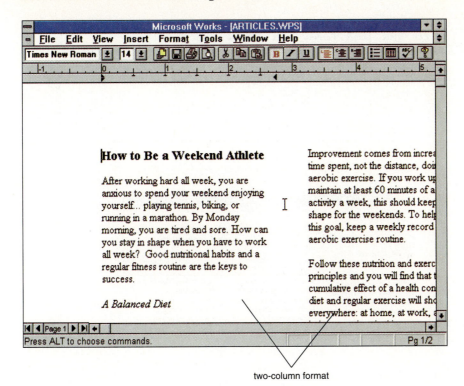

two-column format

FIGURE 4-18

WORD PROCESSING

The text is displayed as two columns. In Normal view the text would be displayed as a single long column. To reduce the character size so that both columns are visible in the window,

Choose: View>Zoom>75%>OK

To move around the columns, click anywhere in the text if you are using the mouse. If you are using the keyboard, the same keys you use in normal text display are used to move within a column. It is difficult to move between columns without a mouse; therefore, if you need to edit text while in column layout, use Normal view.

Scroll to the end of the newsletter to see how the two-column layout looks. Move back to the top of the document.

Hyphenating Text

Scroll the document to the bottom of page 1.

Now that the layout is columns, you notice that many of the lines have very uneven right margins. On lines of text where there are several short words, the wrapping of text to the next line is not a problem. However, on lines that contain long words, the long word is wrapped to the next line, leaving a large gap on the previous line. Allowing Works to hyphenate words will help solve this problem.

Return to the top of the document.

To turn on the hyphenation feature,

Choose: Tools>Hyphenation

Your screen should be similar to Figure 4-19.

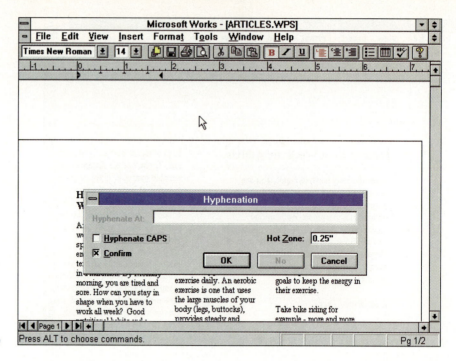

FIGURE 4-19

The Hyphenation dialog box displays the default hyphenation settings. The Hot Zone text box displays the default hyphenation zone setting of .25 inch. The hot zone is an unmarked space along the right margin. Making the hot zone narrower reduces raggedness by hyphenating more words, while making the hot zone larger hyphenates fewer words. When hyphenation is turned on, Works examines words that have been wrapped to the next line to see if part of them can be moved to the previous line. If a word starts before the left boundary of the hot zone and extends past the right boundary, Works inserts a special hyphen called an **optional hyphen** in the word and moves the first part of the word to the preceding line. If text is added or deleted, the optional hyphens are adjusted accordingly.

The default Hot Zone setting is satisfactory and does not need to be changed.

The Confirm option will display each word Works is considering hyphenating and how it would be hyphenated. Then you can confirm the change before it is made. If this option is not checked, Works automatically hyphenates the words. The Confirm option is on by default. To use this option and begin hyphenation,

Choose: OK

The first word that can be hyphenated is located. The blinking light in the Hyphenate At text box shows where Works proposes placing the hyphen. You can use the →
and ← keys to position the hyphen at another location if you do not agree with the proposed hyphenation.

Choose: Yes

The next word that can be hyphenated is located. Although it is safest to confirm each proposed hyphenation, generally Works proposes correct hyphenation placement. To make it faster to hyphenate an entire document, you can turn off Confirm and Works will automatically place hyphens in the rest of the document. To do this,

Choose: Confirm
Choose: Yes

Works moves through the entire document, examining each line and determining where to hyphenate. Finally, a message box indicates that hyphenation is complete. To close the message box,

Choose: OK

Your screen should be similar to Figure 4-20.

If you did not begin hyphenation at the top of the document, Works will ask if you want to continue hyphenating from the beginning when it reaches the end of the document.

FIGURE 4-20

WORD PROCESSING

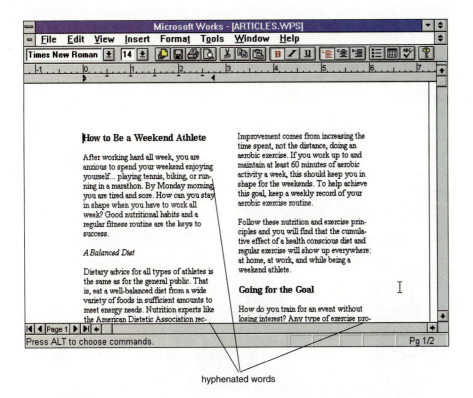

hyphenated words

Hyphenating the newsletter has made the right column margins much less ragged.

If you do not like how Works hyphenates a word, you can remove optional hyphens using the Replace command on the Edit menu. The Find text for an optional hyphen is ^-. The Replace box is left empty.

Save the file as FALLNEWS.WPS.

Adding a Drawing

Note: If you do not have a mouse, skip to the next section, Adding an Outline Border.

Next you want to add a drawing to the newsletter. The drawing is of sports equipment and will complement the text in the first article. You would like the drawing to appear on the left side of the first paragraph.

Move to the beginning of the first paragraph ("After...") on page 1.

Almost any drawing from another software package can be added to a Works word processing document. You will add a drawing contained in a file on your data disk. To insert the drawing,

Choose: Insert>Drawing

The Microsoft Draw dialog box is used to create your own drawings or open and modify previously created drawings. To insert an existing drawing,

Choose: File>Import Picture
Select: SPORTS.WMF
Choose: OK

If necessary change to the directory containing your data file.

Your screen should be similar to Figure 4-21.

FIGURE 4-21

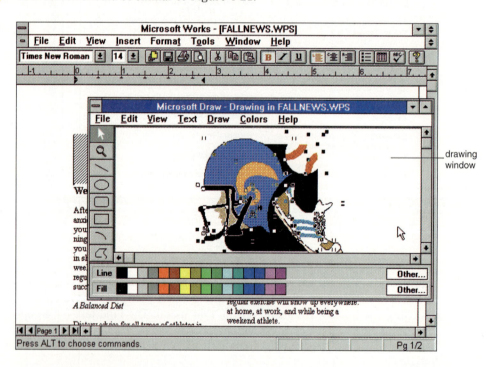

drawing window

The sports drawing is displayed in the Microsoft Draw dialog box. To insert it into the FALLNEWS document,

Choose: File>Exit and Return to FALLNEWS.WPS

In response to the prompt to update the FALLNEWS document,

Choose: Yes

Your screen should be similar to Figure 4-22.

insertion point —

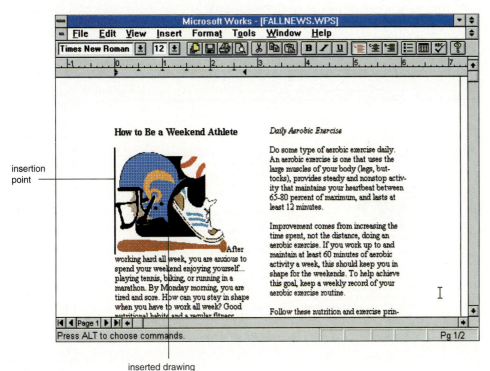

inserted drawing

FIGURE 4-22

WORD PROCESSING

The drawing is inserted in the document at the location of the insertion point. The drawing is inserted as a full-size figure that is larger than you need in the newsletter. Once a drawing is inserted, you can manipulate it in many ways. For example, you can change its size and position in the text, add captions, and change or remove the line and fill pattern. You want to make the drawing smaller.

Select the drawing.

The drawing is surrounded by an outline and eight gray boxes called **handles**. The handles are used to size and move the drawing as you do a window. The mouse changes shape depending upon its position on the drawing. The shapes indicate the following:

> To select a drawing, click on it.

Mouse Shape	Action
	Changes size of drawing
	Moves drawing

Point to the bottom right corner handle.

The mouse pointer changes to 🔲, indicating the drawing can be sized. The arrow shows in which directions you can drag the mouse to change the size of the drawing.

Drag the mouse up and to the left until the outline of the drawing is approximately 1.5 inches square. (See Figure 4-23 for the finished size.)

Your screen should be similar to Figure 4-23.

FIGURE 4-23

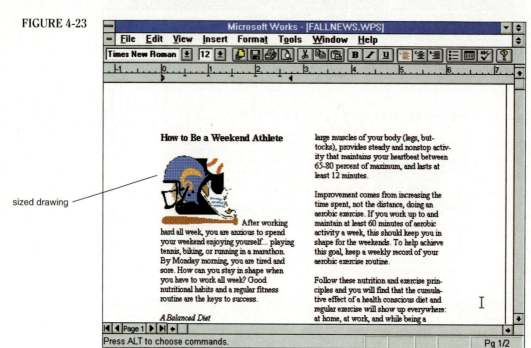

sized drawing

The figure is a smaller size, which allows the first two words of text on the line to appear on the right side of the drawing.

Deselect the drawing. The handles are no longer displayed.

> Click anywhere outside the drawing to deselect it.

Adding an Outline Border

The next item you want to add to the newsletter is an outline border around the list of upcoming events. The list of events is located at the bottom of column 2 on page 2.

Move to: "C" of "Celebrity" in the upcoming events list

First you want to reduce the font size and bold the list.

Highlight the text to the end of the column. Change the font size to 10pt and bold. Clear the highlight.

You also want the dates to line up correctly.

Adjust the dates so the month names line up beneath each other (as in Figure 4-24).

Now you are ready to create the border around the text.
Select the heading "UPCOMING EVENTS" and text to the end of column 2.
To add the outline border,

Choose: Forma**t**>**B**order>**O**utline>OK

Clear the highlight.
Your screen should be similar to Figure 4-24.

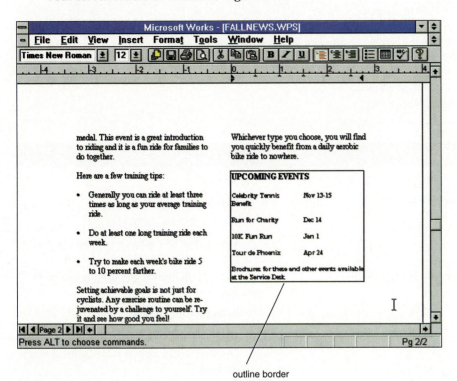

FIGURE 4-24

outline border

A single-line border surrounds the selection.
Move to the bottom of page 2, column 2 and enter your name and the current date. Resave the newsletter as FALLNEWS.
If necessary, select the appropriate printer for your computer system and prepare your printer for printing. Preview the FALLNEWS and NSLTITLE files.
Print the files. Exit Works.

WORD PROCESSING

Key Terms

manual page break (108)
point (109)
cpi (characters per inch) (109)
monospaced (109)
proportional (109)
scalable (109)
style (109)
footnote (113)
pane (113)
header (118)
footer (118)
optional hyphen (132)
handles (135)

Command Summary

Command	Action
Insert>**S**pecial Character>**C**urrent Date	Inserts current date
Insert>Page **B**reak	Inserts manual page break
Forma**t**>**F**ont and Style	Changes appearance of characters on printed page
Forma**t**>**P**aragraph>**Q**uickFormats>Hanging indent	Indents all lines of paragraph except first line
Insert>**F**ootnote	Adds footnote to text
View>**F**ootnotes	Displays/hides footnote pane
View>Page Layout	Displays document as it will appear when printed
View>**H**eaders and Footers	Adds headers and footers to document
Forma**t**>**P**aragraph>Breaks and **S**pacing>Keep paragraph **w**ith next	Keeps related text together on a page
File>Create **N**ew File	Opens Startup dialog box
Insert>**W**ordArt	Allows text to be changed into different shapes and effects
Forma**t**>**B**order	Adds borders to text
Forma**t**>**C**olumns	Displays text in columns
T**o**ols>**H**yphenation	Hyphenates text
Insert>Drawing	Opens Draw dialog box
File>**I**mport Picture	In Microsoft Draw, inserts picture in document
File>E**x**it & Return to <file name>	Exits Microsoft Draw

Matching

1. hot zone _____ a. characters per inch
2. pane _____ b. feature that allows you to apply special effects to text, such as arching, rotation, and shadows
3. cpi _____ c. line of text at top of each page just below top margin
4. handles _____ d. line of text at bottom of each page just above bottom margin
5. monospaced _____ e. each character takes up same amount of space
6. footer _____ f. used to resize drawings
7. WordArt _____ g. fonts that can be printed in almost any point size
8. footnote _____ h. a division of a window
9. header _____ i. source references placed at bottom of page
10. scalable _____ j. area surrounding right margin whose size determines whether fewer or more words will be hyphenated

Practice Exercises

1. The Southwest Regional Manager has prepared an article for the newsletter. He wants you to edit and format it. Open the file FLUIDS.WPS.

   a. Change the font and increase the size of the article title to Arial 14pt.

   b. Center the title line.

   c. Change the layout to two columns with .7 inch between the columns.

   d. Hyphenate the text using the default hot zone.

   e. Add an outline border around the four items at the end of the last paragraph.

   f. Enter your name and the current date at the end of the second column.

   g. Save the document as FLUIDS1. Select your printer. Preview and print the document.

2. Marianne Lopez, a physical education major, is working on a report about water exercises. Open the file WATER.WPS. This file contains the body of a report on water exercises.

   a. Center the main title, "Aquatic Fitness Routine." Change the font to Arial 18pt.

   b. Add a footer that will display your name and the page number at the bottom center of each page.

c. Change the following headings to Arial, 14pt, bold:

Warm-up Stretches

Aerobic Warm-up Exercises

Conditioning Activities

Cool-down Activities

Toning

d. Search the document for headings that are separated from the following text by a page break. Use the Keep With Next Paragraph option to correct any such occurrences.

e. Place the following footnote at the end of the Aerobic Warm-up Exercises paragraph:

McEnvoy, Joseph, *Fitness Swimming: Lifetime Programs*, **Princeton: Princeton Book Company Publishers, 1985.**

Place the following footnote at the end of the last paragraph of the report:

President's Council on Physical Fitness and Sports, *AquaDynamics: Physical Conditioning Through Water Exercise*, **Booklet, Washington, DC: Government Printing Office, 1-33, 1981.**

f. Save the file as WATEREXC. Preview and print the report.

3. You have been assigned to write a report on the topic of children and computers. You are in the final stages of finishing the report. Open the file COMPUTER.WPS. You will complete the layout of this report on children and computers.

a. Bold and enlarge the font to of the following titles to 14pt:
Computers Make Learning Fun
Future Kids
Software For Kids

b. Italicize the following names:
By Andy Rathbone
By Gary S. Dannenbaum

c. Bold the following text:
Computers at Home
Computers in the Classroom
Reader Rabbit 2
Oregon Trail
Where in the World is Carmen Sandiego?
New Math Blaster
Kidworks

d. Add a new page above the body of the report. On the new page center the title "Children and Computers" using WordArt. Add a shadow to the title. Bold the title and change the font to Courier 18pt.

e. Center your name and the current date on separate lines one line below the main title. Change the font for your name and the date to Courier 14pt.

f. Add a footer to display page numbers at the bottom right corners of the pages. Do not display a page number on the title page.

g. Insert the drawing DISK.WMF from your data disk. Place and size the figure to the right of the title "Computers Make Learning Fun."

h. Search the document for headings that are separated from the following text by a page break. Use the Keep With Next Paragraph option to correct any such occurrences.

i. Save the report as KIDSCOMP. Preview and print the report.

4. You work in the advertising department of the Southwestern Discount Store. You need to create a sales brochure to be mailed to all preferred customers.

a. In a new document window, enter the company name "The Southwestern Discount Store" as the first line of text. Center the line and change the font to Helv Italic 18pt.

b. Enter the next line, "Sales Update," as WordArt. Add a shadow. If you are using a mouse, select a shape. Change the font size to Helv 14pt.

c. Enter three blank lines. Enter the third title line, "For Customers of the Southwestern Discount Store." Add a border line above and below this line.

d. Insert the drawing TROPICS.WMF from your data disk. Place and size the figure centered below the first two lines of the title. (The third title line should be below the drawing.)

e. Save the file as SWDTITL. Preview and print the file.

f. Open the file DISCOUNT.WPS. This file contains some new items for the Southwestern Discount Store Update. Bold the uppercase description of each item. Bold the discount store price line for each item.

g. Change the layout to two columns with .5 inch of space between columns. Hyphenate the document.

h. Change the font for the first paragraph to Helv 10pt.

i. Adjust the layout of the columns so that item E starts at the top of the second page.

j. Add a border outline around the paragraph that begins "Check our values" and the ordering information text that follows.

k. Enter your name below the last paragraph of the document. Save the update as SALES.

l. Select your printer. Preview and print the update.

5. Write a paper. The paper can be a paper you have written in the past. It must be a minimum of five pages. You must demonstrate the following:

   a. Title page
- **1)** Center the title of the paper using any WordArt features of your choice to enhance the text.
- **2)** Select a font for the title two sizes larger than the default font for your printer.
- **3)** Center your name and the current date (using the current date special character) near the bottom of the title page.

   b. Body of the report
- **1)** There must be a minimum of three pages of text.
- **2)** Include section heads and subheads that are in a different font and size than the main text.
- **3)** Enter a minimum of four footnotes.

   c. Report layout
- **1)** Display page numbers on the top right corner of every page. Do not number the title page.
- **2)** Search the document for headings that are separated from the following text by a page break. Use the Keep With Next Paragraph option to correct any such occurrences.

   d. Preview and print the report.

6. In this exercise you will create a two-page newsletter on any subject that interests you. Include at least the following layout features:

   a. Enter the text for the newsletter in a new document. Set the page layout to three columns. Set the space between columns appropriately. Include heads and subheads that are formatted to make them stand out from the main text. Add an outline border around an area of text.

   b. Create a newsletter title in a separate document. Use WordArt to enhance the appearance of the title. Select a font of your choice for the title and make it a larger font size. Include a line border in the title. Explore the Insert>ClipArt command and insert one of the ClipArt figures included in the Works ClipArt gallery to enhance the title.

   c. Include your name in both documents. Save and print the newsletter and title.

Electronic Spreadsheets

In contrast to a word processor, which manipulates text, an electronic spreadsheet manipulates numerical data. The first electronic spreadsheet software program (VisiCalc) was offered on the market in 1979. Since then millions of electronic spreadsheet programs of differing brands have been sold. In a 15-year period, spreadsheets have revolutionized the business world.

Definition of Electronic Spreadsheets

The electronic spreadsheet, or worksheet, is an automated version of the accountant's ledger. Like the accountant's ledger, it consists of rows and columns of numerical data. The intersection of a row and column creates a cell where data is entered. Unlike the accountant's ledger, which is created on paper using a pencil and a calculator, the electronic spreadsheet is created using a computer system and an electronic spreadsheet applications software program.

The electronic spreadsheet eliminates the paper, pencil, and eraser. With a few keystrokes the user can quickly change, correct, and update the data. Even more impressive is the spreadsheet's ability to perform calculations—from very simple sums to the most complex financial and mathematical formulas. The calculator is replaced by the electronic spreadsheet. Analysis of data in the spreadsheet has become a routine business procedure. Once requiring hours of labor and/or costly accountants' fees, data analysis is now available almost instantly using electronic spreadsheets.

Nearly any job that uses rows and columns of numbers can be performed using an electronic spreadsheet. Typical uses of electronic spreadsheets are for budgets and financial planning in both business and personal situations.

Advantages of Using an Electronic Spreadsheet

Like a word processor, the speed of entering the data into the worksheet using the keyboard is not the most important advantage gained from using an electronic spreadsheet. This is because the speed of entering data is a function of the typing speed of the user and the user's knowledge of the software program. The advantages are in the ability of the spreadsheet program to quickly edit and format data, perform calculations, create charts or graphs, and print the spreadsheet.

The data entered in an electronic spreadsheet can be edited and revised using the program commands. Numeric or text data is entered into the worksheet in a location called a cell. These entries can then be erased, moved, copied, or edited. Formulas can be entered that perform calculations using data contained in specified cells. The results of the calculations are displayed in another cell.

The design and appearance of the spreadsheet can be enhanced in many ways. There are several commands that control the format or display of a numeric entry in a cell. For instance, numeric entries can be displayed with dollar signs or with a specified number of decimal places. Text or label entries in a cell can be displayed centered or left- or right-aligned to improve the spreadsheet appearance. Columns and rows can be inserted and deleted. The cell width can be changed to accommodate entries of varying lengths.

Many spreadsheet programs let you further enhance the appearance of the spreadsheet by changing the type style and size. You can emphasize different parts of the spreadsheet by using bold or italics and adding underlines, borders, boxes, drop shadows, and shading around selected cells. The ability to see these styles and format changes on the screen as they will appear when printed is called WYSIWYG ("what you see is what you get") pronounced "wizywig."

You have the ability to "play" with the values in the worksheet, to see the effect of changing specific values on the worksheet. This is called "what-if" or sensitivity analysis. Questions that once were too expensive to ask or took too long to answer can now be answered almost instantly, and with little cost. Planning that was once partially based on instinct has been replaced to a great extent with facts. However, any financial planning resulting from the data in a worksheet is only as accurate as that data and the logic behind the calculations. Incorrect data and faulty logic only produce worthless results.

Most electronic spreadsheets also have the ability to produce a visual display of the data in the form of graphs or charts. As the values in the worksheet change, a graph referencing those values automatically reflects the new values. These graphs are a tool for visualizing the effects of changing values in a worksheet. Thus they are analytic graphs. Many spreadsheet programs let you include a graph with the spreadsheet data. This way you can display and print it with the data it represents. You can also enhance the appearance of a graph by using different type styles and sizes, adding three-dimensional effects, and including text and objects such as lines and arrows.

Another new feature of many spreadsheet programs is the ability to open and use multiple spreadsheet files at the same time. Additionally you can create multiple spreadsheets within a file. This is called 3-D spreadsheets. Even more important is the ability to create formulas that link one spreadsheet file to another file. This linking capability lets you change data in one file and automatically update the data in the other.

Alignment: The position of an entry in a cell to the left, centered, or right in the cell space.

Cell: The space created by the intersection of a horizontal row and a vertical column. It can contain a label, value, or formula.

Chart: The visual representation of ranges of data in the worksheet. Also called a graph. Some chart types are line, bar, stacked-bar, and pie.

Column: The vertical block of cells in the spreadsheet identified by letters.

Copy: A feature that duplicates the contents of a cell or range of cells to another location in the worksheet.

File linking: A feature that creates a connection between two files in order to share data.

Format: The styles applied to a cell that control how entries in the spreadsheet are displayed (currency, percent, number of decimal places, and so on).

Formula: An entry that performs a calculation.

Function: A built-in or preprogrammed formula.

Label: An entry that consists of text (alphanumeric characters).

Move: A feature that relocates the contents of a cell (or range of cells) to another area in the worksheet.

Row: The horizontal block of cells in the worksheet identified by numbers.

3-D spreadsheet: A spreadsheet file that contains more than one spreadsheet.

Value: An entry that is a number or the result of a formula or function.

What-if analysis: A process of evaluating the effects of changing one or more values in formulas to help in decision making and planning.

Case Study

In this series of labs, as you continue in your job as a management trainee for The Sports Company, you are working in a retail store as an assistant to the store manager.

In Labs 5 and 6, you will create an operating budget for the retail store. You will learn how to use the spreadsheet program to enter descriptive labels, values, formulas, and functions. You will also learn how to format the spreadsheet to improve its appearance.

Lab 7 demonstrates how to freeze row and column titles and split windows to manage large worksheets. It also shows you how to use the operating budget worksheet to perform what-if analysis.

In Lab 8 you decide you want to analyze the sales data by sport at the store. To better visualize the changes in sales over time, you learn how to create several charts of the data.

SPREADSHEET

5 Creating a Spreadsheet: Part 1

CASE STUDY

Your next assignment with The Sports Company as a management trainee is to develop an operating budget for the retail store. You will use the Works for Windows spreadsheet tool to enter data and analyze the budget. In this lab you will learn how to plan and design a spreadsheet and how to enter descriptive row and column labels, enter numbers and formulas, copy data, and print the spreadsheet.

Examining the Spreadsheet Window

Load Windows and the Works program. Put your data disk in the appropriate drive for your computer system.

The Works Startup dialog box is displayed. To create a new spreadsheet,

Choose: Spreadsheet

If necessary maximize the spreadsheet window.

SPREADSHEET

Your screen should be similar to Figure 5-1.

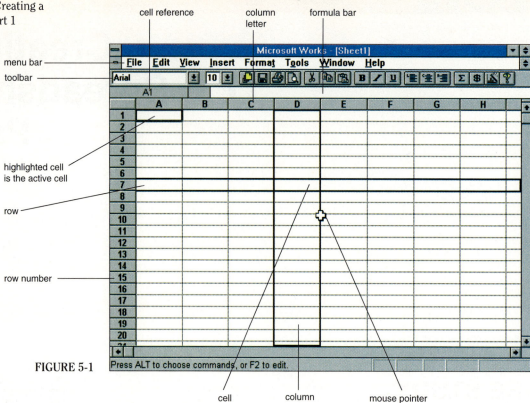

menu bar

toolbar

cell reference

column letter

formula bar

highlighted cell is the active cell

row

row number

FIGURE 5-1

cell

column

mouse pointer

As in the word processing tool, the Works application window is divided into four areas: the menu bar at the top of the window, the toolbar below it, the spreadsheet document window in the workspace, and the status bar and message line at the bottom. The default spreadsheet file name, Sheet1, is displayed in the title bar. The menu bar, the status bar, and message line perform as they did in the word processing tool.

The spreadsheet toolbar contains buttons that are shortcuts to many spreadsheet commands. Several of the buttons are the same as in the word processing tool. Others are specific to the spreadsheet tool. The toolbar operates the same as in the word processor. The buttons will be introduced throughout the labs as they are used.

Below the toolbar is the **formula bar**. The formula bar is used to display entries as they are made and edited in the spreadsheet. Because the spreadsheet is empty, the formula bar is blank.

The spreadsheet window is used to create and display a spreadsheet document. The **spreadsheet** consists of a rectangular grid of **rows** and **columns**. The **row numbers** along the left side of the spreadsheet area identify each row in the spreadsheet. The **column letters** across the top of the spreadsheet area identify the columns. The intersection of a row and column creates a **cell**. The cell that is highlighted (surrounded with a dark border) on your display is called the **active cell**. This is the cell your next entry or procedure affects.

Each cell has a unique name consisting of a column letter followed by a row number. This is called the **cell reference**. The cell reference of the active cell is

The number of rows and columns in your spreadsheet may be different than in Figure 5-1. This is because different display screen settings can display different amounts of information on the screen.

displayed in the box on the left side of the formula bar. Currently it is A1, the cell at the intersection of column A and row 1.

The scroll bars and other mouse symbols are the same as those described in the word processing tool.

Moving Around the Spreadsheet

Either the mouse or the keyboard can be used to move from one cell to another in the spreadsheet. Follow the instructions in the mouse or keyboard sections as appropriate.

In the spreadsheet window, the mouse pointer is a . Other shapes you will see and what they mean are:

Mouse Pointer	Effect
↖	Chooses a button, menu, scroll arrow
↖ DRAG	Moves or copies selection
↔	Adjusts column width
↕	Adjusts row height
I	Edits entry

To move the highlight within the spreadsheet, point to the cell you want to move to and click the mouse button.

Move to: E3

The directional keys on your keyboard are used to move the highlight around the spreadsheet. If you are using the arrow keys on the numeric keypad area, make sure the Number Lock feature is off.

To move to cell E3,

Press: ↓ (2 times)
Press: → (4 times)

Your screen should be similar to Figure 5-2.

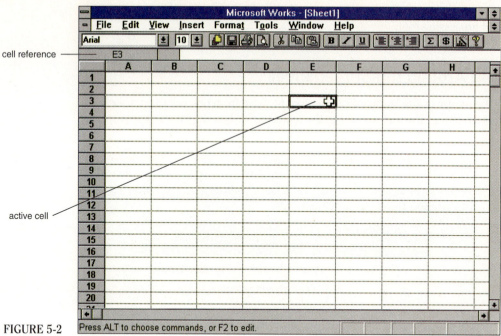

cell reference

active cell

FIGURE 5-2

The highlight is in cell E3, making this cell the active or selected cell. The formula bar reflects the new location of the highlight in the spreadsheet by displaying the cell reference E3 (column E, row 3).

To practice moving around the spreadsheet window using the mouse or keyboard,

Move to: G15
Move to: B4
Move to: D10

To return quickly to the upper left corner, cell A1, of the spreadsheet,

Press: [Ctrl] + [Home]

Wherever you are in the spreadsheet, pressing [Ctrl] + [Home] will move the highlight to the upper left corner of the spreadsheet.

The spreadsheet is much larger than the part you are viewing in the spreadsheet window. The spreadsheet actually extends many columns to the right and many rows down. A Works spreadsheet has 256 columns and 16,384 rows. The spreadsheet window currently displays rows 1 through 20 and columns A through H of the spreadsheet. To view the next full window of cells to the right of column H,

Press: [Ctrl] + [Page Down]

> If your spreadsheet window displays a different number of rows and columns, this is because of the display screen settings on your computer system.

Your screen should be similar to Figure 5-3.

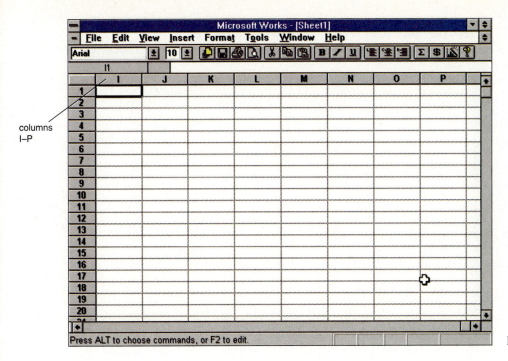

columns
I–P

FIGURE 5-3

Columns I through P and rows 1 through 20 of the spreadsheet are now displayed in the window. To return to the previous window,

Press: Ctrl + Page Up

Columns A through H are visible again. To move down one full window on the spreadsheet,

Press: Page Down

Your screen should be similar to Figure 5-4.

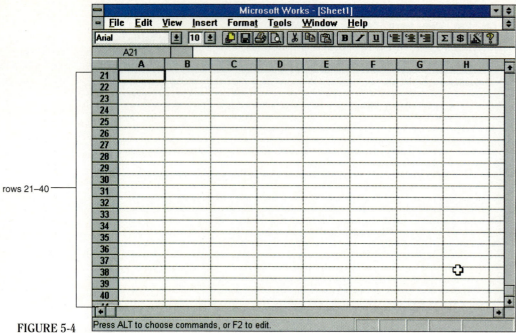

rows 21–40

FIGURE 5-4

The window is positioned over rows 21 through 40 of the spreadsheet. Columns A through H have remained the same. To move up a window on the spreadsheet,

Press: Page Up

Rows 1 through 20 of the spreadsheet are again displayed in the document window.

Scrolling the Spreadsheet

Either the mouse or the keyboard can be used to quickly move through or scroll the spreadsheet. If you have a mouse, you will learn to scroll using both methods.

If you hold down the arrow keys, the Ctrl + Page Down or Ctrl + Page Up keys, or the Page Up or Page Down keys, you can quickly scroll through the spreadsheet. As you scroll the window using the keyboard, the highlight moves to the new location. To move to cell A45,

Press: ↓ and hold down for several seconds until the highlight is on cell A45

You quickly scrolled the window line by line. Cell A45 is now the active cell.

Press: Ctrl + Page Down (hold down for several seconds)

You quickly scrolled the spreadsheet window by window horizontally. To return to cell A1,

Press: Ctrl + Home

The Ctrl key followed by an arrow key will move the highlight to the last used cell of the current row or column. In an empty spreadsheet, this key combination will move the highlight to the last cell of that row or column. To quickly move the highlight to the last row of column A in the spreadsheet,

Press: Ctrl + ↓

The highlight moved to the last row, 16,384, of column A in the spreadsheet. To move to the rightmost column in row 16,384,

Press: Ctrl + →

Your screen should be similar to Figure 5-5.

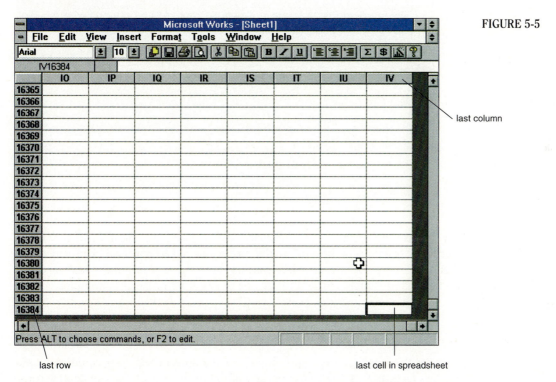

FIGURE 5-5

last column

last row

last cell in spreadsheet

The highlight is positioned in cell IV16384. This is the last cell in the Works spreadsheet. Columns are labeled A to Z, AA to AZ, BA to BZ, and so on, through IA to IV. To return to cell A1,

Press: Ctrl + Home

The ⊡ and ⊡ scroll arrows in the vertical scroll bar and the ⊡ and ⊡ scroll arrows on the horizontal scroll bar will scroll the spreadsheet vertically or horizontally. Just as in Windows and the word processor tool, to scroll continuously hold down the mouse button while pointing to a scroll arrow.

Click: ⊡ scroll arrow (3 times)

SPREADSHEET

Cell A4 should be in the upper left corner of the spreadsheet. Notice that the highlight is not visible. This is because the active cell is still cell A1. Scrolling the spreadsheet with the mouse does not move the highlight. You can confirm the location of the active cell by looking at the cell reference in the formula bar.

Scroll down continuously until row 45 comes into view in the window. Click on cell A45.

The highlight is now positioned on cell A45.

Scroll the spreadsheet window to the right until column P is displayed in the window. Click on cell P45.

The highlight is now positioned on cell P45. To move the window up one window at a time, click on the scroll bar above the scroll box.

Click above the scroll box.

The window displays one full window above the previous window. To move cell A1 back into view, you can drag the scroll box to the top of the vertical scroll bar and to the left in the horizontal scroll bar. Then click on cell A1. This has the same effect as pressing Ctrl + Home. Using the mouse,

Move to: A1

Practice moving around the spreadsheet using the mouse procedures presented above.

When you are ready to go on,

Move to: A1

You can use the mouse or the keyboard with most of the exercises in these labs. Specific instructions on how to use the mouse or the keyboard will be provided only when new topics are introduced. As you use both the mouse and the keyboard, you will find that it is more efficient to use one or the other in specific situations.

Using the Go To Command

To move the highlight to a specific cell in the spreadsheet, you could scroll the windows as demonstrated above; or, as you did in the word processor tool, you can use the Go To command on the Edit menu. The Edit menu commands in the spreadsheet tool perform similar functions as those in the word processor tool Edit menu. The command names however, reflect the structure of the spreadsheet tool. For example, instead of selecting text, you select cells.

To use the Go To command to move the highlight to a specific cell in a spreadsheet,

F5 is the Go To command shortcut as it was in the word processor tool.

Choose: Edit>Go To
➢   F5 GO TO

Your screen should be similar to Figure 5-6.

Go To dialog box

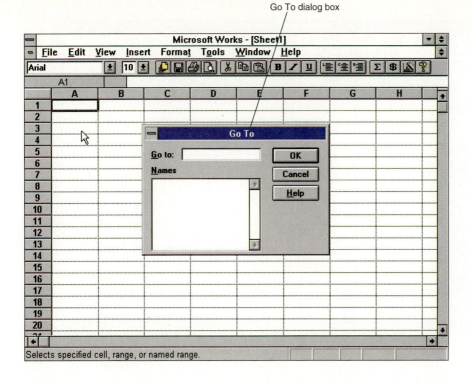

Selects specified cell, range, or named range.

FIGURE 5-6

The same Go To dialog box as in the word processor tool is displayed. In the Go To text box you enter the cell reference of the cell you want to move the highlight to. The cell reference can be entered in either upper- or lowercase letters. To move the highlight to cell AL55,

Type: **AL55**

To complete the command,

Choose: **OK**

Reminder: You can press
(←Enter) to choose OK.

SPREADSHEET

Your screen should be similar to Figure 5-7.

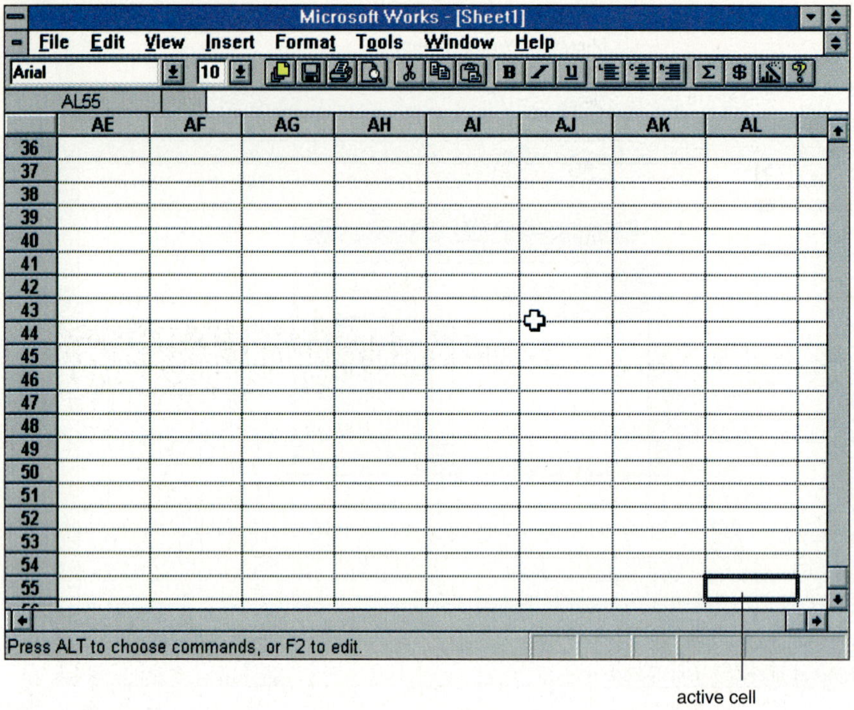

FIGURE 5-7

active cell

The highlight is positioned in cell AL55.

To review, the following keys are used to move around the spreadsheet:

Keys	Action
Arrow keys (↓ ↑ → ←)	Move highlight one cell in direction of arrow
Ctrl + Page Down	Moves highlight right one full window
Ctrl + Page Up	Moves highlight left one full window
Page Down	Moves highlight down one full window
Page Up	Moves highlight up one full window
Ctrl + Home	Moves highlight to cell in upper left corner of spreadsheet
Ctrl + →	Moves highlight to last-used cell in a row
Ctrl + ↓	Moves highlight to last-used cell in a column
Edit>Go To or F5	Moves highlight to specified cell

The following mouse features are used to move around the spreadsheet:

Mouse	Action
Click cell	Moves highlight to selected cell
Click scroll arrow	Moves one row/column in direction of arrow
Click above/below scroll box	Moves one window up/down
Click right/left scroll box	Moves one window right/left
Drag scroll box	Moves multiple windows up/down or right/left

Practice moving the highlight around the spreadsheet using each of the keys and mouse procedures presented on the previous page.

When you are ready to go on,

Move to: A1

Planning a Spreadsheet

Now that you know how to move around the spreadsheet, you will begin creating the six-month budget for The Sports Company.

The first step to creating a spreadsheet is to develop the spreadsheet design. A well-designed spreadsheet produces accurate results, is clearly understandable by the users, is easily adapted to changing needs, and is efficient in terms of its ease of use and in its memory requirements. To achieve these objectives, a spreadsheet plan must be developed. There are four steps in this planning process.

1. **Specify purpose.** As your first step, you must decide exactly what you want the spreadsheet to do. This means a clear identification of the data that will be input and the output that is desired.

2. **Design and build.** You can design the spreadsheet on paper or directly in Works for Windows. Your design should include a spreadsheet title and row and column labels that identify the input and output. Sample data is used to help generate the formulas needed to produce the output.

3. **Test.** Once your design is complete, you are ready to test the spreadsheet for errors. Several sets of real or sample data are used as the input, and the resulting output is verified. The input data should include a full range of possible values for each data item to ensure the spreadsheet can function successfully under all possible conditions.

4. **Document.** Well-designed spreadsheets typically are documented within the spreadsheet. Documentation is important to ensure that whoever uses the spreadsheet will be able to clearly understand its objectives and procedures.

As the complexity of the spreadsheet increases, the importance of following the design process increases. Even for simple spreadsheets like the one you will create in this lab, the design process is important.

After reviewing past budgets and consulting with the store manager, you have designed the basic layout for the half of the budget for the retail store, as shown in Figure 5-8 on page 158.

	A	B	C	D	E	F	G	H	I
1									
2				**1996 First Half Budget**					
3									
4		January	February	March	April	May	June	TOTAL	AVG.
5	*SALES*								
6	Clothing	$140,000	$125,000	$200,000	$210,000	$185,000	$185,000	$1,045,000	$174,167
7	Hard Goods	$94,000	$85,000	$120,000	$145,000	$125,000	$125,000	$694,000	$115,667
8	Total Sales	$234,000	$210,000	$320,000	$355,000	$310,000	$310,000	$1,739,000	$289,833
9									
10	*EXPENSES*								
11	Advertising	$9,360	$8,400	$12,800	$14,200	$12,400	$12,400	$69,560	$11,593
12	Cost of Goods	$135,720	$121,800	$185,600	$205,900	$179,800	$179,800	$1,008,620	$168,103
13	Salary	$32,000	$32,000	$32,000	$32,000	$32,000	$32,000	$192,000	$32,000
14	Lease	$19,000	$19,000	$19,000	$19,000	$19,000	$19,000	$114,000	$19,000
15	Miscellaneous	$16,000	$16,000	$16,000	$16,000	$16,000	$16,000	$96,000	$16,000
16	Overhead	$22,000	$22,000	$22,000	$22,000	$22,000	$22,000	$132,000	$22,000
17	Total Expenses	$234,080	$219,200	$287,400	$309,100	$281,200	$281,200	$1,612,180	$268,697
18									
19	*INCOME*	($80)	($9,200)	$32,600	$45,900	$28,800	$28,800	$126,820	$21,137
20									
21									
22									
23									

text entries ⟵ (column A)

numerical data ⟶ (columns B–I)

FIGURE 5-8

The title in row 2 describes the data displayed in the spreadsheet. The column headings in row 4 are descriptive entries that define the structure of the spreadsheet. The column headings consist of the six months, January through June, and a Total (sum of entries over six months) and Average (average of entries over six months). The month headings indicate the time periods the data in the columns represents.

The row headings in column A describe the following:

SALES
Clothing	Income from clothing sales
Hard Goods	Income from equipment, machines, and miscellaneous sales
Total Sales	Sum of clothing and hard goods sales

EXPENSES
Advertising	Monthly advertising costs (4 percent of total sales)
Cost of Goods	Cost of items sold (58 percent of total sales)
Salary	Personnel expenses
Lease	Monthly lease expense
Miscellaneous	Monthly expenses for phone, electricity, water, trash removal, and so on
Overhead	Monthly payment to corporate headquarters
Total Expenses	Sum of advertising, cost of goods, salary, lease, miscellaneous, and overhead expenses

INCOME   Total Sales minus Total Expenses

The title and row and column headings clearly identify the information in the spreadsheet.

The information in cells B5 through I19 is the numerical data that represents the sales and expenses for the six months.

The information entered into a spreadsheet can be text, numbers, dates and times, or formulas. Generally, entries into a spreadsheet that are descriptive entries are **text entries**. Text entries can contain a combination of letters, numbers, and any other special characters. **Numeric entries**, like those in cells B5 through I19, can include only the digits 0 to 9, and any of the special characters, + – ( ) , . $ %. Text entries are commonly called labels and numeric entries are commonly called values. **Date** and **time entries** are also interpreted as numbers. Numeric entries are used in calculations. A **formula** entry performs a calculation. If an entry includes any characters other than numbers or the special characters listed above or is not interpreted as a date, time, or formula, Works interprets the entry as text.

Entering Text

To create the structure for this spreadsheet, you will begin by entering the row headings. The row heading "SALES" will be entered in cell A3.

Move to: A3

To enter the heading in all capital letters,

Press: Caps Lock

As in the word processor tool, the indicator "CAPS" appears in the status bar to remind you that the Caps Lock key is on. The Caps Lock key affects only the letter keys. To produce the characters above the number and punctuation keys, you must use ⇧Shift in combination with the character. Type the row heading exactly as it appears in Figure 5-9 on page 160.

Type: **SALES**

If you made an error while typing the entry, use the Backspace key to erase the characters back to the error. Then retype the entry correctly.

SPREADSHEET

Your screen should be similar to Figure 5-9.

Cancel button   Enter button   insertion point

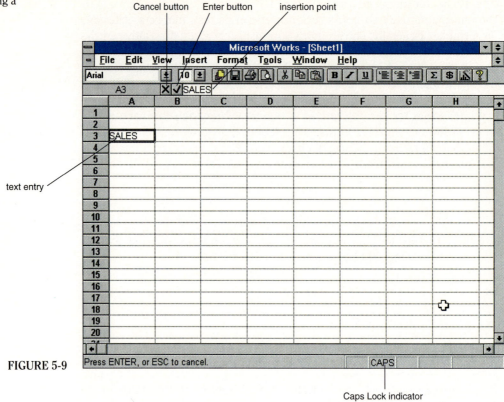

text entry

FIGURE 5-9

Caps Lock indicator

Several changes have occurred in the window. As you type, the entry is displayed in the active cell and in the formula bar. They should display "SALES." The insertion point appears in the formula bar and marks your location in the entry. In addition, two new buttons, Cancel ✗ and Enter ✓, appear in the formula bar. They can be used by the mouse to complete your entry or cancel it.

Although the entry is displayed in both the active cell and the formula bar, it has not yet been completed. The ←Enter key or Enter button ✓ is used to complete your entry and enter it into the cell. If you press Esc or choose the Cancel button ✗, the entry is cleared from the formula bar and the cell. Since your hands are already on the keyboard, it is quicker to press ←Enter. To complete the entry,

Press: ←Enter

Your screen should be similar to Figure 5-10.

double quotation mark
identifies entry as text

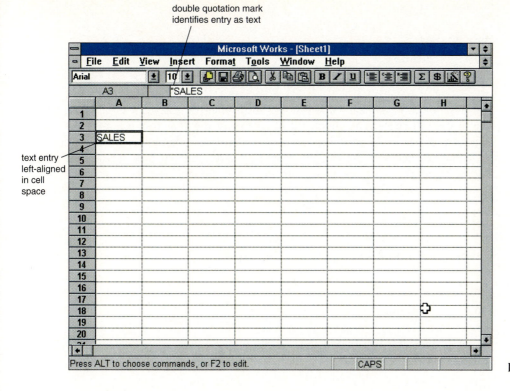

text entry
left-aligned
in cell
space

FIGURE 5-10

The entry "SALES" is displayed in cell A3. Because the highlight is positioned on a cell containing an entry, the contents of the cell are also displayed in the formula bar. The insertion point and the Cancel and Enter buttons are no longer displayed in the formula bar. Notice the double quotation mark (") before the entry in the formula bar. The double quotation mark is entered automatically by Works to show that the cell contents have been interpreted as a text entry. You can also manually enter the double quotation mark before a numeric entry that you want Works to interpret as text; then it cannot be used in calculations. For example, the year entry, 1996, is a date (number) that could be entered as text by typing the entry as "1966. The double quotation mark is displayed only in the formula bar and not in the cell.

Clearing an Entry

After looking at the entry, you decide you want the row headings to begin in row four, rather than in row three. This will leave more space above the column headings for the spreadsheet title.

The Clear command on the Edit menu will clear the contents from the highlighted cell. The shortcut for this command is [Delete]. To remove the entry from cell A3, with the highlight on the entry to be removed,

Choose: Edit>Clear

➤   [Delete]

The cell entry is no longer displayed in the cell or in the formula bar. To enter the heading in cell A4,

Move to: A4
Type: **SALES**
Press: ⏎Enter

The label "SALES" is displayed in cell A4. Notice that the entry is aligned to the left side of the cell space. The alignment of entries in the cell space is similar to the alignment of text in the word processor. The difference is that text in a word processor is aligned between the margin settings, whereas entries in a spreadsheet are aligned within the cell space. By default text entries are displayed left-aligned.

To turn off Caps Lock,

Press: Caps Lock

To enter the next row label,

Move to: A5
Type: **Clothing**

The next entry you will make is in cell A6, one cell down. To complete the label entry and move to the next cell,

Click: A6
or
Press: ↓

> You can click any cell to complete the entry and move to the cell.

Using ↓ entered the heading into the cell and moved the highlight. Moving the highlight to any other cell will complete the entry.

You are now ready to enter the label "Equipment" into cell A6.

Type: **Equipment**
Press: ⏎Enter

Changing an Entry

You would like to change the heading from "Equipment" to "Hard Goods." An entry in a cell can be entirely changed or partially changed. To completely change the entry, move to the cell you want to change and retype the entry the way you want it to appear. As soon as a new character is entered, the existing entry is cleared. To change the entire entry,

Type: **Hard Good**
Press: ⏎Enter

Now you notice that you forgot to enter the "s" at the end of "Good." Generally, if you need to change only a part of an entry, it is quicker to partially edit the entry. To edit an entry, Works changes to the Edit mode.

To change to Edit mode, click the formula bar.

The insertion point appears in the formula bar. Notice that the mouse pointer changes to an I-beam when positioned in the formula bar. The mouse pointer can now be used to position the insertion point in the entry.

If the insertion point is not at the end of the entry, move it there.

The F2 key is called the Edit key. It is used to change to Edit mode.

Press: F2 EDIT

Your screen should be similar to Figure 5-11.

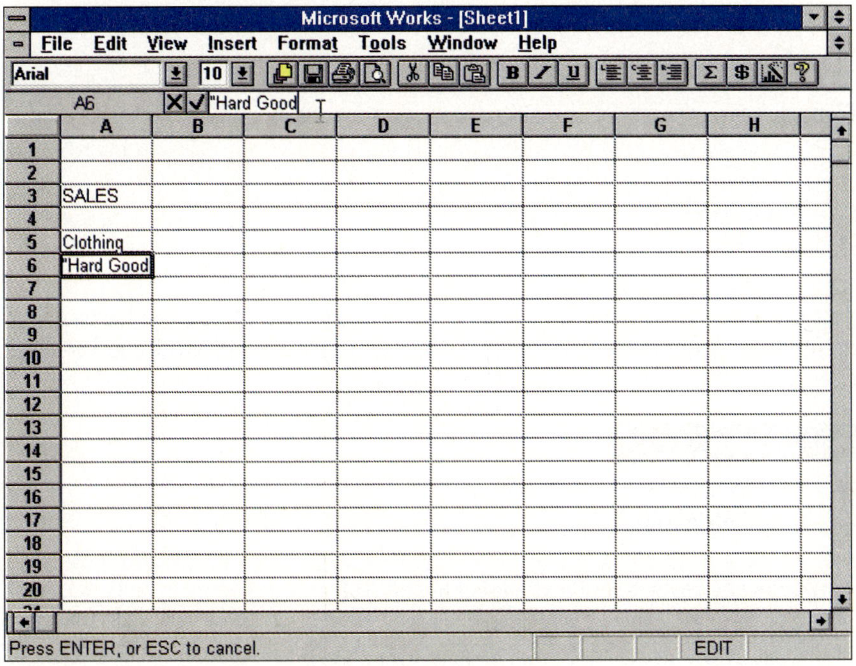

FIGURE 5-11

The insertion point is positioned at the end of the entry in the formula bar. Notice that the status bar displays "EDIT."

In the Edit mode, the following keys can be used:

Key	Action
Home	Moves insertion point to beginning of entry
End	Moves insertion point to end of entry
Del	Erases character at insertion point
Backspace	Erases character to left of insertion point
→	Moves insertion point one character right
←	Moves insertion point one character left

If you have a mouse, you can also move the insertion point anywhere in the entry by positioning the I-beam at the location and clicking the mouse.

To correct the entry,

Type: s

The "s" is added to the label. To complete the edit,

Press: ↓

"EDIT" no longer appears in the status bar. You are now ready to enter the next label.

Type: **Total Sales**
Press: ↓

Continue by entering the next two labels in the cells specified. Enter the labels using uppercase letters where indicated and use ↓ to complete each entry and move to the next cell.

Cell	Label
A9	**EXPENSES**
A10	**Advertising**

You should now be ready to enter the label in cell A11.

Type: **Cost of Goods** (do not press ←Enter or ↓ yet)

Your screen should be similar to Figure 5-12.

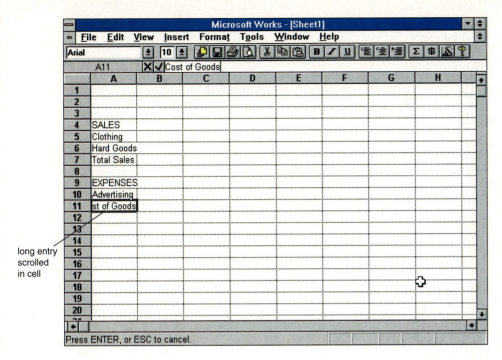

long entry
scrolled
in cell

FIGURE 5-12

Notice that the first two letters of the entry are not displayed in the cell space. This is because the cell space is not wide enough to display the entire entry. By default the cell is 10 spaces wide. Because the entry is longer than 10 spaces, the text has scrolled in the cell highlight. The complete entry is displayed in the formula bar.

Press: ⎆Enter

Now the entry is fully displayed in the spreadsheet because the overlapping part is displayed in cell B11. When a label is longer than the cell's width, it is called a **long entry**. Works will display as much of the label as it can. If the cells to the right are empty, the whole label will be displayed. If the cells to the right contain an entry, the overlapping part of the label will not be displayed.

Continue by entering the rest of the labels in the cells specified. Enter the labels using uppercase letters where indicated. Use ↓ to complete each entry and move to the next cell.

Cell	Label
A12	**Payroll Salaries**
A13	**Lease**
A14	**Miscellaneous**
A15	**Overhead**
A16	**Total Expenses**
A18	**INCOME**

SPREADSHEET

Click on the formula bar or press F2 to change to Edit.

After looking over the labels, you decide to change the entry in cell A12 to "Salary." To edit it,

Move to: A12

Change to Edit mode.

To move the insertion point to the beginning of the entry,

Click: the " in the formula bar
or
Press: Home

The insertion point moved to the beginning of the entry. Then to delete the word Payroll,

Press: Del (9 times)

The word is removed. To move to the end of the entry and change "Salaries" to "Salary,"

Press: End
Press: Backspace (3 times)
Type: **y**

To complete the entry and see how it appears in the cell space,

Press: ←Enter

Your screen should be similar to Figure 5-13.

FIGURE 5-13

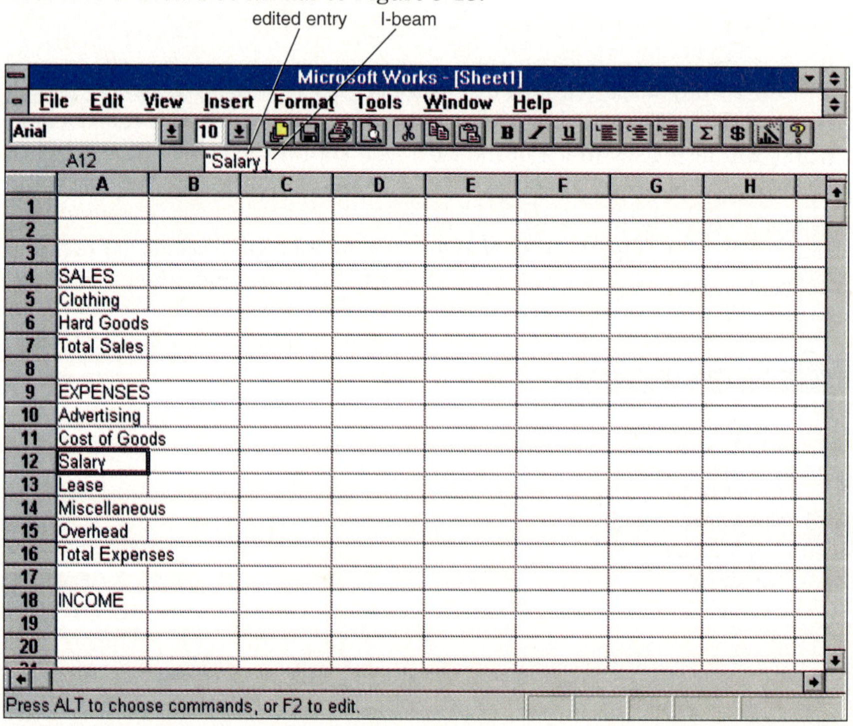

As you can see, editing is particularly useful with long or complicated entries.

Finally, the last text entry you want to enter is a title in row 2 above the column labels.

Move to: C2

Type: 1996 First Half Budget

Press: ←Enter

Your screen should be similar to Figure 5-14.

long entry

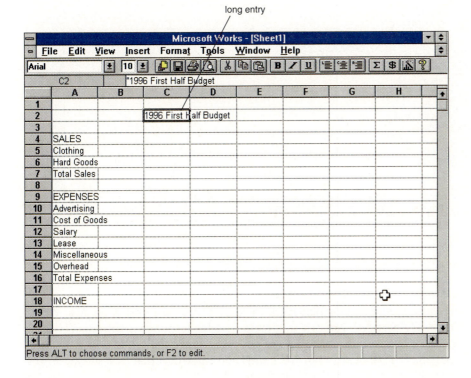

FIGURE 5-14

Notice that the spreadsheet title is a long entry and is fully displayed because the cells to the right of C2 are empty.

Entering Month Labels

Next the month labels for January through June need to be entered in cells B3 through G3.

Move to: B3

Type: jan

Press: ←Enter

SPREADSHEET

Your screen should be similar to Figure 5-15.

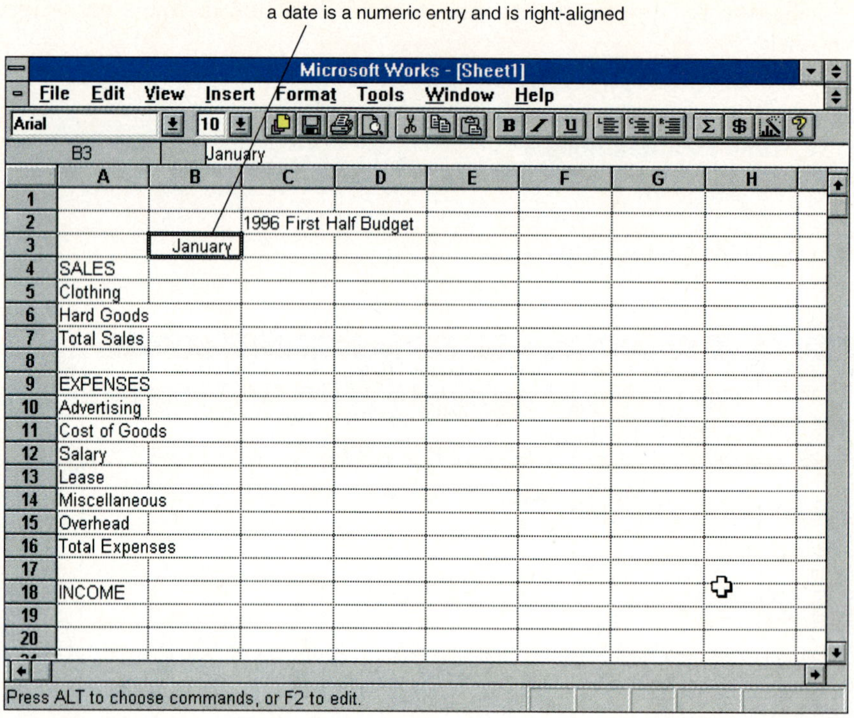

a date is a numeric entry and is right-aligned

FIGURE 5-15

Although you typed "jan," the spreadsheet displays "January." This is because Works recognized the entry as a date. Several changes occur when an entry is interpreted as a date. First, the full month name is displayed. Next, notice the entry is not preceded by a double quotation mark in the formula bar. This is because Works automatically changes entries it interprets as dates to numeric entries. Works assigns each month a numerical value so you can include the cell in a mathematical calculation. The date entry, not the underlying numeric value, is displayed in the cell. Finally, the date is displayed right-aligned in the cell space. This is the default alignment for numeric entries.

If you wanted the month labels to appear abbreviated, such as JAN, you would need to begin the entry with a double quotation mark to make Works accept the entry as a text entry. To try this, for the February month label,

Move to: C3
Type: "Feb
Press: ⏎Enter

Your screen should be similar to Figure 5-16.

text entry left-aligned

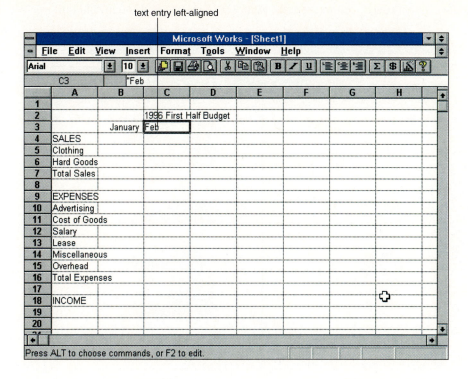

FIGURE 5-16

The entry did not change and is displayed as a text entry in the cell exactly as you entered it.

Although you will not use the months in calculations, you decide to use the default month display, as in cell B3, anyway. To delete the entry from cell C3,

Press: Del

The entry is cleared from the cell.

Entering a Series

To enter the remaining month headings, you could type each one individually. A quicker way is to use the Fill Series command on the Edit menu. This command lets you automatically fill any number of cells with a series of numbers or dates.

Before using this command, you must first enter the starting value or date into the first cell. You have done this already by entering January in cell B3.

Next you need to select (highlight) the cell with the starting value and the cells to the right or below it where you want the series entered. Highlighting cells in a spreadsheet defines a **range**. A range is a rectangular block of cells. It can be a single cell or a row or column of cells. Figure 5-17 shows valid and invalid ranges.

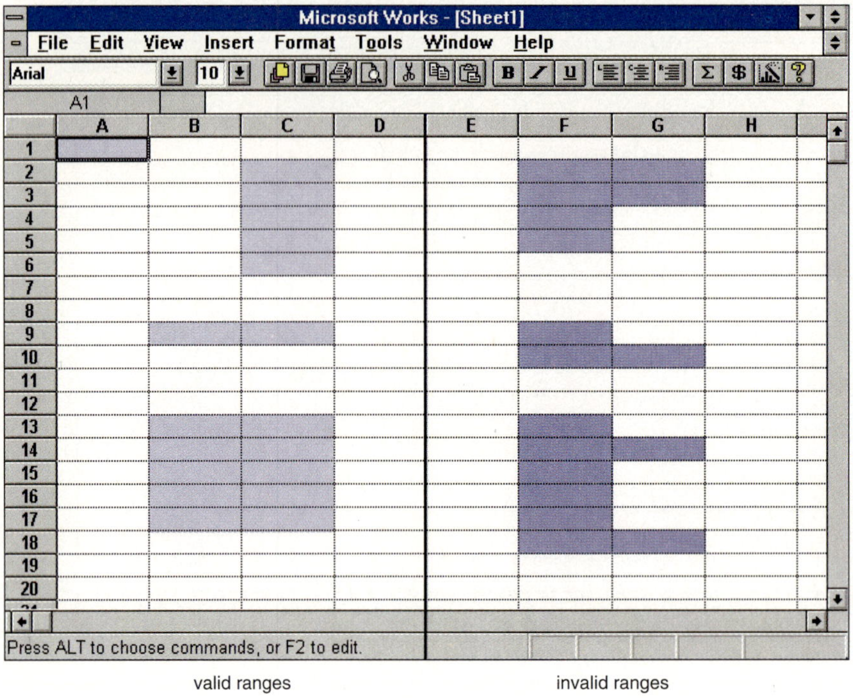

FIGURE 5-17

valid ranges   invalid ranges

Move to: B3

The five cells to the right of cell B3 (C3 through G3) will hold the month labels for February through June.

> The mouse pointer should be ✛ not ⬚ when you highlight a range.

To highlight a range using the mouse, point to the cell beginning the range and drag the mouse pointer to the last cell of the range.

Highlight cells B3 through G3.

> You can also press F8 to turn on Extend and then extend the highlight using the directional keys.

A range is highlighted by using ⇧Shift in combination with a directional key as you did when highlighting in the word processor. The highlight should be positioned on a cell at the upper left or lower right corner of the group of cells before extending the highlight. With the highlight on cell B2,

Press: ⇧Shift + → (5 times)

Your screen should be similar to Figure 5-18.

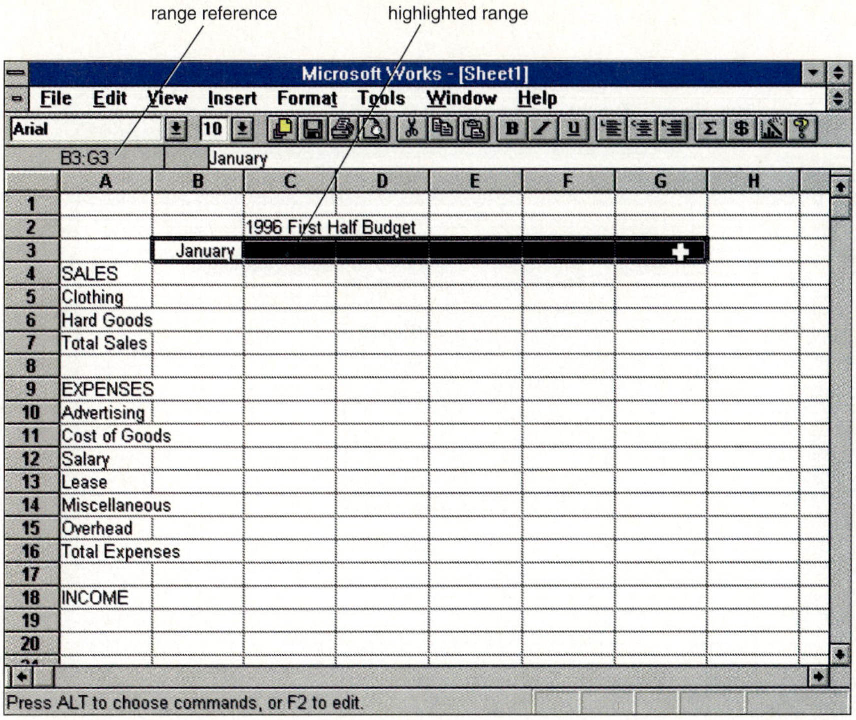

range reference   highlighted range

	A	B	C	D	E	F	G	H	
			B3:G3	January					
1									
2			1996 First Half Budget						
3		January							
4	SALES								
5	Clothing								
6	Hard Goods								
7	Total Sales								
8									
9	EXPENSES								
10	Advertising								
11	Cost of Goods								
12	Salary								
13	Lease								
14	Miscellaneous								
15	Overhead								
16	Total Expenses								
17									
18	INCOME								
19									
20									

Press ALT to choose commands, or F2 to edit.

FIGURE 5-18

The range of cells, B3 through G3, is highlighted. The **range reference** of the selected range is displayed in the cell reference area of the formula bar. A range reference identifies a range by using the upper left and lower right corner cells in the range separated by a colon. When a cell or range is highlighted, this tells Works that you want to work with those cells. To fill the highlighted range with a series of dates,

Choose: Edit>Fill Series

Your screen should be similar to Figure 5-19.

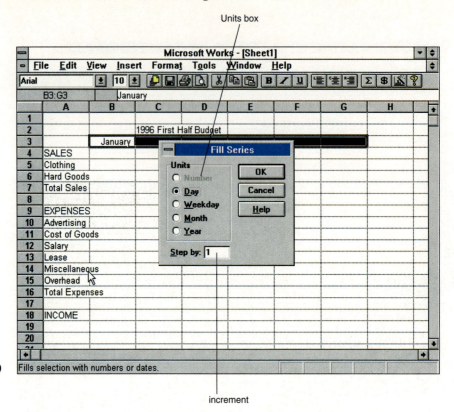

FIGURE 5-19

The Fill Series dialog box is displayed. In the Units box, you specify the type of series you want to create. To specify the type of unit to be months,

Choose: Month

In the "Step by" box, you set the increment to be used in the series. If you wanted Works to increase the series by an increment other than 1, you would specify the number. In this case you want to increase the months one at a time, so you do not need to enter a value. To complete the command,

Choose: OK

Your screen should be similar to Figure 5-20.

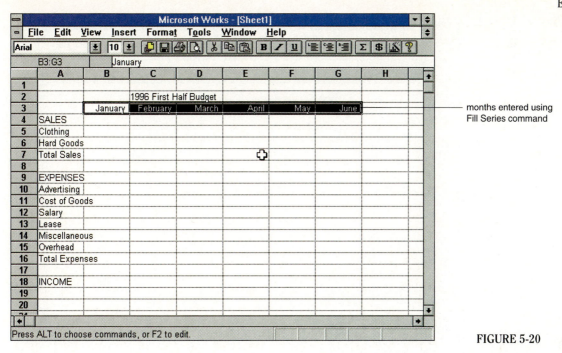

months entered using
Fill Series command

FIGURE 5-20

The highlighted cells have been filled with a series of consecutive months.

Clear the highlight.

> To clear a highlight, click
> anywhere in the spreadsheet
> or use any directional key.

Entering Numbers

Next you will enter the expected clothing sales numbers for January through June into cells B5 through G5.

Move to: B5

To enter the expected clothing sales of $140,000 for January,

Type: 140000
Press: ⟶

Your screen should be similar to Figure 5-21.

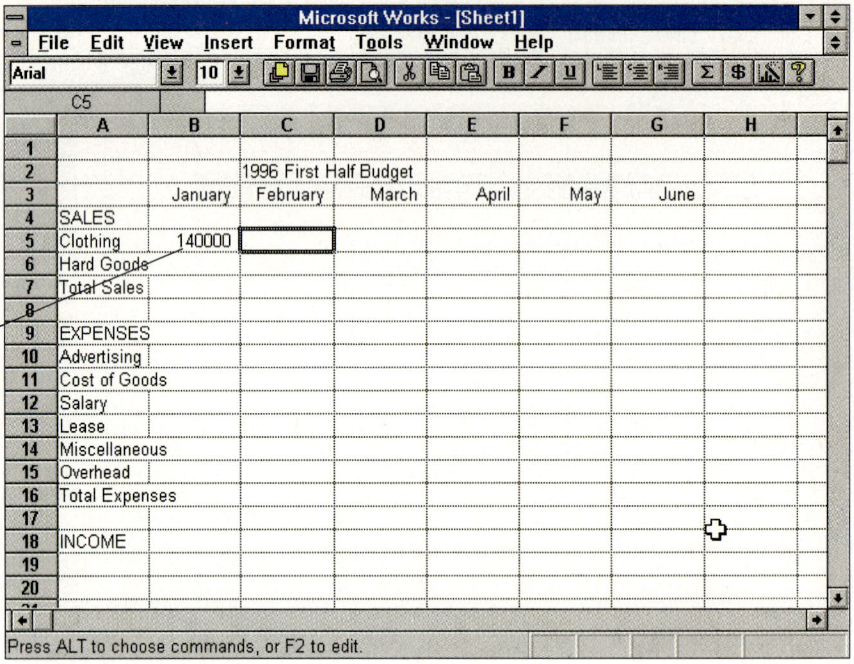

right-aligned numeric entry

FIGURE 5-21

The number 140000 is displayed right-aligned in cell B5. Numeric entries are displayed right-aligned by default.

To enter the expected clothing sales for February,

Type: 125000

Press: →

Reminder: Use the numeric keypad to quickly enter numbers.

In the same manner, enter the remaining clothing sales shown below in the specified cells:

Cell	Value
D5	200000
E5	210000
F5	185000
G5	185000

Next you will enter the hard goods sales for the six months in row 6.

In the same manner, enter the numbers shown below in the specified cells:

Cell	Value
B6	99000
C6	85000
D6	120000
E6	145000
F6	125000
G6	125000

Your screen should be similar to Figure 5-22.

```
┌─────────────────────────────────────────────────────────────────┐
│ ─          Microsoft Works - [Sheet1]              ▼ ▲           │
│ ─  File  Edit  View  Insert  Format  Tools  Window  Help    ▲ ▲ │
│ Arial          ± 10 ±  ⬜⬛⬛⬛⬛ ✂⬛⬛ B I U ≡≡≡ Σ $ ⬛ ? │
│     G6              125000                                         │
│      │    A    │   B   │   C    │   D    │   E    │   F   │   G   │   H   │    ▲ │
│  1   │         │       │        │        │        │       │       │       │      │
│  2   │         │       │1996 First Half Budget│    │       │       │       │      │
│  3   │         │January│February│ March  │ April  │  May  │ June  │       │      │
│  4   │SALES    │       │        │        │        │       │       │       │      │
│  5   │Clothing │140000 │125000  │200000  │210000  │185000 │185000 │       │      │
│  6   │Hard Goods│99000 │85000   │120000  │145000  │125000 │125000 │       │      │
│  7   │Total Sales│     │        │        │        │       │       │       │      │
│  8   │         │       │        │        │        │       │       │       │      │
│  9   │EXPENSES │       │        │        │        │       │       │       │      │
│ 10   │Advertising│     │        │        │        │       │       │       │      │
│ 11   │Cost of Goods│  │        │        │        │       │       │       │      │
│ 12   │Salary   │       │        │        │        │       │       │       │      │
│ 13   │Lease    │       │        │        │        │       │       │       │      │
│ 14   │Miscellaneous│  │        │        │        │       │       │       │      │
│ 15   │Overhead │       │        │        │        │       │       │       │      │
│ 16   │Total Expenses│ │        │        │        │       │       │       │      │
│ 17   │         │       │        │        │        │       │       │       │      │
│ 18   │INCOME   │       │        │        │        │       │   ✛   │       │      │
│ 19   │         │       │        │        │        │       │       │       │      │
│ 20   │         │       │        │        │        │       │       │       │   ▼ │
│ Press ALT to choose commands, or F2 to edit.                                    │
└─────────────────────────────────────────────────────────────────┘
```

FIGURE 5-22

Entering Formulas

Now that the sales values are complete, you can enter the monthly total sales values.

Move to: B7

The calculation of this value can be made automatically for you by entering a formula in the spreadsheet. As you learned earlier, a formula is an entry that directs Works to perform a calculation using the values in the formula or in cells referenced in the formula. The result of the calculation is displayed in the spreadsheet cell. For more information about formula entries, you will use Help.

Choose: Help>Contents>Spreadsheet>Spreadsheet basics>Formulas

Read the Help information on this topic. When you are done, exit the Help window.

Three types of formulas can be entered in a spreadsheet: numeric, text, and logical. Numeric formulas perform calculations with values, text formulas manipulate text entries, and logical formulas evaluate a condition. You will use a numeric formula to calculate the sum of the clothing sales for January through June. To enter a numeric formula, the following **arithmetic operators** are used:

+   for addition
−   for subtraction
/   for division
*   for multiplication
^   for exponentiation

In a formula that contains more than one operator, Works performs the calculation in a specific **order of precedence**. First exponentiations are performed, then multiplications and divisions, and finally additions and subtractions. This order can be overridden by enclosing the operation you want performed first in parentheses. Works evaluates operations in parentheses working from the innermost set of parentheses out. If two or more operators have the same order of precedence, calculations are performed in order from left to right. For example, in the formula =5*4–3, Works first multiplies 5 times 4 to get 20, and then subtracts 3, for a total of 17. If you enter the formula as =5*(4–3), Works first subtracts 3 from 4 because the operation is enclosed in parentheses. Then Works multiplies the result, 1, by 5, for a final total of 5.

A formula always begins with an equal sign (=), which defines the entry as a numeric entry. Numbers or cell references that contain numbers can be used in a formula. Most commonly cell references are used, and when the values in the referenced cell(s) change, the value calculated by the formula is automatically recalculated. A formula is the power behind the spreadsheet.

The formula you will enter will calculate the total sales for January. The cells containing the sales numbers for January are cells B5 through B6. The total number will be displayed in cell B7. To sum the numbers in these cells, enter the following formula in cell B7. Cell references can be typed in either upper- or lowercase letters.

> If you enter a formula using the wrong format, Works will display a message and change to Edit mode to let you correct your entry.

Type: **=B5+B6**

Press: [←Enter]

Your screen should be similar to Figure 5-23.

FIGURE 5-23

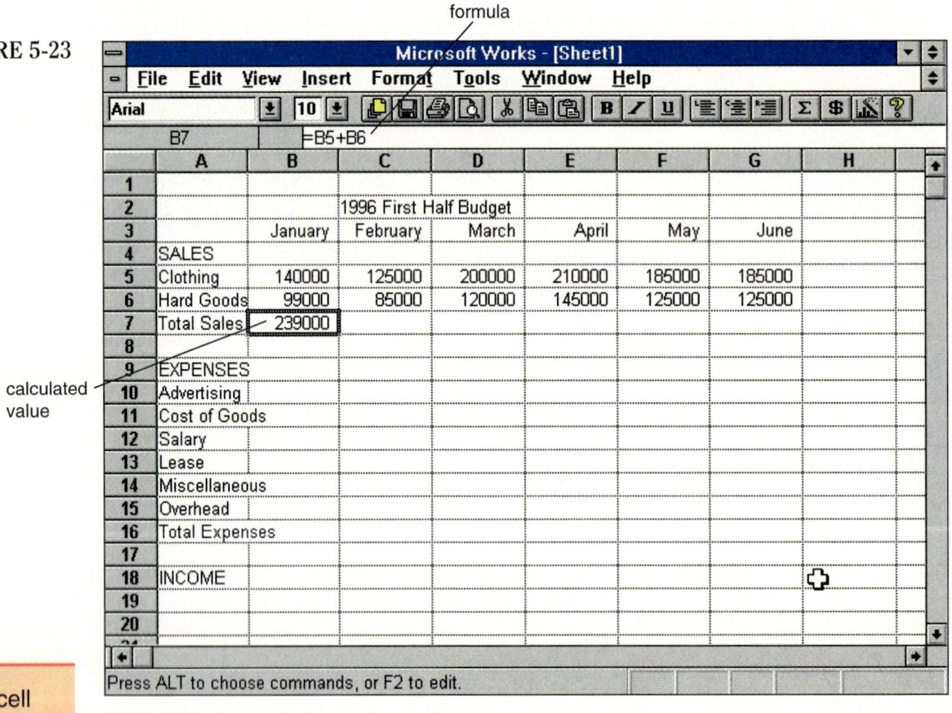

formula

calculated
value

> If you see B4+B5 in the cell rather than the calculated value, you forgot to begin the formula with an = symbol. Edit the formula.

The result of the formula, 239000, is displayed in cell B7. The formula, not the calculated result, is displayed in the formula bar.

Recalculating the Spreadsheet

Now that the total for January has been calculated, you see that you entered the number for the estimated sales for hard goods incorrectly. The correct value is 94,000.

Change the number in B6 to 94000.

The total formula in cell B7 has been automatically recalculated. The number displayed is now 234000. The **automatic recalculation** of a formula when a number in a referenced cell in the formula changes is one of the most powerful features of electronic spreadsheets. When Works recalculates a spreadsheet, only those formulas directly affected by a change in the data are recalculated. This is called **minimal recalculation**. Without this feature, in large spreadsheets it could take several minutes to recalculate all formulas each time a number is changed in the spreadsheet. The minimal recalculation feature decreases the recalculation time by recalculating only affected formulas.

In the next lab, you will complete the spreadsheet by entering the remaining numbers and formulas.

Documenting and Saving a Spreadsheet

To document the spreadsheet, enter your first initial and last name in cell A1. Put the date in cell A2 (for example, 11/11/95).

Always save your spreadsheet before closing a file or leaving the Works program. As a safeguard against losing your work if you forget to save the changes, Works will remind you to save them before closing the file or exiting the program. Because this is a new file, you can use the Save or Save As commands on the File menu to save the file to disk. The procedure is the same as saving a word processing file. You will use the Save command and save your work as FIRST1.

Choose: File>Save
  ➤ Ctrl + S
or
Click: 💾 Save

The Save As dialog box is displayed. To replace the default file name with a new file name, in the File Name text box,

Type: **FIRST1**

Select the drive (A or B) from the Drives list where you want Works to save the file.

Choose: OK

The new file name with the extension .WKS is displayed in the spreadsheet window title bar. The spreadsheet data that was on your screen and in the computer's memory is now saved on your data disk in a new file called FIRST1.WKS.

Make it a habit to save your work often to avoid losing your work due to equipment or power failure.

The spreadsheet file extension, .WKS, is added to the file name automatically.

A file name can contain eight or fewer characters.

SPREADSHEET

Previewing and Printing a Spreadsheet

Before printing, it is a good idea to preview how the spreadsheet will appear on the printed page. This is the same as previewing in the word processor tool. To do this,

Choose: File>Print Preview
or
Click: 🔍 Print Preview

Your screen should be similar to Figure 5-24.

FIGURE 5-24

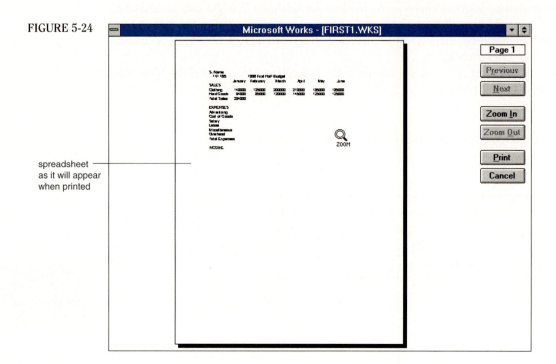

spreadsheet
as it will appear
when printed

The spreadsheet for the first six months is displayed as it will appear when printed. Notice that the spreadsheet gridlines are not displayed and will not appear when the spreadsheet is printed. You will learn more about previewing a spreadsheet in the next lab. To close the preview window,

Choose: Cancel

If you have printer capability, you can print a copy of the spreadsheet using the Print command on the File menu. To begin the Print command,

Choose: File>Print
    ➤   Ctrl + P

Your screen should be similar to Figure 5-25.

Print tool button

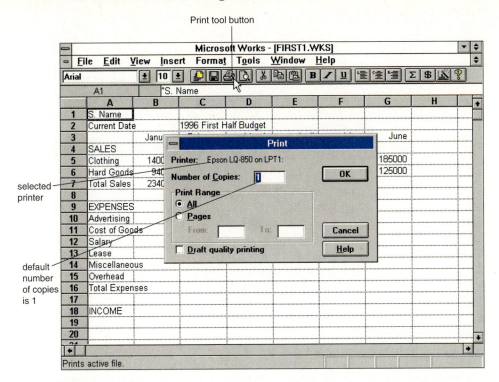

FIGURE 5-25

The default settings print one copy of all pages of the selected sheet. The default settings are satisfactory for now. The name of the printer displayed in the Printer information line of the dialog box should be your printer.

Note: If you need to select a different printer, cancel the Print dialog box, choose Printer Setup in the File menu, select the appropriate printer, and choose OK. Then open the Print dialog box again.

To print the spreadsheet,

Choose: OK

Your printer should be printing out the spreadsheet.
To close the FIRST1.WKS file,

Choose: File>Close

Works prompts you to specify whether you want to save the changes to the file before closing the file. The only changes made to the file since last saving it were to specify print settings. Since they are default settings, you do not need to resave the file.

Choose: No

> You can also double-click on the Close box to close a file.

SPREADSHEET

The Startup dialog box is displayed again. If you want to quit or exit the Works for Windows program at this time,

Choose: Cancel
Choose: File>Exit Works

You have exited from the Works program. The Program Manager window is displayed.

Key Terms

formula bar (148)	date entry (159)
spreadsheet (148)	time entry (159)
row (148)	formula (159)
column (148)	long entry (165)
row number (148)	range (170)
column letter (148)	range reference (171)
cell (148)	arithmetic operators (175)
active cell (148)	order of precedence (176)
cell reference (148)	automatic recalculation (177)
text entry (159)	minimal recalculation (177)
numeric entry (159)	

Command Summary

Command	Shortcut	Button	Action
Edit>Go To	F5		Moves to specified cell
Edit>Clear	Del		Clears contents from highlighted cell
Edit>Fill Series			Automatically fills any number of cells with a series of numbers or dates
File>Save	Ctrl + S	💾 Save	Saves file using same file name
File>Print	Ctrl + P	🖨 Print	Prints file
File>Close			Closes file
File>Exit Works			Exits Works

Matching

1.	minimal recalculation	_____	**a.** moves highlight to specified cell
2.	*	_____	**b.** moves highlight to upper left corner of spreadsheet
3.	F5	_____	**c.** only those formulas directly affected by a change in data are recalculated
4.	Ctrl + Home	_____	**d.** indicates the beginning of a formula entry
5.	.WKS	_____	**e.** a cell reference
6.	F2	_____	**f.** a label longer than cell's width
7.	C19 + A21	_____	**g.** an arithmetic operator
8.	long entry	_____	**h.** accesses Edit mode
9.	D11	_____	**i.** a formula summing two cells
10.	=	_____	**j.** a spreadsheet file extension

Fill-In Questions

1. In the following spreadsheet, several items are identified by letters. Enter the correct term for each item in the spaces below. The first one has been identified for you.

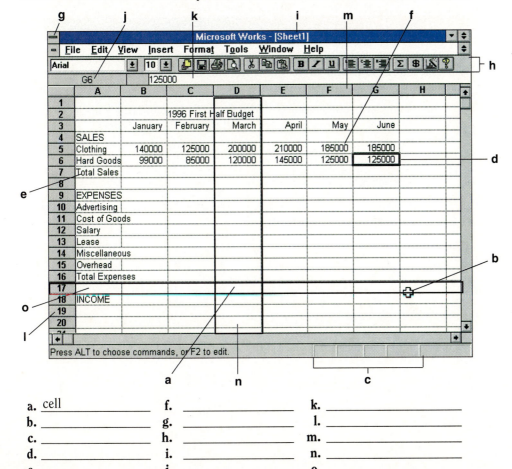

a. cell	**f.** _____	**k.** _____
b. _____	**g.** _____	**l.** _____
c. _____	**h.** _____	**m.** _____
d. _____	**i.** _____	**n.** _____
e. _____	**j.** _____	**o.** _____

SPREADSHEET

2.   Complete the following statements by filling in the blanks with the correct terms.

a.   A(n) _____ is a rectangular block of cells.

b.   The spreadsheet displays a rectangular grid of _____ and _____.

c.   The _____ tells you that a certain key or program condition is in effect.

d.   The intersection of a row and column creates a(n)_____.

e.   _____ are text entries that are used to create the structure of the spreadsheet.

f.   A text entry that is longer than the width of a cell is called a(n) _____.

g.   The digits 0 through 9 and the special characters _____ define an entry as a number.

h.   A(n) _____ is an entry that performs a calculation.

i.   The _____ _____ of a formula when a number in a referenced cell changes is one of the most powerful features of electronic spreadsheets.

j.   The _____ command on the File menu will save the current file to disk with a different file name.

Practice Exercises

1.   Open the file PAPERBK.WKS on your data disk. This is a spreadsheet file for a small bookstore. It is similar to the spreadsheet you created in this lab, but it contains several errors. Complete the following steps to locate and correct the errors.

a.   Complete row 3, columns B through G, by using the Fill Series command. Change the text entry in cell H3 to all capital letters.

b.   Edit the row headings in column A, rows 5 through 7 and 10 through 16, so that the first letter of each word in the row heading is capitalized.

c.   Correct any number that has been entered as text.

d.   Check the formulas in row 7. Correct any that reference the wrong cells or were entered incorrectly.

Your completed spreadsheet should be similar to the spreadsheet below.

	A	B	C	D	E	F	G	H	
1			The Paperback Book Company Budget						
2									
3		January	February	March	April	May	June	Total	
4	SALES:								
5	Best Sellers	1400	1230	1750	2100	1850	1850	10180	
6	Classics	940	850	120	1350	1250	1250	5760	
7	Total Sales	2340	2080	1870	3450	3100	3100	15940	
8									
9	EXPENSES:								
10	Advertising								
11	Cost of Goods								
12	Salary	900							
13	Lease	300							
14	Miscellaneo	100							
15	Overhead	50							
16	Total Expen								
17									
18	INCOME:								

e. Enter your name in cell A1 and the current date in cell A2. Save the spreadsheet as PAPERBK1. Preview and print the spreadsheet.

You will complete this problem as Practice Exercise 2 in Lab 6.

2. Open the file CANDY.WKS. This spreadsheet contains the sales figures for Glenda's Homemade Candy Store. It contains many errors. Follow the steps below to correct the spreadsheet.

a. Enter the month column headings using the Fill Series command. Change the heading in cell H3 to all uppercase letters.

b. Edit the row headings so only the first letter of each word is capitalized.

c. Use the editing features you learned in this lab to correct the numbers and formulas that are incorrectly entered.

Your completed spreadsheet should be similar to the spreadsheet below.

	A	B	C	D	E	F	G	H	
1			Glenda's Homemade Candy Store Sales						
2									
3		January	February	March	April	May	June	TOTAL	
4									
5	SALES:								
6	Hard Candy	783	1230	1750	3200	1850	1850	10663	
7	Soft Candy	378	432	398	189	732	348	2477	
8	Chocolate	1890	2390	1200	1350	2380	1250	10460	
9	Seasonal	85	65	95	450	74	23	792	
10									
11	Total Sales	3136	4117	3443	5189	5036	3471	24392	
12									

d. Enter your name in cell A1 and the current date in cell A2.

e. Save the file as CANDY1. Preview and print the spreadsheet.

3. Susan Anderson has just moved. She is considering three different apartments: Sun Lakes, Apple Way, and Valley Vista. Susan has estimated the expenses for both one- and two-bedroom units at each complex. Her data is shown below.

	A	B	C	D	E	F	G	H	
1	Student Name								
2	Date								
3			Apartment Analysis For Susan Anderson						
4			Sun Lakes		Apple Way		Valley Vista		
5			BDRM 1	BDRM 2	BDRM 1	BDRM 2	BDRM 1	BDRM 2	
6	Rent		300	350	400	450	375	425	
7	Telephone		35	35	45	45	25	25	
8	Electricity		75	85	65	75	60	85	
9	Deposit		300	300	200	225	375	425	
10									
11	TOTAL COST		710						
12									
13									
14									
15									

Create the spreadsheet shown above by completing the following steps.

a. Enter the spreadsheet title in cell C3.

b. Enter the headings **Sun Lakes**, **Apple Way**, and **Valley Vista** in cells C4, E4, and G4.

c. Enter the headings **BDRM 1** in cells C5, E5, and G5; and **BDRM 2** in cells D5, F5, and H5.

d. Enter the row headings in cells A6 through A9. Enter the heading **TOTAL COST** in cell A11.

e. Enter the numbers shown above in cells C6 through H9.

f. Enter the formula to total column C only in cell C11.

g. Enter your name in cell A1 and the current date in cell A2. Save the spreadsheet as APTMT1. Preview and print the spreadsheet.

You will complete this exercise as Practice Exercise 3 in Lab 6.

4. The Director of Parks and Recreation needs to prepare a financial summary for the years 1994, 1995, and 1996.

  a. Create the spreadsheet shown below by entering the text and numbers in the appropriate cells. Use the Fill Series command to enter the year column headings.

	A	B	C	D	E	F	G	H
1				PARKS AND RECREATION DEPARTMENT				
2				FINANCIAL STATEMENT				
3								
4			1994	1995	1996	TOTAL	AVERAGE	
5	Revenues							
6	Operating		234220	339382	332928			
7	Fund Raising		193910	283819	389238			
8	Interest Income		23088	48493	28382			
9	TOTAL REVENUE							
10								
11	Expenses							
12	Operating		219000	290182	289300			
13	Capital Projects		193983	87363	76939			
14	Fund Raising		158992	167391	142821			
15	TOTAL EXPENSES							
16								
17	RESERVE							
18								

  b. Use edit to change the entries in cells A5 and A11 to all uppercase letters.

  c. Enter the formulas to calculate total revenue (C9) and total expenses (C15) for 1994.

  d. Save the spreadsheet as PARKFIN. Preview and print the spreadsheet.

You will continue working on this spreadsheet as Practice Exercise 4 in Lab 6.

5. Create a simple six-month budget for yourself. Include any income such as wages and monthly allowances. Estimate your expenses for food, clothing, transportation expenses, and so on. Include any planned savings. Be realistic and experiment a bit with your income and expenses. Save and print the spreadsheet.

SPREADSHEET

6 Creating a Spreadsheet: Part 2

CASE STUDY

In the previous lab, you defined the row and column headings for The Sports Company budget spreadsheet. You also entered the expected sales figures and a formula to calculate the total sales for January.

In this lab you will continue to build the spreadsheet. The data for the expenses and the formulas to calculate the advertising, cost of goods sold, total expenses, and income still need to be entered into the spreadsheet. You will also improve the appearance of the spreadsheet by adjusting column widths, inserting and deleting rows and columns, formatting values, adding bold and underlining, and changing font sizes and styles.

Copying Cell Contents

Load Works for Windows. Put your data disk in the appropriate drive for your computer system.

Open the spreadsheet FIRST2.WKS from your data disk. If necessary maximize the spreadsheet window.

This spreadsheet should be the same as the spreadsheet you created in Lab 5 and saved as FIRST1.WKS on your data disk. In addition the January expense values for the salary, lease, miscellaneous, and overhead expenses have already been entered for you.

Notice that the text entry in cell A14, Miscellaneous, is not fully displayed in the cell. It is a long text entry, and because the cell to the right now contains an entry, the overlapping part of the heading is not displayed. The entry in cell B14 causes the display of the text entry to be interrupted.

Move to: A14

Your screen should be similar to Figure 6-1.

complete entry
displayed in
formula bar

interrupted
entry

	A	B	C	D	E	F	G	H
1								
2			1996 First Half Budget					
3		January	February	March	April	May	June	
4	SALES							
5	Clothing	140000	125000	200000	210000	185000	185000	
6	Hard Goods	94000	85000	120000	145000	125000	125000	
7	Total Sales	234000						
8								
9	EXPENSES							
10	Advertising							
11	Cost of Goods							
12	Salary	32000						
13	Lease	19000						
14	Miscellane	16000						
15	Overhead	22000						
16	Total Expenses							
17								
18	INCOME							
19								
20								

FIGURE 6-1

The formula bar displays the complete entry; only the display of the heading in cell A14 has been interrupted. You will learn shortly how to change the width of a column so that the entire entry can be displayed.

Now, you need to enter the estimated expenses for salary, lease, miscellaneous, and overhead for February through June. To begin, you will enter the salary values.

When you entered the sales numbers for January through June, you entered them individually into each cell because the numbers changed from month to month. However, the number in cell B12 is the same number that needs to be entered in cells C12 thought G12. You could type the same amount into each month, or you can copy the number in B12 into the other cells. When you copy a cell, you duplicate the cell contents and paste them in a new location.

There are several methods you can use to copy in a spreadsheet. One method is the Copy command on the Edit menu, which you used in the word processor tool. This command copies a selection to the Clipboard. Then you use the Paste command to copy the contents of Clipboard to a new location.

To use the Copy command, you first must select the cell or cells containing the data to be copied. This is called the **source**. You want to copy the entry in cell B12. To copy this cell,

> The keyboard shortcut for Copy is Ctrl + C and the toolbar equivalent is 📋.

Move to: B12

Choose: Edit>Copy

➤   Ctrl + C

or

Click: 📋 Copy

The contents of the selection have been copied to the Clipboard. Next you need to select the **destination**, which is the cell or cells where you want to paste the contents of the Clipboard. The destination can be any cell or range of cells in the same spreadsheet or any other Works or Windows-based spreadsheet application. The destination is the range of cells C12 through G12.

Highlight the range C12 through G12 using the mouse or the keyboard.

The destination range is highlighted. Next you will paste the contents of the Clipboard into the destination range.

Choose: Edit>Paste
➢   Ctrl + V
Click: 🗐

Your screen should be similar to Figure 6-2.

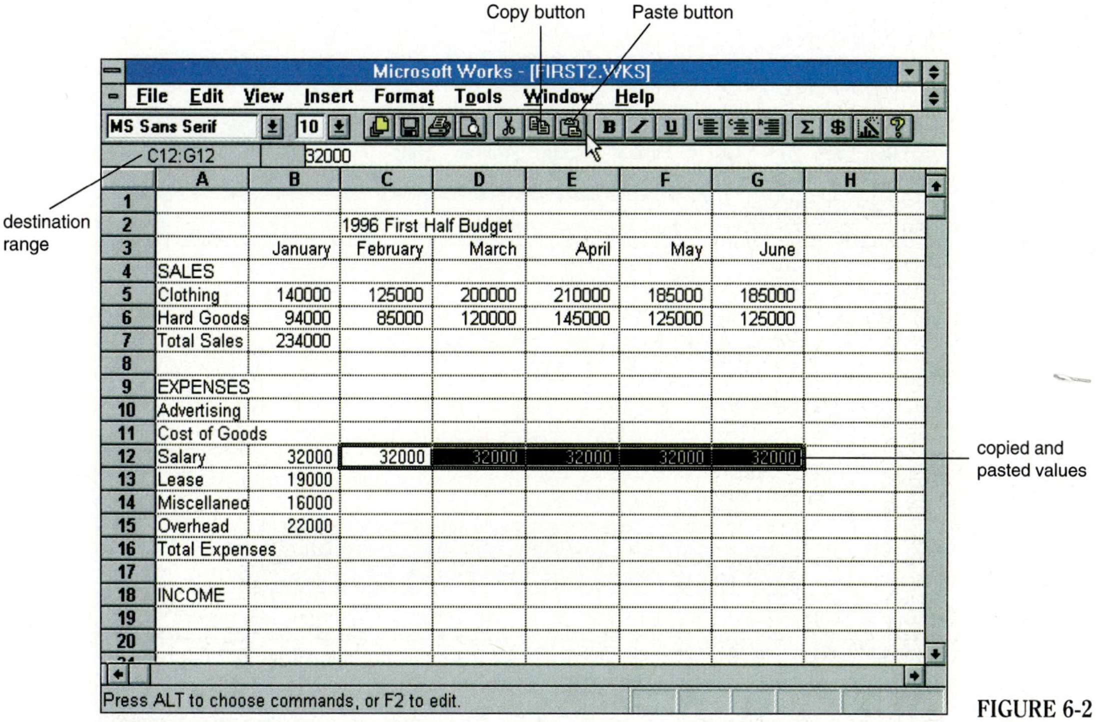

FIGURE 6-2

Works copies the data from the Clipboard and pastes it into the destination range and as a result, the number 32000 is entered into cells C12 through G12.

Because the data you copied is stored in the Clipboard, you can paste the contents of the Clipboard immediately after using Copy or at a later time. You can also paste multiple copies of the same data into different locations. The data that was copied to the Clipboard is stored in the Clipboard until it is replaced by new data or until you exit the program.

As you can see, copying and pasting data is very fast and it also eliminates the possibility of typing errors. However, you should be careful when pasting because any existing entries in the destination range will be replaced by the contents of the Clipboard.

The destination range is still highlighted. It will clear as soon as you move to another cell.

Drag the mouse or use ⇧Shift plus the arrow keys to highlight the range.

The keyboard shortcut for Paste is Ctrl + V and the toolbar equivalent is 🗐.

Copying to Adjacent Cells

Next you will copy the January expense numbers for the lease, miscellaneous, and overhead (cells B13 through B15) to February through June (C13 through G15). You would like to copy all three values at the same time.

Another way to copy cell contents is to use the Fill Down or Fill Right commands on the Edit menu. These commands copy a selection into adjacent cells below or to the right of the source cells.

You want to copy the contents of cell B13 through B15 to the right to cells C13 through G15. To do this you select the source and destination range before choosing the Fill Right command. This is called **preselecting** a range.

Using either the mouse or keyboard, highlight the range B13 through G15.

Next, to fill the cells to the right of the cell whose contents you want to copy,

Choose: Edit>Fill Right

Your screen should be similar to Figure 6-3.

FIGURE 6-3

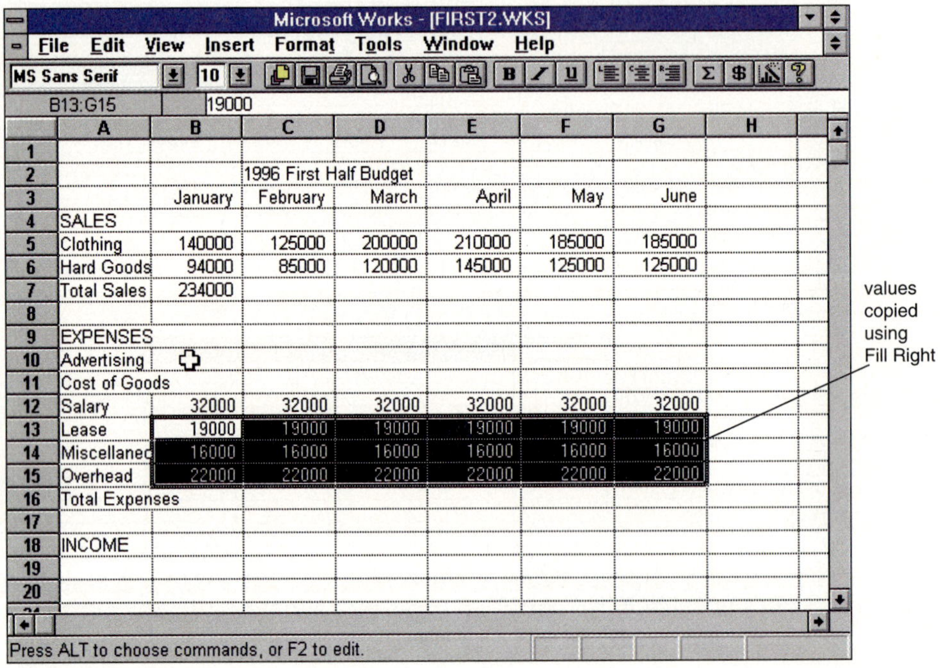

values
copied
using
Fill Right

The entries in cells B13 through B15 are copied into cells C13 through G15. The Fill Down and Fill Right commands do not copy the source to the Clipboard. Therefore they can only be used within the same spreadsheet.

Copying Formulas

Now that you know how to copy in a spreadsheet, you will copy the total sales formula from the January column to the February through June columns. Just like text and numeric entries, you can copy formulas from one cell to another. To quickly copy the formula in cell B7 to the adjacent cells to the right, C7 through G7,

Preselect: the range B7 through G7
Choose: Edit>Fill Right

The calculated numbers are displayed in the specified cell range.
    To look at the formulas as they were copied into the cells,

Move to: C7

Your screen should be similar to Figure 6-4.

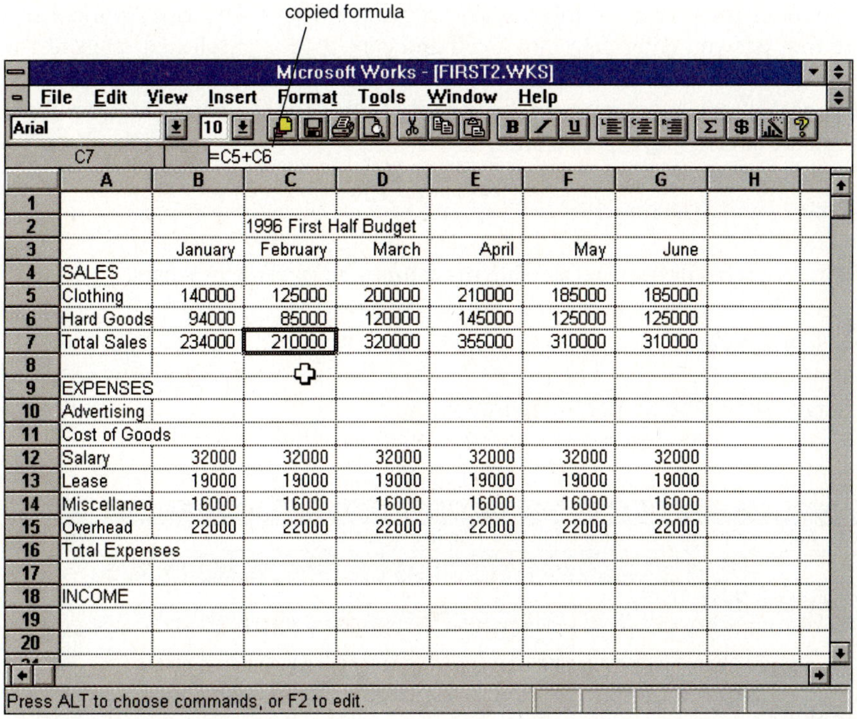

copied formula

FIGURE 6-4

The number 210000 is displayed in the cell.
    Look at the formula displayed in the formula bar.
    It is =C5+C6. The formula to calculate the February total sales is not an exact duplicate of the formula used to calculate the January total sales (=B5+B6). Instead the cell referenced in the formula has been changed to reflect the new column location. This is because the formula uses a **relative cell reference**. A relative cell reference is a cell or range in a formula whose location is interpreted by Works as relative to the cell that contains the formula. When the formula in B7 was copied, the referenced cell in the formula was automatically adjusted to reflect the new column location so that the relative relationship between the referenced cell and the new column location is maintained.

Move to: D7

Look at the formula as it appears in the formula bar.

The formula has changed to reflect the new column location and it appropriately calculates the number based on the March sales.

Entering and Copying Simultaneously

Next you will enter the formulas to calculate the advertising and cost of goods sold. These numbers are estimated by using a formula to calculate the number as a percent of total sales. As a general rule, The Sports Company figures advertising at 4 percent of sales and cost of goods at 58 percent of sales. The formula to make these calculations for January takes the value in cell B7 and multiplies it by the percentage.

To make the process of entering and copying entries even easier, Works has a feature that lets you enter data into a cell and copy it to a preselected range at the same time. You will use this feature to enter the formulas to calculate the advertising and cost of goods expenses for January through June. To enter the formula to calculate the advertising expenses first,

Preselect: B10 through G10

Next you enter the formula to calculate the January advertising expenses.

Type: =B7*4%

Your screen should be similar to Figure 6-5.

FIGURE 6-5

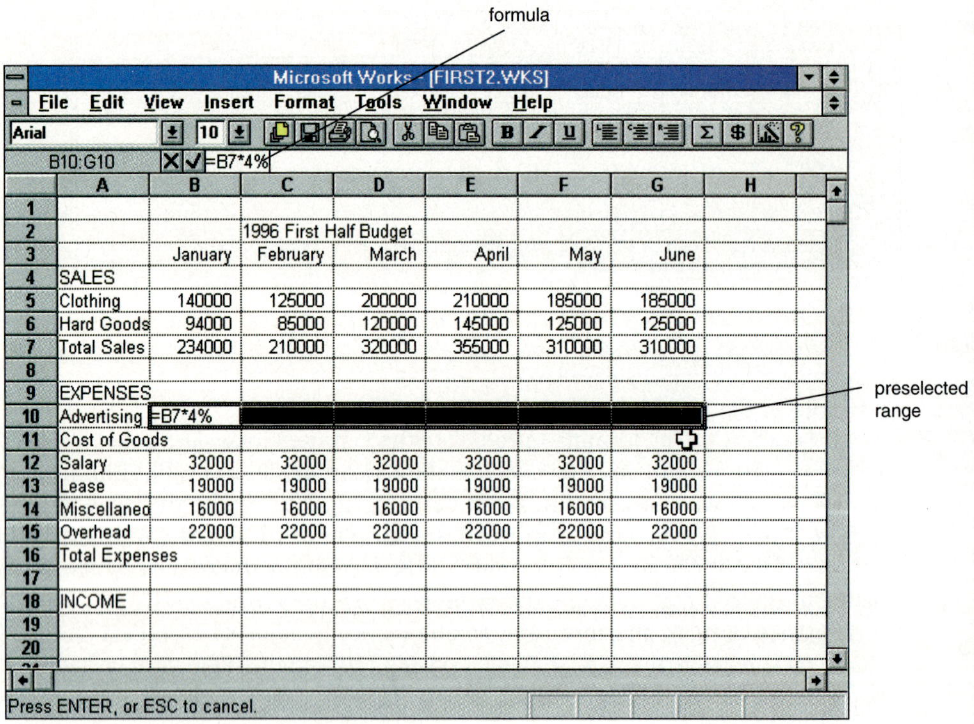

Microsoft Works - [FIRST2.WKS]

	A	B	C	D	E	F	G	H
1								
2			1996 First Half Budget					
3		January	February	March	April	May	June	
4	SALES							
5	Clothing	140000	125000	200000	210000	185000	185000	
6	Hard Goods	94000	85000	120000	145000	125000	125000	
7	Total Sales	234000	210000	320000	355000	310000	310000	
8								
9	EXPENSES							
10	Advertising	=B7*4%						
11	Cost of Goods							
12	Salary	32000	32000	32000	32000	32000	32000	
13	Lease	19000	19000	19000	19000	19000	19000	
14	Miscellaneo	16000	16000	16000	16000	16000	16000	
15	Overhead	22000	22000	22000	22000	22000	22000	
16	Total Expenses							
17								
18	INCOME							
19								
20								

formula

preselected range

Press ENTER, or ESC to cancel.

To complete the entry and have it copied to the preselected range,

Press: ⌐Ctrl⌐ + ⌐←Enter⌐

The formula was quickly copied to the preselected range. To calculate the cost of goods sold,

Preselect: B11 through G11
Type: =

Rather than typing the cell reference into the formula, you will enter the cell reference by selecting the spreadsheet cell. This is called **pointing**. To tell Works to use the number in cell B7,

Click: B7
or
Press: ↑ (4 times)

Your screen should be similar to Figure 6-6.

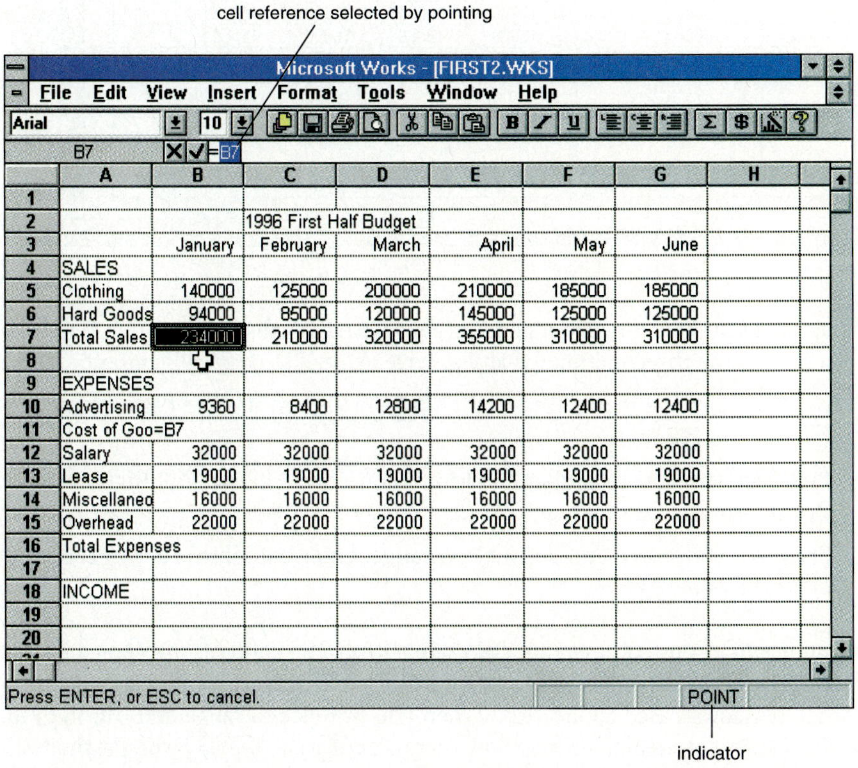

If you press ⌐←Enter⌐ without holding down ⌐Ctrl⌐, the formula will appear in the active cell only.

cell reference selected by pointing

	A	B	C	D	E	F	G	H
1								
2			1996 First Half Budget					
3		January	February	March	April	May	June	
4	SALES							
5	Clothing	140000	125000	200000	210000	185000	185000	
6	Hard Goods	94000	85000	120000	145000	125000	125000	
7	Total Sales	234000	210000	320000	355000	310000	310000	
8								
9	EXPENSES							
10	Advertising	9360	8400	12800	14200	12400	12400	
11	Cost of Goo=B7							
12	Salary	32000	32000	32000	32000	32000	32000	
13	Lease	19000	19000	19000	19000	19000	19000	
14	Miscellaneo	16000	16000	16000	16000	16000	16000	
15	Overhead	22000	22000	22000	22000	22000	22000	
16	Total Expenses							
17								
18	INCOME							
19								
20								

Press ENTER, or ESC to cancel.   POINT

FIGURE 6-6

SPREADSHEET

indicator

The indicator in the status bar displays "POINT." When POINT is displayed, you can move the highlight to any spreadsheet cell. Works will enter the cell reference of the highlighted cell into the cell containing the formula. Because the highlight is on B7, the formula displays the cell reference, B7, in the formula bar and the beginning cell in the range.

To complete the formula,

Type: *58%

Press: Ctrl + ←Enter

Your screen should be similar to Figure 6-7.

FIGURE 6-7

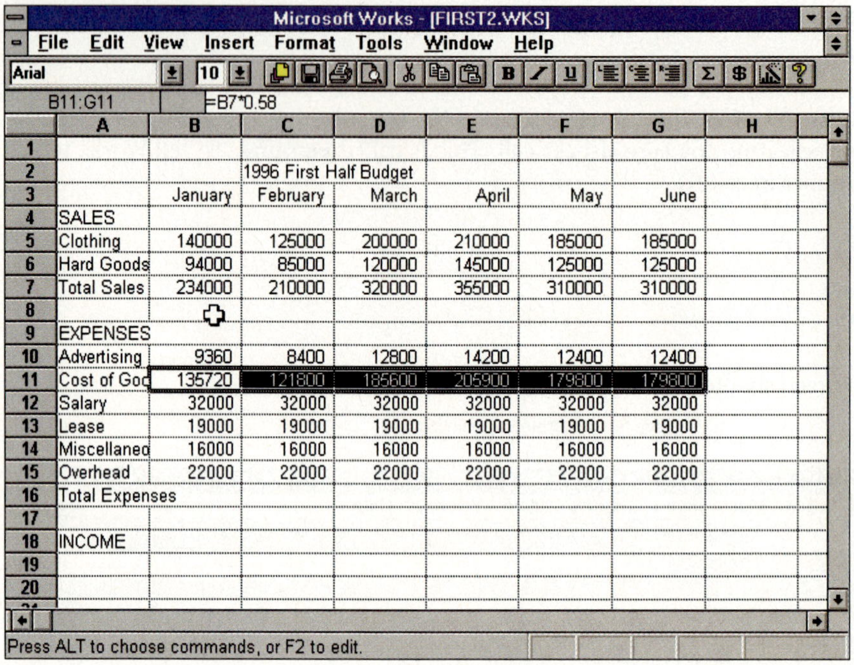

The calculated numbers for cost of goods are displayed in cells C11 through G11.
    To review, the three methods that you have learned to copy cell contents are:

1.   Use the Copy command (Ctrl + C or 🗐 Copy) then use the Paste command
     (Ctrl + V or 🗐 Paste).

2.   Preselect the source and destination range and choose Fill Right or Fill
     Down from the Edit menu.

3.   Preselect the source and destination range, enter data in the active cell, and
     press Ctrl + ←Enter.

When you use the Copy command or 🗐 Copy button, the contents are copied to the
Clipboard and can be copied to any location in the spreadsheet, another spreadsheet,
or another Windows-based application. When you preselect a range and use the Fill
Right, Fill Down commands on the Edit menu, or Ctrl + ←Enter, the destination
must be adjacent to the source and the contents are not copied to the Clipboard.

Entering a Function

Now that all the expenses have been entered into the spreadsheet, the total expenses can be calculated. The formula to calculate the total expenses for January needs to be entered in the spreadsheet in cell B16 and copied across the row through June.

Move to: B16

You could use a formula similar to the formula used to calculate the total sales (B7). The formula would be =B10+B11+B12+B13+B14+B15. However, it is faster to use one of Works's built-in formulas, called **functions**, which perform certain types of calculations automatically. In this case the SUM function would be used.

The **syntax** or rules of structure for entering all functions is:

=Function Name(Argument0, Argument1...)

All functions begin with the = sign followed by the function name. The function name identifies the type of calculation to be performed. Most functions require that you enter one or more arguments following the function name. The **argument** specifies the data the function uses to perform the calculation. The type of data the function requires depends upon the type of calculation being performed. Most commonly, arguments consist of numbers or range references to cells that contain numbers. The argument is enclosed in parentheses, and multiple arguments are separated by commas.

Several very common functions and the results they calculate are shown below.

Function	Calculates
=SUM()	Total of all numbers in the arguments
=AVG()	Average of the arguments
=MAX()	Maximum value in a data set
=MIN()	Minimum value in a data set
=COUNT()	Tally of the arguments that are numbers

You will use the SUM function to calculate the total expenses. The function to calculate the total expenses is =SUM(B10:B15). The argument in this function is the range reference B10:B15.

Because the SUM function is the most commonly used function, it has its own shortcut for both the mouse and keyboard. To use the shortcut to calculate the total expenses for January,

Click: [Σ] Autosum
or
Press: [Ctrl] + M

Your screen should be similar to Figure 6-8.

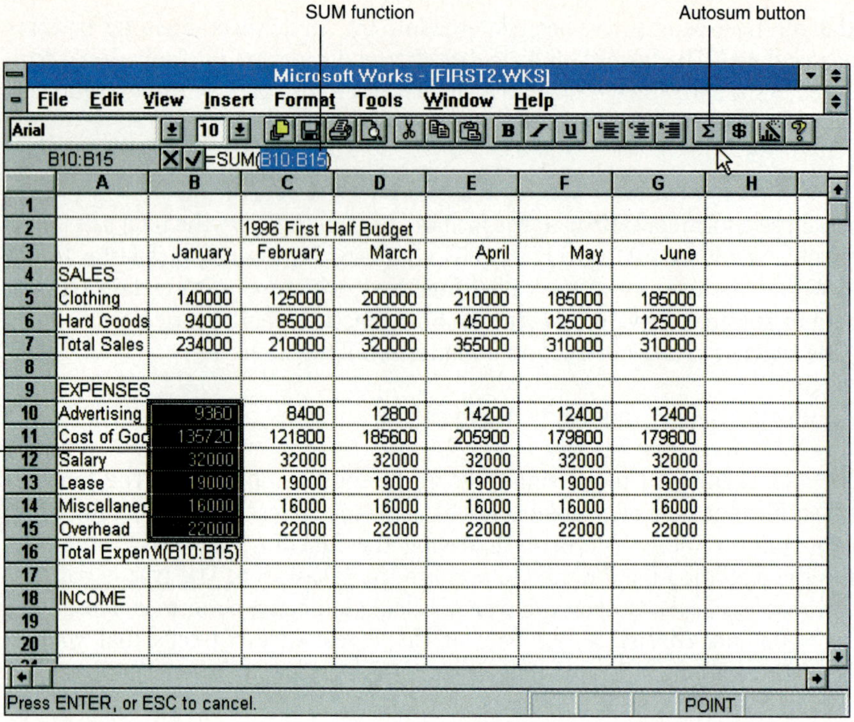

FIGURE 6-8

The SUM function followed by a proposed range reference enclosed in parentheses is entered in the current cell and displayed in the formula bar. In addition the proposed range reference is highlighted. Works automatically proposes a range reference for the SUM function based upon the data located above or to the left of the active cell. Because the cell to the left contains a text entry, Works selected the cells above the current cell as the range to sum. You can modify the proposed range or select another. Since this is the correct range, to accept the range and enter the function,

Press: ←Enter

The result, 234080, calculated by the function is displayed in cell B16.
Use the Fill Right command to copy the function to cells C16 through G16.

Move to: C16

Your screen should be similar to Figure 6-9.

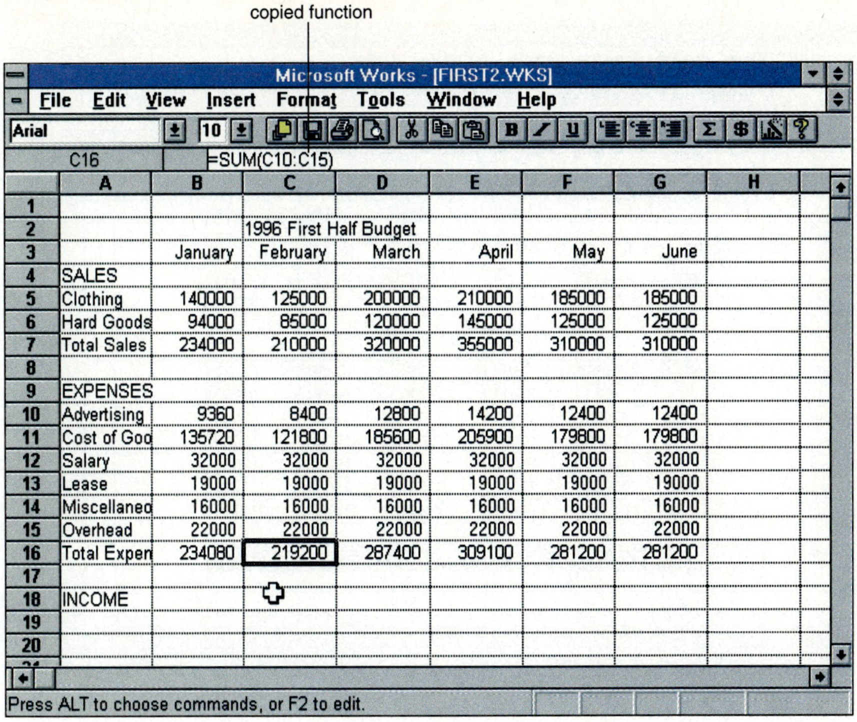
copied function
Microsoft Works - [FIRST2.WKS]
File Edit View Insert Format Tools Window Help
Arial 10
C16 =SUM(C10:C15)
A B C D E F G H
1
2 1996 First Half Budget
3 January February March April May June
4 SALES
5 Clothing 140000 125000 200000 210000 185000 185000
6 Hard Goods 94000 85000 120000 145000 125000 125000
7 Total Sales 234000 210000 320000 355000 310000 310000
8
9 EXPENSES
10 Advertising 9360 8400 12800 14200 12400 12400
11 Cost of Goo 135720 121800 185600 205900 179800 179800
12 Salary 32000 32000 32000 32000 32000 32000
13 Lease 19000 19000 19000 19000 19000 19000
14 Miscellaneo 16000 16000 16000 16000 16000 16000
15 Overhead 22000 22000 22000 22000 22000 22000
16 Total Expen 234080 219200 287400 309100 281200 281200
17
18 INCOME
19
20
Press ALT to choose commands, or F2 to edit.

FIGURE 6-9

The result, 219200, calculated by the SUM function is displayed in cell C16.

Look at the function displayed in the formula bar.

It is =SUM(C10:C15). When a function is copied, it is adjusted relative to the new cell location just like a formula.

Now that the total expenses are calculated, the formula to calculate income can be entered. This number is the difference between sales and total expenses.

To enter this formula in cells B18 through G18, preselect the range B18 through G18. Enter the formula =B7–B16.

Press: Ctrl + ←Enter

SPREADSHEET

Your screen should be similar to Figure 6-10.

	A	B	C	D	E	F	G	H
1								
2			1996 First Half Budget					
3		January	February	March	April	May	June	
4	SALES							
5	Clothing	140000	125000	200000	210000	185000	185000	
6	Hard Goods	94000	85000	120000	145000	125000	125000	
7	Total Sales	234000	210000	320000	355000	310000	310000	
8								
9	EXPENSES							
10	Advertising	9360	8400	12800	14200	12400	12400	
11	Cost of Goo	135720	121800	185600	205900	179800	179800	
12	Salary	32000	32000	32000	32000	32000	32000	
13	Lease	19000	19000	19000	19000	19000	19000	
14	Miscellaneo	16000	16000	16000	16000	16000	16000	
15	Overhead	22000	22000	22000	22000	22000	22000	
16	Total Expen	234080	219200	287400	309100	281200	281200	
17								
18	INCOME	-80	-9200	32600	45900	28800	28800	
19								
20								

FIGURE 6-10

The calculated income numbers are displayed in cells B18 through G18. The income numbers for January and February show a loss, while March through June show positive numbers.

Changing Column Widths

Now that the data in the spreadsheet is complete, you want to improve the spreadsheet's appearance by adjusting column widths, using underlining, and displaying dollar signs and commas. The Format menu contains commands that allow you to enhance the appearance of the spreadsheet.

After entering the numbers for January in column B, any long headings in column A were cut off or interrupted. To allow the long headings to be fully displayed, you can increase the **column width** or the number of characters that can be displayed in column A. The column width can be any number from 1 to 79. This number represents the number of characters that can be displayed in a cell using the standard spreadsheet font of Arial and type size of 10 points. The default column width is 10. The cell containing the longest heading in column A is A16.

Move to: A16

How you change the width of an individual column varies if you are using the mouse or the keyboard.

The column width can be quickly adjusted by dragging the line at the right edge of a column heading. Dragging it to the left decreases the column width, while dragging it to the right increases the width.

Point to the line to the right of the column letter A.

The mouse pointer changes to .

Drag the mouse pointer to the right. (Continue to hold down the mouse button.)

As you drag, a temporary reference column line is displayed to show your new column width.

When the temporary line reaches the "n" in "January," release the mouse button.

The Column Width command on the Format menu is used to change the column width. Begin by positioning the highlight anywhere in the column whose width you want to change or by selecting a range of columns. The highlight should already be in cell A16.

Choose: Format>Column Width

The Column Width dialog box is displayed. The default column width setting of 10 is displayed in the width text box. To enter the new column width,

Type: 14
Choose: OK

SPREADSHEET

Your screen should be similar to Figure 6-11.

adjusted column width

	A	B	C	D	E	F	G	H
1								
2			1996 First Half Budget					
3		January	February	March	April	May	June	
4	SALES							
5	Clothing	140000	125000	200000	210000	185000	185000	
6	Hard Goods	94000	85000	120000	145000	125000	125000	
7	Total Sales	234000	210000	320000	355000	310000	310000	
8								
9	EXPENSES							
10	Advertising	9360	8400	12800	14200	12400	12400	
11	Cost of Goods	135720	121800	185600	205900	179800	179800	
12	Salary	32000	32000	32000	32000	32000	32000	
13	Lease	19000	19000	19000	19000	19000	19000	
14	Miscellaneous	16000	16000	16000	16000	16000	16000	
15	Overhead	22000	22000	22000	22000	22000	22000	
16	Total Expenses	234080	219200	287400	309100	281200	281200	
17								
18	INCOME	-80	-9200	32600	45900	28800	28800	
19								
20								

Cell reference A16, content "Total Expenses". Title bar: Microsoft Works - [FIRST2.WKS]. Menu: File Edit View Insert Format Tools Window Help. Font: Arial 10. Status bar: Press ALT to choose commands, or F2 to edit.

FIGURE 6-11

Column A now completely displays all entries. The number of characters that can actually be displayed in the column and printed is also affected by the capitalization and style characteristics, such as bold, that are applied to the characters. If part of a character touches the column line, it may not be printed, even though it is displayed in the cell.

Next you want to see if decreasing the column widths of all the other columns (B through G) in the spreadsheet improves the appearance of the spreadsheet. You can decrease the width of each column individually, but it would be faster to change the width of all the columns at once.

> You can select an entire row (to column IV) by clicking on the row number.

To select the columns,

Click on the column letter B.

The entire column through row 16,384 is highlighted. To select a range of columns,

Drag the mouse across the column border until columns B through G are selected.

To select a range of columns, you can use any row in the columns whose width you want to change.

Using row 16, select columns B through G.

To change the widths of the selected columns,

Choose: Forma**t**>Column **W**idth

The Column Width dialog box is displayed. The largest value displayed in the spreadsheet is six digits. To decrease the column width to 6 and see the effect on the spreadsheet display,

> You cannot drag the column line to change the width for a selected range of columns.

Type: 6
Choose: OK

To clear the selection,

Move to: A16

Your screen should be similar to Figure 6-12.

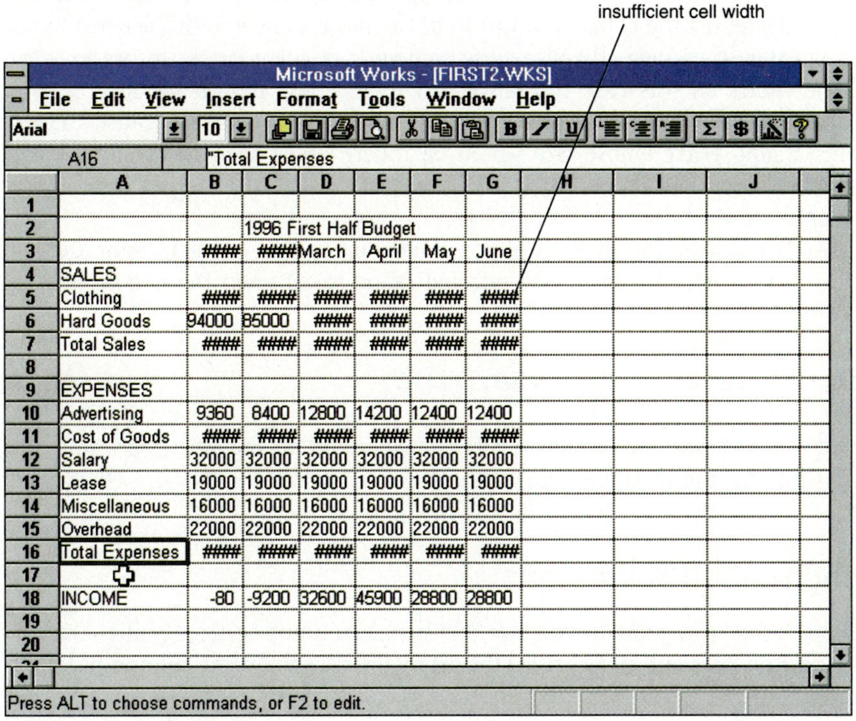

insufficient cell width

FIGURE 6-12

All the cells in the selected columns have changed to six characters. Number signs (#####) appear in many of the spreadsheet cells. Whenever the width of a cell is too small to display the entire number in that cell, a series of number signs or scientific notation is displayed. Scientific notation displays a number with one digit to the left of the decimal point. The next digit is followed by a capital E and a (+) sign, followed by the number of numbers after the decimal place. For example, 12345678 is displayed as 1.2E+07. Notice that number signs also appear in the month headings. This is because the months are numeric entries.

This new column width is much too small. To cancel the most recent operation and restore the spreadsheet to how it was prior to your change,

Choose: Edit>Undo Column Width
➤   `Ctrl` + Z

The effects of the column width command are reversed and the columns are restored to the prior column width setting.

Just as in the word processor tool, Undo must be used before executing another command or making an entry that changes the document. This is because Works creates a backup copy of your existing spreadsheet each time you make a change to the spreadsheet. When you use Undo, Works redisplays the spreadsheet that was stored in memory.

The Undo feature is primarily used to undo errors and is an important safeguard against mistakes that may take a lot of time to fix. When the Undo feature is selected, it reverses the most recent action performed.

Rather than guessing what the correct width should be, you can let Works automatically adjust the column widths to fit the largest entry in the selected range. The range should include all cells whose contents you want Works to use to determine the width. In this case the range will include the month headings and all values. You do not want to include the title in cell C2. This is because the cell contains a long entry whose size would be much larger than the column width needs to be.

Highlight the range B3 through G18.

The Best Fit option in the Column Width dialog box will determine the column width for each column in the selected range based upon the largest entry in each column.

Choose: Format>Column Width>Best Fit>OK

The width of the columns automatically adjusted, and all the entries are fully displayed using the minimum column width.

Changing Cell Alignment

Next you decide you want to add two additional columns to display the sum and average for the sales and expenses for the six months. To enter the column headings,

Move to: H3
Type: TOTAL
Move to: I3
Type: AVG.
Press: `←Enter`

The entries are displayed left-aligned in the cell space. As you learned in Lab 5, the default alignment of text entries in the cell space is left aligned, and of date and numeric entries is right-aligned. You can left-, center-, or right-align text and numeric entries in a similar manner to aligning text in a word processor.

The Alignment command options in the Format menu or the keyboard or toolbar shortcuts shown below will align an entry in the cell space.

Alignment	Shortcut	Effect
Left	📄 Ctrl + L	Left-aligns entry in cell
Center	📄 Ctrl + E	Centers entry in cell
Right	📄 Ctrl + R	Right-aligns entry in cell

You will change the column headings in cells H3 and I3 to right-aligned.
Highlight cells H3 and I3.

Choose: Format>Alignment>Right>OK
  ➤   Ctrl + R
or
Click: 📄

Your screen should be similar to Figure 6-13.

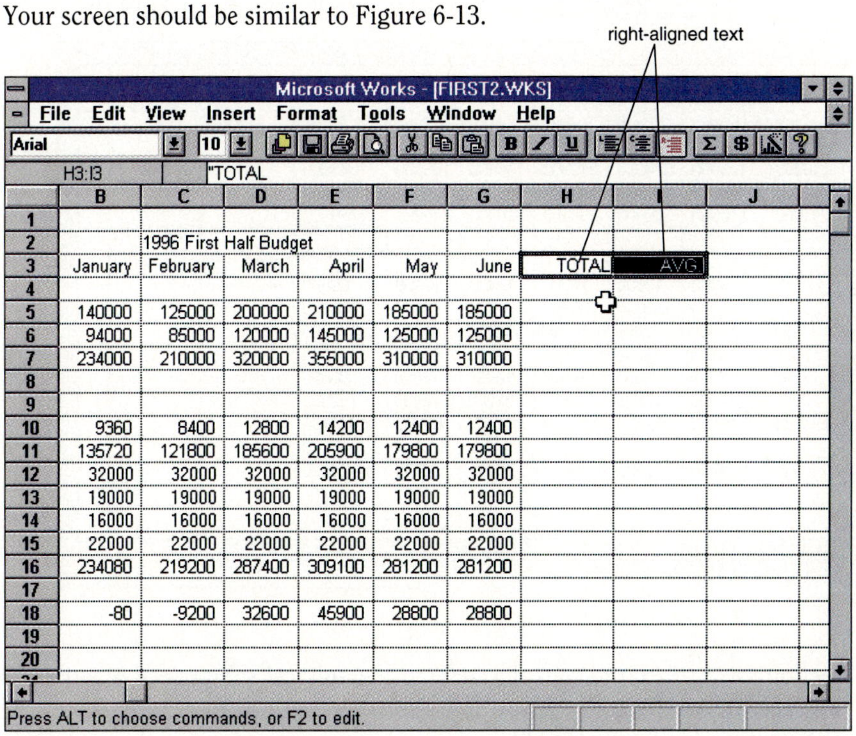

FIGURE 6-13

TOTAL and AVG. are now right-aligned in the cell space.

The functions to calculate the totals for the six months for sales and expenses need to be entered next. To enter the function to calculate the total clothing sales for January through June,

Move to: H5
Click: Σ Autosum
or
Press: Ctrl + M

The Autosum command first looks up then left for cells to sum. If it cannot locate entries, it enters SUM() in the cell. Then you can type in or select the range reference. In this case AutoSum located and highlighted the values to the left of the current cell. To accept the highlighted range,

Press: ⎵Enter

Use the Fill Down command on the Edit menu to copy this function to cells H6 through H18.
   Notice that cells H8 and H9 display zeros.

Move to: H8

Your screen should be similar to Figure 6-14.

FIGURE 6-14

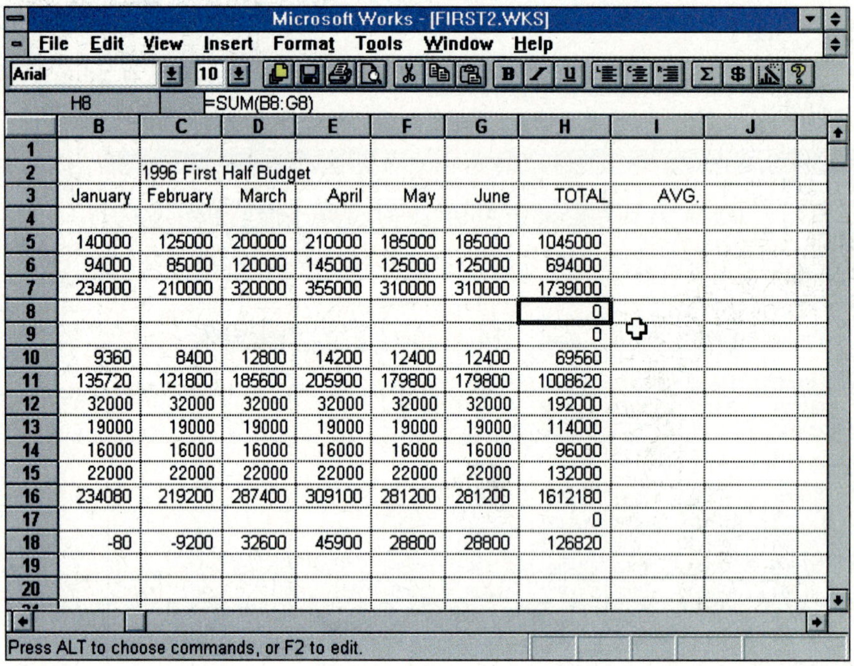

	B	C	D	E	F	G	H	I	J
1									
2		1996 First Half Budget							
3	January	February	March	April	May	June	TOTAL	AVG.	
4									
5	140000	125000	200000	210000	185000	185000	1045000		
6	94000	85000	120000	145000	125000	125000	694000		
7	234000	210000	320000	355000	310000	310000	1739000		
8							0		
9							0		
10	9360	8400	12800	14200	12400	12400	69560		
11	135720	121800	185600	205900	179800	179800	1008620		
12	32000	32000	32000	32000	32000	32000	192000		
13	19000	19000	19000	19000	19000	19000	114000		
14	16000	16000	16000	16000	16000	16000	96000		
15	22000	22000	22000	22000	22000	22000	132000		
16	234080	219200	287400	309100	281200	281200	1612180		
17							0		
18	-80	-9200	32600	45900	28800	28800	126820		
19									
20									

The function was copied into cells that reference empty cells. You need to erase the function from these cells.
   Highlight cells H8 through H9.

Choose: Edit>Clear
or
Press: Del

The function is erased from the cells and consequently the number 0 is no longer displayed.
   Erase the function from cell H17.

You can cancel a deletion by using Undo.

Inserting Functions from a List

Next you need to enter the function to calculate the average for the sales and expenses.

Move to: I5

To enter this function, you could type the function directly into the cell, or you can insert it by selecting the function from a list. To insert the average function,

Choose: Insert>Function

Your screen should be similar to Figure 6-15.

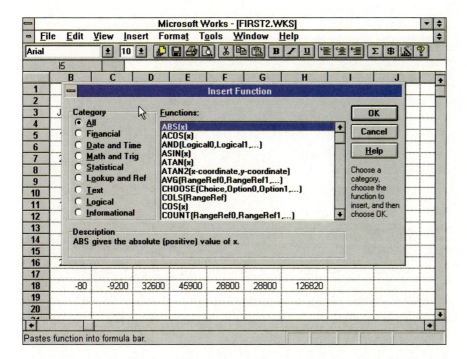

FIGURE 6-15

The Insert Function dialog box is displayed. From this box you select the type of function you want to use. The Category box displays the names of the function categories. The Functions list box displays the names of the functions in the selected category. The currently selected category is All. This category displays the names of all functions in alphabetical order.

Select the AVG function from the Functions list box.

Choose: OK

The Average function and its range reference argument are displayed in the formula bar. The first range reference argument (RangeRef0) is highlighted. You need to replace the argument with the actual numbers or the cell references containing the numbers to be used in the function. They can be entered in the function directly by typing the range reference, or can be entered by selecting the cell or range from the

spreadsheet. You will select the range B5 through G5 from the spreadsheet. This
avoids the accidental entry of incorrect references.

Select: B5 through G5 (do not include cell H5)

Your screen should be similar to Figure 6-16.

inserted   argument replaced with
function   range reference   argument

FIGURE 6-16

The selected range is entered in the function in place of the highlighted argument.
This is the only range reference this function will use. The additional argument
needs to be removed before the function can be completed. To do this,

Highlight and delete ",RangeRef,..." (do not include the closing
parenthesis).

Before you can remove the extra argument, you must be in Edit mode.

Press: F2

Highlight and delete ",RangeRef,..." (do not include the closing
parenthesis).

The function should be =AVG(B5:G5). To complete the function,

Press: ⏎Enter

Note: If a "Reference not valid or wrong operand type" error message box is displayed, choose OK to clear the box. Then edit the function in the formula bar until it is =AVG(B5:G5).

The average clothing sales for the six months are calculated and displayed in cell I5. The average value is 174166.67. The default display of numbers displays as many decimal places as cell space allows and rounds the value appropriately.

Copy the function down the column and if necessary clear the function from any cells that display the error message "ERR," because they reference blank cells.

Your screen should be similar to Figure 6-17.

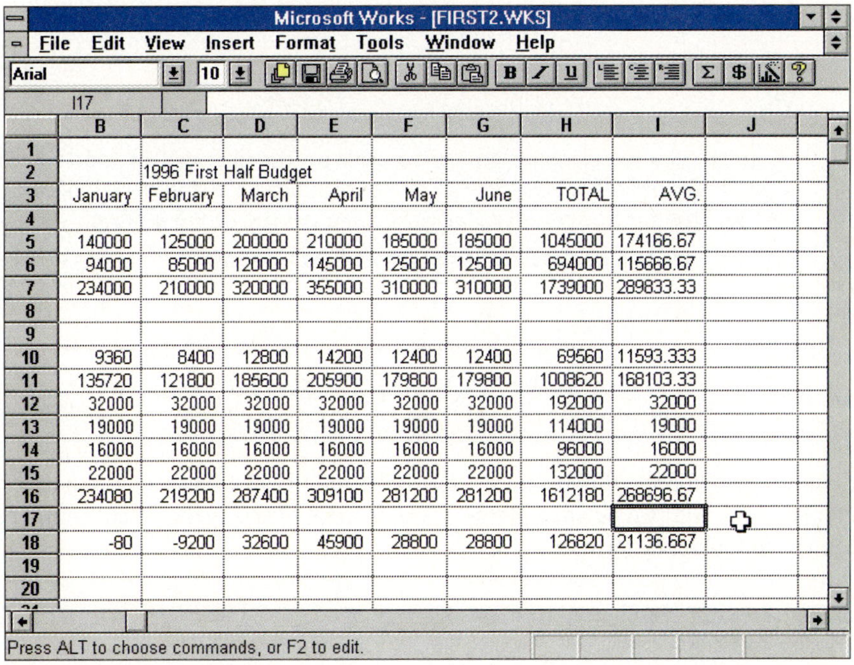

FIGURE 6-17

	B	C	D	E	F	G	H	I	J
1									
2		1996 First Half Budget							
3	January	February	March	April	May	June	TOTAL	AVG.	
4									
5	140000	125000	200000	210000	185000	185000	1045000	174166.67	
6	94000	85000	120000	145000	125000	125000	694000	115666.67	
7	234000	210000	320000	355000	310000	310000	1739000	289833.33	
8									
9									
10	9360	8400	12800	14200	12400	12400	69560	11593.333	
11	135720	121800	185600	205900	179800	179800	1008620	168103.33	
12	32000	32000	32000	32000	32000	32000	192000	32000	
13	19000	19000	19000	19000	19000	19000	114000	19000	
14	16000	16000	16000	16000	16000	16000	96000	16000	
15	22000	22000	22000	22000	22000	22000	132000	22000	
16	234080	219200	287400	309100	281200	281200	1612180	268696.67	
17									
18	-80	-9200	32600	45900	28800	28800	126820	21136.667	
19									
20									

Press ALT to choose commands, or F2 to edit.

Formatting Numbers

You want to improve the appearance of the spreadsheet by changing the format of numbers in the spreadsheet. **Formats** determine how information is displayed in a cell. Formats include such features as font, color, patterns, and number formats such as commas and dollar signs.

You think the spreadsheet would look better if the numbers were displayed in currency format. This is a numeric format. The table below shows examples of some common numeric formats.

Formatted Number	Format Setting
10,000	Comma
$10,000	Currency with no decimal places
$10,000.00	Currency with two decimal places
10/10/10	Long International Date
9:10	Time
90%	Percent with no decimal places
90.05%	Percent with two decimal places

You want the values to be displayed with dollar signs, commas, and two decimal places. The range of cells you want to format is B5 through I18.

A quick way to select a range is to click on the first cell of the range and then to hold down ⇧Shift while clicking on the last cell of the range. This method is particularly useful when the range is large.

Use this method to preselect the range B5 through I18.

Preselect the range B5 through I18.

Next you want to change the format of cells B5 through I18 to display as currency, with dollar signs and two decimal places. (Two decimal places is the default number of decimals for currency format.)

Choose: Format>Number>Currency>OK

➢ Ctrl + 4

or

Click: 🔳 Currency

You can also set the format for a cell to currency or percent by typing the $ symbol before the number or the % symbol following the number.

Your screen should be similar to Figure 6-18.

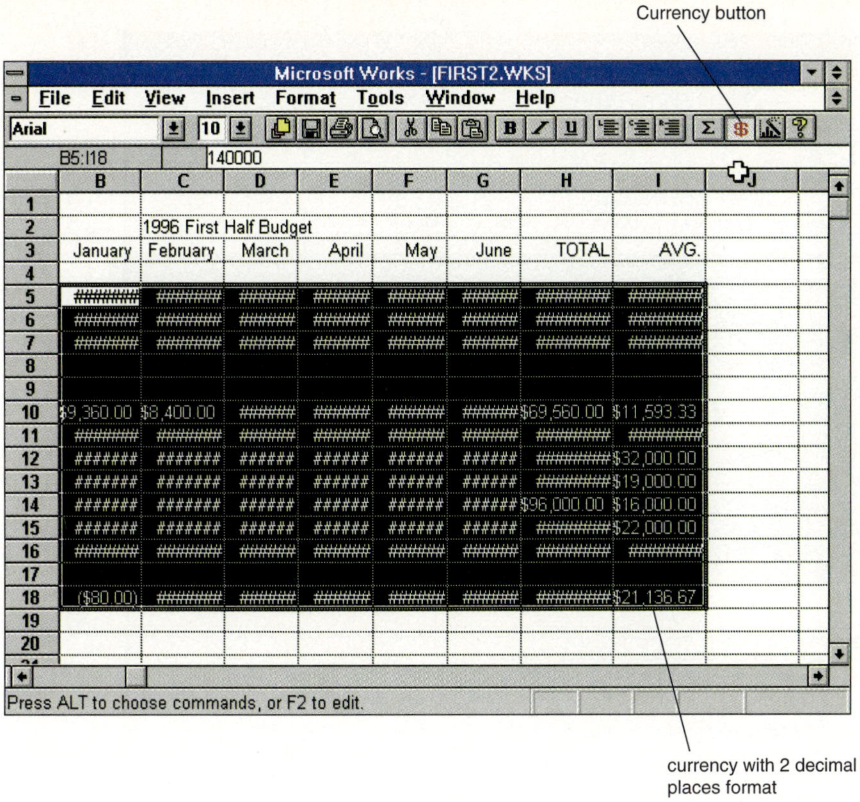

Currency button

FIGURE 6-18

currency with 2 decimal
places format

The numbers in the selected range of the spreadsheet are displayed with dollar signs and two decimal places. However, most numbers cannot be displayed because the cell width is too small to accommodate the $ symbol, comma, and extra decimal places.

Notice that the preselected range is still active. This lets you continue to use the range and select other commands without having to redefine the range each time. Since most of the values are whole numbers, and the values are estimates, you decide to change the format to currency with zero decimal places.

Choose: Format>Number>Currency

In the Number of decimals text box,

Type: **0** (zero)
Choose: OK

Although most of the values are fully displayed in the cell spaces, some are not. While the range is still highlighted,

Choose: Format>Column Width>Best Fit>OK

Your screen should be similar to Figure 6-19.

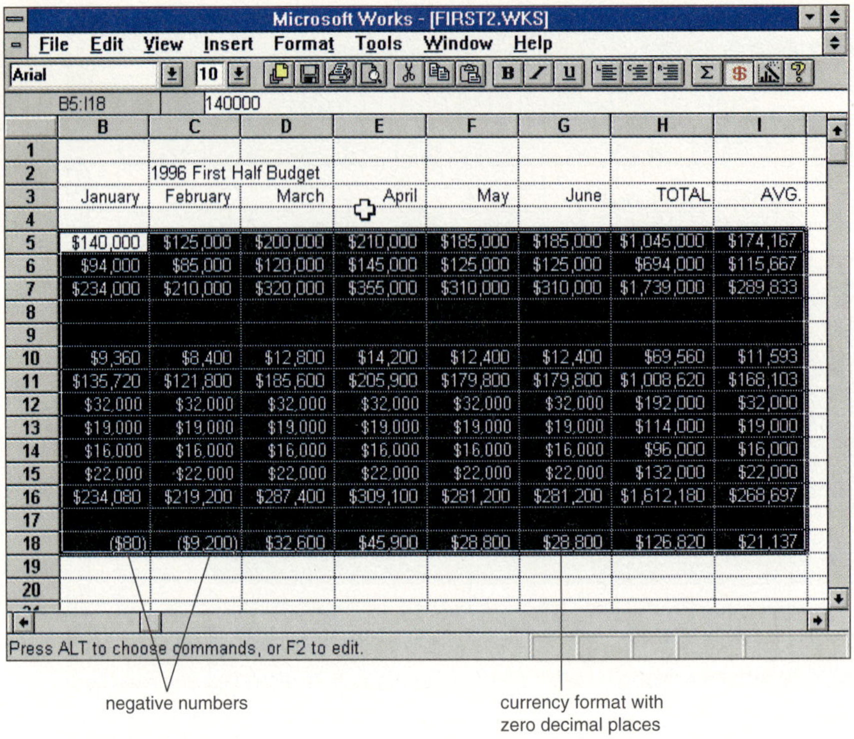

FIGURE 6-19

negative numbers

currency format with
zero decimal places

Now the numbers in the selected range are fully displayed in the columns. Notice that the negative numbers in cells B18 and C18 are displayed in parentheses in currency format.

Press: Home

The spreadsheet is now wider than the width of the window and requires that you scroll the window if you want to see the Average column of data.

Inserting and Deleting Rows

The appearance of the spreadsheet is greatly improved already. However, you still feel that it looks crowded and could be improved by inserting a blank row below the spreadsheet title as row 3.

To insert a blank row into the spreadsheet, begin by moving the highlight to the row where the new blank row will be inserted.

Move to: A3
Choose: Insert>Row/Column>Row>OK

Your screen should be similar to Figure 6-20.

inserted
row

	A	B	C	D	E	F	G	H
1								
2			1996 First Half Budget					
3								
4		January	February	March	April	May	June	TOTA
5	SALES							
6	Clothing	$140,000	$125,000	$200,000	$210,000	$185,000	$185,000	$1,045,00
7	Hard Goods	$94,000	$85,000	$120,000	$145,000	$125,000	$125,000	$694,00
8	Total Sales	$234,000	$210,000	$320,000	$355,000	$310,000	$310,000	$1,739,00
9								
10	EXPENSES							
11	Advertising	$9,360	$8,400	$12,800	$14,200	$12,400	$12,400	$69,56
12	Cost of Goods	$135,720	$121,800	$185,600	$205,900	$179,800	$179,800	$1,008,62
13	Salary	$32,000	$32,000	$32,000	$32,000	$32,000	$32,000	$192,00
14	Lease	$19,000	$19,000	$19,000	$19,000	$19,000	$19,000	$114,00
15	Miscellaneous	$16,000	$16,000	$16,000	$16,000	$16,000	$16,000	$96,00
16	Overhead	$22,000	$22,000	$22,000	$22,000	$22,000	$22,000	$132,00
17	Total Expenses	$234,080	$219,200	$287,400	$309,100	$281,200	$281,200	$1,612,18
18								
19	INCOME	($80)	($9,200)	$32,600	$45,900	$28,800	$28,800	$126,82
20								

Press ALT to choose commands, or F2 to edit.

FIGURE 6-20

A new blank row has been inserted into the spreadsheet at the highlight location. Everything below row 3 has moved down one row. All formulas and functions have been automatically adjusted to their new row locations. When inserting rows into the spreadsheet, note that the new row will be added at the highlight position, moving the current row and all others down.

The procedure to insert a column is the same as inserting a row, except that you select Column rather than Row in the Insert dialog box. When a column is added, the current column and all other columns will move to the right. To delete a row or column, choose Delete Row/Column from the Insert menu and select the option from the dialog box. Be very careful when using the Delete option because any information in the selected range will be deleted.

> Multiple rows or columns can be inserted or deleted by preselecting a range.

Moving and Aligning Entries Across Columns

Next you want the spreadsheet title to be centered over the spreadsheet data and in a larger font. The Alignment command on the Format menu lets you align text across a selection. To use this feature, the text you want aligned must be in the leftmost cell of the range. You can use the Cut and Paste commands on the Edit menu to move the spreadsheet title to cell A2, or, if you have a mouse, you can use the drag-and-drop feature.

Move to: C2

Drag-and-drop in the spreadsheet operates just like it does in the word processor.

Point to the border of the highlight until the pointer changes to .

When the mouse pointer is ▨, this indicates that you can drag the mouse to specify the location where you want to move or copy the cell contents. To move cell contents, simply drag the mouse. To copy cell contents, hold down ⌨Ctrl⌨ while dragging. The mouse pointer changes to ▨ when the contents are being moved or ▨ when the contents are being copied.

Drag the mouse and point to cell A2. Release the mouse button when the cell outline appears in cell A2.

Choose: Edit>Cut

➤   ⌨Ctrl⌨ + X

The contents of cell C2 are removed from the spreadsheet and placed in the Clipboard. If the Clipboard already contains information, it is replaced by the new data. To specify the destination location and enter the contents of the Clipboard at this location,

Move to: A2

Choose: Edit>Paste

➤   ⌨Ctrl⌨ + V

The contents of the Clipboard are copied into the current cell. If you cut and paste cells containing formulas, the formulas are adjusted relative to their new spreadsheet location.

Now you can use the alignment command to center the spreadsheet title over the spreadsheet across cells A2 through I2.

Preselect: A2 through I2
Choose: Format>Alignment>Center across selection>OK

Your screen should be similar to Figure 6-21.

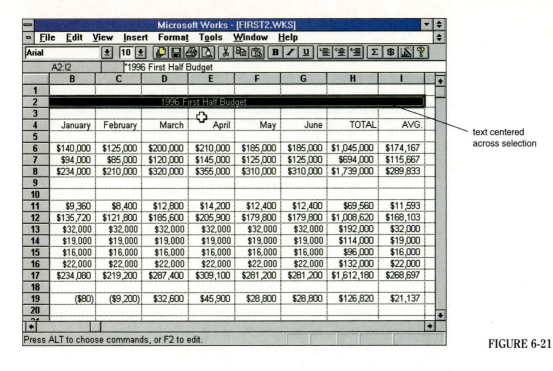

text centered
across selection

FIGURE 6-21

The text in the leftmost cell of the selection is centered across all selected blank cells to the right. The title now appears balanced over the spreadsheet columns. However, the text entry is still in cell A2. The formula bar displays the text entry.

Changing Fonts

Finally, you want to enlarge and bold the spreadsheet title. Changing fonts is the same as in the word processor.

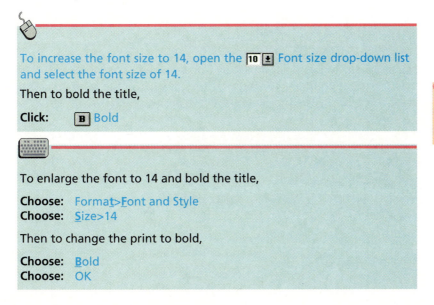

To increase the font size to 14, open the `10 ±` Font size drop-down list and select the font size of 14.

Then to bold the title,

Click: `B` Bold

To enlarge the font to 14 and bold the title,

Choose: Format>Font and Style
Choose: Size>14

Then to change the print to bold,

Choose: Bold
Choose: OK

Click `±` to the right of the
`10 ±` Font Size button to
open the list.

SPREADSHEET

To clear the highlight,

Press: [Ctrl] + [Home]

Your screen should be similar to Figure 6-22.

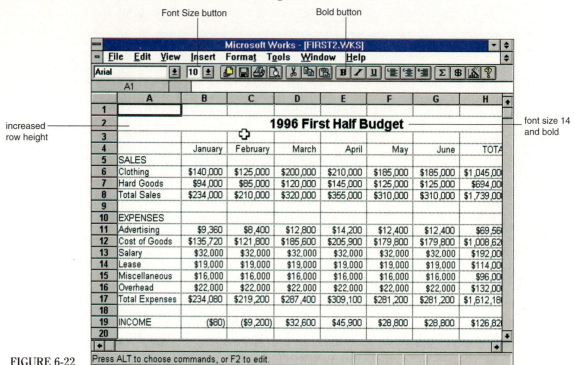

FIGURE 6-22

Notice that the title is much larger than the other characters in the spreadsheet and that the height of the entire row has increased in order to accommodate the larger character size of the heading in that row. The title is also bold.

Adding Underlines and Italics

You also want to add bold, italics, and underlines to several other spreadsheet entries. The same shortcuts for these features as used in the word processor are used in the spreadsheet. The shortcuts are shown below.

Feature	Shortcut	Button
Bold	[Ctrl] + B	**B**
Italics	[Ctrl] + I	_I_
Single underline	[Ctrl] + U	U

First you want to bold and italicize the row labels in cells A5, A10, and A19.

Move to: A5

Click: **B** Bold

Click: *I* Italic

or

Press: Ctrl + B

Press: Ctrl + I

In the same manner, bold the contents of cells A10 and A19.

    Next you want to bold and underline the column headings.

Preselect: B4 through I4

Click: **B** Bold

        U Underline

or

Press: Ctrl + B

        Ctrl + U

To quickly move to the first cell in a row,

Press: Home

Your screen should be similar to Figure 6-23.

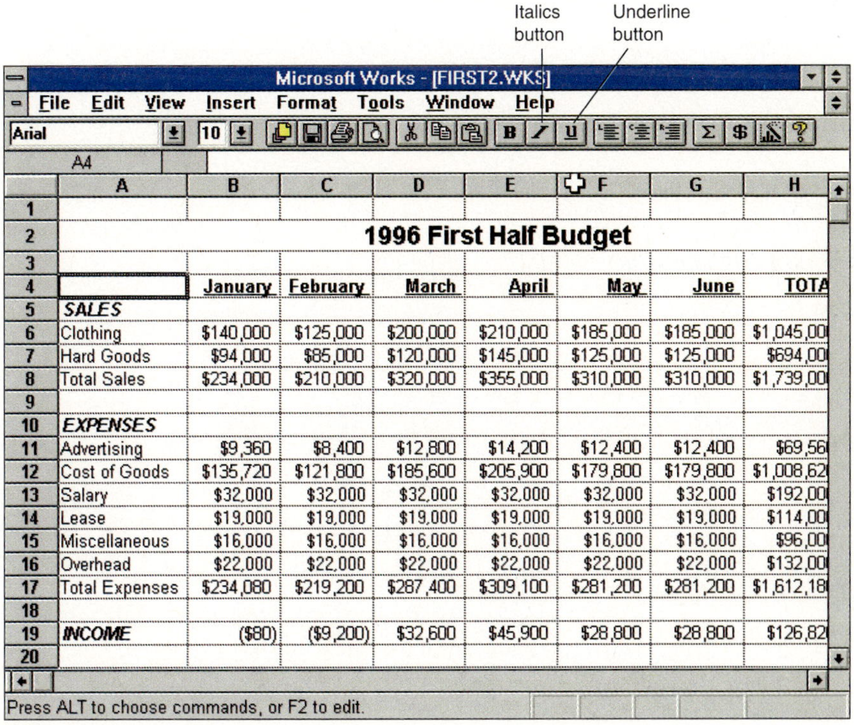

Italics button   Underline button

FIGURE 6-23

SPREADSHEET

The six-month budget is now complete.

    Enter your first initial and last name in cell A1.

Entering the System Date

The current date as maintained by your computer system can be entered automatically into a spreadsheet using the NOW function. Because the spreadsheet title is in cell A2, you will enter the date in cell A3.

Move to: A3
Type: **=NOW()**
Press: [←Enter]

The NOW function displays the serial number equivalent until the cell is formatted as a date. The **serial number** is a number assigned to each day between January 1, 1900 and June 3, 2079. To change the display of this cell to a date format,

Choose: Forma**t**>**N**umber>**D**ate

The date formats are displayed in the Options list box. You want the date displayed as month/day/year. The highlighted option in the list box displays the date in this format.

Choose: OK

The date is displayed in cell A1. Now whenever you open this spreadsheet, it will display that day's date.

> Save the spreadsheet as FRSTHALF.

The shortcut [Ctrl] + ; will insert the current date, but it will not update the date in the spreadsheet.

Zooming a Spreadsheet

Before printing, to preview how the spreadsheet will appear,

Choose: **F**ile>Print Pre**v**iew
or
Click: 🔍 Print Preview

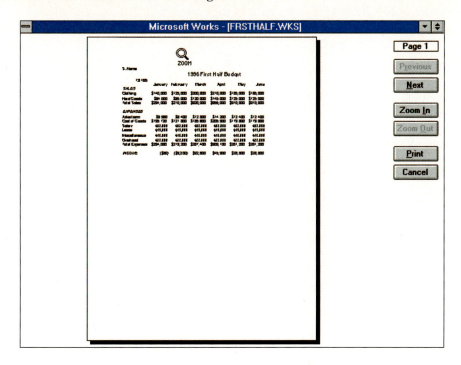

FIGURE 6-24

The spreadsheet for the first six months is displayed as it will appear on the printed page. This is called the full-size view, but it is difficult to read. While previewing a spreadsheet, you can enlarge the display by "zooming" the Preview window.

Move the mouse pointer onto the spreadsheet.

The mouse pointer changes to a 🔍. The location of the 🔍 in the Preview window determines the area of the document that will be displayed in the window when you zoom the display.

Position the 🔍 over the row labels in column A and click the mouse button.

The onscreen size of the characters increases. To enlarge the text to the actual size it will appear when printed,

With the 🔍 still in the same location, click the mouse button again.

Choose: Zoom In

The size of the print increases, making the spreadsheet easier to read. To enlarge the text to the actual size it will appear when printed,

Choose: Zoom In

Clicking 🔍 cycles through all
sizes in order.

When the Preview window is actual size, you may need to scroll the screen using the scroll bars or the arrow keys to see parts of the spreadsheet that are not visible. To return the display to the previous size,

Choose: Zoom **O**ut

Now you can see that the Total and Average columns of data will not fit on the page. To see the next page,

Choose: **N**ext

Printing with Landscape Orientation

Note: Not all printers can print with landscape orientation. If your printer cannot, skip this section. Your printed output will be on two pages.

The two columns of data appear on the second page. You decide to change the orientation of the spreadsheet on the page so that the entire spreadsheet can be printed on one page. To close the Preview window,

Choose: Cancel

To change the orientation,

Choose: **F**ile>Page Setup

The three Page Setup tab folders are used to change how the spreadsheet is printed on a page.

Choose: **S**ource, Size, and Orientation

The default orientation is **portrait**. This setting prints across the width (8½" side) of a page. The other orientation option, **landscape**, prints the spreadsheet sideways across the length (11" side) of the page. To change the orientation,

Select: **L**andscape

Your screen should be similar to Figure 6-25.

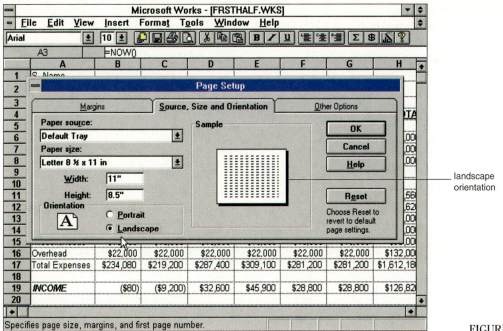

landscape
orientation

FIGURE 6-25

The Sample box shows how changing the orientation to landscape will change the page layout.

Choose: OK

Note: You will be printing in this section. If necessary first select the correct printer for your computer (**F**ile>P**r**inter Setup).

To see how the new orientation setting has affected the spreadsheet,

Choose: **F**ile>Print Pre**v**iew
or
Click: Print Preview

The spreadsheet data is displayed across the length of the page. Consequently there is plenty of space for the Total and Average columns to be printed on the same page as the rest of the First Half budget.
　　To print the spreadsheet,

Choose: **P**rint
Choose: OK

The printer should begin printing the spreadsheet.
　　When you are ready, close the file, save the changes to the file, and exit Works.

SPREADSHEET

Key Terms

source (188)
destination (189)
preselect (190)
relative cell reference (191)
pointing (193)
function (195)
syntax (195)
argument (195)
column width (198)
format (207)
serial number (216)
portrait (218)
landscape (218)

Command Summary

Command	Shortcut	Button	Action
Edit>**C**opy	Ctrl + C	📋	Copies contents of selected cell(s) to Clipboard
Edit>**P**aste	Ctrl + V	📋	Pastes data from Clipboard to selected cell(s)
Edit>Fill Ri**gh**t			Copies selected cell contents to adjacent cells to right
Insert>**F**unction>SUM	Ctrl + M	Σ	Totals all numbers in range reference
Forma**t**>Column **W**idth			Changes width of selected columns
Edit>**U**ndo	Ctrl + Z		Undoes last editing or formatting change
Forma**t**>Column **W**idth>**B**estFit			Changes width of columns so largest entry is displayed
Forma**t**>**A**lignment>**R**ight	Ctrl + R	▤	Right-aligns selected cells
Forma**t**>**N**umber>C**u**rrency		$	Displays numbers with dollar signs
Insert>**R**ow/Column			Inserts a blank row or column
Edit>Cu**t**	Ctrl + X	✂	Places cell contents in Clipboard
Forma**t**>**A**lignment>Center **a**cross selection			Centers cell contents across preselected cells
Forma**t**>**F**ont and Style			Changes font and attributes of cell contents
Forma**t**>**N**umber>**D**ate			Changes cell display to a date format
File>Print Pre**v**iew		🔍	Displays spreadsheet as it will appear when printed
File>Pa**g**e Setup>**S**ource, Size and Orientation>**L**andscape			Prints spreadsheet sideways across length of page

LAB REVIEW

Matching

1. Fill Right _____ a. function to add series of numbers
2. Copy _____ b. inserts row or column
3. point _____ c. copies contents of cell to new location
4. Print Preview _____ d. indicates insufficient cell width
5. Landscape _____ e. method of entering a cell or range reference into a formula
6. Best Fit _____ f. copies contents of cell to adjacent cells to right
7. SUM _____ g. cancels most recent operation
8. Edit>Insert _____ h. displays spreadsheet as it will be printed
9. ###### _____ i. prints text across length of page
10. Edit>Undo _____ j. adjusts column width to display all entered characters

Fill-In Questions

1. Complete the following statements by filling in the blanks with the correct terms.

a. _____ are built-in formulas that perform certain types of calculations automatically.

b. To display more characters in a cell, you would increase the _____.

c. When a formula is copied, and the row and column reference adjusts to the new location, the formula is using a(n) _____.

d. When text is displayed darker than other text in the spreadsheet, it is _____.

e. The _____ command copies the topmost cells into adjacent cells below it.

f. When column widths are adjusted based on their contents, the _____ command is used.

g. _____ appear when a cell width is too small to display the entire number in that cell.

h. _____ reverses the effects of the most recently executed command or action.

i. A(n) _____ is the data the function uses to perform the calculation.

j. The _____ command centers a cell's content across a preselected range.

Practice Exercises

1. Kevin Hemstreet has been working on his personal budget. He has been having some problems. Open the spreadsheet file PERBDGT.WKS.

    a. The entries in row 5 are Kevin's monthly interest income. These figures are incorrect. Clear the numbers from these cells.

    b. Enter the number 35 for interest income in cell B5. Copy the number from February through June.

    c. In cell H5, total the Interest Income row.

    d. Insert two blank rows as rows 1 and 2. In cell A1, enter the title PERSONAL BUDGET FOR FIRST HALF OF 1996 in a font type and size of your choice. Bold the title. Center the title across columns A through H.

    e. Increase the width of column A to completely display the row headings. Bold and italicize the entries in cells A5, A9, and A18.

    f. Bold and underline the column headings.

    g. Format the numbers to currency with two decimal places.

Your completed spreadsheet should be similar to the spreadsheet shown below.

	A	B	C	D	E	F	G	H
1		PERSONAL BUDGET FOR FIRST HALF OF 1996						
2								
3		JAN	FEB	MAR	APR	MAY	JUN	TOTAL
4								
5	*Income:*							
6	Wages	$1,900.00	$1,900.00	$1,900.00	$1,900.00	$1,900.00	$1,900.00	$11,400.00
7	Interest Income	$35.00	$35.00	$35.00	$35.00	$35.00	$35.00	$210.00
8								
9	*Expenses:*							
10	Rent	$450.00	$450.00	$450.00	$450.00	$450.00	$450.00	$2,700.00
11	Food	$200.00	$200.00	$200.00	$200.00	$200.00	$200.00	$1,200.00
12	Clothing	$100.00	$100.00	$100.00	$100.00	$100.00	$100.00	$600.00
13	Telephone	$35.00	$35.00	$35.00	$35.00	$35.00	$35.00	$210.00
14	Car Payment	$200.00	$200.00	$200.00	$200.00	$200.00	$200.00	$1,200.00
15	Insurance	$45.00	$45.00	$45.00	$45.00	$45.00	$45.00	$270.00
16	Savings	$200.00	$200.00	$200.00	$200.00	$200.00	$200.00	$1,200.00
17								
18	*Total Expenses*	$1,230.00	$1,230.00	$1,230.00	$1,230.00	$1,230.00	$1,230.00	$7,380.00
19								
20								

    h. Enter your name in cell A2 and the current date in cell A3. Change the orientation to landscape. Save the spreadsheet as PERBDGT2. Preview and print the spreadsheet.

2. To complete this problem, you must have completed Practice Exercise 1 in Lab 5. Open the file PAPERBK1.WKS. Complete the budget by following these steps:

    a. In cell B10, enter the formula to calculate the advertising expense as 10 percent of January total sales. In cell B11, calculate cost of goods expenses as 35 percent of January total sales. Copy the formulas to February through June.

    b. Copy the remaining expense values in B12 through B15 to February through June.

c. In row 16, use SUM functions to calculate the total expenses for January through June.

d. Enter a formula in cell B18 to calculate the income for January (=B7– B16). Copy the formula to February through June.

e. Complete the remaining total calculations for the total column (column H).

f. Best Fit column A to fully display the row headings.

g. Right-align the Total column heading in cell H3. Bold all column headings in row 3. Bold the title.

h. Insert a blank row under the column headings.

i. Format the values as currency with zero decimal places.

j. Underline the entries in cells A5, A10, and A19. Underline the values in rows 7 and 16.

Your completed spreadsheet should be similar to the spreadsheet shown below.

	A	B	C	D	E	F	G	H
1	Student Name		The Paperback Book Company Budget					
2	Date							
3		January	February	March	April	May	June	Total
4								
5	SALES:							
6	Best Sellers	$1,400	$1,230	$1,750	$2,100	$1,850	$1,850	$10,180
7	Classics	$940	$850	$120	$1,350	$1,250	$1,250	$5,760
8	Total Sales	$2,340	$2,080	$1,870	$3,450	$3,100	$3,100	$15,940
9								
10	EXPENSES:							
11	Advertising	$234	$208	$187	$345	$310	$310	$1,594
12	Cost of Goods	$819	$728	$655	$1,208	$1,085	$1,085	$5,579
13	Salary	$900	$900	$900	$900	$900	$900	$5,400
14	Lease	$300	$300	$300	$300	$300	$300	$1,800
15	Miscellaneous	$100	$100	$100	$100	$100	$100	$600
16	Overhead	$50	$50	$50	$50	$50	$50	$300
17	Total Expenses	$1,350	$2,286	$2,192	$2,903	$2,745	$2,745	$14,220
18								
19	INCOME:	$990	($206)	($322)	$548	$355	$355	$1,720
20								
21								
22								

k. Enter the current date in cell A2. Preview and print the spreadsheet.

l. Save the spreadsheet as PAPERBK2.

3. Open the file APTMT1.WKS you created in Lab 5, Practice Exercise 3. You will continue to build the spreadsheet to analyze the expenses at the three different apartment complexes.

a. Copy the total formula in cell C11 across the row to total the cost of each apartment.

b. Insert two blank rows under the main title. Insert one blank row between the column headings and the values.

c. Increase the width of column A to completely display the row headings. Delete column B.

d. Right-align and underline the BDRM column headings. Center the apartment complex names over the two columns. Bold the complex names.

e. Move the spreadsheet title to cell A3 and center it across columns A through G. Bold the title.

f. Underline the values in row 12.

g. Format the TOTAL COST row to currency with zero decimal places.

Your completed spreadsheet should be similar to the spreadsheet shown below.

	A	B	C	D	E	F	G	H
1								
2								
3			Apartment Analysis For Susan Anderson					
4								
5								
6		Sun Lakes		Apple Way		Valley Vista		
7		BDRM 1	BDRM 2	BDRM 1	BDRM 2	BDRM 1	BDRM 2	
8								
9	Rent	300	350	400	450	375	425	
10	Telephone	35	35	45	45	25	25	
11	Electricity	75	85	65	75	60	85	
12	Deposit	300	300	200	225	375	425	
13								
14	TOTAL COST	$710	$770	$710	$795	$835	$960	
15								
16								
17								
18								
19								
20								

h. Enter the current date in cell A2. Preview and print the spreadsheet.

i. Save the file as APTMT2.

4. To complete this problem you must have created the spreadsheet in Practice Exercise 4 in Lab 5. Open the spreadsheet file PARKFIN.WKS. You will continue to build the spreadsheet for the three-year financial statement for the Parks and Recreation Department Director.

a. To make the spreadsheet easier to read, insert a blank row below the column headings. Insert an additional blank row as rows 10 and 17 (in that order).

b. Increase the width of column A to completely display all the row headings.

c. Delete column B.

d. Copy the formulas to calculate total revenue and total expenses from 1994 to 1995 and 1996.

e. Enter the formula to calculate reserve in cell B20 (=B11–B18). Copy the formula to calculate the reserve for 1995 and 1996.

f. Enter functions to calculate the total and average for the three years in cells E7 and F7, respectively. Copy the functions down the column. Erase the functions from the cells that reference empty cells. Format the Average column to fixed with zero decimal places. (Use Help for information on the Fixed number format.)

g. Underline rows 9 and 16, columns B through F. Increase the size of the first and second title lines. Center the title lines over columns B through F. Bold all row headings in column A and column headings in row 4. Right-align the entries in cells E4 and F4.

Your completed spreadsheet should be similar to the spreadsheet shown below.

	A	B	C	D	E	F	G	H
1	Student Name	PARKS AND RECREATION DEPARTMENT						
2	Date	FINANCIAL STATEMENT						
3								
4		1994	1995	1996	TOTAL	AVERAGE		
5								
6	Revenues							
7	Operation	234220	339382	332928	906530	302177		
8	Fund Raising	193910	283819	389238	866967	288989		
9	Interest Income	23088	48493	28382	99963	33321		
10								
11	TOTAL REVENUE	451218	671694	750548	1873460	624487		
12								
13	Expenses							
14	Operating	219000	290182	289300	798482	266161		
15	Capital Projects	193983	87363	76939	358285	119428		
16	Fund Raising	158992	167391	142821	469204	156401		
17								
18	TOTAL EXPENSES	571975	544936	509060	1625971	541990		
19								
20	RESERVE	-120757	126758	241488	247489	82496		

h. Clear the old date from cell A2 and enter the current date. Change the orientation to landscape. Save the spreadsheet as PARKFIN2. Preview and print the spreadsheet. This problem is continued in Practice Exercise 2 of Lab 7.

5. April Murphy owns a small cafe. To help her make a decision about expanding the cafe, she wants to create a simplified budget. Open the spreadsheet file FLOWER.

a. Change the width of column A to fully display the headings. Right-align the column heading in cell H6.

b. Copy the January fixed expenses (rows 16 through 19) to February through June.

c. Enter the formulas to calculate food and beverage expenses as 30 percent of the food and beverage sales for January. Copy the formulas to the February through June food and beverage expense columns.

d. Use the SUM function to calculate total sales (B11) and total expenses (B20) for January. Copy the functions to February through June.

e. Use the SUM function to calculate the Total column (H). Copy the function down the column. Clear the functions that reference blank cells.

f. Format the numbers to display currency with zero decimal places. Adjust the column widths using the Best Fit feature.

g. Move the title lines to cells A3 and A4. Center the title lines above columns A through H. Make the title a larger font size than the other characters in the spreadsheet. Bold the title and column headings. Underline the beverage sales and direct expense values.

Your completed spreadsheet should be similar to the spreadsheet shown below.

	A	B	C	D	E	F	G	H	I
1									
2									
3			April's Flower Garden Cafe						
4			Six Month Budget						
5									
6		January	February	March	April	May	June	Total	
7									
8	SALES								
9	Food	$3,490	$4,000	$4,200	$4,900	$5,100	$5,500	$27,190	
10	Beverage	$320	$450	$460	$500	$520	$600	$2,850	
11	Total Sales	$3,810	$4,450	$4,660	$5,400	$5,620	$6,100	$30,040	
12									
13	EXPENSES								
14	Food	$1,047	$1,200	$1,260	$1,470	$1,530	$1,650	$8,157	
15	Beverage	$96	$135	$138	$150	$156	$180	$855	
16	Payroll	$2,200	$2,200	$2,200	$2,200	$2,200	$2,200	$13,200	
17	Lease	$200	$200	$200	$200	$200	$200	$1,200	
18	G&A	$175	$175	$175	$175	$175	$175	$1,050	
19	Direct	$1,000	$1,000	$1,000	$1,000	$1,000	$1,000	$6,000	
20	Total Expenses	$4,718	$4,910	$4,973	$5,195	$5,261	$5,405	$30,462	

h.   In cells A1 and A2, enter your name and the date. Preview and print the spreadsheet. Save the spreadsheet as CAFEBDGT.

6.   Compare the cost of traveling to four major cities in different areas of the United States (use information in the travel section of a newspaper, travel magazine, or a local travel agency). Create a spreadsheet to help you analyze the costs as if you needed to visit the cities with only one week's notice. Include the cost of travel using all practical modes of transportation such as air, rail, and car. The cost may also include hotel accommodations, car rental, meals, and other expenses. Figure your spending money as a percent of the total cost.

Enter your name in cell A1 and the current date in cell A2. Save and print the spreadsheet.

LAB

7 Managing a Large Spreadsheet

CASE STUDY

You presented the completed first half of the estimated operating budget to The Sports Company store manager. The manager is pleased with the six-month analysis and has asked you to create a separate spreadsheet showing the annual budget. In addition, the manager wants you to calculate the profit margin for the store over the 12 months. At the end of 12 months, the profit margin should be 13 percent. You will make these adjustments to the budget.

Locating a Circular Reference

After presenting the budget to the manager, you made several of the changes requested, and saved them in a file called ANNUAL.WKS.

Load Works. Place your data disk in the appropriate drive for your computer system. To see your revised and expanded budget, open the spreadsheet file ANNUAL.WKS. If necessary maximize the spreadsheet window.

Competencies

After completing this lab, you will know how to:

1. Locate a circular reference.
2. Freeze titles.
3. Calculate a percentage.
4. Perform what-if analysis.
5. Split windows.
6. Use absolute cell references.
7. Add borders.
8. Add headers.
9. Set margins, font size, and print area.

Your screen should be similar to Figure 7-1.

	A	B	C	D	E	F	G	H
	Microsoft Works - [ANNUAL.WKS]							
	File Edit View Insert Format Tools Window Help							
	Arial 10							
	A1							
1								
2							**The Sports Comp**	
3								
4		January	February	March	April	May	June	J
5								
6	SALES							
7								
8	Clothing	$140,000	$125,000	$175,000	$210,000	$185,000	$185,000	$200,
9	Hard Goods	$94,000	$85,000	$120,000	$145,000	$125,000	$125,000	$135,
10	Total Sales	$234,000	$210,000	$295,000	$355,000	$310,000	$310,000	$335,
11								
12	EXPENSES							
13								
14	Advertising	$9,360	$8,400	$11,800	$14,200	$12,400	$12,400	$13,
15	Cost of Goods	$135,720	$121,800	$171,100	$205,900	$179,800	$179,800	$194,
16	Salary	$32,000	$32,000	$32,000	$32,000	$32,000	$32,000	$32,
17	Lease	$19,000	$19,000	$19,000	$19,000	$19,000	$19,000	$19,
18	Miscellaneous	$16,000	$16,000	$16,000	$16,000	$16,000	$16,000	$16,
19	Overhead	$22,000	$22,000	$22,000	$22,000	$22,000	$22,000	$22,
20	Total Expenses	$234,080	$219,200	$271,900	$309,100	$281,200	$281,200	$296,

Press ALT to choose commands, or F2 to edit.   CIRC

FIGURE 7-1

The spreadsheet now contains values for 12 months and a new row heading for profit margin. The spreadsheet extends beyond column H and below row 20.

Note: Although there are quicker ways to move to cells in the spreadsheet, use the arrow keys when directed. Your screen will then show the same rows and columns as the figures in the text.

To see the rest of the row headings, using ⬇,

Move to: A24

The row heading "PROFIT MARGIN" is now visible on the screen. The formula to calculate this value still needs to be entered into the spreadsheet. Notice that the column headings are no longer visible in the window. This makes it difficult for you to know which column of data corresponds to which month.

To see the rest of the spreadsheet to the right of column H, using ➡,

Move to: N24

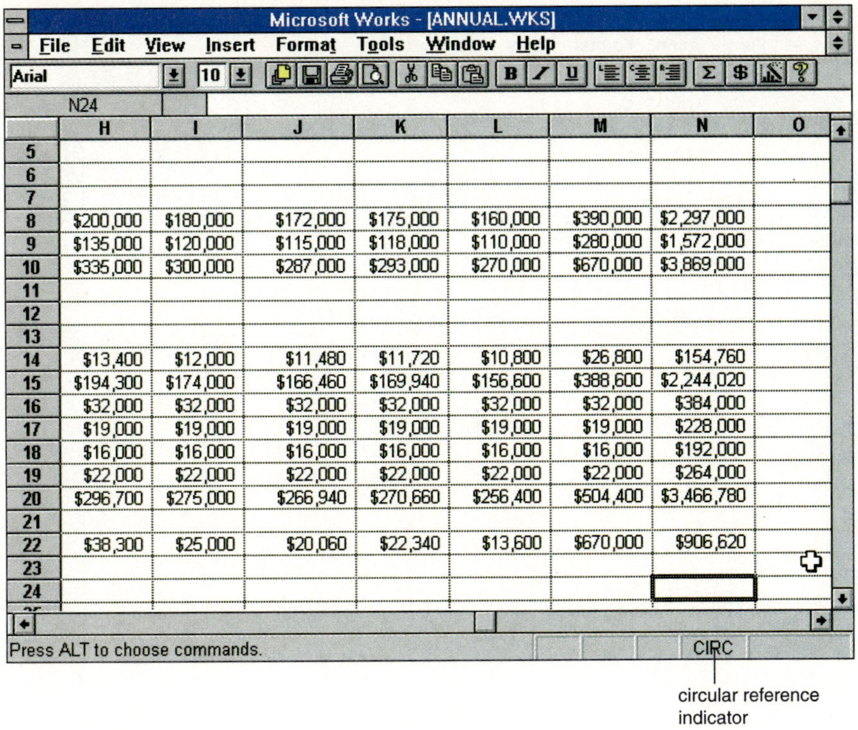

	H	I	J	K	L	M	N	O
5								
6								
7								
8	$200,000	$180,000	$172,000	$175,000	$160,000	$390,000	$2,297,000	
9	$135,000	$120,000	$115,000	$118,000	$110,000	$280,000	$1,572,000	
10	$335,000	$300,000	$287,000	$293,000	$270,000	$670,000	$3,869,000	
11								
12								
13								
14	$13,400	$12,000	$11,480	$11,720	$10,800	$26,800	$154,760	
15	$194,300	$174,000	$166,460	$169,940	$156,600	$388,600	$2,244,020	
16	$32,000	$32,000	$32,000	$32,000	$32,000	$32,000	$384,000	
17	$19,000	$19,000	$19,000	$19,000	$19,000	$19,000	$228,000	
18	$16,000	$16,000	$16,000	$16,000	$16,000	$16,000	$192,000	
19	$22,000	$22,000	$22,000	$22,000	$22,000	$22,000	$264,000	
20	$296,700	$275,000	$266,940	$270,660	$256,400	$504,400	$3,466,780	
21								
22	$38,300	$25,000	$20,060	$22,340	$13,600	$670,000	$906,620	
23								
24								

Microsoft Works - [ANNUAL.WKS]

File Edit View Insert Format Tools Window Help

Arial 10 N24

Press ALT to choose commands. CIRC

circular reference
indicator

FIGURE 7-2

The Total column and the values for the months of July through December are now visible.

Looking at the values in the spreadsheet, you may find it difficult to remember what the values stand for when the row headings in column A or the month headings in row 4 are not visible in the window. For example, look at the value in cell K19. The value in this cell is 22000. Is this value a lease expense or a miscellaneous expense or an overhead expense? Is it form the month of September, October, or November? Without seeing the row and column headings, it is difficult to know. You will learn shortly how to manage a spreadsheet that extends beyond a single window.

Notice the indicator "CIRC" displayed in the status bar. This indicator is a warning that a **circular reference** has been located in the spreadsheet. This means that a formula in a cell either directly or indirectly references itself. For some special applications, a formula containing a circular reference may be valid, but these cases are not very common. Whenever you see this message displayed, stop and locate the cell or cells containing the reference.

Locating the formula containing a circular reference in a spreadsheet can be very difficult. Each formula needs to be checked. Sometimes a value in a cell that is much larger or smaller than other values in the same category can point you to the location of the error.

Move to: M22

The number in this cell, $670,000, is much larger than the other numbers in this row. Notice that the formula in the formula bar is =M10–M22. The formula in cell M22 incorrectly references itself, M22, as part of the computation. The formula in this cell should calculate the profit for December using the formula =M10–M20.

Correct the formula in cell M22 to be =M10–M20.

SPREADSHEET

Your screen should be similar to Figure 7-3.

	H	I	J	K	L	M	N	O
5								
6								
7								
8	$200,000	$180,000	$172,000	$175,000	$160,000	$390,000	$2,297,000	
9	$135,000	$120,000	$115,000	$118,000	$110,000	$280,000	$1,572,000	
10	$335,000	$300,000	$287,000	$293,000	$270,000	$670,000	$3,869,000	
11								
12								
13								
14	$13,400	$12,000	$11,480	$11,720	$10,800	$26,800	$154,760	
15	$194,300	$174,000	$166,460	$169,940	$156,600	$388,600	$2,244,020	
16	$32,000	$32,000	$32,000	$32,000	$32,000	$32,000	$384,000	
17	$19,000	$19,000	$19,000	$19,000	$19,000	$19,000	$228,000	
18	$16,000	$16,000	$16,000	$16,000	$16,000	$16,000	$192,000	
19	$22,000	$22,000	$22,000	$22,000	$22,000	$22,000	$264,000	
20	$296,700	$275,000	$266,940	$270,660	$256,400	$504,400	$3,466,780	
21								
22	$38,300	$25,000	$20,060	$22,340	$13,600	$165,600	$402,220	
23								
24								

Microsoft Works - [ANNUAL.WKS]
File Edit View Insert Format Tools Window Help
Arial   10
M22   =M10-M20
Press ALT to choose commands, or F2 to edit.

FIGURE 7-3

The CIRC indicator has disappeared, and the affected spreadsheet formulas were recalculated. The new calculated value of $165,600 is displayed in cell M22. This was a simple example of a circular reference error; others may be much more complex. In any case, whenever this indicator appears, locate the circular reference and determine whether it is valid or not.

Freezing Row and Column Titles

Now you want to enter the formula to calculate the profit margin. As noted earlier, however, it is difficult to read the spreadsheet when the row headings in column A and the column headings in row 4 are not visible in the window. To make it easier to read the spreadsheet as the spreadsheet scrolls in the window while entering this formula, you can **freeze** specified rows or columns (or both) on the window.

Press: Ctrl + Home

Although the headings are visible again, you cannot see the numbers in columns I through N or the rows containing the income and profit margin. To keep the row headings in column A visible in the window at the same time you are viewing the values in columns I through N, you will freeze column A in the window. To do this the Freeze Titles command in the Format menu is used. The "titles" can consist of any number of columns or rows along the top or left edge of the window.

The location of the highlight in the spreadsheet controls where the titles will be frozen in the window. Freezing affects all cells above and to the left of the highlight. To freeze columns of titles only, move the highlight to row 1 and to the right of the columns you want to freeze. Since you want to freeze column A on the window,

Move to: B1
Choose: Format>Freeze Titles

A solid dark line appears separating columns A and B to show where the spreadsheet is frozen.

Watch the movement of the columns in the window as you use → to,

Move to: N1

Your screen should be similar to Figure 7-4.

FIGURE 7-4

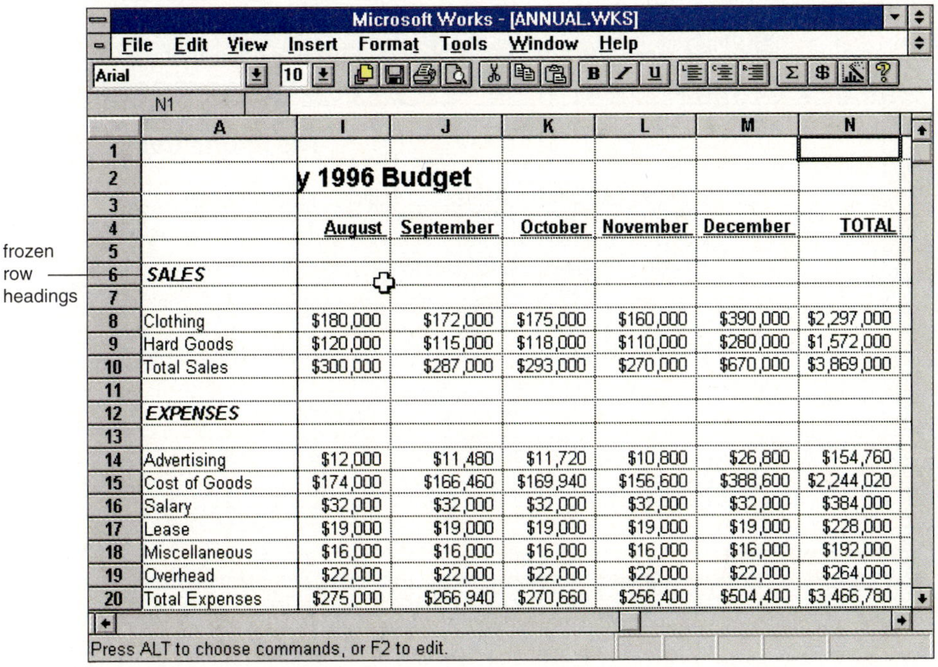

frozen
row
headings

	A	I	J	K	L	M	N
1							
2		y 1996 Budget					
3							
4		August	September	October	November	December	TOTAL
5							
6	SALES						
7							
8	Clothing	$180,000	$172,000	$175,000	$160,000	$390,000	$2,297,000
9	Hard Goods	$120,000	$115,000	$118,000	$110,000	$280,000	$1,572,000
10	Total Sales	$300,000	$287,000	$293,000	$270,000	$670,000	$3,869,000
11							
12	EXPENSES						
13							
14	Advertising	$12,000	$11,480	$11,720	$10,800	$26,800	$154,760
15	Cost of Goods	$174,000	$166,460	$169,940	$156,600	$388,600	$2,244,020
16	Salary	$32,000	$32,000	$32,000	$32,000	$32,000	$384,000
17	Lease	$19,000	$19,000	$19,000	$19,000	$19,000	$228,000
18	Miscellaneous	$16,000	$16,000	$16,000	$16,000	$16,000	$192,000
19	Overhead	$22,000	$22,000	$22,000	$22,000	$22,000	$264,000
20	Total Expenses	$275,000	$266,940	$270,660	$256,400	$504,400	$3,466,780

Press ALT to choose commands, or F2 to edit.

Column A remains frozen in the window while columns I through N scroll into view. This makes reading the spreadsheet much easier.

To unfreeze or clear the frozen column,

Choose: Format>Freeze Titles

> The checkmark next to Freeze Titles shows that this option is in use.

Columns B through H are displayed again. The highlight however, is still in cell N1. To confirm that column A is unfrozen,

Press: Home

Column A is no longer frozen, and the highlight is positioned in cell A1.

SPREADSHEET

Titles can also be frozen across a row as easily as they are frozen down a column. To indicate the row to freeze, move the highlight one row below the row to be frozen. To freeze the column headings in row 4,

Move to: A5

Choose: Forma**t**>Freeze **T**itles

A solid vertical line below row 4 shows where the window is frozen.

Move to: A29

Your screen should be similar to Figure 7-5.

FIGURE 7-5

frozen column
headings

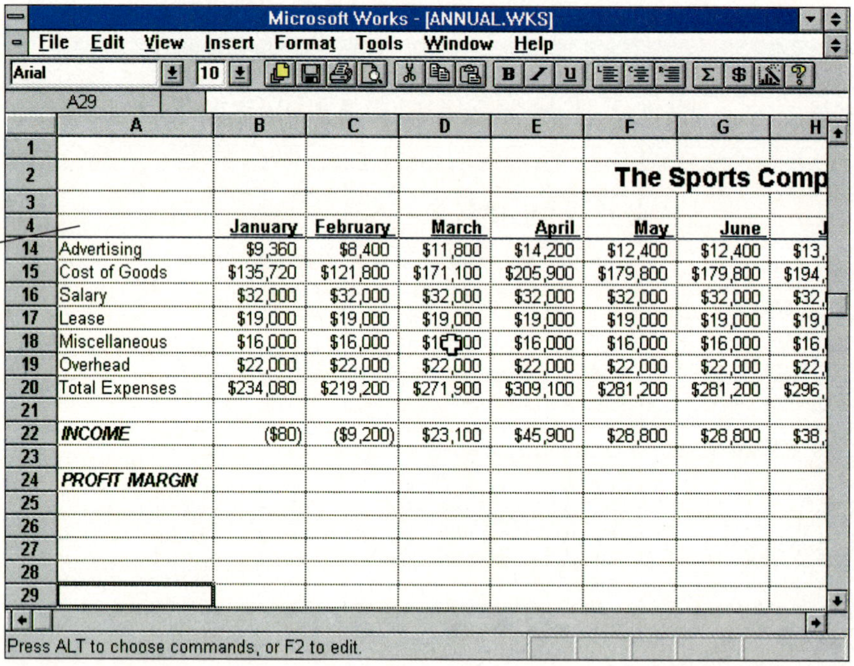

Rows 1 through 4 remain stationary in the window as you scrolled down through the spreadsheet.
Using ➡,

Move to: N29

Although the month headings have remained stationary in the window with the row headings unfrozen, it is again difficult to read the spreadsheet. Conveniently both column and row titles can be frozen at the same time. To quickly return to cell A5,

When the spreadsheet has frozen titles, the Home position is the upper-left corner of the unfrozen spreadsheet area.

Press: Ctrl + Home

Clear the frozen titles.

To freeze both the row and column titles at the same time, move the highlight one row below the rows to be frozen and one column to the right of the columns to be frozen.

Move to: B5
Choose: Format>Freeze Titles

The rows above and the column to the left of the highlight position are frozen. Solid vertical and horizontal lines appear to show the location where the spreadsheet is frozen. Watch your screen carefully as you use your arrow keys to,

Move to: N5
Move to: N29

Your screen should be similar to Figure 7-6.

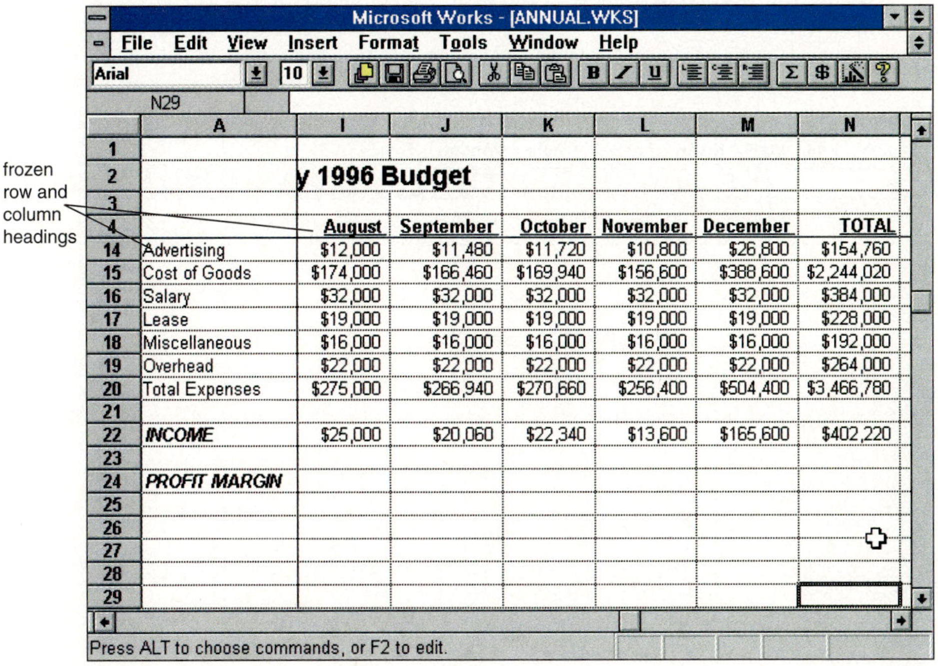

FIGURE 7-6

frozen row and column headings

	A	I	J	K	L	M	N
1							
2		y 1996 Budget					
3							
4		**August**	**September**	**October**	**November**	**December**	**TOTAL**
14	Advertising	$12,000	$11,480	$11,720	$10,800	$26,800	$154,760
15	Cost of Goods	$174,000	$166,460	$169,940	$156,600	$388,600	$2,244,020
16	Salary	$32,000	$32,000	$32,000	$32,000	$32,000	$384,000
17	Lease	$19,000	$19,000	$19,000	$19,000	$19,000	$228,000
18	Miscellaneous	$16,000	$16,000	$16,000	$16,000	$16,000	$192,000
19	Overhead	$22,000	$22,000	$22,000	$22,000	$22,000	$264,000
20	Total Expenses	$275,000	$266,940	$270,660	$256,400	$504,400	$3,466,780
21							
22	*INCOME*	$25,000	$20,060	$22,340	$13,600	$165,600	$402,220
23							
24	*PROFIT MARGIN*						
25							
26							
27							
28							
29							

Press ALT to choose commands, or F2 to edit.

Both the row and column titles remain stationary in the window as you scroll through the spreadsheet.

Press: Ctrl + Home

The Home position is now the upper left corner of the unfrozen rows and columns, cell B5.

SPREADSHEET

Calculating a Percentage

Now you are ready to enter the formula to calculate the profit margin in cell B24. Using ⬇,

Move to: B24

The formula to calculate the monthly profit margin divides the monthly total sales by the monthly income.

Enter the formula =B22/B10 in cell B24.

The number –0.0003419 is displayed in cell B24. You want to change the display of this number to a percent with two decimal places. To do this,

Choose: Forma**t**>**N**umber>**P**ercent>OK

The profit margin for January is now displayed as –0.03%.

Using Fill Right, copy the formula in cell B24 across the row through the Total column (N24).

Your screen should be similar to Figure 7-7.

FIGURE 7-7

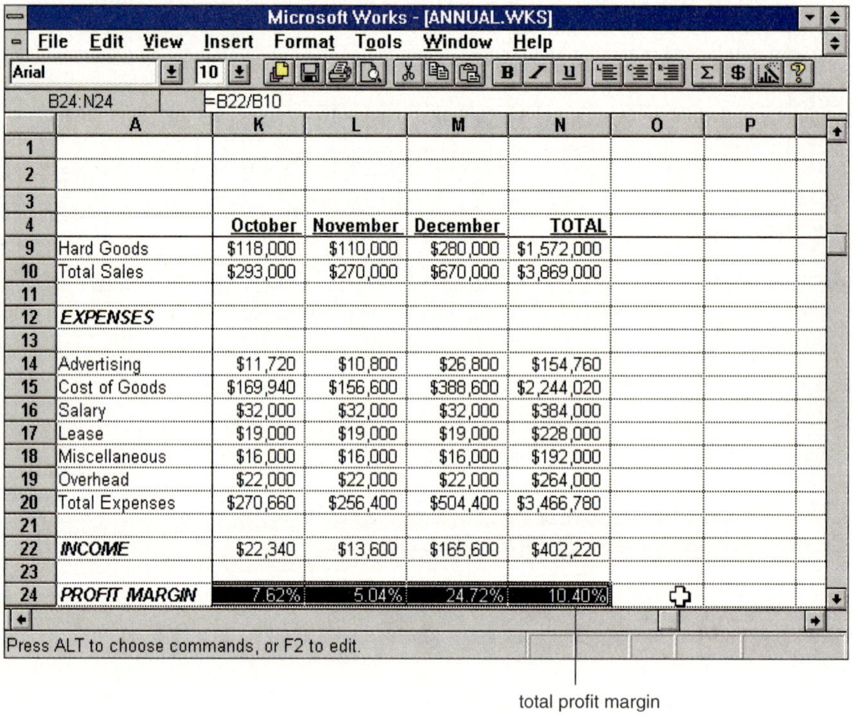

	A	K	L	M	N	O	P
1							
2							
3							
4		October	November	December	TOTAL		
9	Hard Goods	$118,000	$110,000	$280,000	$1,572,000		
10	Total Sales	$293,000	$270,000	$670,000	$3,869,000		
11							
12	EXPENSES						
13							
14	Advertising	$11,720	$10,800	$26,800	$154,760		
15	Cost of Goods	$169,940	$156,600	$388,600	$2,244,020		
16	Salary	$32,000	$32,000	$32,000	$384,000		
17	Lease	$19,000	$19,000	$19,000	$228,000		
18	Miscellaneous	$16,000	$16,000	$16,000	$192,000		
19	Overhead	$22,000	$22,000	$22,000	$264,000		
20	Total Expenses	$270,660	$256,400	$504,400	$3,466,780		
21							
22	INCOME	$22,340	$13,600	$165,600	$402,220		
23							
24	PROFIT MARGIN	7.62%	5.04%	24.72%	10.40%		

Press ALT to choose commands, or F2 to edit.

total profit margin

Notice that not only was the formula copied, but also the cell format. The total profit margin for the year displayed in cell N24 is 10.40%.

As you can see, the frozen titles make it much easier to use a large spreadsheet.

Using What-If Analysis

The manager wants the store to show a total profit margin of 13 percent. Using the figures as budgeted for the year, the total profit margin of 10.40 percent is below this objective.

After some consideration, you decide that the only way to increase the total profit margin is to reduce expenses. Salary expenses can be reduced by scheduling fewer employees to work during slow periods.

The process of evaluating what effect reducing the salary expenses will have on the total profit margin is called **what-if analysis**. What-if analysis is a technique used to evaluate the effects of changing selected factors in a spreadsheet. You want to know what would happen if salary expenses decreased a set amount each month.

First you want to see the effect of reducing the salary expenses to $30,000 per month.

Move to: B16

Type: 30000

Press: ←Enter

Your screen should be similar to Figure 7-8.

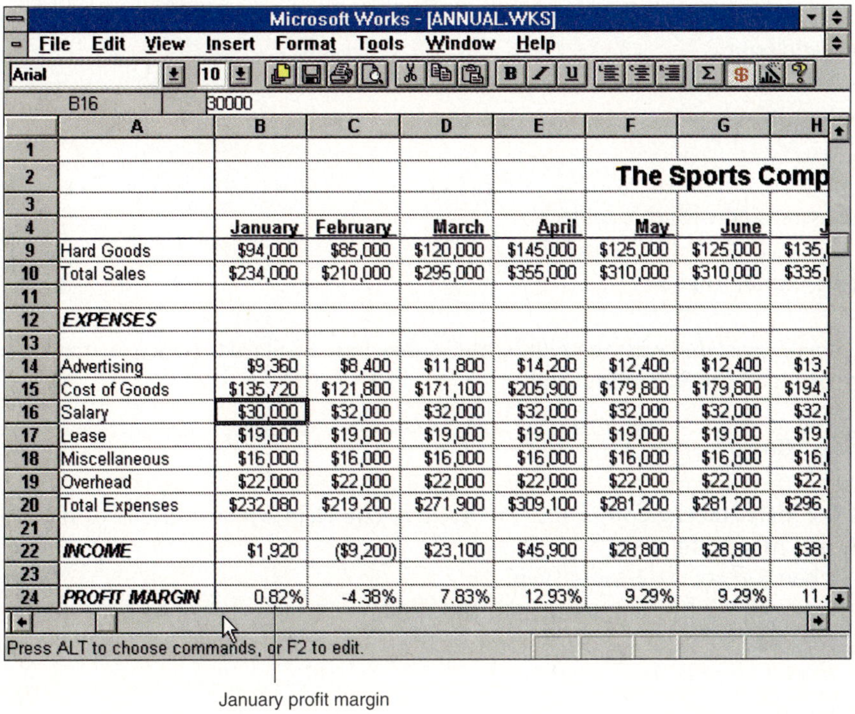

FIGURE 7-8

January profit margin

The January profit margin has changed from –.03 percent to .82 percent.

To quickly move to the last used cell in this row to see how this change has affected the total profit margin,

Press: End

The total profit margin (in cell N24) increased from 10.40 to 10.45 percent.

Splitting the Window

Although the frozen titles greatly improve the readability of the spreadsheet, it is still difficult to compare the values in columns that cannot be viewed in the same window. Rather than having to keep scrolling the window to see the effect on the total profit margin, you would like column N to remain visible in the window while you change the salary expense numbers. This way you can easily compare the numbers in each month to the numbers in the Total column. To do this you can split the window into two or four areas called **panes**.

Before splitting the window, you must unfreeze the Titles.
Clear the frozen titles.

Press: [Home]

The Split command on the Window menu lets you split the window horizontally and vertically into panes. You can divide the window into two side-by-side panes, two upper and lower panes, or four panes. For Help information about this feature,

Choose: Help>Search for Help on
Type: S

Notice that the list box has jumped to words that begin with S. To continue to move to the Help topic,

Type: PL

The Splitting Document Windows subject area is displayed in the list box. To see the topics associated with this subject,

> You can double-click on the subject to display the topics.

Choose: Show Topics

Two topics associated with the highlighted subject are displayed. To display the Help information on the Split command,

> You can double-click on the topic to select and go to the Help window on the topic.

Choose: Go To

Read the Help information about this feature. The Help window discusses how to create and move split panes.
When you are done, close Help.
You will use this feature to split the window into four panes so that you can easily compare the values in each month to the values in column N, TOTAL.

Choose: Window>Split

Your screen should be similar to Figure 7-9.

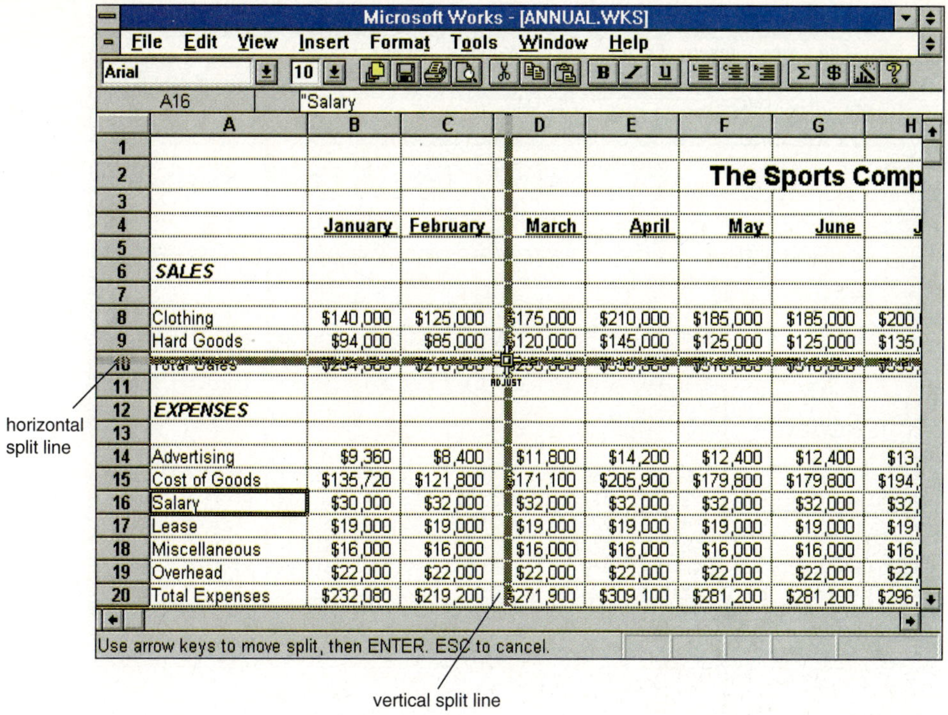

FIGURE 7-9

horizontal split line

vertical split line

Horizontal and vertical split lines appear in the window. The split lines divide the window into quarters. To create panes you position the split lines where you want the panes to be displayed in the window.

The status line displays information about how to move split lines. You move the horizontal split line by using the ⬆ and ⬇ keys and the vertical split line by using the ➡ and ⬅ keys.

Press: ➡ (10 times)

The vertical split line has moved 10 spaces to the right.

Press: ⬆ (2 times)

The horizontal split line has moved up two rows.

Position the vertical split line between columns F and G and the horizontal split below row 4 (see Figure 7-10 on the next page).

To complete the command,

Press: ←Enter

Instead of using the arrow keys, you can drag the split lines to the location where you want a split.

SPREADSHEET

Your screen should be similar to Figure 7-10.

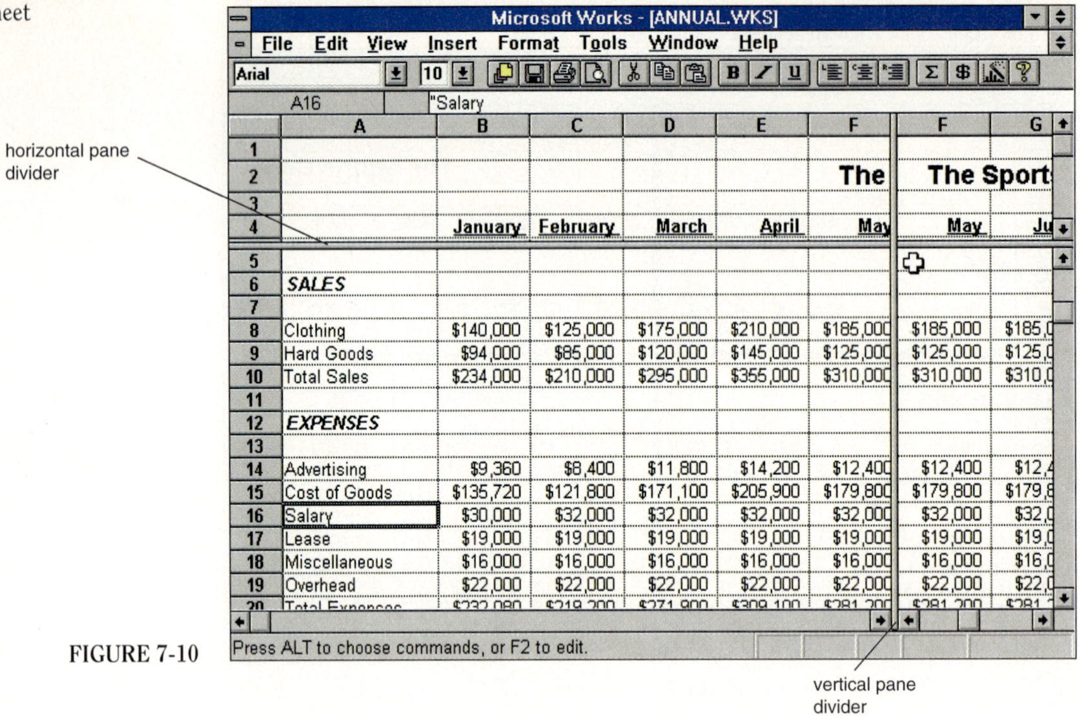

horizontal pane
divider

	A	B	C	D	E	F	F	G
1								
2						The	The Sport	
3								
4		January	February	March	April	May	May	Ju
5								
6	SALES							
7								
8	Clothing	$140,000	$125,000	$175,000	$210,000	$185,000	$185,000	$185,0
9	Hard Goods	$94,000	$85,000	$120,000	$145,000	$125,000	$125,000	$125,0
10	Total Sales	$234,000	$210,000	$295,000	$355,000	$310,000	$310,000	$310,0
11								
12	EXPENSES							
13								
14	Advertising	$9,360	$8,400	$11,800	$14,200	$12,400	$12,400	$12,4
15	Cost of Goods	$135,720	$121,800	$171,100	$205,900	$179,800	$179,800	$179,8
16	Salary	$30,000	$32,000	$32,000	$32,000	$32,000	$32,000	$32,0
17	Lease	$19,000	$19,000	$19,000	$19,000	$19,000	$19,000	$19,0
18	Miscellaneous	$16,000	$16,000	$16,000	$16,000	$16,000	$16,000	$16,0
19	Overhead	$22,000	$22,000	$22,000	$22,000	$22,000	$22,000	$22,0
20	Total Expenses	$232,080	$219,200	$271,900	$309,100	$281,200	$281,200	$281

A16   "Salary

Press ALT to choose commands, or F2 to edit.

FIGURE 7-10

vertical pane
divider

The window is divided into four panes. The upper panes still display the months. Each pane has its own scroll bar. The highlight is positioned in the bottom left pane. This is the **active pane**.

Watch your screen carefully as you use ↓ to

Move to: A24

Your screen should be similar to Figure 7-11.

FIGURE 7-11

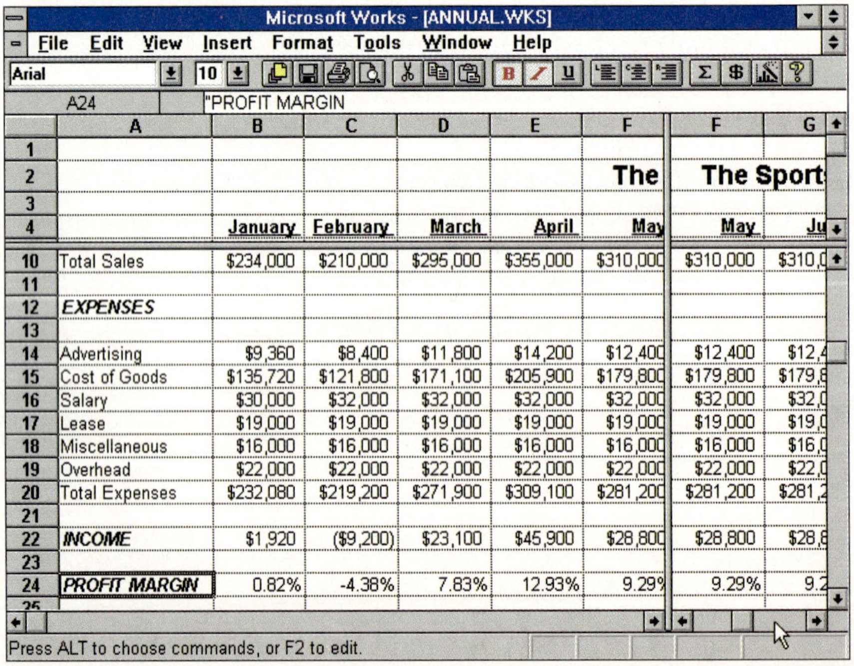

A24   "PROFIT MARGIN

	A	B	C	D	E	F	F	G
1								
2						The	The Sport	
3								
4		January	February	March	April	May	May	Ju
10	Total Sales	$234,000	$210,000	$295,000	$355,000	$310,000	$310,000	$310,0
11								
12	EXPENSES							
13								
14	Advertising	$9,360	$8,400	$11,800	$14,200	$12,400	$12,400	$12,4
15	Cost of Goods	$135,720	$121,800	$171,100	$205,900	$179,800	$179,800	$179,8
16	Salary	$30,000	$32,000	$32,000	$32,000	$32,000	$32,000	$32,0
17	Lease	$19,000	$19,000	$19,000	$19,000	$19,000	$19,000	$19,0
18	Miscellaneous	$16,000	$16,000	$16,000	$16,000	$16,000	$16,000	$16,0
19	Overhead	$22,000	$22,000	$22,000	$22,000	$22,000	$22,000	$22,0
20	Total Expenses	$232,080	$219,200	$271,900	$309,100	$281,200	$281,200	$281,2
21								
22	INCOME	$1,920	($9,200)	$23,100	$45,900	$28,800	$28,800	$28,8
23								
24	PROFIT MARGIN	0.82%	-4.38%	7.83%	12.93%	9.29%	9.29%	9.2
25								

Press ALT to choose commands, or F2 to edit.

The rows in both bottom panes scroll together. The upper panes do not move.

You can move the highlight from one pane to the other using `F6` to move clockwise through the panes or `⇧ Shift` + `F6` to move counter-clockwise.

Click: cell F24 in the lower right pane
or
Press: `⇧ Shift` + `F6`

If you have a mouse you can switch from one pane to another by clicking anywhere in the pane you want to make active.

Note: If you accidentally press `F6`, you will move into the upper pane. The rows in the upper pane will adjust to the same rows as the lower panes. To reset the rows to show the months, scroll to row 1. Then return to the lower left pane by pressing `⇧ Shift` + `F6`.

The highlight is positioned in cell F24 in the lower right pane.

Press: `End`

The Total column is visible in the pane. The columns in the left pane do not move as the highlight moves across the row in the right pane. Now the January through May data displayed in the left pane can easily be compared to the total values displayed in the right pane. Splitting the window into panes lets you view different parts of the same spreadsheet. Any changes made in one pane are made to the entire spreadsheet and can be seen in either pane.

To return to the lower left pane,

Click: A24
or
Press: `F6`

Now you are ready to see what effect reducing the salary expenses to $30,000 for each month has on the total profit margin.

To see the effect of reducing the salary expenses to $30,000 for each month on the total profit margin, copy the January salary value to the February through December salary cells.

Your screen should be similar to Figure 7-12.

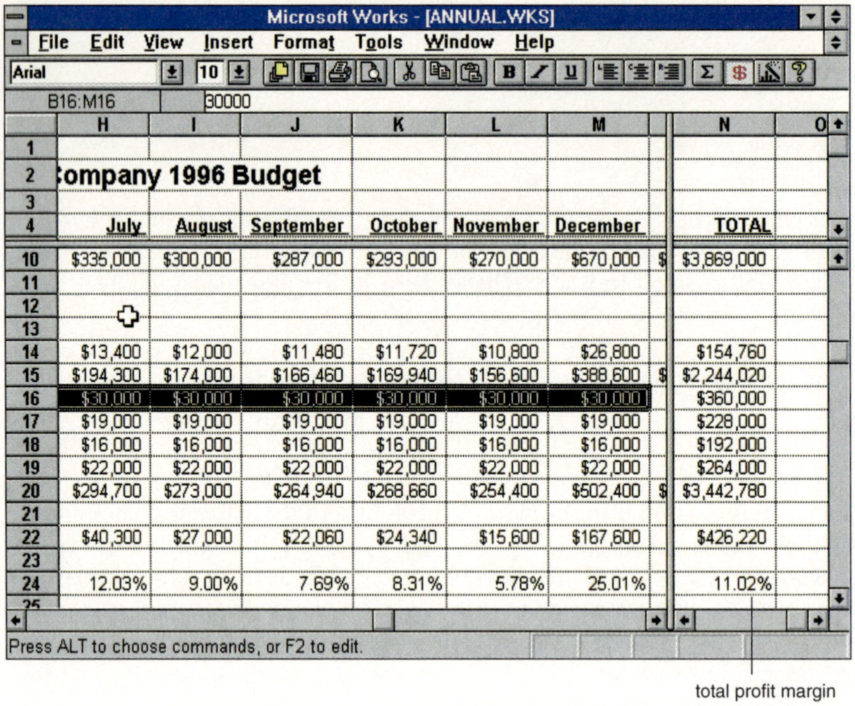

FIGURE 7-12

total profit margin

The spreadsheet has been recalculated. Reducing the salary expenses to $30,000 per month has increased the total profit margin from 10.45 to 11.02 percent. This is still not enough.

You realize that it may take several tries before you reduce the salary expenses enough to arrive at a total profit margin of 13 percent. Each time you change the salary expense, you have to copy the value across the entire row. A quicker way to enter different salary expense values into the spreadsheet is by using any blank cell outside of the spreadsheet area to hold the what-if value.

You will use cell B26 in the lower left pane to hold the what-if value. First, you will enter a descriptive label in A26.

Move to: A26
Type: Salary Value
Press: →

This time you will decrease salary expenses to $26,000 per month. To enter this number in the what-if cell,

Type: 26000
Press: ←Enter

The what-if value needs to be copied into the salary expense cells in the spreadsheet. To do this, a formula referencing cell B26 is entered in the salary expense cells. This formula will tell the program to enter the value in cell B26 into the cell.

Move to: B16

To enter the formula =B26 in cell B16, using pointing,

Type: **=**

Move to: **B26**

Press: ⬅Enter

Your screen should be similar to Figure 7-13.

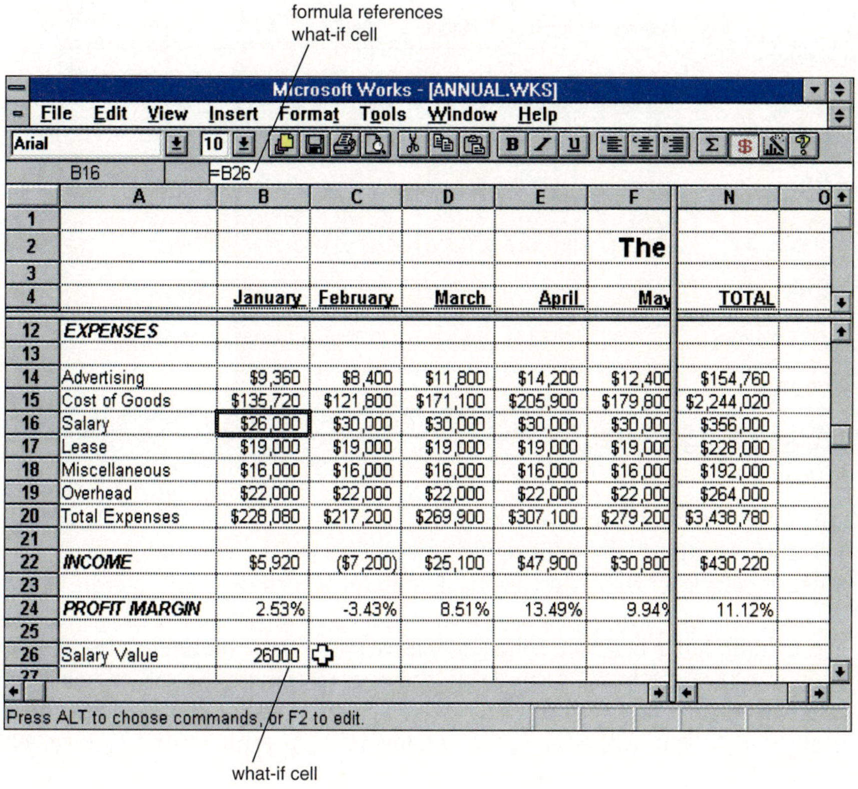

formula references
what-if cell

FIGURE 7-13

	A	B	C	D	E	F	N	O
	B16		=B26					
1								
2						The		
3								
4		January	February	March	April	May	TOTAL	
12	EXPENSES							
13								
14	Advertising	$9,360	$8,400	$11,800	$14,200	$12,400	$154,760	
15	Cost of Goods	$135,720	$121,800	$171,100	$205,900	$179,800	$2,244,020	
16	Salary	$26,000	$30,000	$30,000	$30,000	$30,000	$356,000	
17	Lease	$19,000	$19,000	$19,000	$19,000	$19,000	$228,000	
18	Miscellaneous	$16,000	$16,000	$16,000	$16,000	$16,000	$192,000	
19	Overhead	$22,000	$22,000	$22,000	$22,000	$22,000	$264,000	
20	Total Expenses	$228,080	$217,200	$269,900	$307,100	$279,200	$3,438,780	
21								
22	INCOME	$5,920	($7,200)	$25,100	$47,900	$30,800	$430,220	
23								
24	PROFIT MARGIN	2.53%	-3.43%	8.51%	13.49%	9.94%	11.12%	
25								
26	Salary Value	26000						
27								

Press ALT to choose commands, or F2 to edit.

what-if cell

The value of $26,000 is entered in cell B16.

Copy the formula in the January salary cell to the February through December salary cells using Fill Right.

To clear the highlight,

Press: ⬅

The spreadsheet again has been recalculated. However, there is something wrong. The number 26,000 should appear in cells C16 through M16. Instead 0 appears in those cells.

Move to: **C16**

Your screen should be similar to Figure 7-14.

copied formula with
relative cell reference

	A	B	C	D	E	F	N	O
1								
2						The		
3								
4		January	February	March	April	May	TOTAL	
12	EXPENSES							
13								
14	Advertising	$9,360	$8,400	$11,800	$14,200	$12,400	$154,760	
15	Cost of Goods	$135,720	$121,800	$171,100	$205,900	$179,800	$2,244,020	
16	Salary	$26,000	$0	$0	$0	$0	$26,000	
17	Lease	$19,000	$19,000	$19,000	$19,000	$19,000	$228,000	
18	Miscellaneous	$16,000	$16,000	$16,000	$16,000	$16,000	$192,000	
19	Overhead	$22,000	$22,000	$22,000	$22,000	$22,000	$264,000	
20	Total Expenses	$228,080	$187,200	$239,900	$277,100	$249,200	$3,108,780	
21								
22	INCOME	$5,920	$22,800	$55,100	$77,900	$60,800	$760,220	
23								
24	PROFIT MARGIN	2.53%	10.86%	18.68%	21.94%	19.61%	19.65%	
25								
26	Salary Value	26000						
27								

Press ALT to choose commands, or F2 to edit.

FIGURE 7-14

The formula bar shows the formula in this cell to be =C26, which is a blank cell. Since it contains nothing, the value of 0 is entered in C16.

Move to cells D16, E16, and F16. Look at how the formula changes from =D26 to =E26 and =F26.

The column letter has been adjusted relative to the new column location of the formula in row 16. Each of the formulas in the cells references the cell one column to the right of the previous formula. They were adjusted relative to their location in the spreadsheet. As you learned in Lab 6, the formula was copied using relative cell references.

Using Absolute Cell References

The formula in B16 needs to be entered so that the column in the referenced cell, B26, will not change when the formula is copied. To do this, you will use an **absolute cell reference**.

Move to: B16

To change the formula in B16 to have an absolute cell reference, enter a $ (dollar sign) character in front of the column letter. You can enter the dollar sign character by typing it in directly or you can use the F4 key. Pressing F4 repeatedly cycles a cell address through all possible combinations of cell reference types. When using F4 you must be using pointing to specify the cell reference in the formula. To reenter the formula,

Point must be displayed in the status bar in order for the F4 key to function.

Type: =
Move to: B26

The POINT indicator appears in the status bar.

To change this cell reference in the formula bar to absolute,

Press:　F4

The cell reference now displays a $ character before both the column letter and row number (B26). Because a dollar sign is entered before both the column letter and row number, this cell address is absolute.

Press:　F4

The cell reference has changed to display a dollar sign before the row number only (B$26). This is a **mixed cell reference** because only the row number is preceded by a $ character, not the column letter. A mixed cell reference contains both relative and absolute cell references.

Press:　F4

Again this is a mixed cell reference. This time the $ character precedes the column letter.

Press:　F4

The formula returns to relative cell references. You have cycled the cell reference through all possible combinations of cell reference types.

To review, the table below shows an example of absolute, mixed, and relative referencing using cell B16 and the results when it is copied to cell E13.

Cell	Copied To	Results	Type of Reference
B16	E13	B16	Absolute cell reference
B$16	E13	E$16	Mixed cell reference
$B16	E13	$B13	Mixed cell reference
B16	E13	E13	Relative cell reference

To stop the relative adjustment of the column in the formula when it is copied from one column location to another in the same row, the formula needs to be a mixed cell reference with the column letter absolute. To make this change,

> The cell reference could also be changed to absolute and it would perform correctly.

Press:　F4　(3 times)

To accept the formula as displayed in the formula bar (=$B26),

Press:　←Enter

Copy this formula from the January salary cell to the February through December salary cells using Fill Right.

To clear the highlight,

Press:　←

The number $26,000 appears in each cell in row 16.

Move to:　C16

SPREADSHEET

Your screen should be similar to Figure 7-15.

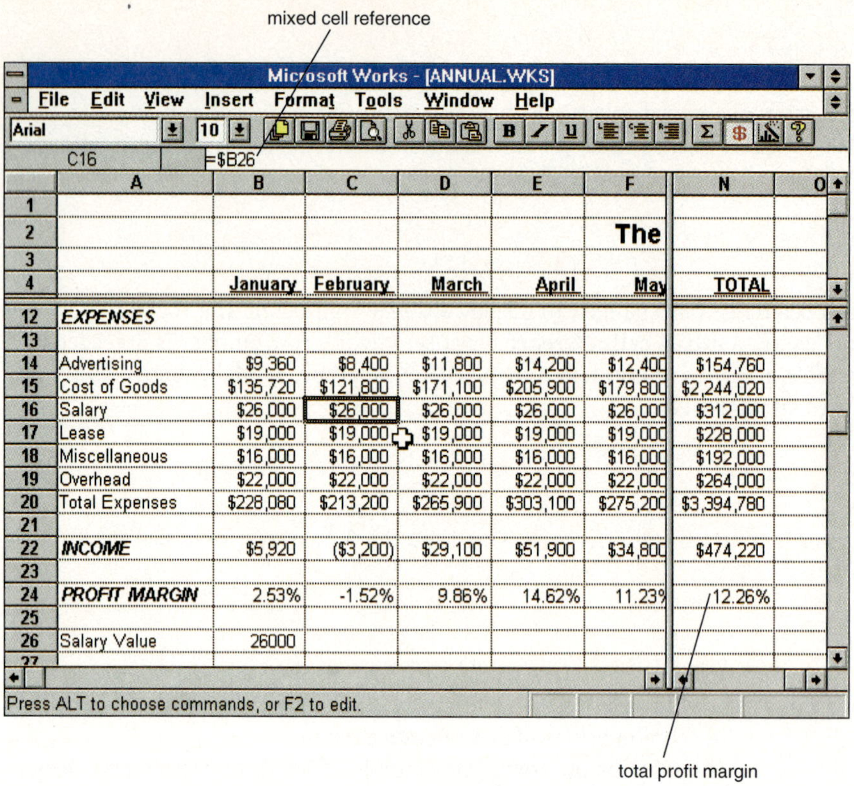

mixed cell reference

	A	B	C	D	E	F	N	O
2						**The**		
3								
4		January	February	March	April	May	TOTAL	
12	EXPENSES							
13								
14	Advertising	$9,360	$8,400	$11,800	$14,200	$12,400	$154,760	
15	Cost of Goods	$135,720	$121,800	$171,100	$205,900	$179,800	$2,244,020	
16	Salary	$26,000	$26,000	$26,000	$26,000	$26,000	$312,000	
17	Lease	$19,000	$19,000	$19,000	$19,000	$19,000	$228,000	
18	Miscellaneous	$16,000	$16,000	$16,000	$16,000	$16,000	$192,000	
19	Overhead	$22,000	$22,000	$22,000	$22,000	$22,000	$264,000	
20	Total Expenses	$228,080	$213,200	$265,900	$303,100	$275,200	$3,394,780	
21								
22	INCOME	$5,920	($3,200)	$29,100	$51,900	$34,800	$474,220	
23								
24	PROFIT MARGIN	2.53%	-1.52%	9.86%	14.62%	11.23%	12.26%	
25								
26	Salary Value	26000						

C16 =$B26

Press ALT to choose commands, or F2 to edit.

FIGURE 7-15

total profit margin

The formula displayed in the formula bar is an exact duplicate of the formula in B16. It references cell B26. Using a mixed cell reference in the formula easily solved the problem. It stopped the relative adjustment of the cells in the copied formula by maintaining the particular cell coordinate.

The result of decreasing the salary expenses to $26,000 each month has increased the total profit margin to 12.26 percent (cell N24). This is closer to the 13 percent management objective, but it is still not good enough.

Decrease the salary expense value in cell B26 to $23,000.

Your screen should be similar to Figure 7-16.

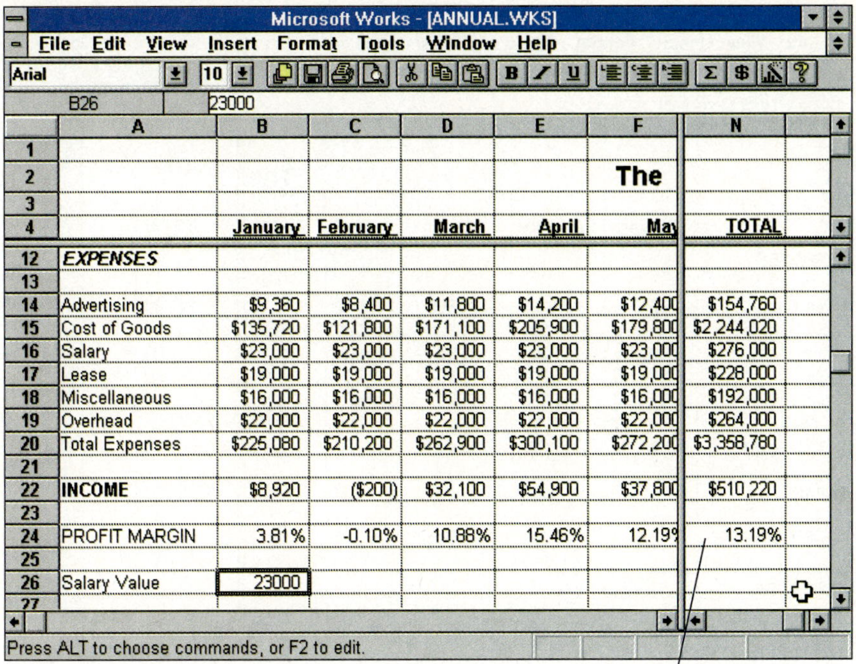

```
┌────────────────────────────────────────────────────────────────────────┐
│ ═                    Microsoft Works - [ANNUAL.WKS]              ▼  ♦    │
│ ═  File   Edit   View   Insert   Format   Tools   Window   Help      ♦  │
│ Arial        ± 10 ±  🗀 🖫 🖨 🔍  ✂ 📋 📋  B I U ≣ ≣ ≣ Σ $ 📊 ？       │
│     B26              23000                                               │
│        A          B        C        D         E         F        N     ♦ │
│  1                                                                       │
│  2                                             The                       │
│  3                                                                       │
│  4            January February  March    April    May    TOTAL        ♦ │
│ 12  EXPENSES                                                           ♦ │
│ 13                                                                       │
│ 14 Advertising   $9,360   $8,400  $11,800  $14,200  $12,400  $154,760   │
│ 15 Cost of Goods$135,720 $121,800 $171,100 $205,900 $179,800 $2,244,020 │
│ 16 Salary       $23,000  $23,000  $23,000  $23,000  $23,000  $276,000   │
│ 17 Lease        $19,000  $19,000  $19,000  $19,000  $19,000  $228,000   │
│ 18 Miscellaneous$16,000  $16,000  $16,000  $16,000  $16,000  $192,000   │
│ 19 Overhead     $22,000  $22,000  $22,000  $22,000  $22,000  $264,000   │
│ 20 Total Expenses$225,080 $210,200 $262,900 $300,100 $272,200 $3,358,780│
│ 21                                                                       │
│ 22  INCOME       $8,920   ($200)  $32,100  $54,900  $37,800  $510,220   │
│ 23                                                                       │
│ 24 PROFIT MARGIN  3.81%   -0.10%  10.88%   15.46%   12.19%   13.19%     │
│ 25                                                                       │
│ 26 Salary Value   23000                                             ⊕   │
│ 27                                                                       │
│ ♦ ◄                                              ►  ◄            ►      │
│ Press ALT to choose commands, or F2 to edit.                            │
└────────────────────────────────────────────────────────────────────────┘
```

total profit margin

FIGURE 7-16

The value in B26 was quickly entered into the salary expense cells in row 16 for each month and the spreadsheet was recalculated. By using a cell to hold the what-if value and referencing the cell in a formula in the spreadsheet using absolute cell referencing, changing the what-if value becomes a simple process.

The total profit margin is now 13.19 percent. This is too much. Try 24000.

The total profit margin is now 12.88 percent. That is too low. You know the appropriate salary expense level is between $23,000 and $24,000. Try 23500. The total profit margin is now 13.03 percent. Now try 23600.

Your screen should be similar to Figure 7-17.

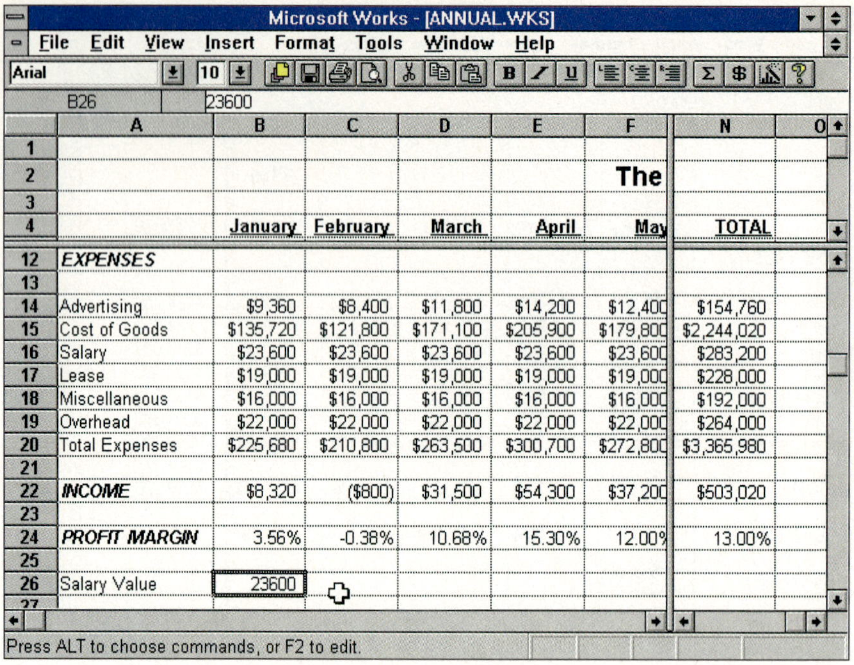

FIGURE 7-17

That's it! The total profit margin is 13 percent.

Now that you are finished, you can remove the split panes from the window.

Choose: Window>Split

The horizontal and vertical split lines needs to be moved out of the work area. To do this quickly,

> You can drag the split line out of the window.

Press: Home

Press: ←Enter

The window is no longer divided into panes.

To return to cell A1,

Press: Ctrl + Home

Adding Borders

Before presenting the spreadsheet to the store manager, you want to enhance its appearance by adding an outline border around the title and a bottom border below several rows of data.

An outline border adds a border line around the outer edge of the selected cell or range. To add an outline border around the range of cells displaying the spreadsheet title,

Select: F2 through J2

Choose: Format>Border

The Border dialog box options are the same options as those in the Border command in the word processor tool. In the spreadsheet the selected border type is added to the cell or range. The default border is Outline. This is the appropriate setting.

The sample box displays the default border line style. It is a single light line. To change the border style to the heaviest line style, from the Line Style box,

Select: heaviest single-line style (last option in list)
Choose: OK

To clear the highlight,

Press: ← (2 times)

Your screen should be similar to Figure 7-18.

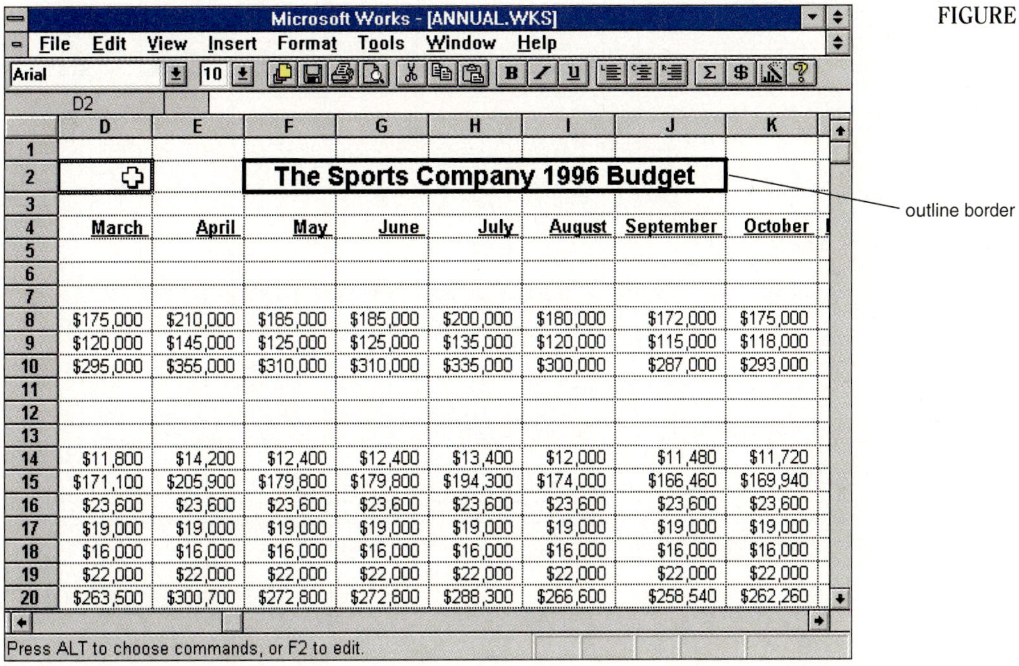

FIGURE 7-18

The range of cells containing the spreadsheet title is outlined with a heavy single-line border.

Next you want to add a single line below the Hard Goods row of data to separate it from the Total Sales row of data.

Select: B9 through N9
Choose: Format>Border>Bottom>OK

Press: Home

> To remove a border, choose the command again and choose the first line style (blank).

The range displays a solid line along the bottom border of the range. The solid line creates a visual separation between the numbers being summed and the total sales numbers.

Next you want to add the same type of line below the Overhead row of data to separate it from the Total Expenses row.

Add a single-line border below the Overhead row of data.

The solid line is added below the selected range of cells.

Finally, you want to add a double line below the income numbers in cells B22 through N22.

Add a double-line border below the Income row of data.

Move to: A22

Your screen should be similar to Figure 7-19.

FIGURE 7-19

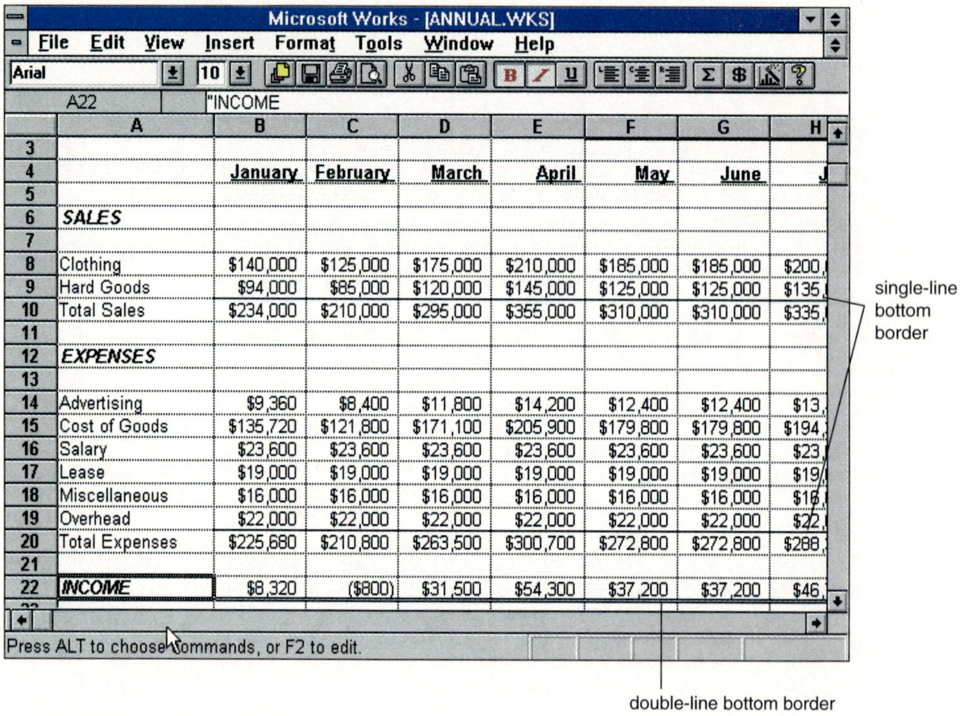

single-line bottom border

double-line bottom border

Adding Headers

Now that the spreadsheet is complete, you need to add your name and the date as the spreadsheet documentation. Instead of entering them in a spreadsheet cell, you will add the information to be printed as a header. This is the same as adding a header to a word processing document. To add a header,

Choose: View>Headers and Footers

The Headers and Footers dialog box is displayed. In the Header text box,

The codes are the same as in the word processor. For information about the codes, refer to page 119.

Type: [Your Name] - &d
Choose: OK

Setting Up the Printed Page

Note: You will be printing in this section. If necessary first select the correct printer for your computer (File>Printer Setup).

Note: Not all printers can print using landscape orientation or in smaller font sizes. If your printer does not have these capabilities, print your spreadsheet on two pages.

You want to print the entire budget on one page. Because the spreadsheet is very wide, you will have to change the orientation (layout of the printed worksheet on the paper) of the spreadsheet to print across the length of the paper (landscape style). To specify landscape,

Choose: File>Page Setup>Source, Size and Orientation>Landscape>OK

Next, to see if this change allows the entire spreadsheet to print on a page,

Choose: File>Print Preview

or

Click: 📷 Print Preview

Your screen should be similar to Figure 7-20.

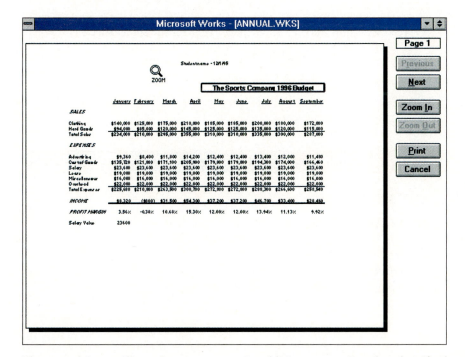

FIGURE 7-20

The spreadsheet still requires two pages. In addition, you notice the what-if value at the bottom of the spreadsheet. You do not want the printout to include the what-if value. To see the next page,

Choose: Next

Several columns of data still appear on this page. To close the Preview window,

Choose: Cancel

You want to change the print settings to exclude the what-if value, and to reduce the margins and the print size to try to fit the spreadsheet on one page. To set the print range so the what-if cell does not print,

Select: A1 through N24
Choose: Forma**t**>**S**et Print Area>OK

Then, to reduce the size of the margins,

Choose: **F**ile>Pa**g**e Setup>**M**argins

The default left and right margins are 1.25 inches.
   Change the left and right margins to .5 inch.

Choose: OK

   Finally, to reduce the print size of the characters, excluding the title,

Select: A3 through N24

Reduce the type size to 8. Best Fit the selection to adjust the column widths. Clear the highlight.
   To see how these changes have affected the printout, preview the spreadsheet. The spreadsheet now fits on a single page. To print the spreadsheet,

Choose: **P**rint

Save the spreadsheet as BUDGET. Exit Works.

> The margins folder is the same as in the Word Processor tool.

Key Terms

circular reference (229)
freeze (230)
what-if analysis (235)
pane (236)
active pane (238)
absolute cell reference (242)
mixed cell reference (243)

Command Summary

Command	Action
Forma**t**>Freeze **T**itles	Freezes/unfreezes titles to top and left of active cell
Forma**t**>**N**umber>**P**ercent	Displays numbers followed by a % sign
Help>**S**earch for Help on	Searches for help on any command or feature
Window>**S**plit	Splits window into panes
Forma**t**>**B**order>**O**utline	Adds border around entire cell or range
Forma**t**>**B**order>Botto**m**	Adds border to bottom edge of selected cell or range
View>**H**eaders and Footers	Adds headers and/or footers to the file
Forma**t**>**S**et Print Area	Restricts area to print to selected range
File>Pa**g**e Setup>**M**argins	Changes size of page margins

LAB REVIEW

Matching

1. CIRC _____ a. an absolute cell reference
2. pane _____ b. cycles cell reference through all possible cell reference types
3. $C25 _____ c. technique used to evaluate effects of changing selected factors
4. outline border _____ d. one fourth of a divided window
5. F4 _____ e. indicator for circular reference
6. what-if analysis _____ f. command that divides window into panes
7. C25 _____ g. command that fixes specified rows and/or columns in window
8. Window>Split _____ h. moves to next pane
9. Format>Freeze Titles _____ i. adds a border around all sides of selection
10. F6 _____ j. mixed cell reference

Fill-In Questions

1. Complete the following statements by filling in the blanks with the correct terms.

   a. A(n) _____ is displayed in the status bar when a formula in a cell either directly or indirectly references itself.

   b. When a column or row is _____, it is visible in the window all the time.

   c. A spreadsheet window can be split into two or four _____.

   d. To evaluate the effects of different values in a spreadsheet, you could use _____.

e. To stop a cell reference in a formula from adjusting relative to its new location when copied, you would use a(n) _____.

f. The _____ border option will draw a line around the entire selection.

g. When only one part of a cell reference is absolute, it is a(n) _____ cell reference.

h. The pane that displays the highlight is called the _____ pane.

i. The code _____ enters the date in a header.

j. To print only the highlighted cells, use the _____ command.

Practice Exercises

1. Barclay Jones has been working on an income statement for his custom framing and print gallery, ArtWorks. He has been having some problems. Open the file ART.WKS to see the spreadsheet Barclay has created.

a. Enter your name in cell A1 and the current date in cell A2.

b. Scroll the column headings so they are the top row in the window and freeze the column and row headings at cell B6.

c. In cell N7, enter the function to sum columns B through M. Copy the function down to cell N22. Clear any functions that reference blank cells.

d. The spreadsheet contains two additional columns, MAX and MIN. These columns will display the maximum and minimum values in each row of data. Enter the functions to calculate the maximum and minimum values in columns B through M. (Use Help for information on the MAX and MIN functions.) Copy the functions down the columns to row 22 and remove the formulas that reference blank cells.

e. Format all values to display as currency with two decimal places.

f. Enter the formula =(C22–B22)/C22 in cell C24 to calculate the percent change (increase or decrease) in February over January's net after taxes. Format the cell to display percent with zero decimal places. Copy the formula from cell C24 to cells D24 through M24.

g. Create a single-line top border above the values in the Gross Margin and Total Expenses rows of data. Create a double-line bottom border below the values in the Federal Taxes row of data.

h. Unfreeze the titles. Increase the font size of the titles in cells B1 through B3. Center the titles across columns B through P.

i. Decrease the font size of the row headings to 8pt. Decrease the font size of the column headings and the spreadsheet values to 6pt. Best Fit the columns. Change the left and right margins to .75. Change the orientation to landscape.

j. Preview the spreadsheet. Print the entire spreadsheet on one page. (Adjust margins and font sizes again if necessary.)

k. Save the spreadsheet as ARTWORKS.

2. To complete this problem, you must have created the spreadsheet in Practice Exercise 4 of Lab 6. Open the file PARKFIN2.WKS. You will extend and expand the spreadsheet for the three-year financial statement for the Parks and Recreation Director. The Director would like the financial statement to project the next three years, 1997, 1998, and 1999.

a. Format the spreadsheet to display currency with zero decimal places. Format the Average column to currency with two decimal places. Adjust the column widths to fully display the numbers.

b. Insert three columns between the 1996 and Total columns to hold the data for the projected years 1997, 1998, and 1999. Enter column headings for the three years (columns E, F, and G). Bold the new column headings.

c. Move the column headings to row 5. Enter the heading <<<<<<<<Projected>>>>>>>> centered above the years 1997 through 1999.

d. Freeze the row and column headings.

e. Enter formulas to calculate the projected expenses for the years 1997 through 1999. Operating expenses are expected to increase 17 percent each year over the previous year, capital projects 15 percent, and fund raising 6 percent.

f. Enter formulas based on the following information to calculate the projected income values for the years 1997 through 1999. The revenues projections are that operating revenues will increase 20 percent over the previous year, and interest income 18 percent. The fund-raising projected income is directly related to the amount of money allocated to fund-raising activities (row 16). For each dollar spent, they expect to raise $2.50.

g. The operating reserve (row 20) is calculated using the same formula as in previous years. Copy it across to the three projected years.

h. Copy the formulas to calculate the total revenue and total expenses for the years 1997 through 1999.

i. Change the formulas used to calculate the total and average to include the new columns. Unfreeze the titles. Underline rows 9 and 16, columns E through G.

In 1999 the Parks and Recreation Department plans to build five new swimming pools. The total cost of this project is $1.2 million. After looking at the results of the projected statement on the operating reserve, you realize that there will not be enough money for the new project. Currently the amount allocated toward fund raising is based upon a 6 percent increase over the previous year.

j. Using a what-if cell, adjust the amount that needs to be raised per dollar spent for cells E8, F8, and G8 until the total operating reserve is at least $1.2 million by the end of 1999.

k. Insert a blank row as row 1. Erase your name and date from cells A2 and A3. Center the spreadsheet title between columns A through I. Using the Format>Border feature, create a heavy outline border around the spreadsheet title.

l. Enter your name and the current date in a header. Save the spreadsheet as PARKFIN3.WKS.

m. Print the spreadsheet using landscape orientation. Do not include the what-if cell.

3.   Open the file CAFE.WKS. This is a spreadsheet of a one-year income statement for April's Flower Garden Cafe. The formulas in the spreadsheet are:

Row 10   Gross Margin = Sales – Cost of Goods Sold
Row 15   Total Expense = Marketing + Administrative + Miscellaneous Expenses
Row 17   Net Income Before Taxes = Gross Margin – Total Expense
Row 18   Federal Taxes = Net Income Before Taxes *.52
Row 19   Net Income After Taxes = Net Income Before Taxes – Federal Taxes

a.   Enter your name and the current date in a header.

b.   Bold and underline the month headings. Bold and enlarge the spreadsheet title lines to 12pt. Center the two title lines across the spreadsheet.

c.   Complete the Total column by summing the year's totals. Format the numbers to currency with no decimal places.

April wants to calculate the cost of goods sold as a percent of sales. She estimates that the cost of goods sold is about 35 percent of sales.

d.   Enter the formula to calculate the cost of goods sold (B8*.35) in cell B9.

e.   Copy the formula across the row. To see how this change affected total net income after taxes, look at the number in cell N19. What is the number?

April thinks she may have been too high in her estimate for the percent cost value. She wants to see the effect on the total of changing the percentage.

f.   Split the window into four panes so that the lower right pane displays the total column. Use cell B21 as the what-if cell. Enter the label Cost of Goods Sold in cell A21. Enter 35% in the Cost of Goods Sold what-if cell. Change the formulas in row 9 to reference the what-if cell for the percentage value. Check the value of cell N19.

g.   Change the what-if cell to calculate the cost of goods sold as 30 percent of sales.

April would also like to see the effect of changing the marketing, administrative, and miscellaneous expenses. By calculating these values as a percentage of the gross margin, she feels she will be able to plan and budget better for the future.

h.   Using the following percentages, label and create what-if cells and enter the formulas to calculate the expenses as a percentage of the gross margin:

MKT .08

ADM .04

MISC.02

i.   Copy the formulas across the rows. Check the total net income again.

j.   Adjust the what-if cell for the expenses until cell N19 is as close to 7900 as possible. Clear the window split.

    k. Change the orientation to landscape. Reduce the left and right margins and use a smaller font size as needed in order to print the spreadsheet on one page. Save the spreadsheet as CAFE1. Print the spreadsheet.

4. Bill Baron has been working on a six-month income statement for his model train shop. He has been having some problems. Open the file TRAIN.WKS to see the spreadsheet Bill has created.

    a. Enter your name in cell A1 and the current date in cell A2.

    b. Locate the source of the CIRC reference and correct the formula or function causing it. (*Hint:* Look in row 10.) Does the CIRC indicator disappear? If not, again locate the source of the CIRC reference and correct it until it disappears. (*Hint:* Look in rows 16 and 17.)

    c. Complete the TOTAL column by entering the function to sum columns B through G. Clear the function from any cells in column H that reference blank cells.

    d. Complete the MAX and MIN columns by using the functions to calculate the maximum and minimum values in columns B through G for each row. (Use Help for information about these functions.) Clear the function from any cells in columns I and J that reference blank cells.

    e. In cell C24 enter the formula to calculate the percentage increase (or decrease) in the February sales in row 7 over the January sales (C7–B7)/ B7. Format the cell to display as a percent with zero decimal places. Copy the formula from cell C24 to cells D24 through G24.

    f. Change the spreadsheet values to display as currency with zero decimal places. Best Fit the column widths to display the values.

    g. Insert two additional rows below the bottom title line. Move the titles in cells D1 through D3 to A3 through A5. Center the titles across columns A through J. Increase the font size and bold the first title line. Italicize the third title line. Bold and underline the column headings.

    h. Add a header to display the file name centered on the page and a footer to display a page number centered on the page. (Use Help for information about the header and footer codes.)

    i. Change the orientation to landscape. Preview the spreadsheet. Verify that all columns fit on the page.

    j. Save the spreadsheet as TRAIN3. Print the spreadsheet.

5. Open the file THERMO.WKS. The upper section of this spreadsheet (A9:E15) contains data from a study showing the percentage cost savings you may expect if you use a programmable thermostat to turn your thermostat down in winter or up in summer.

    To find out what your energy savings might be, you will use two cells (B19 and D19) to hold what-if values representing varying annual heating or cooling costs. Then you will use the what-if values in the lower section of the spreadsheet (A24:D30) to calculate the savings.

    a. The what-if cell for annual cooling costs is cell B19. Enter 850 in this cell. The what-if cell for the annual heating costs is cell D19. Enter 1000 in this cell.

b.   Add a double-line border around the what-if cell area (B17:D19).

Next you will enter a formula to calculate the dollar savings for each city. The calculated values will be displayed in cells B24 through D30. The formula takes the value in the what-if cell and multiplies it by the percent values from the upper section of the spreadsheet. For example, to calculate the cooling savings in Denver in summer, you would enter the formula B19*B9 in cell B24.

c.   Enter the formula =B19*B9 in cell B24.

d.   Copy the formula in cell B24 to B25:B30 to calculate the savings for the other cities. The calculated value of $93.50 shows that if your annual cooling costs are $850.00 and you live in Denver, you will save $93.50 on your cooling bill if you set the thermostat 5 degrees higher.

e.   In a similar manner, enter the formulas to calculate the dollar savings for heating (C24 through C30 and D24 through D30).

f.   Change the value in the cooling what-if cell (B19) to 500 and in the heating cell (D19) to 900. How do the results in B24:D30 change? Then change both what-if values to values that reflect your annual heating and cooling costs. Now you can see what your savings would be by looking at the values in one of the cities that is nearest to you or has a climate similar to yours. Add a border around this row of data.

g.   Enter your name in cell A1 the current date in cell A2. Save the spreadsheet as THERMO1. Preview and print the spreadsheet.

6.   As the Vice President of Finance for the Future Business Executives Club, you are responsible for preparing the annual income statement. The club currently has 280 members and has an annual membership dues of $20.00. Throughout the academic year, the club plans monthly meetings with guest speakers. They also sponsor several fund raisers to raise money for the annual banquet and to cover operating costs.

a.   Create a full-year income statement including all possible sources of income (member dues, fund raisers, and so on) and all expenses (mailings, posters, banquet, speakers, awards, and so on).

b.   Enter your name and the current date in a header.

c.   Save the spreadsheet. Preview and print the spreadsheet.

8 Creating and Printing Charts

CASE STUDY

You have noticed over the past few months while working at The Sports Company that sales are increasing in some sports and declining in others. While looking through the store sales records, you have found sales data by sport for the past several years—1992 through 1995—as well as projected sales data for the following year, 1996. You decide to create a spreadsheet of the data to see if the data supports your observations. Although the data in the spreadsheet shows the trends in sales, you feel the use of several charts would make it easier to see the trends and growth patterns over the years. In this lab you will create several different charts of the sales data.

Formatting Tables with AutoFormat

Load Works for Windows. Place your data disk in the appropriate drive for your system.

To see the spreadsheet of sales data, open the file SALES.WKS. If necessary maximize the spreadsheet window.

Your screen should be similar to Figure 8-1.

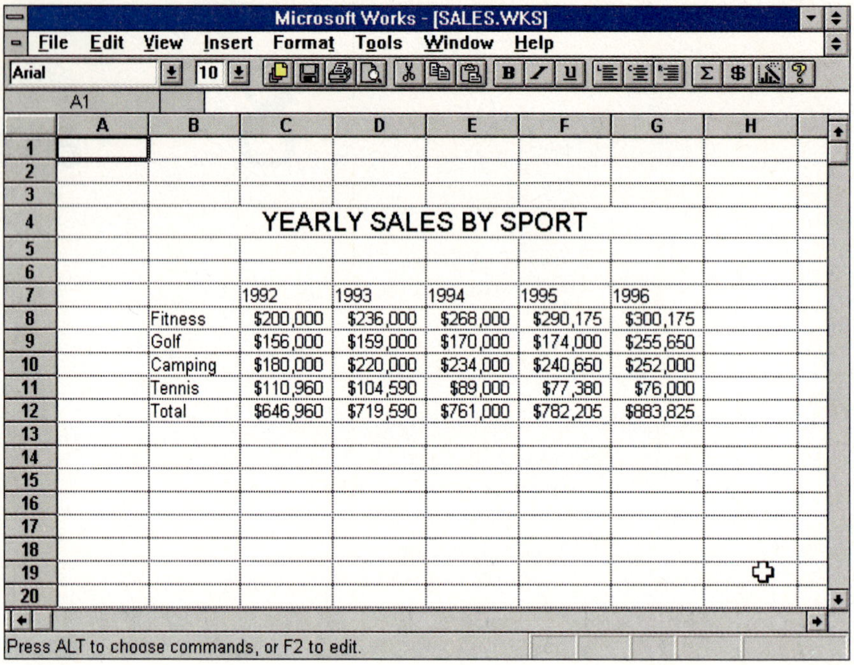

FIGURE 8-1

The spreadsheet lists four sports categories and a total as row headings in column B. The total is the sum of the sales for the four sports categories for each year. The four past years—1992 through 1995—are displayed in row 7. In addition you have included the projected sales for the four sports categories for 1996.

Before creating the charts, you would like to improve the appearance of the spreadsheet. Works includes a feature called AutoFormat that contains 14 built-in table formats. The table formats consist of a collection of number formats, fonts and attributes, colors, patterns, borders, frames, and alignment settings. To use this feature you first specify the range you want formatted.

> AutoFormat can only be used to format adjacent cells.

Select: B7 through G12

Choose: Format>AutoFormat

The AutoFormat dialog box displays the names of the 14 different format styles in the Table Format list box. The Sample box shows an example of how the selected format will appear.

To preview the formats, highlight each format name and look at the table layout in the Sample box.

You think the Colorful 2 format would be appropriate for the data in the SALES spreadsheet. To format the spreadsheet using this layout,

> If you have a monochrome monitor, Works shows the format as different shades of gray.

Select: Colorful 2

Choose: OK

To clear the highlight,

Press: [Home]

Your screen should be similar to Figure 8-2.

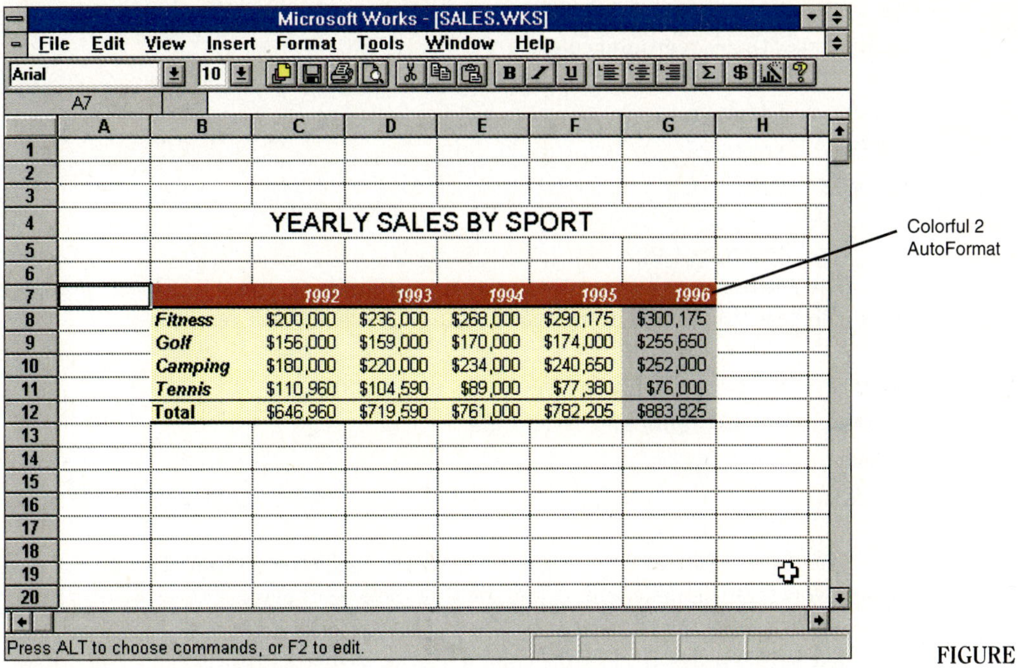

Colorful 2
AutoFormat

FIGURE 8-2

The Colorful 2 format layout has been applied to the selected range. This format includes the use of color and shading, italics, and border lines. In addition the labels have been aligned and the column widths sized to the largest entry.

Next you want to add a heading above the 1996 column of data to clarify that this data represents projected sales for 1996.

Enter the heading "Projected" in G6. Center, bold, and italicize the entry.

Because the entire table is formatted, this heading does not look like part of the table. To include the heading in the table, you will make the row containing this heading the same color as the row containing the years in the table.

Select: B6 through G6
Choose: Format>Patterns

In the Patterns dialog box, you specify the shading to be applied to the selection and the color. First you need to tell Works to add a pattern to the cells in the selection. To specify a solid pattern,

Select: Pattern

A drop-down list of patterns is displayed. The default setting of None displays no shading.

Select: the solid pattern (second option in the list)

SPREADSHEET

Next you can specify the color you want the selection to display. The Foreground option controls the color of the pattern and the Background option controls the color of the shading behind the pattern. However, selecting a solid pattern displays only the Foreground color.

Select:	Foreground
Select:	Dark Red
Choose:	OK

Clear the highlight.

The entire row is the same color as row 6. However, the text is black, and you want it to be white, as it is in the year headings. To change the text color,

Move:	G6
Choose:	Format>Font and Style>Color
Select:	White
Choose:	OK

The text is white and the entire row and text looks the same as the AutoFormat layout. Now that the table is in color, the title looks very plain. In a similar manner, change the color of the text in the title in cell B4 to Dark Red.

The title appears in the same color as in the formatted table.

Understanding Charts

Although the spreadsheet shows the sales numbers for each sports category, it is hard to see how the different categories have changed over time. A visual representation of data in the form of a graph or **chart** would convey that information in an easy-to-understand and attractive manner. Works creates a chart from any data you highlight in a spreadsheet.

The basic parts of a two-dimensional chart are illustrated in Figure 8-3. The bottom boundary of the chart is the **X axis**. It is used to label the data being charted, such as a point in time or a category. The **category labels** are displayed along the X axis. The spreadsheet range that contains the category labels is the **category series**. The left boundary of the chart is the **Y axis**. This axis is a numbered scale whose minimum and maximum numbers are determined by the data used in the chart.

The selected spreadsheet data is visually displayed within the X- and Y-axis boundaries. Each group of related data, such as the numbers in a row or column of the selected area of the spreadsheet, is called a **value series**. To distinguish one value series from another, different markers, colors, or patterns are used. A **legend** identifies the data displayed in each value series.

A chart can also contain descriptive text, such as **titles**, which explains the contents of the chart. The chart title is displayed centered above the charted data. Titles can also be used to describe the X and Y axes.

In pie charts there are no axes. Instead the spreadsheet data that is charted is displayed as slices in a circle or pie. Each slice is labeled.

In 3-D charts there can also be an additional axis, called the Z axis, which allows you to compare data within a series more easily. This axis is the vertical axis. The X and Y axes delineate the horizontal and vertical surface of the chart, while the Z axis shows depth.

To remove a pattern, choose None as the Patterns setting and all foreground and background settings are cleared.

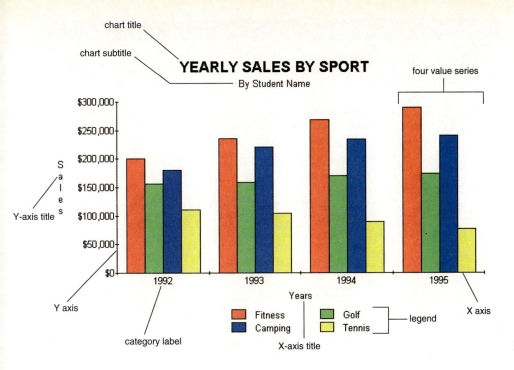

FIGURE 8-3

Works for Windows can produce 12 basic types of charts with many different styles for each type. The basic chart types are:

Type of Chart	Description
	Area charts show the relative importance of a value over time by emphasizing the area under the curve created by each data series.
	Bar charts display the categories vertically and values horizontally, placing more emphasis on comparisons and less on time.
	Line charts are used to show changes in data over time, emphasizing time and rate of change rather than the amount of change.
	Pie charts show the relationship of each value in a data series to the series as a whole. Each slice of the pie represents a single value in the series.
	Stacked-line charts show the relationships between the values of the categories and their totals. The values of each line are added to those of the line below.
	XY (scatter) charts are used to show the relationship between two ranges of numeric data.
	Radar charts display a line or area chart wrapped around a central point. Each axis represents a set of data points.
	Combination charts display bars and lines in the same chart.

SPREADSHEET

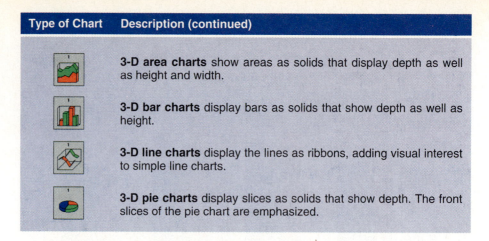

Type of Chart	Description (continued)
	3-D area charts show areas as solids that display depth as well as height and width.
	3-D bar charts display bars as solids that show depth as well as height.
	3-D line charts display the lines as ribbons, adding visual interest to simple line charts.
	3-D pie charts display slices as solids that show depth. The front slices of the pie chart are emphasized.

Selecting the Data to Chart

First you want to create a chart to show the total sales pattern over the past four years. This chart will not display the projected sales data for 1996. All charts are drawn from data contained in a spreadsheet. To create a new chart, you highlight the spreadsheet range containing the data that you want displayed as a chart plus any row or column headings that you want used in the chart. Works then translates the selected data into a chart based upon the shape and contents of the spreadsheet selection. The shape and contents criteria are:

- If the selection has more columns than rows, Works plots the first row as the category series and data in subsequent rows as the value series.

- If the highlight has more rows than columns, Works plots the first column as the category series and data in subsequent columns as the value series.

- If the first row or column contains dates, the dates become the category series, regardless of the dimensions of the selection.

- If the first row or column contains text, Works uses the text entry as a legend label.

The year headings in cells C7 through F7 will label the X axis. The total values to be charted are in cells C12 through F12. In addition the label "Total" in cell B12 will be used as the chart legend, making the entire range B12 through F12. Notice that the two ranges, C7 through F7 and B12 through F12, are not adjacent ranges. When cells or ranges that you want included in the same chart are not adjacent, you first select all the adjacent rows or columns and then add the other ranges to the chart after it is created.

Select: B12 through F12

Next you direct Works to create the chart by choosing the Create New Chart command on the Tools menu or the 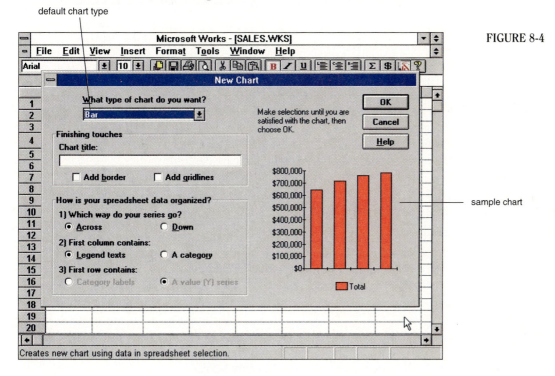 New Chart tool button.

Choose: Tools>Create New Chart

or

Click: New Chart

Your screen should be similar to Figure 8-4.

default chart type

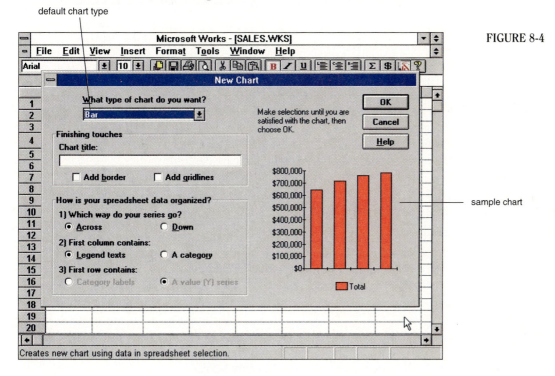

FIGURE 8-4

sample chart

Works plots a sample chart for the highlighted range using the default chart settings and displays it in the New Chart dialog box. By default Works creates a **bar chart** of the data. Works has created the chart based upon the organization of the spreadsheet selection as shown in the "How is your spreadsheet data organized?" section of the dialog box. Works plotted the data series from left to right across the spreadsheet. In this instance, because there was only one row of data in the selection, the contents of the row were plotted as the only data series. In addition, because the first entry in the row is the text entry Total, this is used as the legend label.

You can modify the default chart settings using this dialog box. The only change you want to make is to add a title to the chart. To do this,

Choose: Chart title

Type: THE SPORTS COMPANY SALES

The title appears centered above the chart in the dialog box. To close the dialog box,

Choose: OK

The chart is displayed in a second window, called the **chart window**.

If necessary maximize the chart window.

In addition, the Chart menu and Chart toolbar are displayed. These features are automatically displayed whenever a chart window is active.

The Chart toolbar buttons are identified below.

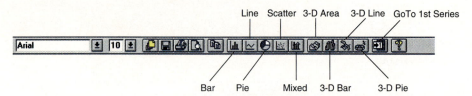

The bar chart shows the change in the total sales over the four years. The height of each bar corresponds to the value in each cell of the selected spreadsheet range. The values along the Y scale are automatically set by Works as a scale of values determined by the lowest and highest numbers in the data range.

The chart is not easy to understand, however, because the X axis does not have category labels and the X and Y axes do not have descriptive titles.

Adding a Value Series

Once a chart is created, you can continue to modify and enhance the chart using the Chart menu and toolbar. The first addition you want to make is to add the value series that will label the X axis of the chart. To do this,

Choose: Edit>Series

> A chart can have up to six Y (value) series.

The Series dialog box shows that the range C12:F12 has been used as the first Y series. The Y series are the ranges that contain the values to be plotted in the chart. To specify the range to use as X-axis category labels,

Select: Category (X) Series
Type: C7:F7
Choose: OK

Your screen should be similar to Figure 8-5.

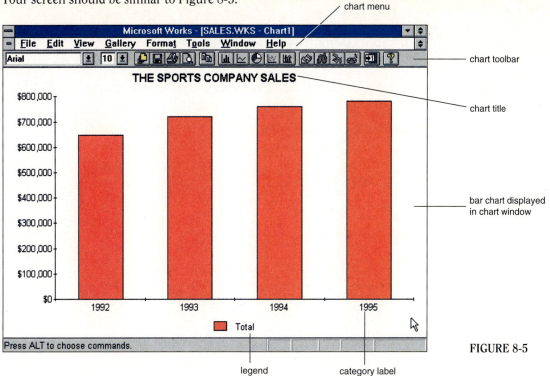

FIGURE 8-5

Works adds the dates contained in the selected range as the X-axis category labels.

Adding Titles

To further clarify the chart data, you can add a subtitle below the main title.

Choose: Edit>Titles

The title you entered in the New Chart dialog box is displayed in the Chart Title text box. To add a subtitle that contains your name,

Press: Tab ⇥
Type: By [Your Name]

> Do not press ←Enter to complete the text entry. If you do, OK is chosen and the command is completed.

You also want to include horizontal (X) and vertical (Y) axis titles to the chart. The X axis shows the change in sales over the four years, and the Y axis shows the sales in thousands of dollars. To add descriptive titles,

Press: Tab ⇥
Type: YEARS
Press: Tab ⇥
Type: SALES

To close the dialog box and place the titles on the chart,

Choose: OK

Your screen should be similar to Figure 8-6.

chart subtitle ——————————————

Y-axis title

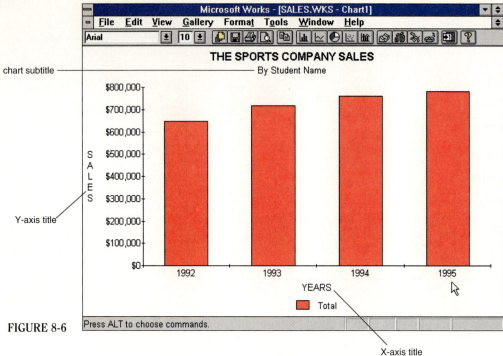

FIGURE 8-6

X-axis title

The chart with the settings you specified is displayed.

Changing the Type of Chart

You would like to see how the same data displayed in the bar chart would look as a line chart. A **line chart** displays data as a line and is used to show trends. Changing the chart type is easily done.

Choose: Gallery>Line
or
Click: ☑ Line

A dialog box of the six different line chart types is displayed. You want to change the bar chart to the standard line chart, option 1. This is the preselected line chart type.

Choose: OK

Your screen should be similar to Figure 8-7.

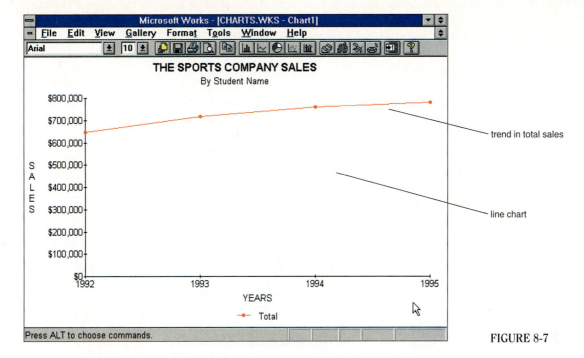

FIGURE 8-7

The bar chart is redrawn as a line chart. The data for the total sales for each year is now displayed as a line. The line chart displays the years along the X axis and the value series as a line within the chart. The line represents the total sales. Although the line chart shows the trend in sales over time, because it only contains one data series, it is not as interesting as the bar chart.

To change the chart type back to the standard bar type,

Choose: Gallery>Bar
or
Click: 📊 Bar

The six types of bar charts that can be created are displayed in the dialog box. The standard bar chart (1) is the preselected type.

Choose: OK

Naming a Chart

Up to eight different charts can be created and stored in a spreadsheet. To create more than one chart in a spreadsheet, each chart is assigned a different name. Naming the chart allows the current chart settings to be stored in the spreadsheet and recalled for later use. The bar chart you just created was assigned the default name, Chart1, by Works. To change the chart name to a more descriptive name,

Choose: Tools>Name Chart

> The chart name is displayed in the title bar.

SPREADSHEET

The Name Chart dialog box is displayed. Works assigns a numbered name to each chart you create, just as it does a file. And just like a file, you can change the name to a one that is more descriptive of the contents of the chart. Since this is the only chart, it is also the selected chart. To rename this chart,

Choose: Name

A chart name can be up to 15 characters long. It will appear exactly as you enter it, including upper- and lowercase characters. To rename the chart BAR,

Type: BAR
Choose: Rename

Your screen should be similar to Figure 8-8.

FIGURE 8-8

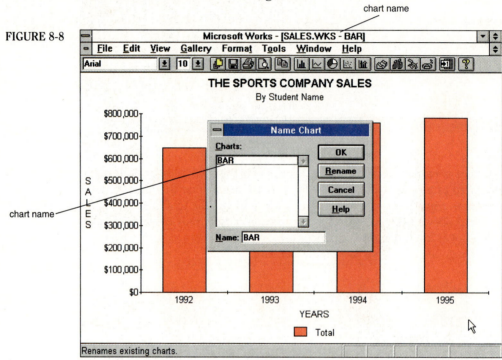

The name Chart1 has been replaced by BAR in the Charts list box and in the title bar. To complete this command,

Choose: OK

The BAR chart settings are stored in the computer's memory for later use. The named chart is not permanently saved on the disk until you save the spreadsheet file using the Save command on the File menu.

Creating a Chart with Multiple Value Series

Now you are ready to continue your analysis of sales trends. You want to create a second chart to display the sales data for each sports category for the four years. You could create a separate chart for each category and then compare the charts. However, to make the comparisons between the categories easier, you will display all the categories on a single chart.

To return to the spreadsheet window,

Choose: View>Spreadsheet

The data for the four years for the four categories is in cells C8 through F11. The year labels (X-axis series) are in cells C7 through F7 and the legend text is in the column of data B8 through B11. Because the data ranges are adjacent, you can select the complete range as the chart series.

Select: B7 through F11 (do not select the total value in row 12 or the projected values in column G)

To create a new chart,

Choose: Tools>Create New Chart
or
Click: New Chart

The New Chart dialog box shows the initial chart created by Works. The four data series are displayed as four bars. Each bar is a different color if you have a color monitor or contains a different pattern if you have a monochrome monitor. The years are the X-axis labels and the text entries in column B are the legend labels.

You would like to change the chart type from the default bar to a line.

Choose: What type of chart do you want?
Select: Line

The chart changes to a line chart. Each line displays a different color to distinguish the four value series. If you have a monochrome monitor, the lines display different data markers.

Again the Chart Title text box is empty. Rather than type the chart title in the text box, you can copy a title from the spreadsheet into the chart. To do this you enter the cell reference for the cell that contains the title in the text box. You will use the spreadsheet title in cell B4 for the chart title.

You can move the dialog box to see the spreadsheet cells.

Choose   Chart title
Type: B4

The label in cell B4 of the spreadsheet is displayed as the chart title. To complete the chart,

Choose: OK

The line chart of the data shows that sales in fitness and camping are increasing, sales in tennis are decreasing, and golf sales are steady.

SPREADSHEET

You think the title would look better if it was displayed in a larger font size. To select the title,

Choose: Edit>Select Title Text
➤   Ctrl + T
or
Click: the title

Increase the size of the text to 16pt. Clear the title selection.

Now all you need to do to complete the chart is to add a subtitle and X- and Y-axis titles. To do this,

Choose: Edit>Titles>Subtitle
Type: By [Your Name]
Press: Tab ⇥
Type: Years
Press: Tab ⇥
Type: Sales
Choose: OK

Your screen should be similar to Figure 8-9.

> Click anywhere or press Ctrl + t to clear the title selection.

FIGURE 8-9

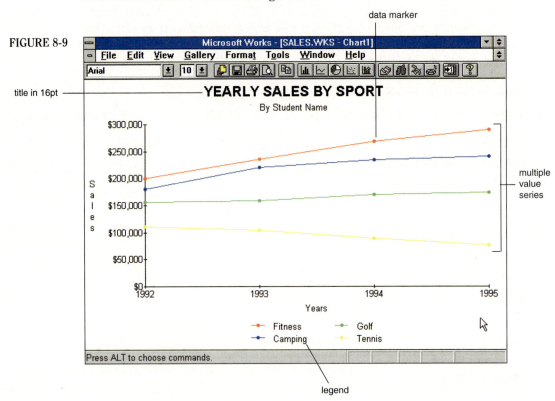

After looking at the chart, you decide you want to modify several of the chart features. Although the line chart clearly shows the sales trends for the four years for the four sports categories, it does not give you a feeling for the magnitude of the change. You feel that a stacked-bar chart or an area chart may better represent the data. Additionally you want to change several other features in the chart, such as adding gridlines and patterns.

First you will change the chart to a **stacked-bar chart**. This type of chart will show the proportion of each type of sport to the total sport sales in each year. To change the chart to a stacked-bar chart,

Choose: Gallery>Bar

or

Click: 📊 Bar

From the Bar dialog box,

Choose: 2>OK

The chart is redrawn. Rather than a group of bars being displayed side-by-side, the bars are stacked upon each other (see Figure 8-10 on the next page). The Y-axis scale has changed to reflect the new range of data. The new Y-axis range is the sum of the four categories, or the same as the total value in the spreadsheet. It is now easy to compare how much each category contributed to the total sales in each year. However, trends over time are not so easy to see anymore.

Adding Gridlines

You want to see if the addition of **gridlines** will improve the readability of the chart. Gridlines are lines that extend horizontally or vertically across the chart. Gridlines make it easier to read the value of a data point or the height of a bar. To add gridlines,

Choose: Format>Vertical (Y) Axis

The Vertical Axis dialog box lets you set the scale and unit of measure for the vertical axis and add gridlines to the chart. To add gridlines,

Choose: Show Gridlines>OK

Your screen should be similar to Figure 8-10.

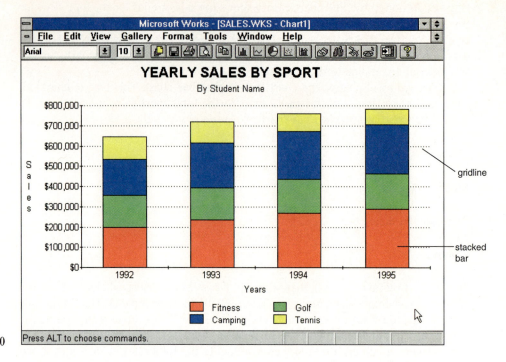

FIGURE 8-10

It is now easy to compare how much each category contributed to the total sales in each year.

The stacked-bar chart shows the amount of change better, but still it is difficult to see trends. To see the data represented as an **area chart**,

Choose: Gallery>Area>OK

Your screen should be similar to Figure 8-11.

FIGURE 8-11

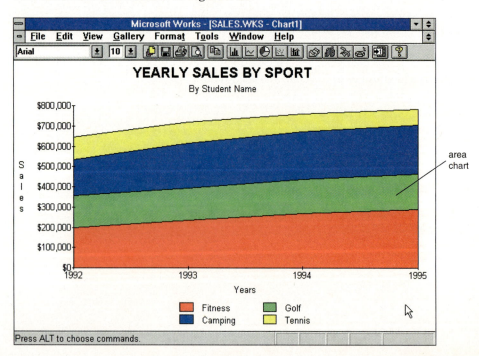

An area chart shows the magnitude of change and the trend from year to year better than the other types of charts.

As you can see, it is very easy to change the chart type and format once the data series are specified. The same data can be displayed in many different ways. Depending upon the emphasis you want the chart to make, a different chart style can be selected.

Rename the chart AREA.

Use Tools>Name Chart to rename the chart.

Adding Patterns

If you have a color monitor, the four areas in your chart are displayed in different colors. If you have a monochrome monitor, the areas are displayed as different black-and-white patterns. To see how the chart will appear when printed,

Choose: View>Display as Printed

The chart appears in colors that are available on your printer or in patterns of black and white if you have a monochrome printer. To turn off this display,

Choose: View>Display as Printed

The chart is displayed in color again if you have a color monitor.

You want to add patterns to each color if you have a color printer, or change the default patterns that are used in each series if you have a black-and-white printer. This will make the chart more attractive and will make it easier to distinguish between the different areas. To add or change patterns, you select each value series and then change the pattern settings.

Choose: Format>Patterns and Colors

The Patterns and Colors dialog box lets you specify colors and patterns for each value series. In addition, if the chart is a line chart, you could specify different markers for each line. The Auto option in both the Colors and Patterns list boxes shows the default settings. To select a pattern for the first value series, Fitness,

Choose: Patterns
Select: XX
Choose: Format

Your screen should be similar to Figure 8-12.

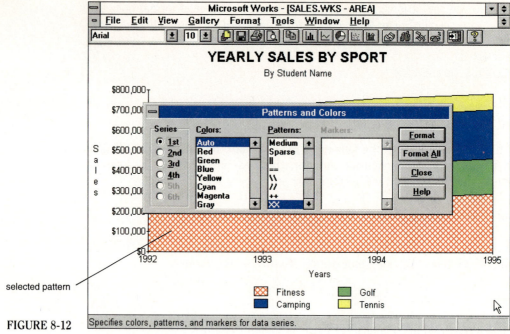

selected pattern

FIGURE 8-12

The chart is redrawn with the Fitness area of the chart displaying the selected pattern. The dialog box is still open so you can change other settings. To change the pattern for the second series,

Choose: 2nd
Select: Light //

In the same manner, select the ++ pattern for the third series and the Light \\ pattern for the fourth series.

The chart displays the selected patterns for the four series. To close the dialog box,

Choose: Close

Now when you print the chart, it will be printed in the selected patterns in color if you have a color printer or in black and white if you have a monochrome printer.

> You can move the dialog box to view the chart.

Creating a Combination Chart

The next chart you will create will show the sales for four years as well as the projected sales for 1996. You want to display the past four years' sales values as lines and the 1996 projected sales as a bar. This type of chart is called a **combination chart** or mixed chart.

Another way to return to the spreadsheet window is to use the Window menu.

Choose: Window>1 SALES.WKS

The spreadsheet window is now active. To create a combination chart,

Select: B7 through G11
Choose: T<u>o</u>ols><u>C</u>reate New Chart
or
Click: 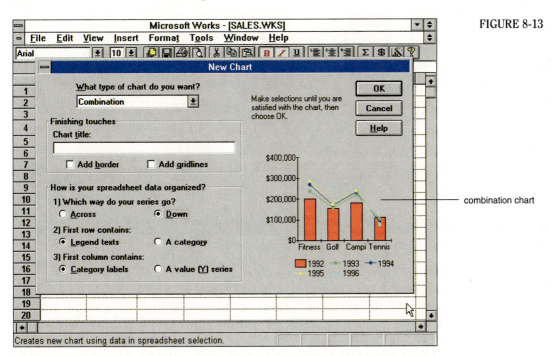 Chart

Change the chart type to a combination chart.
    The first value series (Fitness) is still a bar. All other series (Golf, Camping, and Tennis) are lines. This is the default interpretation of data in a combination chart. Notice that the sample chart displays the year labels along the X axis while the sports categories are displayed in the legend. You would like the chart to display the year labels as the legends and the sports categories as the X-axis labels. To do this you need to change the way the data series are selected from Across to Down.

Choose: <u>D</u>own

Your screen should be similar to Figure 8-13.

FIGURE 8-13

The sample area now displays the chart series as you want them.

Choose: OK

Next you want to change how Works assigned the bars and lines to the value series. You want the projected year, 1996, to be the bar, and all other years as lines. To respecify how the series are displayed,

Choose: Forma<u>t</u>><u>M</u>ixed Line and Bar

The dialog box lets you change each data series to either a line or a bar. To change the first data series to a line,

Select: Line **A**

Then to make the 1996 data series (5th series) a bar,

Select: Bar **K**
Choose: OK

Your screen should be similar to Figure 8-14.

FIGURE 8-14

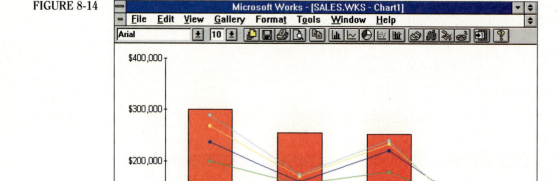

combination chart

The combination chart displays the 1996 value series for the four sports categories as bars and the other four years as lines. A combination chart makes it easy to see comparisons between groups of data or to show different types of data in a single chart. In this case you can easily see how the sales for each category are changing compared to projected sales for each category. In this case you can see that the fitness and camping projections are right on target, but that golf is high and tennis is low.

> Use Edit>Titles to add chart titles.

Add the following titles to the chart:

Chart title:	**Annual vs Projected Sales** (do not press ←Enter)
Subtitle:	**By** [your name]
Horizontal axis:	**Sports Category**
Vertical axis:	**Sales**

Add the Light // pattern to the fifth value series (bar).

Your screen should be similar to Figure 8-15.

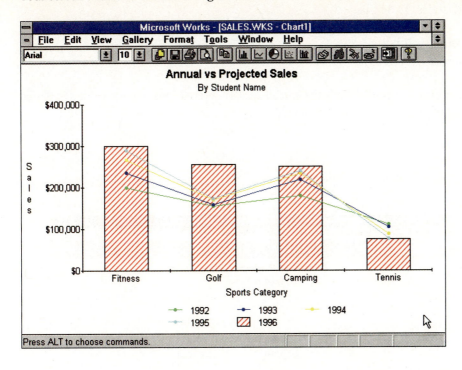

FIGURE 8-15

Rename the chart COMBINE.

Adding Data Labels

You would like to include on the chart the actual numbers being plotted for the projected sales. These are called **data labels**. To add data labels, you copy the numbers from the data range to the chart.

> View the spreadsheet.

To copy the data values for the 1996 projections,

Select: G8 through G11

Choose: Edit>Copy

   ➣   Ctrl + C

or

Click: 🖺 Copy

To return to the Chart window,

Choose: View>Chart>COMBINE>OK

To add data labels,

Choose: Edit>Data Labels

You could also choose the window you want to make active from the Window menu.

SPREADSHEET

The Data Labels dialog box is displayed. You would like to show the values of the fifth series. To do this,

Choose: 5th
Choose: Paste

The range you copied from the spreadsheet is entered into the 5th Value (Y) Series text box. To complete the command,

Choose: OK

Your screen should be similar to Figure 8-16.

FIGURE 8-16

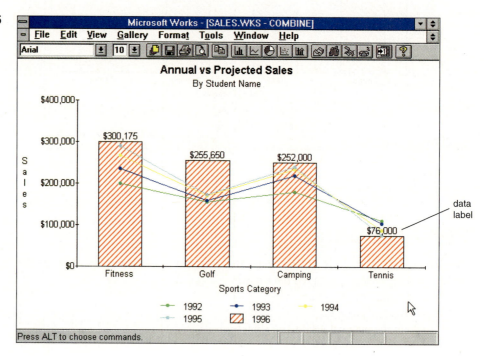

The data labels for the 1996 sales values are displayed above each of the bars.

Creating a Pie Chart

The last chart you would like to make will use the projected sales data. The sales of Fitness items have been increasing and you are particularly interested in next year's sales projections.

View the spreadsheet.

You want to see what portion of all sales for the projected year are fitness sales. The best chart for this purpose is a pie chart. A **pie chart** compares parts to the whole, in a similar manner to a stacked-bar chart. However, each value in the range is a slice of the pie displayed as a percentage of the total.

The use of X (category) and value series settings in a pie chart is different from their use in a bar or line chart. The X series labels the slices of the pie rather than the X axis. The Y series is used to create the slices in the pie. Only one series can be specified in a pie chart.

For this chart the X series (the sports category labels) and the values for the data series (cells G8 through G11) are not in adjacent ranges. To specify the values series first,

Select: G8 through G11

Choose: T**o**ols>**C**reate New Chart

or

Click: 📊 New Chart

Change the chart type to pie. Add the chart title "1996 Projected Sales." Select the Add Border option.

Choose: OK

Your screen should be similar to Figure 8-17.

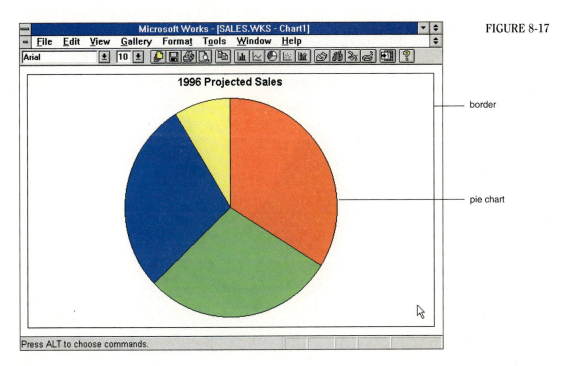

FIGURE 8-17

A basic pie chart is drawn enclosed in a single-line border box. However, because the chart does not contain category labels, the meaning of the chart is unclear. To change the pie chart style to include slice labels and percentages,

Choose: **G**allery>**P**ie

or

Click: 🥧 Pie Chart

The Pie dialog box is displayed. The sixth option will display the pie chart with percentages and labels.

Select: <u>6</u>
Choose: OK

The pie chart is redrawn using the entries in cells G8 through G11 of the preselected range as the labels and percentages. However, you want the labels to be the names of the four categories. To specify the category labels for the slices,

Choose: <u>E</u>dit><u>D</u>ata Labels

To change the cell range to the range containing the labels (B8 through B11),

> You could also copy and paste the range as you did data labels earlier.

Select: Cell <u>R</u>ange
Type: **B8:B11**
Choose: OK

Your screen should be similar to Figure 8-18.

FIGURE 8-18

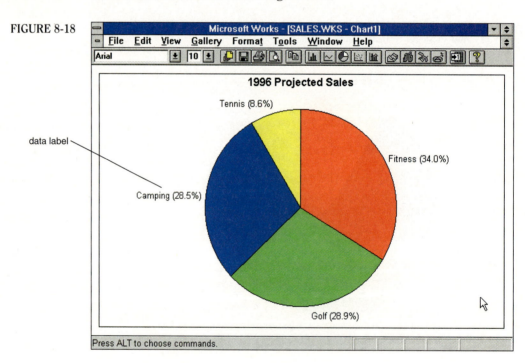

Next, to add your name as the chart subtitle,

Choose: <u>E</u>dit><u>T</u>itles

Notice that the last three title text box labels are dim. Because pie charts do not have X or Y axes these options are not available. To enter a subtitle,

Select: Subtitle
Type: By [Your Name]
Choose: OK

You want the pie chart to be displayed as a three-dimensional shape. To change the pie chart,

Choose: Gallery>3-D Pie
or
Click: 3-D Pie Chart

> You can also change a chart to 3-D using the Make 3-D command in the Format menu.

The sixth 3-D pie option is already selected. To use this selection,

Choose: OK

Your screen should be similar to Figure 8-19.

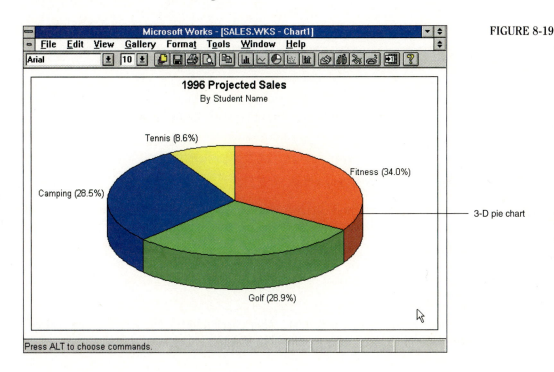

FIGURE 8-19

The chart changes to a three-dimensional pie chart.

Finally, you want to **explode** or separate slightly from the other slices the Fitness slice of the chart to emphasize the data. To do this,

Choose: Format>Patterns and Colors

Since the Fitness slice is the first series,

Choose: Explode Slice>Format>Close

Your screen should be similar to Figure 8-20.

exploded slice ———

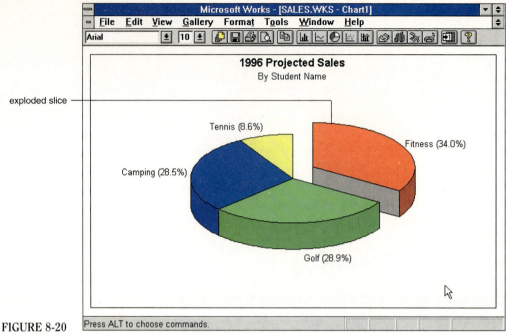

FIGURE 8-20

The slice is separated slightly from the other slices in the pie.

Rename the chart 3D PIE.

Changing the Spreadsheet Data

You notice that the Tennis category represents 8.6 percent of the total and you think this figure is a little high. You want to check the data entered in the spreadsheet for this category.

View the spreadsheet.

Move to: G11

The number in cell G11 is $76,000. After checking your records, you find that you entered the data incorrectly. It should be $70,000.

Type: 70000
Press: ←Enter

The spreadsheet has been recalculated.

To see the effect on the pie chart, view the pie chart.

The pie chart has been redrawn to reflect the change in the 1996 data for the Tennis category. Tennis now accounts for 8 percent of total sales for the projected year, 1996. Since the chart document is linked to the source data, changes to the source data are automatically reflected in the chart.

Printing Charts

You would like to print the combined chart. To make the combined chart active,

Choose: View>Chart>COMBINE>OK

The combined chart whose settings were named and stored in memory is displayed on the screen.

Choose: File>Print Preview
or
Click: 🔍 Print Preview

The combined chart has been enlarged to occupy a full page. You want to change the page layout of the chart so it appears in the same proportions as on the screen.
Cancel the Preview window.

Choose: File>Page Setup>Other Options

To print the chart on a full page and keep the proportions,

Choose: Full page, keep proportions
Choose: OK

Preview the chart again.
Your screen should be similar to Figure 8-21.

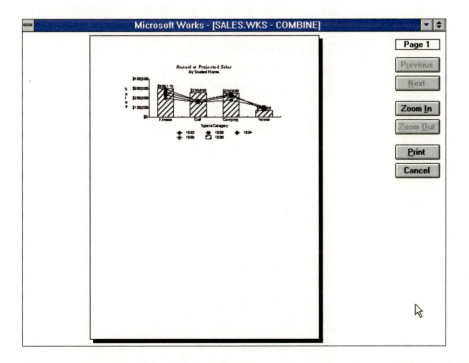

FIGURE 8-21

SPREADSHEET

The chart appears in the same proportions as it was onscreen.
To print the chart,

Choose: Print

Save the spreadsheet and charts as CHARTS. If requested by your instructor, print
the spreadsheet and other charts. Exit Works.

Key Terms

chart (260)
X axis (260)
category labels (260)
category series (260)
Y axis (260)
value series (260)
legend (260)
title (260)
bar chart (263)

chart window (264)
line chart (266)
stacked-bar chart (271)
gridlines (271)
area chart (272)
combination chart (274)
data labels (277)
pie chart (278)
explode (281)

Command Summary

Command	Shortcut	Button	Action
Forma**t**>AutoFo**r**mat			Formats spreadsheet to one of 14 built-in table formats
T**o**ols>**C**reate New Chart		🖾	Creates a new chart from preselected range of data
Edit>**S**eries			Adds value series to chart
Edit>**T**itles			Adds titles to chart
Gallery>**L**ine		📈	Changes chart type to line
Gallery>**B**ar		📊	Changes chart type to bar
T**o**ols>**N**ame Chart			Names current chart
View>**S**preadsheet			Displays active spreadsheet
Edit>Select Title Te**x**t	Ctrl + T		Selects chart title
Forma**t**>**V**ertical [Y]Axis>Show **G**ridlines			Displays gridlines on chart
Gallery>**A**rea			Changes chart type to area
View>Display as **P**rinted			Displays chart as it will appear when printed
Forma**t**>**P**atterns and Colors			Changes color, pattern, and marker for specified value series
Forma**t**>**M**ixed Line and Bar			Creates chart with lines and bars
View>**C**hart			Displays specified chart
Edit>**D**ata Labels			Adds data labels to chart
Gallery>**P**ie		🥧	Changes chart type to pie
Gallery>3-D P**ie**		🥧	Changes chart type to 3-D pie
Forma**t**>**P**atterns and Colors>**E**xplode Slice			Explodes selected data series slice
File>**P**age Setup>**O**ther Options>Full page, **k**eep proportions			Sets chart layout to a full page, keeping proportions

LAB REVIEW

Matching

1.	gridlines	_____	a.	left boundary of chart
2.	value series	_____	b.	bottom boundary of chart
3.	stacked-bar chart	_____	c.	data series containing values to be charted
4.	X axis	_____	d.	used to distinguish one value series from another
5.	explode	_____	e.	vertical or horizontal lines that make chart easier to read
6.	patterns	_____	f.	displays symbols and descriptive labels of data
7.	category labels	_____	g.	labels along X axis
8.	Y axis	_____	h.	shows proportion of each value
9.	legend	_____	i.	separates slice slightly from other slices of pie
10.	pie chart	_____	j.	compares parts to whole in a circle

Fill-In Questions

1. Complete the following statements by filling in the blanks with the correct terms.

   a. A visual representation of data in an easy-to-understand and attractive manner is called a(n) _____.

   b. A(n) _____ describes the symbols used within the chart.

   c. The bottom boundary of a chart is the _____ and the left boundary is the _____.

   d. Works can display _____ value series in a chart.

   e. A(n) _____ displays data as a set of evenly spaced bars.

   f. A(n) _____ and a(n) _____ compare parts to the whole.

   g. The _____ menu and toolbar are automatically displayed when a chart window is active.

   h. The X axis displays the _____.

   i. When a chart is printed in black and white, _____ can be added to the chart to make it easer to distinguish one series from another.

   j. When a slice of a pie chart is separated from the other slices, the slice has been _____.

Practice Exercises

1. Karen has just completed her college degree at age 30. She is interested in what percentage of adults over 25 complete four years of college education. Her supervisor at the Arkansas Department of Higher Education has asked her to submit a report on those findings.

The following data shows the percentages for both the United States and the State of Arkansas.

Completed Higher Education After Age 25 (in percents)			
	1970	1980	1989
Arkansas	7.0	9.95	15.99
United States	10.1	16.00	21.00

a. Create a spreadsheet displaying this data. Use the AutoFormat feature to format the spreadsheet to a format of your choice. Use the titles and row and column headings shown. Do not leave blank columns between the columns of data. Format the numbers as Fixed with two decimal places.

b. Create a bar chart of this data. Use the spreadsheet title as the chart title. Add a border around the chart.

c. Make the following changes to the chart:

- Enter your name as the chart subtitle. Enter "Years" as the X-axis title and "Percentage" as the Y-axis title.

- Enlarge the font size of the chart title.

- Change the chart to a stacked-bar chart (style #2).

- Add patterns to the value series.

- Add gridlines.

d. Name the chart STACKED. Preview and print the chart on a full page, keeping proportions.

e. Save the spreadsheet as EDUCTN. Print the spreadsheet.

2. Sean Rees has a summer internship with the Department of Land Management. He has prepared the following table to compare the leasing cost per acre of private and federal lands.

Average Monthly Leasing Cost Per Acre (in dollars)				
	1975	1980	1985	1990
Federal	2.00	2.40	1.85	1.90
Private	6.00	7.80	8.90	9.00

a. Create a spreadsheet of this data. Use the titles and row and column headings shown. Do not leave blank columns between the columns of data. Format the numbers as Fixed with two decimal places.

b. Create a line chart of the data in the spreadsheet. Enter the chart title "Cost for Leasing Lands."

c. Enter your name as the chart subtitle. Enter "Years" as the X-axis title and "Price per Acre" as the Y-axis title. Enlarge the font of the chart title.

d. Name the chart LANDLINE.

e. Save the spreadsheet as LAND. Preview and print the chart on a full page, keeping proportions.

3. Charlene Reynolds has been on a low-calorie diet for the past few months. Today, however, Charlene attended a luncheon meeting and splurged on her meal. Charlene had autumn roast chicken, Mediterranean salad, two rolls, and apple pie.

As soon as Charlene returned to work, she felt guilty. She went to her calorie converter and exercise guide to see what she could do to burn off those extra calories. Open the file CALORIE to see how many minutes of each exercise would be required to burn off Charlene's lunch.

a. Use the AutoFormat feature to format the spreadsheet to a format of your choice.

b. Create a bar chart showing the amount of time that is required to burn off the calories for each food for each type of exercise activity (C7:F11). Include an appropriate chart title. Add the category (X) series (A7:A11) to label the X axis.

c. Change the chart type to stacked-bar (style #2). Add a subtitle to display your name. Add appropriate horizontal and vertical axis titles. Add patterns and vertical and horizontal gridlines. Name the chart.

d. Create a pie chart to display what percentage of the total calories of Charlene's lunch is made up of each of the four foods she ate. Enter an appropriate chart title and a subtitle that includes your name. Display the names of the foods as the slice labels and display the percent each slice is of the total.

e. Enlarge the title. Add patterns to the pie chart. Name the chart.

f. Save the file as CALCHART. Preview and print both charts on a full page, keeping proportions. Print the spreadsheet.

4. Jennifer Little has created a spreadsheet to track the populations of five cities. Open the file CITY to see the data she has collected.

a. Create a line chart of the data. Include an appropriate chart title, a subtitle displaying your name, and vertical and horizontal axis titles. Enlarge the font of the chart title. Name the chart.

b. Jennifer realizes after looking at the chart that the data for Claremont may be incorrect. She checks her records and realizes that the population for 1995 should be 553,100. Make this change.

c. Create a 3-D pie chart of the average population for the cities. Add appropriate titles (include your name in the subtitle). Enlarge the title. Add data labels and display the city name and the percentage next to each slice. Add patterns. Name the chart.

d. Save the file as CITY1. Preview and print the charts on a full page, keeping proportions.

5. Dave Robson is preparing a report on the candy industry for his marketing class. During the research process he collected the following data:

Percent U.S. Market Share in 1994	
Hershey Foods Corp.	20.8
Jacobs Suchard	7.2
Mars, Inc.	18.5
Nestle, S.A.	7.0
RJR Nabisco	4.7
Other	41.8

a. Create a spreadsheet of this data. Do not leave blank columns between the data.

b. Create a pie chart to show the percentage each company had of the 1994 market. Include an appropriate chart title and a subtitle showing your name.

c. Increase the size of the chart title. Add patterns. Explode the Jacobs Suchard slice of the pie.

d. Name the chart. Save the spreadsheet as MKTRES. Preview and print the chart on a full page, keeping proportions.

6. In this problem you will create a chart of the data in the THERMO1 spreadsheet you created in Practice Exercise 5 of Lab 7. Open the file THERMO1.WKS.

a. Create a bar chart of the data in rows 23 through 30 showing the cities as the X-axis category labels and the percent savings for the three categories as the value series.

b. Enter appropriate chart titles (include your name in the subtitle). Enlarge the font of the chart title. Add patterns to the bars.

c. Name the chart. Save the spreadsheet as THERMO2. Preview and print the chart on a full page, keeping proportions.

Electronic Databases

A word processor helps you enter and manipulate text. An electronic spreadsheet helps you enter and analyze numerical data. A computerized database helps you enter and manage information or data in record format.

Databases have been in existence for many years. Paper records organized in a filing cabinet by name or department are a database. The information in a telephone book, organized alphabetically, is a database. The records maintained by a school—of teachers, classes, and students—are a database.

Before computers most database records were kept on paper. With computers the same data is entered and stored on a disk. The big difference is that an electronic database can manipulate—sort, analyze, and display—the data quickly and efficiently. What took hours of time to pull from the paper files can be extracted in a matter of seconds using a computerized database.

Definition of a Database

A database is an organized collection of related data that is stored in a file. The data is entered as a record that consists of several fields of data. Each record contains the same fields. For example, a school has a database of student records. Each record may contain the following fields of data: name, address, social security number, phone number, classes, and grades. All the records for each student in the school are stored in a single file.

Some database programs only access and manipulate the data in a single file. Others allow the user to access and relate several files at one time. For example, the school may have a second database file containing data for each student's current class schedule. At the end of the semester the grades are posted in this file for each student. The data in one file can then be linked to the other file by using a common field, such as the student's name. The ability to link database files creates a relational database. Relational databases allow you to create smaller and more manageable database files, since you can combine and extract data between files.

The database program contains commands that allow the user to design the structure of the database records and enter the data for each record into the file. This is the physical storage of the data. How this data is retrieved, organized, and manipulated is the conceptual use of the data.

DATABASE

Advantages of Using a Database

A computerized database system does not save time by making the data quicker to enter. This, as in most programs, is a function of the typing speed of the user and his or her knowledge of the program.

One of the main advantages to using a computerized database system is the ability to quickly locate records. Once data is entered into the database file, you can quickly search the database to locate a specific record based on the data in a field. In a manual system, a record usually can be located by knowing one key piece of information. For example, if the records are organized by last name, to find a record you must know the last name. In a computerized database, even if the records were organized by last name, you can still locate the record using information in another field.

A computerized database also makes it easy to add and delete records from a file. Once a record is located, you can edit the contents of the fields to update the record or delete the record entirely from the file. You can also add new records to a database file.

Another advantage to a computerized database system is its ability to arrange the records in the file according to different fields of data. The records can be organized by name, department, pay, class, or whatever else is needed at a particular time. This ability to produce multiple file arrangements helps provide information in a more meaningful manner. The same records can provide information to different departments for different purposes.

A fourth advantage is the ability to perform calculations on different fields of data. Instead of pulling each record from a filing cabinet, recording the piece of data you want to use, and then calculating a total for the field, you can simply have the database program sum all the values in the specified field. It can even selectively use in the calculation only those records meeting certain requirements. Information that was once costly and time consuming to get is now quickly and readily available.

Finally, a database program can produce either very simple or complex professional-looking reports. A simple report can be created by asking for a listing of specified fields of data and restricting the listing to records meeting specified conditions. A more complex, professional-looking report can be created using the same restrictions or conditions as the simple report, but the data can be displayed in a columnar format, with titles, headings, subtotals, and totals.

In manual systems there are often several files containing some of the same data. A computerized database system can allow access by more than one department to the same data. Common updating of the data can be done by any department. The elimination of duplicate information saves space and time.

Database Terminology

Delete: To remove a record from the database file.

Edit: To change or update the data in a field.

Field: A collection of related characters, such as last name, that makes up a piece of information.

Record: A collection of related fields, such as a person's name, classes, and grades.

Report: A listing of specified fields of data for specified records in a file.

Search: To locate a specific record in a file.

Sort: To arrange the records in a file in a specified order.

Case Study for Labs 9–11

Your next assignment with The Sports Company as a management trainee is in the Southwest Regional office as an assistant to the Regional Manager. Your primary responsibility in this position is to use Works for Windows to update the current system of maintaining employee records and to generate related reports.

In Lab 9 you design a database for the employee records and create the structure for the database using Works for Windows. You learn how to enter records, edit records, and set field sizes.

You learn how to maintain and modify a database in Lab 10. Specifically, you learn how to delete records and modify the database structure by adding fields and formatting fields. You also learn to sort a database to organize the information in a more meaningful order. Finally, you will learn to search and query a database to locate information.

In Lab 11, you learn how to create a customized data entry form to make it easier to enter records in the database. In addition, you learn how to create a report of selected database information.

Before You Begin

All figures in these labs reflect the use of a standard VGA display monitor and an Epson FX850 printer. If another monitor is used, there may be more lines of text displayed in the windows than in the figures. This setting can be changed using the Windows Setup. The selected printer also affects how text appears onscreen. If possible, select a printer for which the display matches the figures in the manual.

DATABASE

9

Creating
a Database

CASE STUDY

Your next assignment with The Sports Company as a management trainee is in the Southwest Regional office as an assistant to the Regional Manager. Your primary responsibility in this position is to use Works for Windows to update the current system of maintaining employee records and producing related reports.

In this lab you will learn how to design a database for the employee records and create the structure for the database using Works for Windows.

Competencies

After completing this lab, you will know how to:
1. Plan a database.
2. Create a database form.
3. Enter and edit information.
4. Change the field size.
5. View multiple records.
6. Move around in List view.
7. Change the field width.
8. Print a database.

Exploring the Database Window

Load Works for Windows.
From the Startup dialog box,

Choose: Database

If a message box appears describing how to start a database,

Choose: OK

If necessary, maximize the database window.

DATABASE

Your screen should be similar to Figure 9-1.

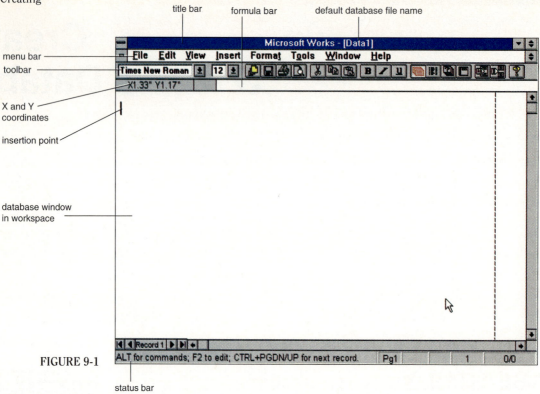

FIGURE 9-1

As in the word processor and spreadsheet tools, the screen is divided into four areas: the menu bar at the top of the screen, the toolbar below it, the **database window** in the workspace, and the status bar at the bottom. The default database file name, Data1, is displayed in the title bar.

The database menu bar and toolbar contain many commands and buttons that are the same as in the word processor and spreadsheet tools. Others are specific to the database tool. The menu and toolbar operate the same as in the word processor and spreadsheet.

Below the toolbar is the formula bar. As in the spreadsheet tool, this area displays entries as they are made or selected. The left end of the formula bar displays the **X and Y coordinates** of the insertion point. The X coordinate specifies the location of the insertion point in inches horizontally from the left edge of the paper, and the Y coordinate specifies its location vertically from the top of the paper. An entry made at the current location of the insertion point would be 1.33 inches from the left edge of the paper and 1.17 inches from the top. This information is helpful if you need to design the database form to match a printed form.

The status bar contains several new items of information.

Pg 1 This indicator tells you that the insertion point is on the first page of the form.

1 This number tells you that the insertion point is on the first record. In this case, the record you will enter will be the first record in the database.

> Do not be concerned if the X and Y coordinates on your screen are slightly different. This is a function of the printer your system is using.

0/0   The first of these two numbers tells you how many records are *displayed* in the database. As you will learn later, records can be hidden from view. When hidden, they are not included in this number. The second number tells you the total number of records (both displayed and hidden) in the database. A Works database can have up to 32,000 records. Since there are no records in the database, it displays 0/0.

The messages in the status bar tell you how to activate the menu bar, edit a record, and move to the next record. Information in the status bar will vary as you use the database tool.

Planning a Database

A **database** is an organized collection of information. For example, the information in your address book is a database. The information in a database consists of fields and records. A **field** is a collection of related characters, such as a person's name. A **record** is a collection of related information, such as a person's name, address, and phone number.

The Sports Company plans to use Works to maintain several different types of databases. The database you will create will contain information about each Sports Company employee. Other plans for using Works include keeping records on preferred customers and inventory. To keep the different types of files separate, a database for each group will be created.

Your first step is to plan the design of your database. You need to decide what information the employee database should contain and how it should be structured or laid out.

This information can be obtained by analyzing the current recordkeeping procedures used throughout the company. You need to understand the existing procedures so that your database reflects the information that is maintained by different departments. You should be aware of the forms that are the basis for the data entered into their records and of the information that is taken from their records to produce periodic reports. You also need to find out what information department managers would like to be able to obtain from the database that may be too difficult to generate using their current procedures.

After looking over the existing recordkeeping procedures and the reports that are created from the information, you decide to include in one database all the information currently maintained in the personnel folder on each employee. This data includes personal information such as the employee's name and address, as well as company information such as department and job title.

After carefully looking at the data currently maintained on each employee and the reports that are generated from this data, you need to decide how to break the information into fields. How you set up the database affects what you can do with the database later on. For example, you could include the employee's first and last names in one field in the database. However, a database designed this way is hard to arrange and makes locating information difficult because too much information is included in one field. Alternatively you could set up two fields for the same information, one for each part of the name. The advantage to creating separate and smaller fields of information is the flexibility it gives you later on to locate and arrange information.

You decide to include the fields shown below:

```
Emp #
Hire Date
Last Name
First Name
Street Address
City
State
Zip Code
Store #
Department
Job Title
Hourly Rate
Hours
```

Creating a Database Form

Once you know what information you want included in the database, you can design the database **form**. A form is used to enter the records into the database. The form consists of the field names and blank entry areas where you enter the field information for each record. The layout of the form can be designed any way you want.

When you open a new database file, Works automatically displays **Form view**. Form view is one of four different views that can be used in the database tool. The different views are used for different purposes. Form view is used to design the form, enter records, and view one record at a time. It is most similar to looking at paper application forms one at a time.

First you want to enter the **label**, THE SPORTS COMPANY EMPLOYEE RECORD, as a form header or title to identify the data contained in the form. A label is a descriptive text entry that is not part of a field. The title will be entered at the top of the form and will appear above each record in Form view.

The insertion point can be moved anywhere within the window using the directional keys, or by clicking on the location in the window with the mouse.

Press:

The X and Y coordinates in the formula bar show the insertion point is 1.33 inches from the left edge of the paper and 1.25 inches from the top of the paper. To enter the label at this location in all capital letters,

Press: Caps Lock

Type: **THE SPORTS COMPANY EMPLOYEE RECORD**

Your screen should be similar to Figure 9-2.

insertion point

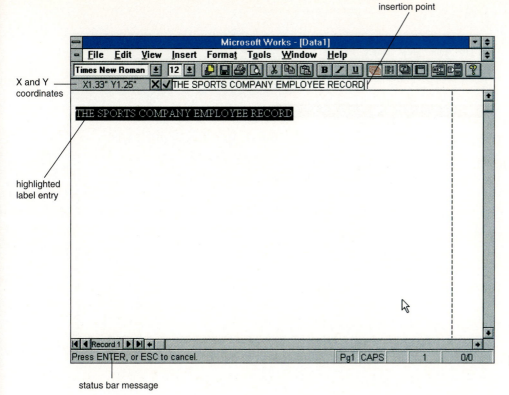

X and Y coordinates

highlighted label entry

status bar message

FIGURE 9-2

As you type, the label is displayed in the formula bar and in the form window. Notice that the insertion point in the window has expanded to highlight the entire label. In the formula bar the insertion point shows you where the next character you type will appear.

To complete the label, following the directions in the status bar,

Press: ←Enter

Your screen should be similar to Figure 9-3.

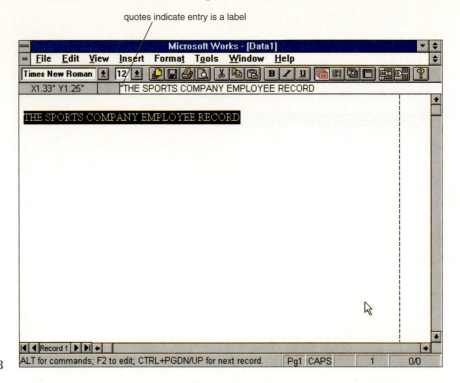

FIGURE 9-3

Notice that the label in the formula bar begins with a double quote, just as does a text entry in a spreadsheet.

To turn off Caps Lock,

Press: `Caps Lock`

Entering Field Names

Next you will create the first field for the employee record form. A field consists of two parts, the **field name** and the **field entry**. Each field name in a database must be unique and should be descriptive of the contents of the field. It can be a maximum of 15 characters and cannot begin with a single or double quotation mark or an apostrophe. The field entry is the information you enter in each field to complete a record. For example, the field name "Last Name" would label the field containing the last name of "Smith," the field entry.

The fields can be entered anywhere in the form window as long as they do not overlap. You want the fields to be a single column along the left edge of the form and to begin two lines below the form header. To move to this location,

Press: ↓ (2 times)

Check the X and Y coordinates to verify that the highlight is positioned at X1.33" Y1.58". If it is not, move it to that location (or as close as possible).

The first field of data you will enter in the database is the employee number. Each new employee is assigned a number that is a maximum of four digits. You have decided to name the first field "Employee Number." The name can be typed in either upper- or lowercase letters. Works will display the characters in the form window as you enter them.

To enter the field name,

Type: **Employee Number**

Because the data you will enter in this field is a maximum of four characters, you decide to shorten the field name to Emp #. This way the field name will be closer in size to the data that will be entered in the field. To change the entry, you will delete the extra characters and type in the new character, #. The ←Backspace key will delete the characters to the left of the insertion point.

Use ←Backspace to erase all characters back to the "p."

Press: Spacebar
Type: #

To show that the field name is complete and to define the entry as a field name, not a label, you type a colon (:).

Type: :
Press: ←Enter

Your screen should be similar to Figure 9-4.

> If you forget the colon, Works will treat the entry as a label, and the Field Size dialog box will not be displayed. Erase the label entry by pressing Delete and reenter the field name correctly.

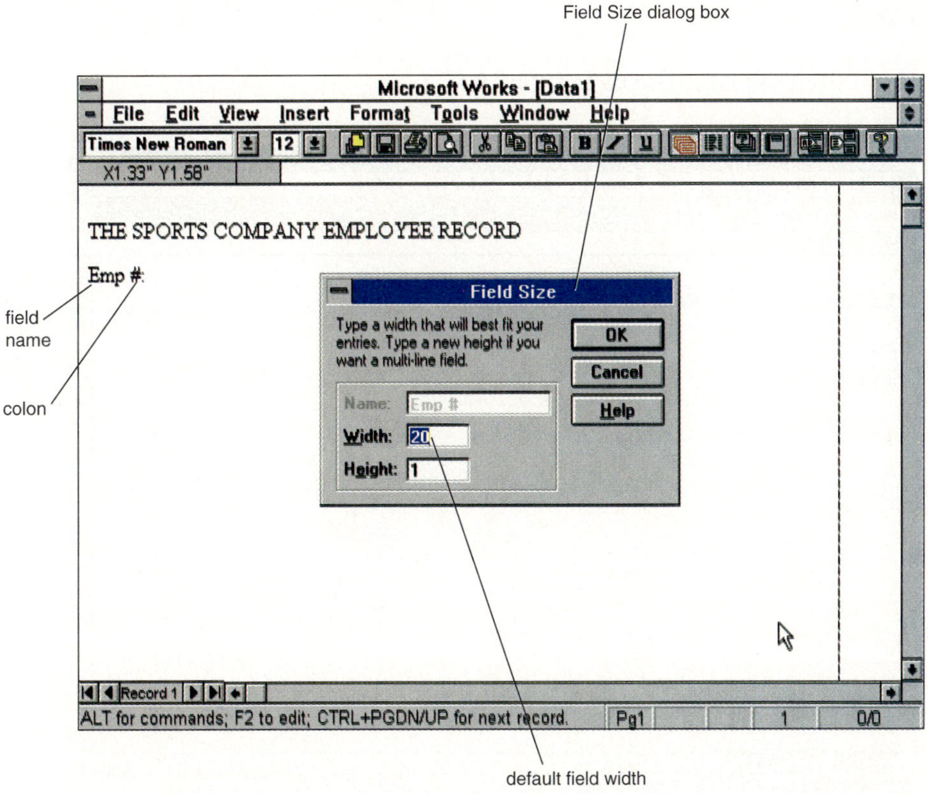

FIGURE 9-4

The Field Size dialog box is displayed to allow you to specify the size of the field entry space. Works proposes the **field width** of 20 spaces and **field height** of 1 line. The field width is the number of spaces needed to display the largest possible entry in that field. The field height is the number of lines needed to display the field entry. The largest employee number is five digits. To change the field size,

> The maximum field width is 325 characters.

Type: 4

The employee number will not require more than one line to display the field entry. Therefore the height setting is acceptable. To complete the command,

> Reminder: You can press ←Enter to choose OK.

Choose: OK

Works displays a line after the Emp # field name to show the location and size of the field entry space. The insertion point moves to the next line in anticipation that you want to add another field. To enter the second field name, Hire Date,

Type: **Hire Date:**
Press: ←Enter

You estimate that the field size needs to be eight spaces to accommodate the date entry.

Type: 8
Choose: OK

Your screen should be similar to Figure 9-5.

FIGURE 9-5

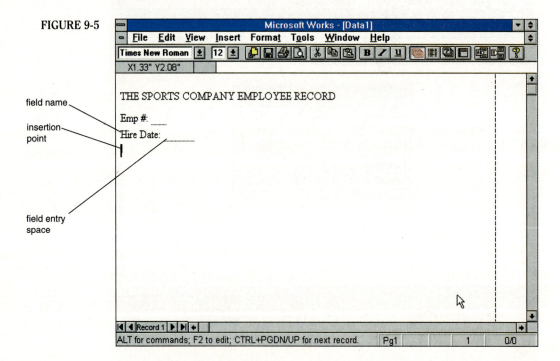

You are ready to define the third field, which will hold the employee's last name. The field name will be Last Name. You estimate the field size will require 18 spaces. When determining field size, make the size as close as possible to the anticipated largest entry. If you make the size too small, the entire entry will not be displayed in the field. To enter the third field,

Type: Last Name:
Press: ↵Enter
Type: 18
Choose: OK

In the same manner, enter the information for the next ten fields.

Field Name	Width
First Name	15
Street	20
City	15
State	2
Zip Code	5
Store #	3
Department	12
Job Title	15
Hourly Rate	5
Hours	3

Do not be concerned if you make a mistake. You will learn how to correct it next.

Your screen should be similar to Figure 9-6.

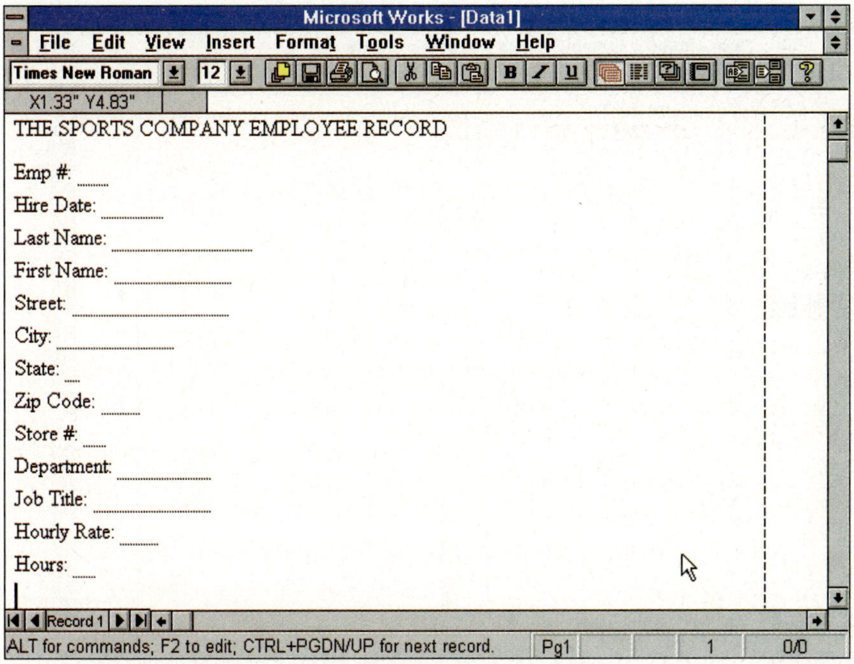

FIGURE 9-6

Editing Field Names

After looking over the field names, you decide to change the Street field name to Street Address. Now that the form contains labels and fields, as you move the insertion point and it is positioned on a field name, field entry, or label, the entire entry is highlighted, indicating it is selected.

Move to: the Street field name

To change the field name, you could completely replace it with the new name, or you can edit it. The F2 EDIT key is used to edit an entry just as in the Spreadsheet tool.

Click: formula bar

or

Press: F2 EDIT

The EDIT indicator appears in the status bar. To add the word "Address" to the field name,

Press: ←

Press: Spacebar

Type: **Address**

Press: ←Enter

Your screen should be similar to Figure 9-7.

> Click on the field name or use the arrow keys to move to the field name.

> The mouse shortcut to turn on Edit is to click the formula bar.

FIGURE 9-7

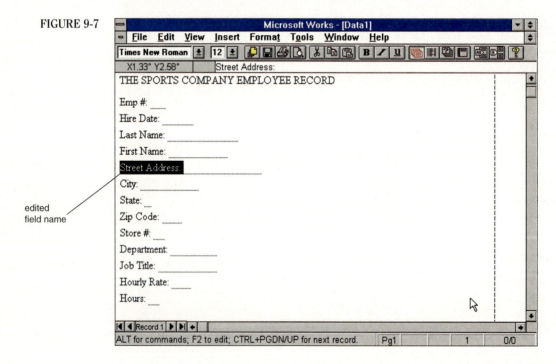

edited
field name

Carefully check your screen to ensure that the field names match exactly those in Figure 9-7. If they do not, correct them now.

Once you are satisfied that your field names are correct, the database form can be saved.

Choose: **F**ile>**S**ave

➤   Ctrl + S

or

Click: 💾 Save

The Save As dialog box is displayed.

Name this file EMPLOYEE. If necessary, change the drive to the drive containing your data disk where you want Works to save the file.

Choose: OK

Entering Information

Next you will enter the information for the first employee record. As mentioned earlier, the information that is stored in each field is called the field entry. The field entries you will be entering for the first record are:

Field Name	Field Entry
Emp #	51
Hire Date	6/14/89
Last Name	Anderson
First Name	Susan
Street Address	4389 S. Hayden Rd.
City	Mesa
State	AZ
Zip Code	84101
Store #	52
Department	Clothing
Job Title	Sales associate
Hourly Rate	6.45
Hours	40

The field entry is entered in the field entry space to the right of the field name. To enter the employee number for the first record,

Move to: the Emp # field entry space

You can move directly to the next field entry space by pressing Tab or the previous field entry space by pressing ⇧ Shift + Tab.

DATABASE

Your screen should be similar to Figure 9-8.

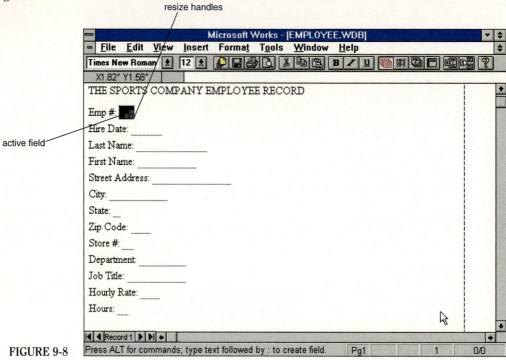

resize handles

active field

FIGURE 9-8

The entry space is highlighted to show that it is an **active field**. An active field is one in which you can enter information. The three shaded squares within the highlight are **resize handles** that are used with a mouse to adjust the field size. You will learn how to use this feature shortly.

You can enter text, numbers, or a formula as a field's entry. The field entry can be up to 325 characters long. To enter the employee number for the first record,

Type: **51**

The entry is displayed in the field and in the formula bar.

To complete the entry,

> If you made an error, use ←Backspace to erase the characters and retype the entry correctly.

Press: ←Enter

Your screen should be similar to Figure 9-9.

field entry
right-aligned numeric entry

```
┌──────────────────────────────────────────────────────────────┐
│             Microsoft Works - [EMPLOYEE.WDB]            ▼  ▲▼ │
├──────────────────────────────────────────────────────────────┤
│ □  File  Edit  View  Insert  Format  Tools  Window  Help   ▲▼│
├──────────────────────────────────────────────────────────────┤
│ Times New Roman ± 12 ± │▢▢▢▢│▢▢▢│ B / U │▢▢▢▢│▢▢▢│ ? │
├──────────────────────────────────────────────────────────────┤
│   X1.82" Y1.56"          51                                   │
├──────────────────────────────────────────────────────────────┤
│ THE SPORTS COMPANY EMPLOYEE RECORD                          ↑│
│                                                              │
│ Emp #: ▓▓                                                    │
│ Hire Date: ..........                                        │
│ Last Name: ..........                                        │
│ First Name: ..........                                       │
│ Street Address: ..........                                   │
│ City: ..........                                             │
│ State: ....                                                  │
│ Zip Code: ......                                             │
│ Store #: ....                                                │
│ Department: ..........                                       │
│ Job Title: ..........                                        │
│ Hourly Rate: ......            ⇖                             │
│ Hours: ....                                                 ↓│
├──────────────────────────────────────────────────────────────┤
│ │◄│◄│Record 1│►│►││◄│                                    →   │
├──────────────────────────────────────────────────────────────┤
│ Press ALT for commands; type text followed by : to create field.  Pg1      1      1/1 │
└──────────────────────────────────────────────────────────────┘
```

FIGURE 9-9

displayed/total
record indicator

The formula bar shows that Works has interpreted this entry as a numeric entry (no quote mark is displayed). Works interprets numeric and text entries in a database the same as in a spreadsheet. Although it is difficult to see because the field size is small, the numeric entry is displayed right-aligned in the entry space.

As soon as you enter data in a record, the status bar updates the number of displayed records over the total number of records indicator. It now displays "1/1" because there is one displayed record in the database, which consists of a total of one record.

To move directly to the next field entry space,

Press: Tab ⇆

If you press ↓ instead of Tab ⇆, the highlight may move to the field name on the next line, or to a blank space in the window, rather than to the field entry space. You would then need to move to the field entry space. Using Tab ⇆ takes you directly to the next field entry.

You are now ready to enter the information for the next field, Hire Date. To enter the hire date for this record,

You can click directly on the field entry space to move to it.

DATABASE

Type: 6/14/89
Press: ←Enter

Creating
a Database

Your screen should be similar to Figure 9-10.

field entry

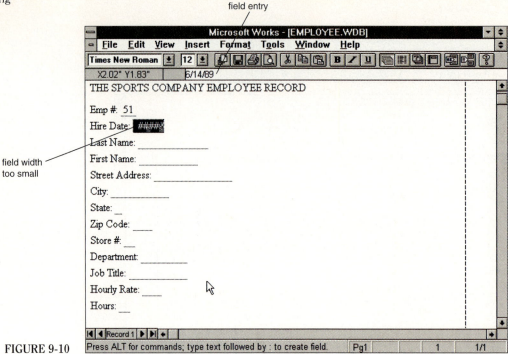

field width
too small

FIGURE 9-10

This entry has been interpreted as a date, as in the Spreadsheet tool, and is a
numeric entry. Although the complete entry is displayed in the formula bar, the
entry space displays #####. The space is too small to fully display the entry, even
though the field width assigned to this field is 8 and the entry is only seven characters. This is because the selected typeface and size affect the number of characters
that can be displayed. The default typeface in Form view is Times New Roman 12pt.
With this font, the field size must be larger than the number of characters in the field
entry to fully display it in the field. You will learn how to adjust the field size shortly.

To move to the Last Name field,

Press: Tab ⇥

Now you are ready to enter the employee's last name. The information you enter in a
text field must be typed just as you want it to appear. In addition it is very important
to be consistent when entering field entries. For example, if you decide to abbreviate
the word "Street" in an address as St., then every record that contains the word
"Street" should be abbreviated in the same way. Also, be careful not to enter a blank
space by pressing Spacebar before or after a field entry. This can cause problems
when using the database to locate information. If information is entered in a consistent manner, it is easier to locate information and to create accurate reports from
the information in the database.

To enter the last name,

Type: **Anderson**
Press: ←Enter

The entry is interpreted as a text entry and is left-aligned in the entry space.

You can also use the `Tab ⇆` key to both enter the data and move to the next field. To enter the first name data using this feature,

Press: `Tab ⇆`

Type: **Susan**

Press: `Tab ⇆`

To enter the information for the next field, Street Address,

Type: **489 S. Hayden Road**

Press: `Tab ⇆`

Your screen should be similar to Figure 9-11.

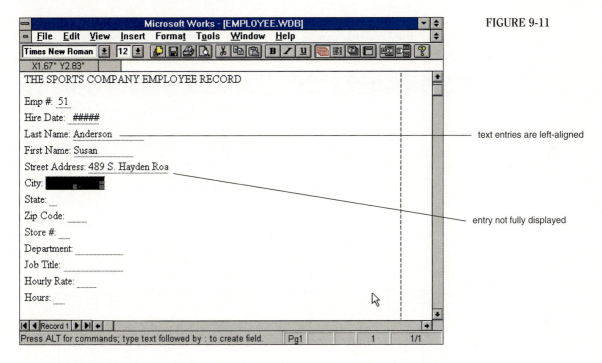

FIGURE 9-11

Notice that the address field entry is longer than the field width, so the entire address cannot be displayed within the field space. Works displays as much of a text entry as possible in the field space.

To return to the Street Address field,

Press: `⇧ Shift` + `Tab ⇆`

The formula bar displays the entire entry. Now you notice that you entered the address incorrectly. It should be 4389 S. Hayden Road. To correct this entry using Edit,

Click: formula bar

or

Press: `F2` EDIT

The house number needs to be corrected. To move the insertion point to the beginning of the entry in the formula bar,

Press: Home

To change the number from 489 to 4389,

Press: → (2 times)
Type: 3

The 3 was inserted into the house number.
    To complete the edit and move to the City field,

Press: Tab

To review, the keys that can be used to enter and edit database records are shown below.

Key	Action
Tab	Moves insertion point to next field entry
⇧Shift + Tab	Moves insertion point to previous field entry
→	Moves insertion point right one field or space; in Edit moves insertion point one space right
←	Moves insertion point left one field or space; in Edit moves insertion point one space left
↑	Moves insertion point up one line
↓	Moves insertion point down one line
Home	In Edit moves insertion point to beginning of entry
End	In Edit moves insertion point to end of entry
Delete	Deletes entry; in Edit deletes character at insertion point
←Backspace	In Edit deletes character to left of insertion point

Enter the next eight fields, typing the information exactly as it appears below. If you make typing errors, practice using the editing keys demonstrated above. When entering the field entry for the last field, Hours, press ←Enter rather than Tab to enter the data. If you press Tab, Works will display a new blank entry form. If this happens, press Ctrl + Page Up to move to the previous record.

Field Name	Data
City	Mesa
State	AZ
Zip Code	84101
Store #	52
Department	Clothing
Job Title	Sales associate
Hourly Rate	6.45
Hours	40 (press ←Enter)

You can also click anywhere in the entry to move the insertion point.

When in Edit, you cannot use Tab to move word by word in the formula bar. This is because pressing Tab is the same as pressing ←Enter; it completes the entry.

Your screen should be similar to Figure 9-12.

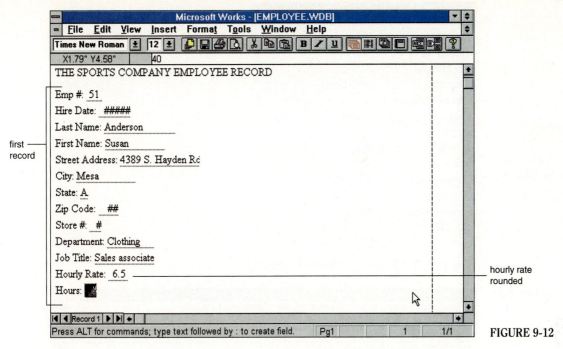

first record

hourly rate rounded

FIGURE 9-12

The data for the first record is now complete. If the hourly rate entry space displays "6.5," this is because the field size is too small to display the complete entry. Whenever there is insufficient space, Works rounds decimals to the largest decimal value that can be displayed rather than display asterisks. Do not be concerned if the fields on your screen display more or fewer characters. The printer and monitor on your system also affect the character display.

As you can see, several of the field entry spaces are too small to display the complete field information. Before increasing the field sizes, however, you will enter a few more records.

Press: Tab ⇆

When you are on the last field in a record, the next record is displayed when you press Tab ⇆. Since there is only one record in the database, a second blank form is displayed. Notice that the status bar displays "2" to show you that the record on the screen is record 2. As records are added to a file, they are assigned a **record number** in the order they are entered. The number of the **active record** (the record you are viewing) is displayed in the status bar.

DATABASE

Enter the following information for the second record.

Field Name	Data
Emp #	434
Hire Date	10/4/90
Last Name	Long
First Name	William
Street Address	947 S. Forest St.
City	Tempe
State	AZ
Zip Code	86301
Store #	47
Department	Operations
Job Title	Cashier
Hourly Rate	6.00
Hours	25 (press ←Enter)

Complete the last field using ←Enter rather than Tab⇆, so that a new blank entry form is not displayed.

Your screen should be similar to Figure 9-13.

FIGURE 9-13

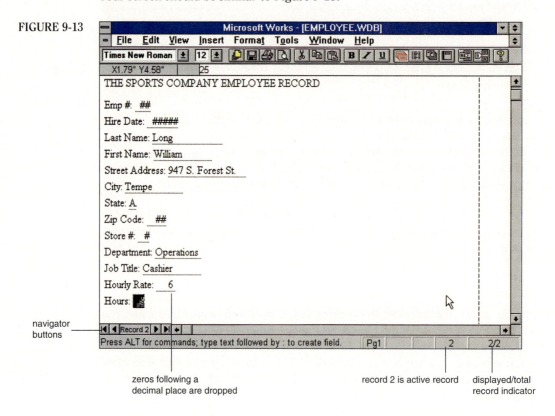

navigator buttons

zeros following a decimal place are dropped

record 2 is active record

displayed/total record indicator

Notice that the hourly rate displays "6." This is because the default number format drops zeros following a decimal point. You will learn how to change the number format in the next lab.

Once you have completed entering record 2, look at the status bar. It shows "2/2." There are now two displayed records in the database file consisting of two records. To view the previous record,

Press: [Ctrl] + [Page Up]

The first record you entered is displayed on the screen. The record number, 1, is displayed in the status bar. Pressing [Ctrl] + [Page Up] or [Ctrl] + [Page Down] will move up or down through the records in the file and display the active record.

Check both records carefully. Edit if necessary.

Since you used abbreviations in the street address for the second record, you want to use abbreviations in the Street Address field in the first record.

Change the street address in record 1 to 4389 S. Hayden Rd.

To move to the end of the database and display a blank entry form,

Click: ▶| Last

or

Press: [Ctrl] + [End]

Pressing [Ctrl] + [End] or clicking ▶| quickly takes you to the end of the file and displays a blank entry form. The highlight is in the same field, Street Address, that it was in in the previous record.

Enter the next record using the information shown below.

Field Name	Data
Emp #	1024
Hire Date	11/12/89
Last Name	Bergstrom
First Name	Drew
Street Address	843 E. Southern Ave.
City	Mesa
State	AZ
Zip Code	84101
Store #	52
Department	Warehouse
Job Title	Stock clerk
Hourly Rate	5.75
Hours	35

Changing the Field Size

As you entered information into the fields, you noticed that some of the field widths were too small to display the entire entry. When a numeric field is too small, it displays number signs just as in the spreadsheet tool. If a text entry field is too small, the entry is interrupted. The first field you will change is the employee number field.

If you have a mouse, you can use the navigator buttons on the left end of the horizontal scroll bar to move to the first ◀|, previous ◀, next ▶, or last ▶| record in the database.

Be careful that you are in the correct field entry space as you are entering the information for each field.

DATABASE

Make the employee number field entry active.
This field needs to be large enough to display an employee number of four digits. Although you defined the field size as 4, it is not large enough to display the current entry of a four-digit number. The procedure for changing the field size in the Database tool is just like changing the column width in the spreadsheet tool.

Choose: Forma**t**

If the Field Size command is dimmed, the field entry area is not selected.

The Field Size command will change the size of the field in Form view.

Choose: Field Si**z**e

Your screen should be similar to Figure 9-14.

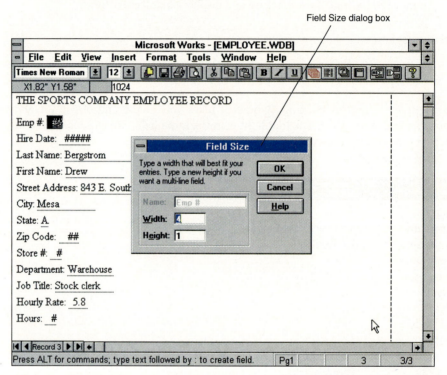

FIGURE 9-14

The Field Size dialog box is displayed. The Field Name option is dimmed because the command you selected lets you change the size only. To increase the field size by 2, in the Width text box,

Type: **6**
Choose: OK

If the field is still too small, increase the width to 7.
The field is now large enough to fully display the employee number. The next field that needs to be enlarged is the Hire Date field.
Make the Hire Date field entry active.

Another way to adjust the field size is to drag the resize handles in the highlight. The handle on the right end of the highlight adjusts the width, the handle on the bottom adjusts the height, and the one in the lower right corner adjusts both width and height.

To increase the width, point to the handle on the right end of the highlight.

When you point to a resize handle, the mouse pointer shape displays an arrow to show you in which direction dragging the handle will affect the size. The shapes and their effects are:

Adjusts width

Adjusts height

Adjusts both width and height

To increase the width, drag the mouse to the right.

As you drag, an outline shows the new field size.

When you think the size is large enough to accommodate the entry, release the mouse button.

If the entry is not fully displayed, increase the width some more.

Using the Field Size command on the Format menu, increase the field size to 10 or as large as needed to fully display the entry on your computer system.

Your screen should be similar to Figure 9-15.

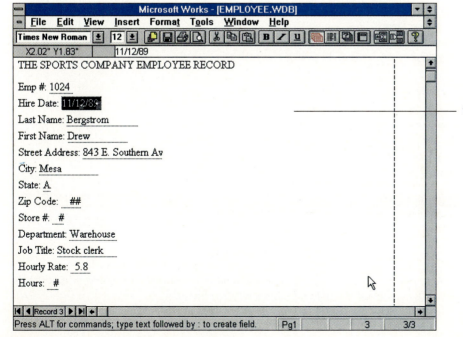

FIGURE 9-15

field size dialog box

If you adjusted the field size by dragging the resize handle, your field may be larger than the field in the figure.

With the default font of Times New Roman 12pt, in Form view the field size needs to be several spaces larger than the entry in order to fully display the entry. If you know the maximum field entry size, you can make the field width just large enough to display the entry. However, where the field size may vary, such as a street address, it is practical to make the field width slightly larger than you think the largest entry will require, so that you do not need to constantly resize fields as new records are added that contain larger entries.

Increase the sizes of the fields to the widths shown below. Depending upon your computer setup, you may need to make several of these fields larger in order to fully display the entries.

> If you are dragging to resize the field, increase the width to approximately the same size.

Field Name	Field Width
Street Address	28
City	18
State	4
Zip Code	8
Store #	4
Department	14
Job Title	18
Hourly Rate	6
Hours	4

Your screen should be similar to Figure 9-16.

FIGURE 9-16

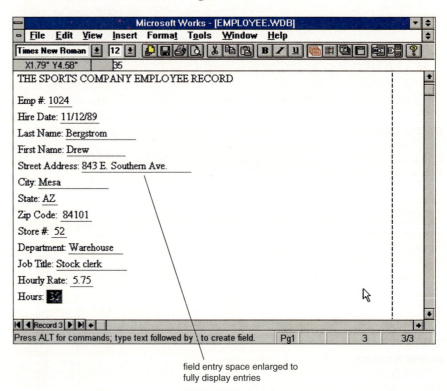

field entry space enlarged to
fully display entries

Look at records 1 and 2 and confirm the field entries are fully displayed in all fields. If they are not large enough, adjust the field width again.

Finally, you would like to enter several more records into the database.

Enter the following two records into the database using the information shown below.

Field Name	Record 4	Record 5
Emp #	728	839
Hire Date	1/15/91	3/14/91
Last Name	Toroyan	Artis
First Name	Lucy	Jose
Street Address	2348 S. Bala Dr.	358 Maple Dr.
City	Tempe	Scottsdale
State	AZ	AZ
Zip Code	85301	85205
Store #	68	57
Department	Warehouse	Sports Equipment
Job Title	Stock clerk	Sales associate
Hourly Rate	7.00	7.50
Hours	40	40

Enter a final record as record 6 using your name in the First and Last Name fields and the information shown below in the fields specified. The information you enter in all other fields can be fictitious.

Field Name	Data
Emp #	9999
Hire Date	(current date)
Store #	52
Department	Operations
Job Title	Mgmt-trainee

When you are done, check each of the records and edit any entries that are incorrect. If necessary, increase the field widths of any fields that are not fully displayed.

Viewing Multiple Records

There are now six records in the database. In Form view only one record is displayed in the window at a time. Many times it is helpful to view many records at once in the window. Works has a second database view called **List view** that lets you do just that.

Move to: Emp # field of record 1

To view all six records on the screen,

Choose: View>List
  ➤   F9 List View
or
Click: List View

Your screen should be similar to Figure 9-17.

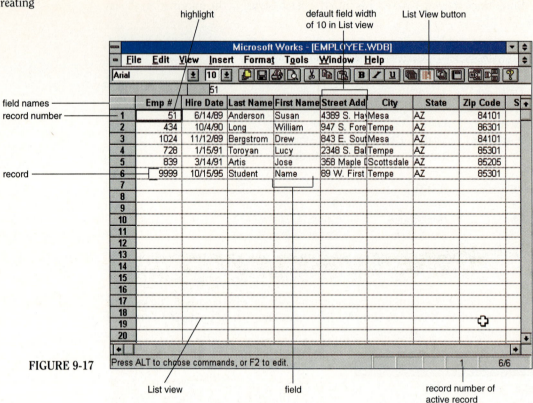

FIGURE 9-17

List view displays the database records as a table, with each record as a row and each field as a column. The field name is displayed centered above each column. Along the left edge of the window, a row number identifies the record number of each record. This view is similar to how data is displayed in a spreadsheet. Up to 20 records can be displayed in List view at a time when the window is maximized. Notice that the form heading, THE SPORTS COMPANY EMPLOYEE RECORD, is not displayed in this view.

The highlight is in the same field and record it was in in Form view. Whichever record you are on in Form view is the first record displayed in List view. Since you were on the first record, record number 1 is at the top of the window.

The menu bar displays the same menu of commands as in Form view. The toolbar also contains the same buttons.

The status bar displays the record number of the active record (the record containing the highlight). It does not display the page number as in Form view. The navigation buttons are not displayed.

Moving Around in List View

Notice that the field widths for all fields in List view are equal and not the same as those in Form view. This is because List view has its own default field width of 10 spaces, just like the spreadsheet. Consequently some of the field names and entries are not fully displayed, and some field widths are much larger than they need to be. When the field is too small, it is difficult to read the information in List view. For example, you cannot see the complete field name or entry for the Street Address field. The only way to read the field entry in interrupted fields is to move the highlight to the field and look at the entry as it is displayed in the formula bar.

To see the Street Address field entry for record 1,

Press: [→] 4 times

Now the complete entry is displayed in the formula bar. You will learn shortly how to increase the field width in List view.

Additionally, because the field entries are displayed across a row, only part of each record can be displayed in the window at a time.

To move around in List view, you use the same keys as in the spreadsheet.

Key	Result
[→],[←],[↑],[↓]	One field or record in direction of arrow
[Page Down]	Down one window
[Page Up]	Up one window
[Ctrl] + [Page Down]	One window right
[Ctrl] + [Page Up]	One window left
[Ctrl] + [End]	End of database
[Ctrl] + [Home]	Beginning of database
[Home]	Leftmost field in active record
[End]	Rightmost field in active record

To scroll the fields to the right into view,

Press: [Ctrl] + [Page Down]

Your screen should be similar to Figure 9-18.

interrupted field names   interrupted field entries

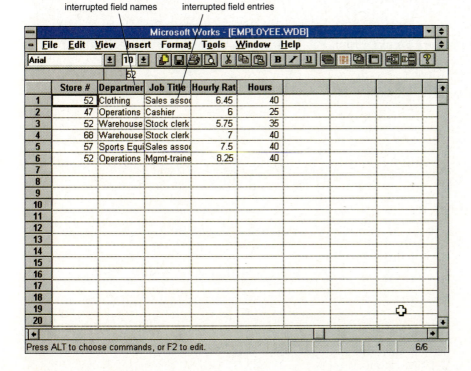

FIGURE 9-18

The fields to the right of the Zip Code field are displayed. As you can see, the Job Title field is too narrow to display the complete entry, and in addition the Department and Hourly Rate field names are interrupted.

To move to the left one window,

Press: Ctrl + Page Up

The first eight fields are displayed again. To move to the last field in a record, you could press Ctrl + Page Down to move a window to the right and then move the highlight to the last field, or you can press End.

Press: End

Pressing End positions the highlight on the rightmost field in a row. The Hours field is now the selected field. To move quickly back to the leftmost field in the row,

Press: Home

Changing the Field Width

You would like to adjust the field widths to better fit the field names and entries. To make the records in List view easier to read, you can increase or decrease the width of the columns. This is similar to changing the field size in Form view. Changing the field width in List view does not affect the field size set in Form view.

The Emp # field is larger than it needs to be. To decrease the width of this field,

Choose: Format

The commands in the List view Format menu are slightly different from those in the Form view Format menu. For example, the command to change the field size is called Field Width rather than Field Size.

Choose: Field Width

Your screen should be similar to Figure 9-19.

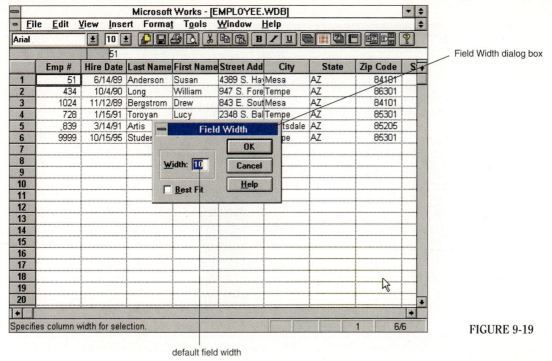

Field Width dialog box

default field width

FIGURE 9-19

The default setting, 10, is displayed in the Field Width dialog box. The Emp # field name entry requires five spaces. As in Form view, the default font affects how many characters can be displayed. In List view the default font is Arial 10pt, as it is in the spreadsheet. To allow extra space in the column head on both sides of the field name, you will decrease the field width to 7.

> In List view the field width can be a maximum of 79 spaces.

Type: 7
Choose: OK

The entire employee number field entry is still displayed, and the field name Emp # has space on both sides in the column head.

The Hire Date, Last Name, and First Name fields are wide enough to display the entries, but the First Name and Last Name field names at the top of the column are crowded.

Increase the Last Name and First Name field widths to 11.

The Street Address field is much too small. Sometimes it is difficult to know how much you need to increase the field width. In that case it is helpful to use the Best Fit option. This feature works just like in the spreadsheet. This command will Best Fit the field based on the size of the currently selected field entry. To best fit all entries in a column, the entire field must be selected.

Move to: Street Address field
Choose: Edit>Select Field
or
Click: Street Address field name

DATABASE

Your screen should be similar to Figure 9-20.

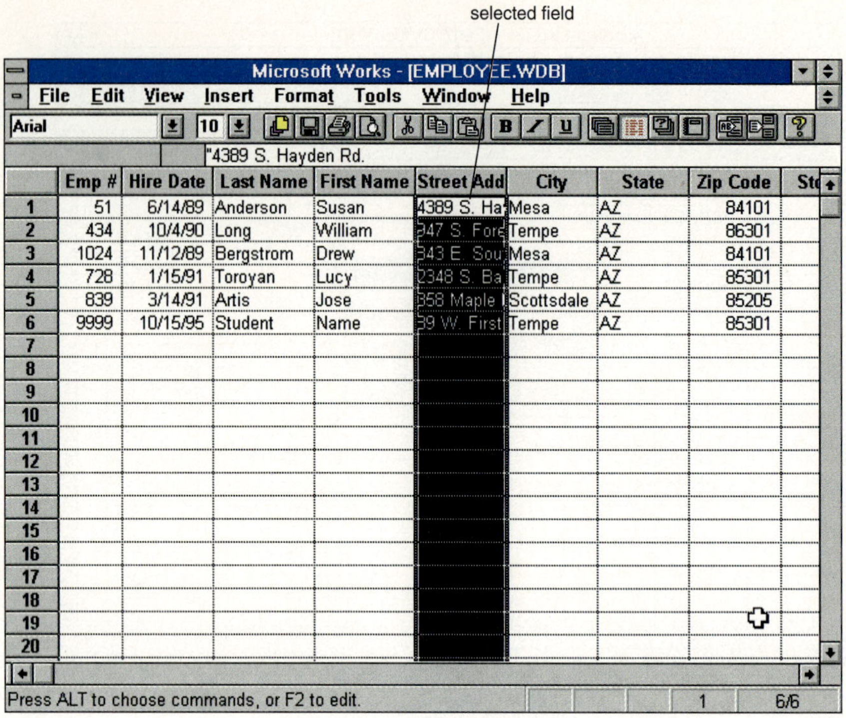

selected field

FIGURE 9-20

Choose: Format>Field **W**idth>**B**est Fit>OK
or
Double-Click: Street Address field name

The width is increased to accommodate the largest entry. In addition, an extra space is automatically added to the right side of the entry to visually separate the field entries from those in the column to the right.

Best Fit does not consider the size of the field name. If the field name is longer than any entries in the field, the field name may be interrupted or there may not be a space between field names. In these cases you need to set the field width manually.

Move to: State field

The State field is larger than it needs to be. However, if you used Best Fit to adjust the column width, the field name would be interrupted.

Decrease the width to fully display the field name and leave a blank space between columns.

In a similar manner, Best Fit or decrease the field widths of the remaining fields so that one space separates the columns and/or there is space on both sides of the field names.

When you are done, the highlight should be in the Hours field.

You can drag the column border to change the field width as you did in the Spreadsheet tool.

Your screen should be similar to Figure 9-21.

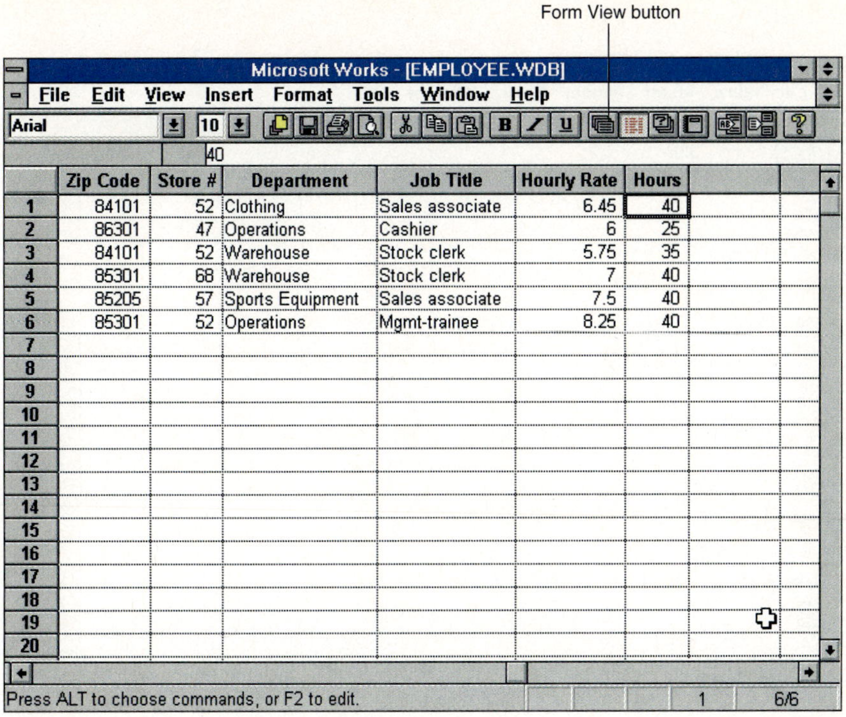

Form View button

	Zip Code	Store #	Department	Job Title	Hourly Rate	Hours		
1	84101	52	Clothing	Sales associate	6.45	40		
2	86301	47	Operations	Cashier	6	25		
3	84101	52	Warehouse	Stock clerk	5.75	35		
4	85301	68	Warehouse	Stock clerk	7	40		
5	85205	57	Sports Equipment	Sales associate	7.5	40		
6	85301	52	Operations	Mgmt-trainee	8.25	40		
7								
8								
9								
10								
11								
12								
13								
14								
15								
16								
17								
18								
19								
20								

Press ALT to choose commands, or F2 to edit.   1   6/6

FIGURE 9-21

The changes you have made to the field widths in List view do not affect the field size settings in the Form view. To verify this you will switch back to Form view. To do this,

Choose: View>Form
 ➤   F9   Form View
or
Click: 🖼 Form View

The F9 key acts as a toggle to switch between Form view and List view.

DATABASE

Your screen should be similar to Figure 9-22.

List View button

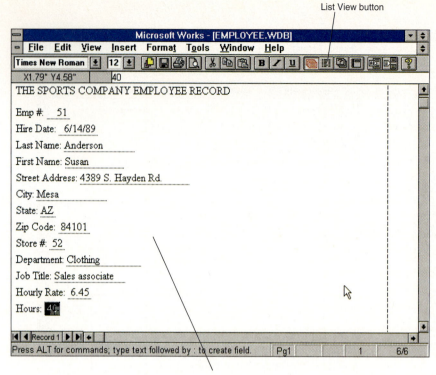

FIGURE 9-22

Form view field sizes are unchanged

Since the highlight was in the Hours field for record 1 in List view, the same record and field are selected in Form view. The Hours field entry space is only five spaces wide in Form view; in List view it is six spaces wide.

Move to each field of this record and verify that the original field sizes you set in Form view were not altered. When you are done, the Emp # field should be active.

To return to List view,

Click:  List View

or

Press: F9 Form View

You need to save the records you have entered into the file and the changes made to the field sizes. To do this,

Choose: File>Save

➤ Ctrl + S

or

Click: 🖫 Save

Works saves the file using the same file name, EMPLOYEE.

Printing the Database

You would like to print a list of the records in this file to show to the store manager.

If necessary prepare your printer for printing.

Just as in the other tools, before printing the file it is a good practice to preview your document.

Choose: File>Print Preview

or

Click: 🔍 Print Preview

Zoom in the Preview window.

Your screen should be similar to Figure 9-23.

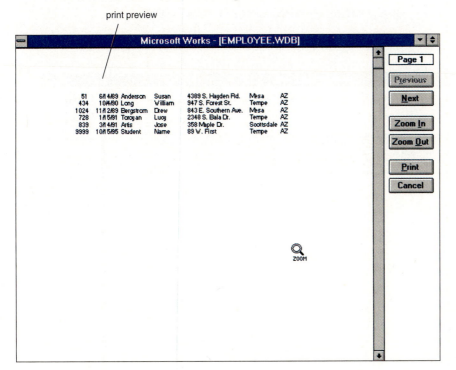

FIGURE 9-23

The Emp # through State fields are displayed on the first page. Notice that the field names and record numbers are not included. To see the next page of the printout,

Choose: Next

The report will require two pages. You want to see if you can adjust the orientation and margins so that it will only require one page. Additionally you want the final printout to display the record numbers and field names.

Close the Preview window.

First you want to make the right and left margins narrower so that as many fields of data can be printed across the width of the page as possible. To do this,

Choose: File>Page Setup>Margins>Left Margin

Set the left and right margins to .25".

To change the orientation of the page to landscape,

Choose: Source, Size and Orientation>Landscape

Finally, to turn on the feature to print the records with field name labels and record numbers,

Choose: Other Options>Print record and field labels>OK

Preview the database again. Your screen should be similar to Figure 9-24.

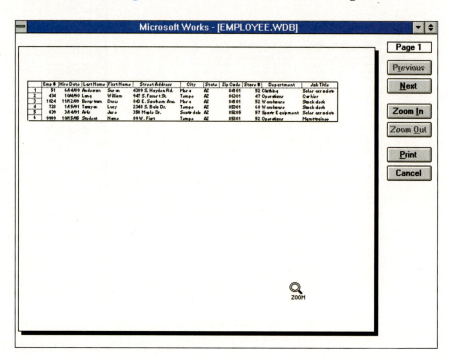

FIGURE 9-24

The entire database now fits on one page. If your database does not fit on one page, reduce the margins as much as necessary to meet this objective. If this is still insufficient, print the database without record and field labels.

To print the database from the Preview window,

Choose: Print

The printer should be printing out the database.

You still are not completely pleased with the appearance of the records. You particularly do not like how the hourly rate values appear. You will learn how to change the display of the data in the next lab.

Close the file. Respond Yes to save the changes. If you are ready, exit Works.

Key Terms

database window (294)
X and Y coordinates (294)
database (295)
field (295)
record (295)
form (296)
Form view (296)
label (296)
field name (298)

field entry (298)
field width (300)
field height (300)
active field (304)
resize handle (304)
record number (309)
active record (309)
List view (315)

Command Summary

Command	Shortcut	Button	Action
File>**S**ave	Ctrl + S	💾	Saves current file
Forma**t**>Field Size			Changes field size in Form view
View>**L**ist	F9		Displays records in List view
Forma**t**>Field **W**idth			Changes width of fields in List view
Edit>Select Fiel**d**			Selects entire field
Forma**t**>Field **W**idth>**B**est Fit			Changes field width to size of largest entry
View>**F**orm	F9		Displays records in Form view
File>Print Pre**v**iew			Displays file as it will appear when printed
File>Pa**g**e Setup			Changes page layout and printing options

LAB REVIEW

Matching

1. Form view _____
2. record _____
3. X and Y coordinates _____
4. ### _____
5. record number _____
6. Home _____
7. field _____
8. 1/4 _____
9. F9 _____
10. field width _____

a. shows horizontal and vertical location of insertion point on the form
b. indicates that numeric entry cannot be fully displayed
c. collection of related information
d. insertion point is on record 1 of four records
e. number assigned to records as they are added to a file
f. number of spaces to display largest field entry
g. displays one record at a time
h. in List view, moves to leftmost field in active record
i. collection of related characters
j. switches between Form and List view

DATABASE

Fill-In Questions

1. Identify the parts of the Works database window by entering the appropriate terms on the lines below.

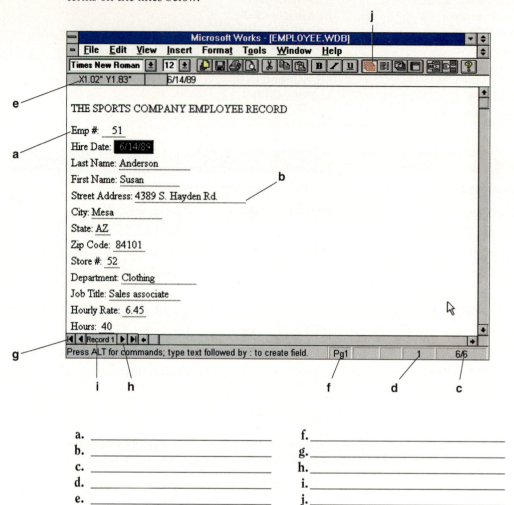

a. _____   f. _____
b. _____   g. _____
c. _____   h. _____
d. _____   i. _____
e. _____   j. _____

1. Cathy owns a small gift shop that sells hand-made crafts. She currently keeps her client orders and payment records in a small accounting ledger. Her business has grown considerably since she started it a year ago, so she has decided to invest in a computer. She wants to keep track of her client orders and payments using Works.

   a. Create a database form using the title "Cathy's Clients" and the field information defined below.

Field Name	Field Size
Client #	5
Last name	12
First name	10
Address	20
City	10
State	2
Zip code	5
Phone	8

   b. Save the form as CRAFTS.

   c. Enter the following records into the database in Form view.

Record 1	Record 2
89342	93432
MaKee	Carpenter
Ryan	Kelly
3846 E. Thomas Rd.	90 W. University Dr.
Claremont	Newport
NH	VT
23745	21543
999-4854	999-0943

   d. Enter a third record using your name in the first and last name fields. Your client number is 74395. The address and phone can be fictitious.

   e. Adjust the field size to fully display all entries.

   f. Switch to List view and adjust the field widths to fully display the field names and field entries.

   g. Print the records in List view with record numbers and field labels using landscape orientation.

   h. Save the database.

2.   Carlos is the manager of the Housesitting Company, a small agency specializing in caring for clients' houses while they're away. One of his responsibilities is to maintain employee records. To help him with this job, he wants to create a database of the employee records using Works.

a.   Create a database form using the title "The Housesitting Company Employee Records" and the field definitions shown below.

Field Name	Field Size
Employee #	3
Last name	15
First name	10
MI	1
Address	45
Date hired	8

b.   Save the form as STAFF1.

c.   Enter the following records into the database in Form view.

Record 1

234
[Your Last name]
[Your First name]
[Your Middle Initial]
34 Maple Dr., San Jose, CA 95157
[Current date]

Record 2

245
Masters
Kevin
W
85 Ash Ave., Danville, CA 94526
September 5, 1994

Record 3

342
Johnson
William
J
3456 Pine St., Santa Ana, CA 92705
October 6, 1994

Record 4

311
O'Hearn
Paul
J
984 Mountain Dr., San Diego, CA 92112
May 18, 1994

d. Adjust the field size to fully display all entries.

e. Switch to List view and adjust the field widths to fully display the field names and entries.

f. Print the records in List view with record and field labels using landscape orientation. If necessary, reduce the margins to fit the records on one page.

g. Save the file.

3. Maryanne works at the local bakery. Her supervisor has asked her to create a database to keep track of the bakery inventory.

a. Create a database form that includes the title "Bakery Inventory" and the following fields.

Field	Field Size
Item #	5
Item name	20
Quantity	2
Cost	6

b. Save the form as BAKEINV.

c. Enter the following records in Form view.

Record 1	Record 2
89333	34567
Flour	Sugar
25	35
45.00	35.00

Record 3	Record 4
43243	21294
Salt	Baking Powder
42	89
23.00	13.50

Record 5	Record 6
33738	83922
Baking Soda	Wheat Flour
13	35
32.00	47.00

d. Enter your name in the Item name field of record 7. Leave all the other fields blank.

e. Adjust the field size to fully display all entries.

f. Switch to List view and adjust the field widths to fully display the field names and entries.

g.   Print the records with record and field labels in List view.

h.   Save the file in List view.

4.   Michael owns a small contracting business. The business is growing and Michael has decided to buy a computer to help him keep track of his clients, employees, and inventory.

   a.   Create a database to help Michael keep track of his clients. The form should include a title and a field for each client's business name, contact person's first and last name, address, telephone number, and type of job. Save the form as CONTRACT.WDB.

   b.   Enter your name and appropriate information as the first record.

   c.   Enter eight additional records using either real or fictitious data.

   d.   Adjust the field sizes in Form view and field widths in List view as necessary.

   e.   Print the records in List view with record and field labels using landscape orientation. If possible, adjust the margins so the printout will require only one page.

   f.   Save the database file in List view.

5.   Karen is a third-year student at a midwestern university. She would like you to create a database form of all the classes she has taken to date. Create a form that contains class information such as class number, title, hours, and any other information you feel would be appropriate. Enter at least 10 records using either real or fictitious data. Save and print the file in List view with record and field labels.

10 Modifying Searching, and Sorting a Database

CASE STUDY

As you continue to add more records to The Sports Company employee database, you realize that you forgot to include a field for the employees' sex. The Regional Manager suggests that you also add a Weekly Pay field to the database form. You will modify the database structure to include these two new fields of data.

In addition, throughout the day you receive several requests for information or notifications of changes that need to be made to the employee records. Updating records and providing information to other departments is a routine part of maintaining and using a database.

Finally, the accounting department manager has asked for a list of employees who are earning less than $6.00 per hour and work in the Clothing or Warehouse departments. You will create a simple report containing this information.

Deleting Records

Load Works. Put your data disk in the appropriate drive for your computer system.

To use the file with the additional employee records, open the database file EMPLOY2.WDB. If necessary, maximize the database window and change to List view.

The database file now contains a total of 42 records. As you look at the records you notice several errors. For example, the sixth record has several errors in the Last Name field and record 11 has several errors in the Street Address field. Also you can see that data for Susan Anderson has been entered twice, as record number 1 and record number 17. The only difference in the records is the employee number. To check the records to see if there are errors in other fields that are not visible on the window,

Press: [Ctrl] + [Page Down]

You do not see any errors in this window. To view the rest of the records in the database,

Press: [Ctrl] + [End]

The highlight is positioned on the last field of the last record.
    In this window you notice that the job title in record 40 contains a data entry error.

Press: [Home]

The rest of the records look good. To return to the first record,

Press: [Ctrl] + [Home]

The first record that needs to be corrected is record 6.
    Move to record 6 and edit the last name to Reynolds.
    In a similar manner, correct the street address for record 11 to be "21 W. Southern Ave."
    The next data entry error is in record 40. You could use the arrow keys to move to the record, but it is faster to use the Go To command on the Edit menu. This command is similar to the Go To command in the Word Processor and Spreadsheet tools.

Choose: Edit>Go To
    ➤   [F5] GO TO

> Press [F2] EDIT or click the formula bar to change to Edit.

> The shortcut key for this command is [F5].

Your screen should be similar to Figure 10-1.

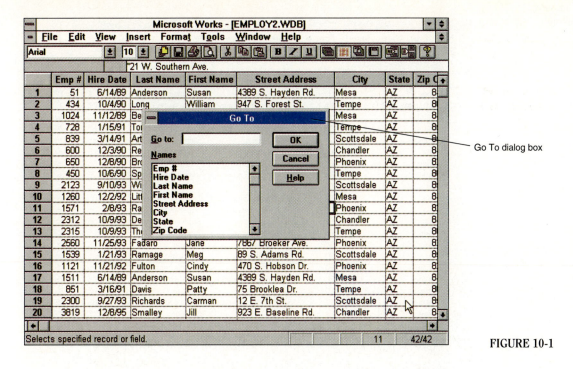

Go To dialog box

FIGURE 10-1

In the Go To text box you can enter a record number or a field name. If you want to move to a field, you can select the name from the Names list box. The highlight will move to the selected field in the active record. To move to record number 40,

Type: 40
Choose: OK

The highlight is now positioned on the Street Address field in record 40.
　　　Using Edit, correct the job title to read "Shipping clerk."
　　　As you noticed, Susan Anderson's record is in the database twice, as record 1 and record 17. After checking the original data input form, you have found that record 1 has the correct employee number. You need to delete record 17. The command to delete a record is in the Insert menu. First the highlight must be on any field in the record to be deleted.
　　　Use the Go To command to move to record 17.
　　　To delete the record,

Choose: Insert>Delete Record/Field>Record>OK

The same command is used to delete a record in Form view.

DATABASE

Your screen should be similar to Figure 10-2.

```
┌─────────────────────────────────────────────────────────────────────────────┐
│                  Microsoft Works - [EMPLOY2.WDB]                        ▼ ▲  │
├─────────────────────────────────────────────────────────────────────────────┤
│  File  Edit  View  Insert  Format  Tools  Window  Help                   ▲  │
│ Arial        ▲ 10 ▲  □□□□□□ ░□□ B I U □□□□□□ ?                               │
│                    "Shipping clerk                                            │
├─────────────────────────────────────────────────────────────────────────────┤
```

	City	State	Zip Code	Store #	Department	Job Title	Hourly Rate	Hour
17	Tempe	AZ	86301	57	Warehouse	Shipping clerk	7	1
18	Scottsdale	AZ	85205	47	Sports Equipment	Sales associate	6.6	3
19	Chandler	AZ	84174	52	Warehouse	Shipping clerk	6.25	4
20	Phoenix	AZ	82891	57	Sports Equipment	Sales associate	5.85	2
21	Phoenix	AZ	82891	68	Clothing	Sales associate	6.45	3
22	Mesa	AZ	84101	52	Operations	Custodian	5.5	2
23	Tempe	AZ	86301	57	Operations	Cashier	6.75	3
24	Chandler	AZ	84174	52	Sports Equipment	Sales associate	6.25	3
25	Scottsdale	AZ	85205	57	Operations	Cashier	6.75	2
26	Mesa	AZ	84101	68	Sports Equipment	Sales associate	5.85	2
27	Mesa	AZ	84101	68	Warehouse	Supervisor	8.85	3
28	Tempe	AZ	86301	47	Operations	Supervisor	8.65	1
29	Phoenix	AZ	82891	57	Warehouse	Stock clerk	5.5	4
30	Scottsdale	AZ	85215	52	Operations	Cashier	6.6	2
31	Phoenix	AZ	82891	57	Warehouse	Stock clerk	5.5	3
32	Tempe	AZ	86301	47	Clothing	Sales associate	6.25	2
33	Phoenix	AZ	82891	52	Sports Equipment	Supervisor	8.45	4
34	Phoenix	AZ	82891	57	Operations	Cashier	6.6	3
35	Scottsdale	AZ	85205	57	Sports Equipment	Sales associate	5.85	3
36	Phoenix	AZ	82891	47	Operations	Cashier	6.45	3

```
┌─────────────────────────────────────────────────────────────────────────────┐
│ ◄│                                                                        │►  │
│ Press ALT to choose commands, or F2 to edit.                  17    41/41   │
└─────────────────────────────────────────────────────────────────────────────┘
```

FIGURE 10-2

The record is permanently removed from the database and the records below have been renumbered. The status bar now shows that there are 41 records in the database.

Formatting Numeric Fields

Next you want to change the display of numeric entries in the Hourly Rate field to currency.

Move to: Hourly Rate field of record 1

Notice that the entries in this field do not display any zeros following the decimal. This is because the default display of numbers in the database, General, drops zeros following the decimal and rounds decimal values when the field width is too small to fully display the value.

As in the Spreadsheet tool, the Format menu commands are used to change how entries are displayed. In the Database tool, the Format menu commands affect the entire field. Therefore it is not necessary to select a range. However, you do need to be positioned on any record in the field you want to change.

To change the format of the hourly rate field to currency,

Choose: Format>Number

The same Number dialog box options as in the Spreadsheet tool are displayed. The default format of General is selected.

Select: Currency

The default decimal place setting of 2 is acceptable.

Choose: OK

Your screen should be similar to Figure 10-3.

numbers displayed in
Currency format

	City	State	Zip Code	Store #	Department	Job Title	Hourly Rate	Hour
1	Mesa	AZ	84101	52	Clothing	Sales associate	$6.45	4
2	Tempe	AZ	86301	47	Operations	Cashier	$6.00	2
3	Mesa	AZ	84101	52	Warehouse	Stock clerk	$5.75	3
4	Tempe	AZ	85301	68	Warehouse	Stock clerk	$7.00	4
5	Scottsdale	AZ	85205	57	Sports Equipment	Sales associate	$7.50	4
6	Chandler	AZ	84174	68	Clothing	Sales associate	$6.60	1
7	Phoenix	AZ	82891	52	Operations	Head cashier	$6.75	3
8	Tempe	AZ	86301	57	Sports Equipment	Sales associate	$5.50	3
9	Scottsdale	AZ	85205	47	Clothing	Sales associate	$5.85	3
10	Mesa	AZ	84101	68	Operations	Head cashier	$6.25	2
11	Phoenix	AZ	82891	57	Warehouse	Stock clerk	$5.50	4
12	Chandler	AZ	84174	52	Sports Equipment	Sales associate	$6.60	1
13	Tempe	AZ	86301	57	Clothing	Sales associate	$6.25	3
14	Phoenix	AZ	82891	52	Operations	Custodian	$7.50	3
15	Scottsdale	AZ	85205	47	Clothing	Sales associate	$5.50	2
16	Phoenix	AZ	82891	68	Operations	Cashier	$5.85	4
17	Tempe	AZ	86301	57	Warehouse	Shipping clerk	$7.00	1
18	Scottsdale	AZ	85205	47	Sports Equipment	Sales associate	$6.60	3
19	Chandler	AZ	84174	52	Warehouse	Shipping clerk	$6.25	4
20	Phoenix	AZ	82891	57	Sports Equipment	Sales associate	$5.85	2

Press ALT to choose commands, or F2 to edit.   1   41/41

FIGURE 10-3

The Hourly Rate field now displays dollar signs and two decimal places. Any new entries made in this field will automatically be displayed in this format.

You also decide to change the display of the numbers in the Emp # field. You want the employee number to appear as four digits for all records. To do this you can change the display to show leading zeros. By default, even if you type a number that begins with a zero, Works drops the leading zero. This can be a problem in a field such as zip code where the leading zero must appear for the number to be correct. To move to the Emp # field,

Press: Home

To format this field to display leading zeros,

Choose: Format>Number>Leading Zeros

The Options area of the dialog box now displays the Number of Digits text box. In this box you specify the total number of digits you want the field to display. Works will then add as many leading zeros to the entries in this field as are needed to fill the entry. The largest number in this field is four. To make all entries in this field four digits, in the Number of Digits text box,

Type: 4

An entire field can also be formatted to display in currency, percent, or fraction format by typing a field entry in the desired format style (for example, $7.10 for currency rather than 7.10).

DATABASE

The Sample area shows how the entry in the current cell will appear in this format.

Choose: OK

Your screen should be similar to Figure 10-4.

field entry

FIGURE 10-4

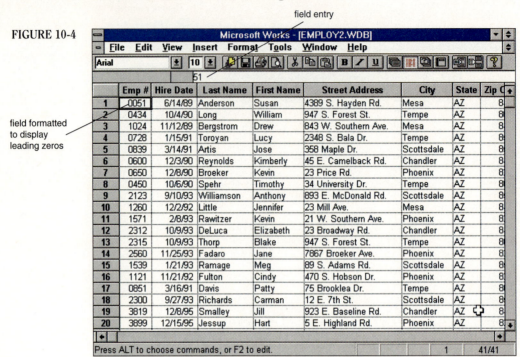

field formatted to display leading zeros

Entries in this field now display leading zeros as necessary to fill up to four digits. The entry in the formula bar is the same as it was initially entered, only the display of the entries has changed.

Inserting a Field in List View

Next you want to add the new field, Sex, to the database. Although it is better to include all the necessary fields when creating the database, it is always possible to add or remove fields at a later time. This can be done in either List view or Form view. To add the field in List view, you create a blank field column and then enter the field name and contents.

The new field will appear between the Zip Code field and the Store # field. Creating a blank field column is much like entering a blank column in a spreadsheet. First you position the highlight anywhere within the column where you want the new column inserted. When the field is inserted, the fields to the right of the new field move right to make room.

Move to: Store # field of record 1

Choose: **I**nsert>**R**ecord/Field>**F**ield>OK

or

Click: Insert Field

A blank column is inserted in the database. The field is automatically assigned the default field width of 10 spaces in List view and 20 spaces in Form view. To enter the field name,

Choose: Edit>Field Name

Your screen should be similar to Figure 10-5.

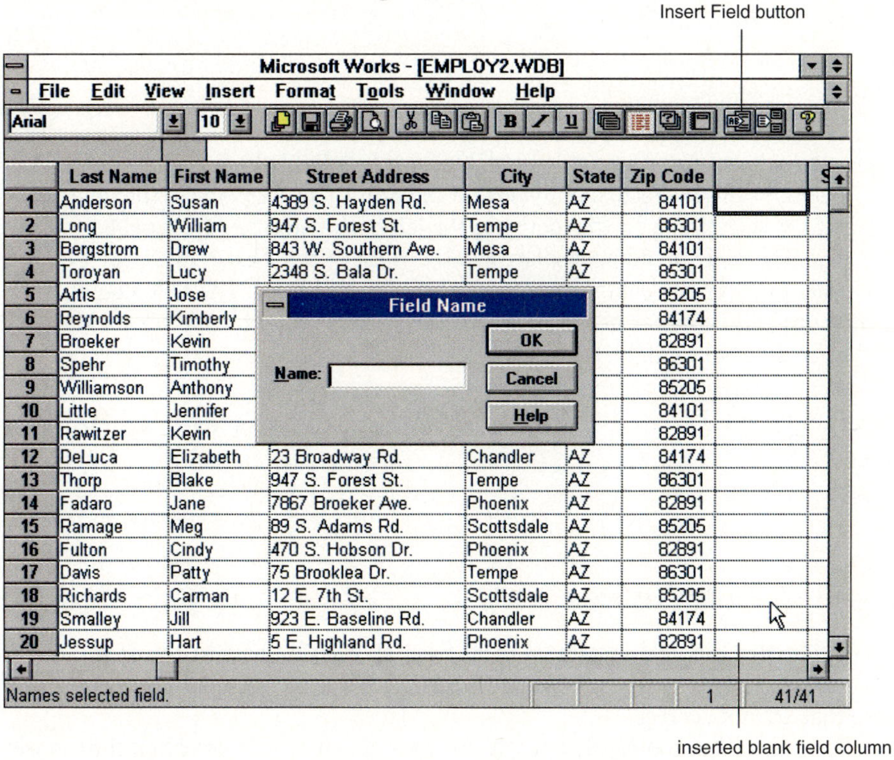

FIGURE 10-5

A dialog box appears for you to enter the field name. You can also use this command to rename an existing field name. The name of the field will be "Sex." You do not need to end the field name with a colon as in Form view.

Type: Sex
Choose: OK

The field name is displayed at the top of the column.

Moving Fields in List View

The information for each record in this field needs to be entered next. In most cases you can determine the sex for each record by looking at the employee's first name. If you were unable to make this determination, you would need to check the original employment form.

The First Name field is on the opposite side of the window from the Sex field. Whenever fields are separated, being able to tell what data belongs with which record is difficult. This is the same problem that happens in large spreadsheets. You can solve the problem by splitting the window as you learned in the spreadsheet labs. However, another way is to move the fields.

You need to enter the data for the Sex field for every record. To make it easier to enter the field contents, you will move the Sex field next to the First Name field. The location of a field can be changed for viewing purposes in List view without affecting Form view. To move a field, the entire field must be selected. To select the Sex field,

Choose: Edit>Select Field

➢   ⇧Shift + F8

or

Click: Sex field name

The entire field column through record 32,000 is highlighted.

Use the Cut and Paste commands on the Edit menu or point to the field name and drag the selection with the mouse to the left of the Street Address field.

The Sex field should be displayed to the right of the First Name field. You are now ready to enter the data for the Sex field for each record. The field contents for each record will be either M for Male or F for Female. To enter the sex for the first employee record in capital letters,

The mouse pointer will change to ▷ when you drag the field to move it.

Press: Caps Lock
Type: F
Press: ←Enter

Copying Field Entries

You could enter the field entries, M or F, for each record individually, or you could copy the same entry down the column through the last record and then change only those that are not correct.

As in the other tools, you can select rows and columns by dragging the mouse, by using ⇧Shift + the directional keys, or F8 Extend.

Select records 1 through 41 of the Sex field.

To fill the selected column with all F's for Female,

Choose: Edit>Fill Down

Your screen should be similar to Figure 10-6.

	Emp #	Hire Date	Last Name	First Name	Sex	Street Address	City	
22	3298	1/15/94	Broeker	Kimberly	F	235 W. Camelback Rd.	Mesa	A
23	1801	2/23/93	Davis	Aaron	F	947 S. Forest St.	Tempe	A
24	1329	1/7/93	Reynolds	Cara	F	432 E. Rider Rd.	Chandler	A
25	2910	11/15/93	Samuals	Scott	F	90 E. Rawhide Ave.	Scottsdale	A
26	1924	8/9/93	Steverson	Todd	F	832 S. William Ave.	Mesa	A
27	1843	7/24/93	Kennedy	James	F	8949 S. Summer St.	Mesa	A
28	2058	8/15/93	Ehmann	Kurt	F	5401 E. Thomas Rd.	Tempe	A
29	3918	12/31/94	Davis	Scott	F	345 W. Mill Ave.	Phoenix	A
30	3195	12/15/93	Cady	Todd	F	235 N. Cactus Dr.	Scottsdale	A
31	4831	1/13/96	Fisher	Sarah	F	984 W. Thomas Rd.	Phoenix	A
32	3800	12/1/94	Granger	Michael	F	564 S. Lemon Dr.	Tempe	A
33	0854	3/18/91	Falk	Nancy	F	298 N. 1st St.	Phoenix	A
34	0283	1/9/87	Briggs	Scott	F	1900 W. Southern Ave.	Phoenix	A
35	0308	12/9/88	Lembi	Damon	F	76 Thomas Rd.	Scottsdale	A
36	0738	4/21/90	Rensmayer	Jeffrey	F	87 E. Aurora Ave.	Phoenix	A
37	0403	1/9/89	Stinkemper	Jacob	F	2348 S. Bala Dr.	Mesa	A
38	0390	12/12/88	Dunn	William	F	491 W. Maple Ave.	Phoenix	A
39	1839	7/21/93	Bond	Jason	F	293 S. Charlette St.	Scottsdale	A
40	3291	1/24/94	McKay	Cody	F	8201 E. Cactus Ave.	Mesa	A
41	3924	8/9/94	Smith	Brent	F	939 E. Rider Rd.	Tempe	A

FIGURE 10-6

entry copied down column

The F in the first cell is copied down the field column. Now all that needs to be done is to change the records that have male first names to M. The first male record is record 2.

Move to the Sex field of record 2.

Type: M
Press: ↓

Continue editing the data for this field, looking at the First Name field to determine whether the employee is male or female (refer to Figure 10-7). When you are done, turn off Caps Lock.

The default field width for the Sex field is wider than it needs to be.

Decrease the width of the Sex field to five spaces.

Your screen should be similar to Figure 10-7.

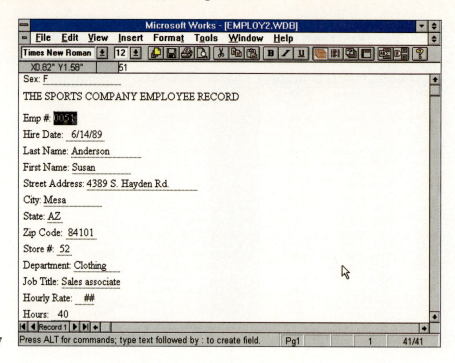

FIGURE 10-7

Move the Sex field back to its original location following the Zip Code field.
To return to the first field of the first record,

> Select the entire field and use Cut and Paste or drag to move it.

Press: Ctrl + Home

Moving and Inserting Fields in Form View

The second field that needs to be added to the database is the Weekly Pay field. You will enter this field in Form view.

Click: ▤ Form View

or

Press: F9   Form View

Your screen should be similar to Figure 10-8.

Form View button

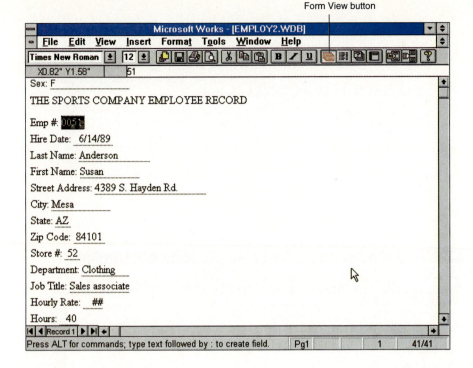

FIGURE 10-8

The first thing you notice is that the Sex field is not in the same location as you entered it in List view. It is displayed above the form title. When a field is added in List view, it is entered in the first available space in the form. You must use Form view to permanently position a field. To move the Sex field,

Move to: Sex field name

Rather than moving the field below the Zip Code field and then having to reposition all fields below it, you will move the Sex field to the right of the Zip Code field.

You can drag a field or use the Position Selection command on the Edit menu to move a field in Form view.

Point to the selected field name.

The mouse pointer changes to ↖. As you move the selection, a dotted outline of the field name and field entry space moves in the form window to show your location. You would like to move the Sex field to the same line and to the right of the Zip Code field.

Drag the selection to the right of the Zip Code (to about X 2.83" Y 3.33").

DATABASE

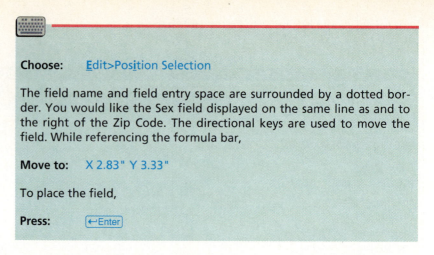

Choose: Edit>Position Selection

The field name and field entry space are surrounded by a dotted border. You would like the Sex field displayed on the same line as and to the right of the Zip Code. The directional keys are used to move the field. While referencing the formula bar,

Move to: X 2.83" Y 3.33"

To place the field,

Press: ←Enter

Your screen should be similar to Figure 10-9.

FIGURE 10-9

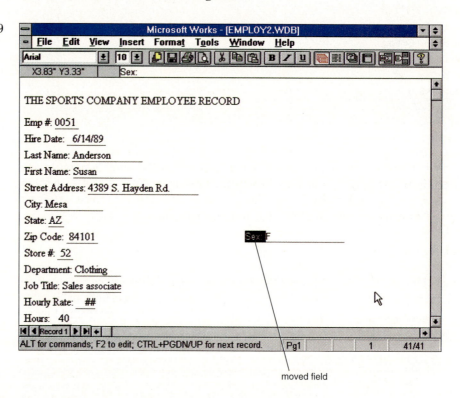

moved field

Moving fields in Form view does not affect where they are displayed in List view.

The Sex field is now displayed next to the Zip Code field.
Notice that the field size is set at the default size of 20 spaces and is much larger than it needs to be.
Select the Sex field entry space and decrease the field size to 3.
Now you are ready to enter the second new field of data as the last field in the form. To do this,

Move to: left margin of blank line below Hours field (approximately X 0.33" Y 4.83")

You have also noticed that the Hourly Rate field space is too small to display the number because it has been formatted to Currency. Increase the field size of the Hourly Rate field until it is large enough to fully display the value.

You can add a new field by typing the field name followed by a colon. You can also add a field using the Field command on the Insert menu or the ▥ toolbar button. To use this method,

Choose: Insert>Field
or
Click: ▣ Insert Field

In the Field Name text box of the Insert Field dialog box,

Type: Weekly Pay

In the Width text box,

Type: 10
Choose: OK

The field is displayed in the form at the location of the insertion point.

Entering a Formula

Now you are ready to enter the data for this field. The data for this field is a value that is calculated by multiplying the Hourly Rate times the Hours.

You can use four types of calculations in the database; addition (+), subtraction (–), multiplication (*) and division (/). Entering a formula in a database is similar to entering a formula in a spreadsheet. With the highlight still on the Weekly Pay entry area,

Type: =

As in the Spreadsheet tool, the equal sign tells Works you are entering a formula. In a database, instead of using cell references, you specify the field names you want Works to use in the calculation. In this case you want to multiply the hours worked times the hourly rate. The field names must be entered exactly as they appear in the entry form (except for case size).

Type: Hourly Rate*Hours

Works displays as much of the entry as possible in the field. The formula bar displays the entire formula.

Press: ⏎ Enter

You cannot use pointing to specify the field names.

If you enter a space before or after the *, Works will delete the space when you complete the formula.

DATABASE

Your screen should be similar to Figure 10-10.

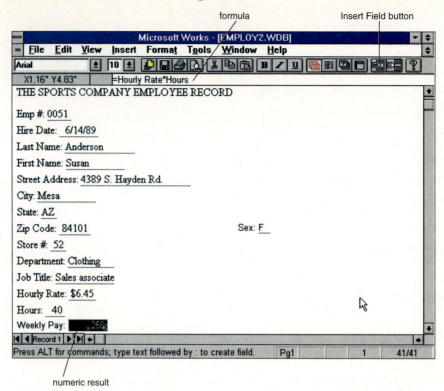

FIGURE 10-10

The calculated value, 258, is displayed in the field. The formula is displayed in the formula bar.

Format the field to display as currency with two decimal places.

To see how this change has affected the other records in the database,

Click: [icon] List View

or

Press: [F9] List View

The Weekly Pay column is displayed. Works calculated the new field for each record in the database. Notice that the field width of 10 spaces is too small to display the entire field name.

Increase the field width to fully display the field name (approximately 12).

To move to the first field of the active record,

Press: [Home]

Searching the Database

While you have been working on the database, you have received several change requests and inquiries from different departments. You want to use the partially completed database to see how quickly Works can provide the answers.

First you need to locate the record for Kimberly Broeker and change her last name to Robson. To locate this record, you could look at the First Name and Last Name fields in List view; however, that can take a lot of time, especially if the database is large. Instead you will use the Find command on the Edit menu to quickly locate a record in the database. To locate Kimberly Broeker's record,

Choose: Edit>Find

In the Find dialog box you type the information you want Works to locate. The Find command will find a record by searching the file for data in a field that matches the text or number you specify. You can enter the text in uppercase or lowercase letters or a combination of the two. Works is not case-sensitive; it will locate the text without regard to the use of uppercase or lowercase characters. Works will also locate the text if it is part of a longer word. In this case you want to locate the record with a last name of Broeker. Because you do not need to be concerned about case sensitivity, the entry can be made in all lowercase letters.

Type: broeker

The Next Record option lets you find the next occurrence of the specified text or number in the database. This is the default setting. To use this setting and tell Works to begin the search,

Choose: OK

Your screen should be similar to Figure 10-11.

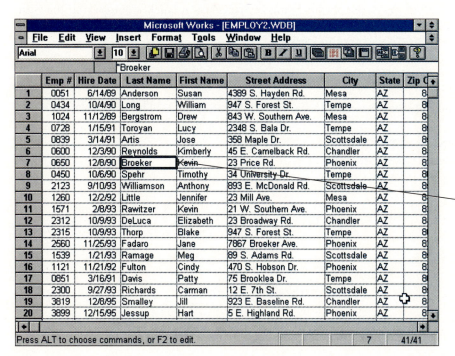

FIGURE 10-11

located record

If the message No Match Found appears, choose OK and reissue the command. Make sure you entered the name correctly.

DATABASE

Works searches forward from your current location in the database. It checks each field of each record in the entire database until it locates the next record matching the search text. This can be slow in a large database.

The first record in the database to exactly match the specified search text of "broeker" is record number 7. The highlight is positioned on the Last Name field of that record. However, this is the record for Kevin Broeker, not Kimberly. To continue the search to look for the next record,

Press: [F7] Find Next

The next record containing the text "broeker" is located, but this time the matching text is found in the Street Address field. When the Find command is used, Works searches for the matching text in all fields of the database.

To continue the search,

Press: [F7] Find Next

Works has located another record containing the text "broeker." This time it is the record for Kimberly Broeker.

Change the last name to Robson.

To return to the first field of the first record,

Press: [Ctrl] + [Home]

The next request on your desk is from the Operations department. It indicates that one of the Operations department employees who lives in Scottsdale is having trouble with mail delivery from the Sports Company because the zip code is incorrect. Unfortunately the note forgot to include the employee's name. You decide to check all the records for employees living in Scottsdale. A quick way to search the entire database or selected area of the database is to use the All Records option in the Find dialog box. To see how this works,

Choose: Edit>Find

The Find What text box displays the text you previously entered. To replace this text,

Type: scottsdale
Choose: All records>OK

	Emp #	Hire Date	Last Name	First Name	Street Address	City	State	Zip C
5	0839	3/14/91	Artis	Jose	358 Maple Dr.	Scottsdale	AZ	8
9	2123	9/10/93	Williamson	Anthony	893 E. McDonald Rd.	Scottsdale	AZ	8
15	1539	1/21/93	Ramage	Meg	89 S. Adams Rd.	Scottsdale	AZ	8
18	2300	9/27/93	Richards	Carman	12 E. 7th St.	Scottsdale	AZ	8
25	2910	11/15/93	Samuals	Scott	90 E. Rawhide Ave.	Scottsdale	AZ	8
30	3195	12/15/93	Cady	Todd	235 N. Cactus Dr.	Scottsdale	AZ	8
35	0308	12/9/88	Lembi	Damon	76 Thomas Rd.	Scottsdale	AZ	8
39	1839	7/21/93	Bond	Jason	293 S. Charlette St.	Scottsdale	AZ	8
42								
43								
44								
45								
46								
47								
48								
49								
50								
51								
52								
53								

matched records

Press ALT to choose commands, or F2 to edit. 5 8/41

FIGURE 10-12

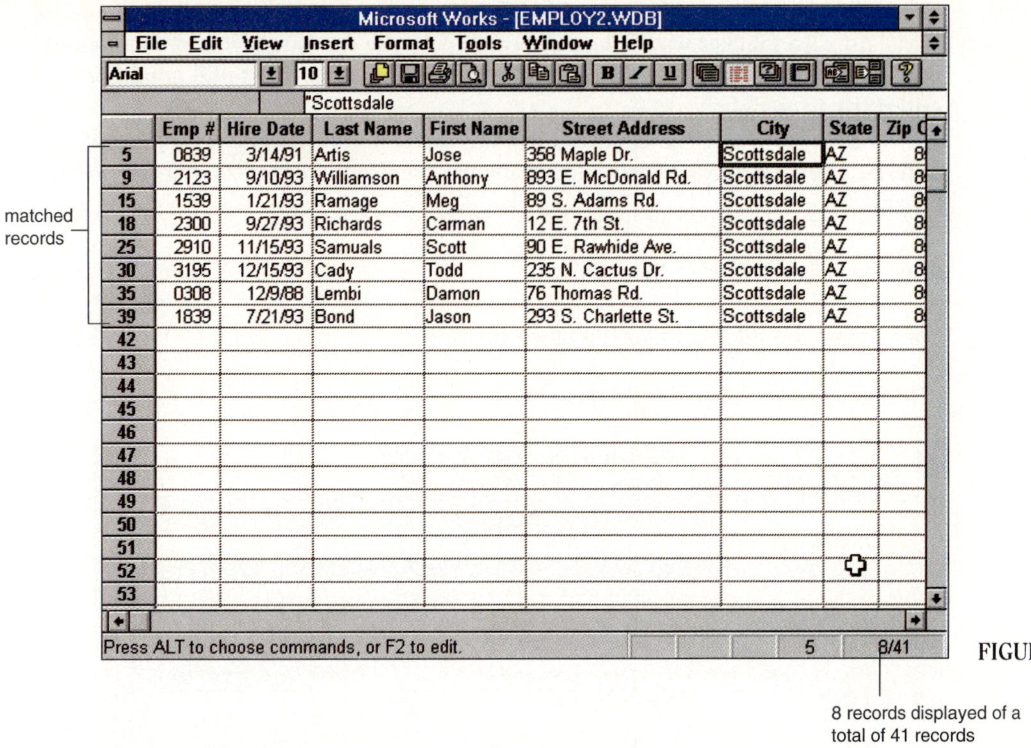

8 records displayed of a total of 41 records

The eight records that match the "find" text are displayed. All the other records in the database are hidden. The status bar shows that 8 of the 41 records (8/41) are displayed.

To see the Zip Code field for the located records,

In Form view, the eight records would be displayed individually.

Move to: Zip Code field

Notice that the zip code for one employee is 85215. It should be 85205.

Change the zip code for record 30 to 85205.

When records are hidden, you can switch the display between the hidden and unhidden records. To display the hidden records and hide the displayed records,

Choose: View>Switch Hidden Records

All records that do *not* match the "find" text are displayed. The status bar shows that you are displaying 33 of 41 records in the database. To display all the records again,

Choose: View>Show All Records

All 41 records are displayed again (41/41).

DATABASE

Querying the Database

Next you need to locate the record for Cara Reynolds and change her last name to Davis. An even quicker way to locate records is to use the Query command. A **query** is a special type of search used to locate groups of records that fulfill conditions or **criteria** that you define.

When you query the database, you are searching for all entries that meet the criteria. The Create New Query command on the Tools menu lets you specify the criteria.

Choose: T̲o̲ols>C̲reate New Query

Your screen should be similar to Figure 10-13.

default query name

FIGURE 10-13

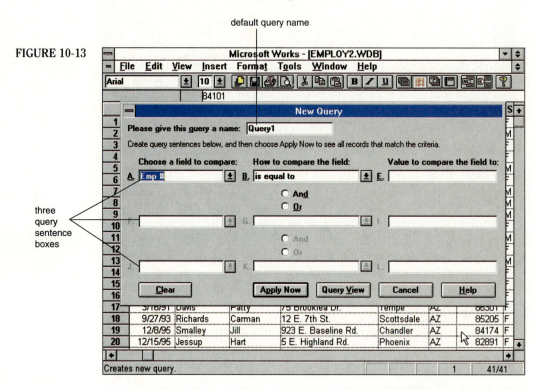

three query sentence boxes

A query name can be a maximum of 15 characters.

The New Query dialog box is used to enter the criteria that you want Works to use to locate the records in the database. You can have up to eight queries in a database. The default name of Query1 is displayed in the text box. To better identify the queries, you can rename them using a more descriptive name.

Replace the default name with Last Name.

Next, you enter the criteria to be used in the query. The three lines of criteria that are entered in the New Query dialog box are called **query sentences**. The New Query dialog box lets you enter a maximum of three query sentences. Each query sentence consists of three parts: the field you want to compare, the type of comparison, and the value you are comparing to. The three boxes in the dialog box are used to define the three parts of each query sentence.

In this case you need to locate the record for Cara Reynolds. You will enter only one query sentence, which will specify the criteria for the Last Name field. To choose the field you want to use for the query sentence,

Select: <u>A</u>

From the Choose A Field To Compare drop-down list,

Select: Last Name

Next you enter the method to be used to make the comparison. **Comparison operators** are used to create instructions that find records that fit within a certain range. The comparison operators are:

Comparison Operators
is equal to
is less than
is greater than
is not equal to
is less than or equal to
is greater than or equal to
contains

The default comparison operator, "is equal to," is displayed in the How To Compare The Field box. This is the operator you want to use because you want the Last Name to be equal to Reynolds.

Finally, to complete this query sentence, you need to enter the value to be located. To locate all records with a last name of Reynolds, in the Value To Compare The Field To box,

Type: reynolds

Keyboard users press Tab↹ or Alt + the letter next to each box to move to the box.

Query is not case-sensitive.

DATABASE

Your screen should be similar to Figure 10-14.

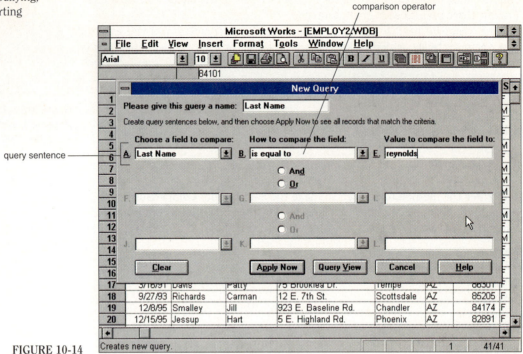

comparison operator

query sentence

FIGURE 10-14

The query sentence is complete. The completed query is called a **query instruction**. The query instruction asks Works to locate all records with a Last Name field entry of Reynolds.

After entering the query instruction in the New Query dialog box, it needs to be applied to the database. To apply the query and see the results,

Choose: Apply Now

Your screen should be similar to Figure 10-15.

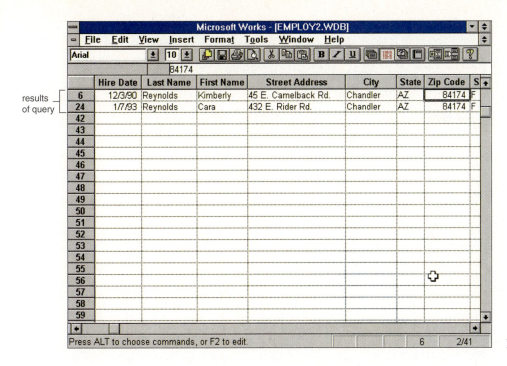

results
of query

FIGURE 10-15

Works has located the records that match the query criteria and displays them in List view. All other records are hidden. As you can see, using Query is quicker than using Find to locate information in a database file.

> Change the last name of Cara Reynolds to Davis.
> To display all the records again,

> If Form view is displayed, switch to List view.

Choose: View>Show All Records
Press: Ctrl + Home

Using Query View

To see the query instructions that were created when you entered the query sentences in the New Query dialog box, you switch to **Query view**.

Choose: View>Query>OK
or
Click: 🔲 Query View

DATABASE

Your screen should be similar to Figure 10-16.

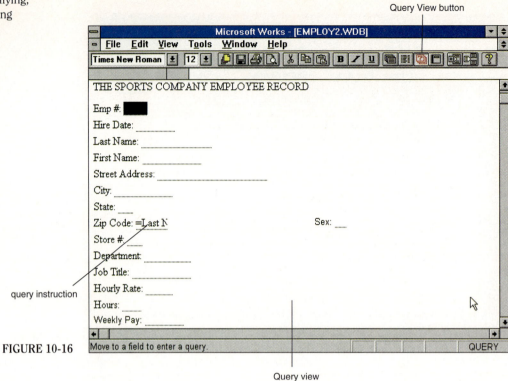

FIGURE 10-16

The Query view window looks like a blank form. In one field you will see the query instructions that were created. Works enters the query instructions in any blank entry area.

Move to: entry line that displays the query instructions

The query instructions displayed in the formula bar are =Last Name="reynolds." The query instruction begins with an equals sign because it is a formula. The selected field name appears exactly as it is in the database. The comparison operator "is equal to" is entered as the mathematical equivalent, =. The value, when it is a text entry, is enclosed in double quotation marks to distinguish it from the field name.

You can use Query view to define a query by entering the value or query instruction in the window. You could have defined this query simply by typing the last name, Reynolds, in the Last Name field entry space of the query window. Generally it is easier and more accurate to use the New Query dialog box. However, if the query is larger than three criteria (more than three query sentences), Query view must be used.

To apply a query from Query view, you need to switch to List view, Form view, or Print Preview.

Switch to List view.

The query is applied again. This time only one record matches the criteria. To redisplay all the records,

Choose: View>Show All Records

Sorting the Database Records

The next request on your desk is from the Accounting department. The manager wants a list of all employees working in the Warehouse or Clothing departments who earn less than $6.00 per hour. The manager would like the list in alphabetical order by last name.

Before creating the query to locate these records, you need to change the order of the records to alphabetical by last name. Works lets you rearrange the order of records in a database into groups of related records based on the contents of the selected field. The field contents on which a database is sorted is called the **sort field**. The Sort Records command on the Tools menu is used to rearrange records in the database.

Choose: Tools>Sort Records

Your screen should be similar to Figure 10-17.

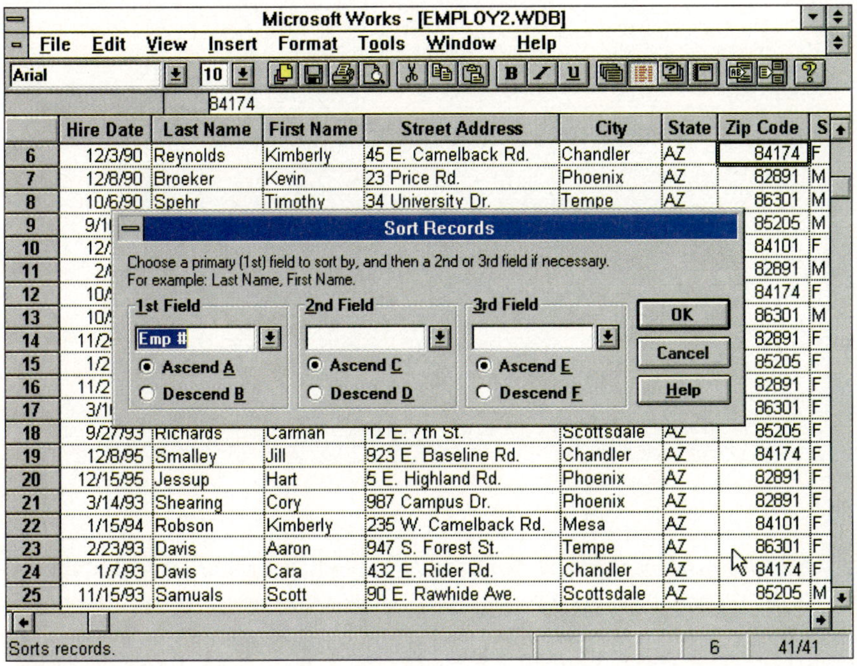

FIGURE 10-17

In the Sort Records dialog box, you enter the name of the field on which you want the records sorted. Works can sort records using up to three fields at a time.

In the 1st Field text box Works has proposed the Emp # field name as the first field to sort on. If the database has not been sorted before, Works displays the first field in the database as the proposed field. If the database had been previously sorted, the proposed field name would be the field name on which the database is currently sorted. To tell Works to sort using the Last Name field, from the 1st Field drop-down list,

Select: Last Name

Below the Field text boxes are the options Ascend and Descend. Works can sort in either ascending (A through Z or 0 through 9) or descending (Z through A or 9 through 0) order. Ascending order is the default setting. Since ascending is how you want the records displayed, you do not need to change the setting. To complete the command,

Choose: OK

Your screen should be similar to Figure 10-18.

FIGURE 10-18

sorted alphabetically by last name

record numbers

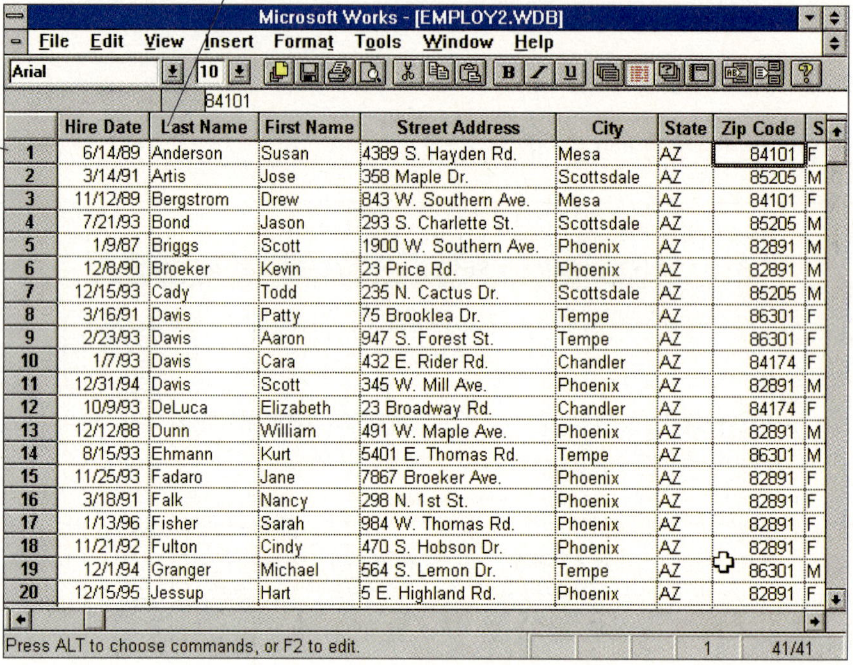

	Hire Date	Last Name	First Name	Street Address	City	State	Zip Code	S
1	6/14/89	Anderson	Susan	4389 S. Hayden Rd.	Mesa	AZ	84101	F
2	3/14/91	Artis	Jose	358 Maple Dr.	Scottsdale	AZ	85205	M
3	11/12/89	Bergstrom	Drew	843 W. Southern Ave.	Mesa	AZ	84101	F
4	7/21/93	Bond	Jason	293 S. Charlette St.	Scottsdale	AZ	85205	M
5	1/9/87	Briggs	Scott	1900 W. Southern Ave.	Phoenix	AZ	82891	M
6	12/8/90	Broeker	Kevin	23 Price Rd.	Phoenix	AZ	82891	M
7	12/15/93	Cady	Todd	235 N. Cactus Dr.	Scottsdale	AZ	85205	M
8	3/16/91	Davis	Patty	75 Brooklea Dr.	Tempe	AZ	86301	F
9	2/23/93	Davis	Aaron	947 S. Forest St.	Tempe	AZ	86301	F
10	1/7/93	Davis	Cara	432 E. Rider Rd.	Chandler	AZ	84174	F
11	12/31/94	Davis	Scott	345 W. Mill Ave.	Phoenix	AZ	82891	M
12	10/9/93	DeLuca	Elizabeth	23 Broadway Rd.	Chandler	AZ	84174	F
13	12/12/88	Dunn	William	491 W. Maple Ave.	Phoenix	AZ	82891	M
14	8/15/93	Ehmann	Kurt	5401 E. Thomas Rd.	Tempe	AZ	86301	M
15	11/25/93	Fadaro	Jane	7867 Broeker Ave.	Phoenix	AZ	82891	F
16	3/18/91	Falk	Nancy	298 N. 1st St.	Phoenix	AZ	82891	F
17	1/13/96	Fisher	Sarah	984 W. Thomas Rd.	Phoenix	AZ	82891	F
18	11/21/92	Fulton	Cindy	470 S. Hobson Dr.	Phoenix	AZ	82891	F
19	12/1/94	Granger	Michael	564 S. Lemon Dr.	Tempe	AZ	86301	M
20	12/15/95	Jessup	Hart	5 E. Highland Rd.	Phoenix	AZ	82891	F

Press ALT to choose commands, or F2 to edit.   1   41/41

The database now displays the records in ascending alphabetical order by last name. Notice that the records have been renumbered. Once a database is sorted, the original record number order in which the records were entered cannot be restored. If the original order of entry is important to you, be sure to save the database file before you sort it; then save the sorted file using a new file name. Alternatively you could create a permanent record number field in which you would enter the original record number of each record. The record number in the field would not be altered when the file is sorted. Then you could resort the records by record number if you wanted to restore the original order.

Look at the records with a last name of Davis.

You want the records sorted so that the first names are alphabetized within same last names. To alphabetize the employees' first names within identical last names, you can specify two sort fields, Last Name and First Name. When a file is sorted on more than one sort field, it is called a **multilevel sort**. To specify a second sort field,

Choose: Tools>Sort Records

When you sort on multiple sort fields, enter the most important sort field as the first sort field. Last Name is the field that will be sorted first, so the first sort field does not need to be changed. To enter a second sort field,

Choose: 2nd Field
Select: First Name

Again, you want the records sorted in ascending order, so you do not need to change the default selection. To complete the command,

Choose: OK

Your screen should be similar to Figure 10-19.

sorted alphabetically by
last name and first name

	Hire Date	Last Name	First Name	Street Address	City	State	Zip Code	S
1	6/14/89	Anderson	Susan	4389 S. Hayden Rd.	Mesa	AZ	84101	F
2	3/14/91	Artis	Jose	358 Maple Dr.	Scottsdale	AZ	85205	M
3	11/12/89	Bergstrom	Drew	843 W. Southern Ave.	Mesa	AZ	84101	F
4	7/21/93	Bond	Jason	293 S. Charlette St.	Scottsdale	AZ	85205	M
5	1/9/87	Briggs	Scott	1900 W. Southern Ave.	Phoenix	AZ	82891	M
6	12/8/90	Broeker	Kevin	23 Price Rd.	Phoenix	AZ	82891	M
7	12/15/93	Cady	Todd	235 N. Cactus Dr.	Scottsdale	AZ	85205	M
8	2/23/93	Davis	Aaron	947 S. Forest St.	Tempe	AZ	86301	F
9	1/7/93	Davis	Cara	432 E. Rider Rd.	Chandler	AZ	84174	F
10	3/16/91	Davis	Patty	75 Brooklea Dr.	Tempe	AZ	86301	F
11	12/31/94	Davis	Scott	345 W. Mill Ave.	Phoenix	AZ	82891	M
12	10/9/93	DeLuca	Elizabeth	23 Broadway Rd.	Chandler	AZ	84174	F
13	12/12/88	Dunn	William	491 W. Maple Ave.	Phoenix	AZ	82891	M
14	8/15/93	Ehmann	Kurt	5401 E. Thomas Rd.	Tempe	AZ	86301	M
15	11/25/93	Fadaro	Jane	7867 Broeker Ave.	Phoenix	AZ	82891	F
16	3/18/91	Falk	Nancy	298 N. 1st St.	Phoenix	AZ	82891	F
17	1/13/96	Fisher	Sarah	984 W. Thomas Rd.	Phoenix	AZ	82891	F
18	11/21/92	Fulton	Cindy	470 S. Hobson Dr.	Phoenix	AZ	82891	F
19	12/1/94	Granger	Michael	564 S. Lemon Dr.	Tempe	AZ	86301	M
20	12/15/95	Jessup	Hart	5 E. Highland Rd.	Phoenix	AZ	82891	F

Press ALT to choose commands, or F2 to edit.　　　　1　　41/41

FIGURE 10-19

Now look at the records with a last name of Davis.

Those records with duplicate last names are further sorted by first names within the Last Name field.

Before you create the employee list for the accounting department, you want to add two more employee records to the database. Although a new record can be entered into the database in either Form or List view, it is easier to use Form view.

Switch to Form view.

To add a record as the last record in the database,

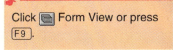

Click 🗐 Form View or press
F9 .

Press: Ctrl + End

A blank record entry form (record 42) is displayed.

DATABASE

Enter the following field contents:

Field	Entry
Emp #	4392
Hire Date	4/15/95
Last Name	Brooks
First Name	Melody
Street Address	2562 Winding Way
City	Mesa
State	AZ
Zip Code	84101
Sex	F
Store #	52
Department	Clothing
Job Title	Stock clerk
Hourly Rate	5.65
Hours	25

As soon as you complete the Pay and Hours fields, the Weekly Pay field is calculated automatically.

Check your entries for this record and edit if necessary. Return to List view.

To display the beginning of the record,

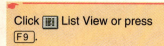

Click 🗐 List View or press
F9.

Press: Home

Melody Brooks' record has been added to the file as record 42. It is not in the correct alphabetical position. Each time a record is added to a sorted file, the file must be resorted in order to maintain the alphabetical order.

As you can see, the Sort Records command has some drawbacks. Each time a file is sorted, the records are renumbered. This makes locating a record by its original record number unlikely. Also, each time a change is made in the data in the sort field or a record is added to the database, the file needs to be resorted. To resort the database,

Choose: Tools>Sort Records

The sort settings you entered are displayed. Since you want to sort the database again using the same fields and order, to continue the command by accepting the settings displayed,

Choose: OK

Your screen should be similar to Figure 10-20.

Insert Record button

	Emp #	Hire Date	Last Name	First Name	Street Address	City	State	Zip C
1	0051	6/14/89	Anderson	Susan	4389 S. Hayden Rd.	Mesa	AZ	8
2	0839	3/14/91	Artis	Jose	358 Maple Dr.	Scottsdale	AZ	8
3	1024	11/12/89	Bergstrom	Drew	843 W. Southern Ave.	Mesa	AZ	8
4	1839	7/21/93	Bond	Jason	293 S. Charlette St.	Scottsdale	AZ	8
5	0283	1/9/87	Briggs	Scott	1900 W. Southern Ave.	Phoenix	AZ	8
6	0650	12/8/90	Broeker	Kevin	23 Price Rd.	Phoenix	AZ	8
7	4392	4/15/95	Brooks	Melody	2562 Winding Way	Mesa	AZ	8
8	3195	12/15/93	Cady	Todd	235 N. Cactus Dr.	Scottsdale	AZ	8
9	1801	2/23/93	Davis	Aaron	947 S. Forest St.	Tempe	AZ	8
10	1329	1/7/93	Davis	Cara	432 E. Rider Rd.	Chandler	AZ	8
11	0851	3/16/91	Davis	Patty	75 Brooklea Dr.	Tempe	AZ	8
12	3918	12/31/94	Davis	Scott	345 W. Mill Ave.	Phoenix	AZ	8
13	2312	10/9/93	DeLuca	Elizabeth	23 Broadway Rd.	Chandler	AZ	8
14	0390	12/12/88	Dunn	William	491 W. Maple Ave.	Phoenix	AZ	8
15	2058	8/15/93	Ehmann	Kurt	5401 E. Thomas Rd.	Tempe	AZ	8
16	2560	11/25/93	Fadaro	Jane	7867 Broeker Ave.	Phoenix	AZ	8
17	0854	3/18/91	Falk	Nancy	298 N. 1st St.	Phoenix	AZ	8
18	4831	1/13/96	Fisher	Sarah	984 W. Thomas Rd.	Phoenix	AZ	8
19	1121	11/21/92	Fulton	Cindy	470 S. Hobson Dr.	Phoenix	AZ	8
20	3800	12/1/94	Granger	Michael	564 S. Lemon Dr.	Tempe	AZ	8

Press ALT to choose commands, or F2 to edit.   1   42/42

FIGURE 10-20

Melody Brooks' record now appears in the correct order (record 7).

Inserting Records

The next record you will enter into the database will contain your first and last name. This time, however, you will insert the record in the correct alphabetical order so that you do not need to resort the file.

To insert a record, position the highlight where you want the record entered into the database. For example, if the new record should be at the record 10 location, the new record becomes record 10 and all the records below are automatically renumbered.

The Record/Field command on the Insert menu or the ⌨ toolbar button is used to insert a record between existing records in List view. The Insert>Record command performs the same task in Form view. The procedure is the same in either view.

To insert your record in List view in the correct alphabetical order, first move the highlight to any field in the record that is in the location where you want your record displayed.

Move to: any field in the record where your name would be in alphabetical order

Choose: Insert>Record/Field>OK

or

Click: ⌨ Insert Record

A blank record row is displayed.

DATABASE

Enter a record using your name in the First and Last Name fields and the information shown below in the fields specified. The data you enter for all the other fields can be fictitious.

Field	Entry
Emp #	9999
Hire Date	(current date)
Store #	52
Department	Operations
Job Title	Mgmt.-trainee
Hourly Rate	8.25
Hours	40

Because you entered the new record in the correct alphabetical order, the database should not need to be resorted. Generally, if you have a lot of records to add to the database, it is easier to add them in Form view at the end of the database and then sort the file.

You should now have 43 records in the database.

Press: Ctrl + Home

Querying on Multiple Criteria

Now you are ready to create the list for the Accounting department showing the employees in the Clothing or Warehouse departments who earn less than $6.00 per hour.

Because you need to locate records that match information in more than one field, you cannot use the Find command. A query is the only way to search for records that meet several criteria. To query the database to locate all employees meeting the criteria described above,

Choose: Tools>Create New Query

Rename the query Accounting.

To enter the first query sentence to locate all employees who work in the Clothing department, from the Choose a Field to Compare list box (item A),

Select: Department

The default selection in the How to Compare the Field list box (item B) of "is equal to" is the comparison you want to use. To enter the department name, in the Value to Compare the Field To box (item E),

Type: clothing

Now you are ready to enter the criteria for the second query sentence to locate employees who work in the Warehouse department. To combine query sentences,

logical operators are used. The logical operators are options in the New Query dialog box and are described below.

Logical Operator	Effect
And	Finds all records that match the criteria in *both* the preceding and next query sentence
Or	Finds all records that match the criteria in *either* the preceding or next query sentence

You want the query to find the records that match the criteria in either the first sentence or the second. To do this,

Choose: Or

The second query sentence will instruct Works to find all records with a department of Warehouse. From the Choose a Field to Compare list box (F),

Select: Department

From the How to Compare the Field box (G),

Select: is equal to

In the Value to Compare the Field To text box (I),

Type: warehouse

You need to add a third query sentence that will instruct Works to locate all records with an hourly rate less than $6.00. To find all records that match the criteria in either of the two preceding sentences and criteria in the third query sentence,

Choose: And

From the Choose a Field to Compare list box (J),

Select: Hourly Rate

The comparison operator for this comparison is "is less than." From the How to Compare the Field list box (K),

Select: is less than

To tell Works to locate records that have hourly rates less than $6.00, in the Value to Compare the Field To list box (L),

Type: 6

You do not need to enter the value as currency.

Your screen should be similar to Figure 10-21.

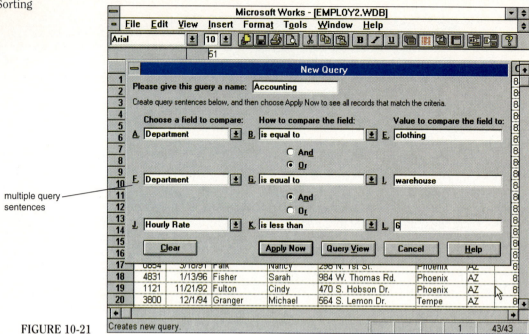

multiple query
sentences

FIGURE 10-21

The query instruction has been created. To apply the query,

Choose: Apply Now

The eight records matching these conditions are displayed. All the other records are hidden.

Scroll the window to display the Department and Hourly Rate fields.

Each record should be either Clothing or Warehouse and the hourly rate and should be less than $6.00.

To see the query instructions that were created,

Choose: View>Query>OK

or

Click: Query View

Move to: entry line that displays the query instructions

The query instruction displayed in the formula bar is:

=Department="clothing"#OR#Department
="warehouse"#AND#Hourly Rate<VALUE("6")

When a multiple-criteria query is defined to select records that meet several criteria, the query instructions are entered in a single field in Query view. To define this same query in Query view, you would enter the query formula as it appears on page 360. In this case it is much easier to define the query using the New Query dialog box.

Switch to List view.

The query is applied again and the same results are displayed in List view.

Printing Selected Records and Fields

The accounting department wants a printout of the employees' names, store numbers, departments, job titles, and hourly rates only. To print only these fields, you will hide the fields you do not want printed. To hide a field, you decrease the field width to 0.

Move to: Emp # field

Choose: Forma**t**>Field **W**idth

The current field width of 7 is displayed in the dialog box. Before hiding fields, it is always a good idea to first write down the field widths of the fields you are hiding. This way when you go to redisplay the field, you will know the correct width to enter. To hide the field,

Type: **0**

Choose: OK

In a similar manner, hide the Hire Date field.

You also need to hide the Street Address, City, State, Zip Code, and Sex fields. To quickly hide the five columns, you will select them first.

Highlight the five columns.

Choose: Forma**t**>Field **W**idth

Notice that the Field Width dialog box displays a field width of 10 even though the columns all have different sizes. To change the width of all the columns to 0,

Type: **0**

Choose: OK

> You can also hide a column by dragging its right border all the way to the left border.

> To highlight, drag the mouse or use ⇧Shift + the directional keys.

DATABASE

Your screen should be similar to Figure 10-22.

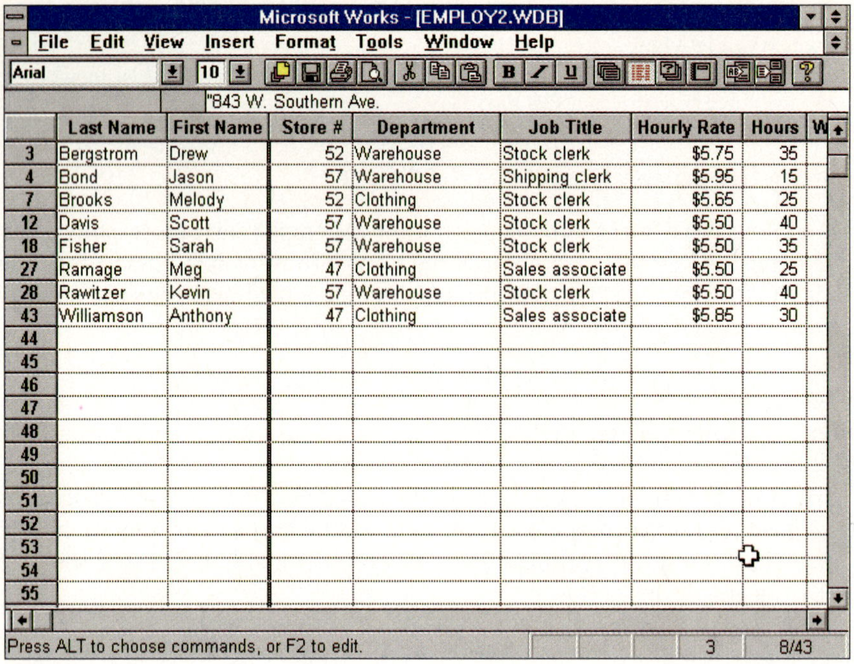

	Last Name	First Name	Store #	Department	Job Title	Hourly Rate	Hours	W
3	Bergstrom	Drew	52	Warehouse	Stock clerk	$5.75	35	
4	Bond	Jason	57	Warehouse	Shipping clerk	$5.95	15	
7	Brooks	Melody	52	Clothing	Stock clerk	$5.65	25	
12	Davis	Scott	57	Warehouse	Stock clerk	$5.50	40	
18	Fisher	Sarah	57	Warehouse	Stock clerk	$5.50	35	
27	Ramage	Meg	47	Clothing	Sales associate	$5.50	25	
28	Rawitzer	Kevin	57	Warehouse	Stock clerk	$5.50	40	
43	Williamson	Anthony	47	Clothing	Sales associate	$5.85	30	
44								
45								
46								
47								
48								
49								
50								
51								
52								
53								
54								
55								

Microsoft Works - [EMPLOY2.WDB]
File Edit View Insert Format Tools Window Help
Arial   10
"843 W. Southern Ave.
Press ALT to choose commands, or F2 to edit.   3   8/43

FIGURE 10-22

The fields are no longer displayed. This same procedure can be used to hide a column of data in a spreadsheet. The highlight is not visible because it is in the hidden field.

> If you switched to Form view, the fields would be displayed.

To redisplay the highlight,

Press: →

In a similar manner, hide the Hours and Weekly Pay fields.

Now you are ready to print a list of the displayed records. You would like this report to have a title. To do this you will use the Headers and Footers command in the View menu to create a header for the page.

Choose: View>Headers and Footers

The Headers and Footers dialog box is displayed. In the Header text box,

Type: Clothing and Warehouse Employees Earning Less Than $6.00 Per Hour

In the Footer text box,

Type: [your name, current date]
Choose: OK

To preview and print the displayed records and fields only,

Choose: File>Print Preview

or

Click: Print Preview

The page setup settings you specified at the end of Lab 9 in the Employee file are the same settings as in the current file, Employ 2. You want to include the record and field labels; however, this printout does not need to have smaller margins or to be printed in landscape orientation.

Close the Preview window. Set the left and right margins back to the defaults (1.25 inches) and change the orientation to portrait. (Use the Reset command button to quickly restore the setting.)

Preview the report again. Zoom in on the window.

Your screen should be similar to Figure 10-23.

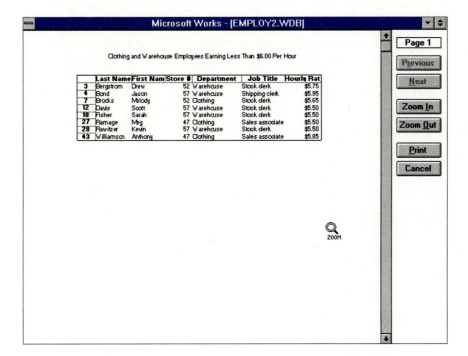

FIGURE 10-23

Zoom in on the window again to enlarge the field names to their full size.

Although the database of employee records is not complete, the sample list will show the Accounting department manager the type of report that Works is capable of producing. To print the report,

Choose: Print

Redisplaying Hidden Fields

Now you want to redisplay the hidden fields of data. To unhide fields you increase the field width to a value greater than zero. In order to do this, however, you must be able to move the highlight into the field you want to change. Since the field is hidden, the only way to position the highlight in the field is to use the Go To command on the Edit menu.

Choose: Edit>Go To
➢   F5 GO TO

DATABASE

To tell Works you want to move to a specific field, you can type in the field name exactly as it appears in the entry from, or you can select the field name from the list of names. Using the list box ensures that you do not enter the field name incorrectly.

Select: Emp #

The field name is displayed in the Go To text box. To complete the command,

Choose: OK

The highlight is no longer displayed in the workspace. That is because it is positioned on the hidden field. You can confirm its location by looking at the formula bar. It displays the entry for the Emp # for record 3.

To reset the field width to 7 spaces,

Choose: Forma**t**>Field **W**idth>**7**>OK

The Emp # field is displayed again.

Move to and unhide the Hire Date, Street Address, City, State, Zip Code, Sex, Hours, and Weekly Pay fields. The original field widths were:

Field	Width
Hire Date	10
Street Address	28
City	10
State	6
Zip Code	9
Sex	6
Hours	7
Weekly Pay	12

Press: Home

Unhiding fields takes a lot of time, because each field width must be respecified individually. It is more efficient to save the file before hiding the fields. Then after you've hidden the fields and created the report, you can close the file without saving it. When you open the original file again, all the fields and records will be displayed because the file was saved before the fields were hidden.

Redisplay all records and save the file as EMPLOY3. Exit Works.

Key Terms

query (348)   Query view (351)
criteria (348)   sort field (353)
query sentence (348)   multilevel sort (354)
comparison operator (349)   logical operators (359)
query instruction (350)

Command Summary

Command	Shortcut	Button	Action
Edit>**G**o To			Moves highlight to selected field
Insert>**D**elete Record/Field			Removes record or field in List view
Forma**t**>**N**umbers>**L**eading Zeros			Displays zeros at beginning of numbers
Insert>**R**ecord/Field			Inserts record or field in List view
Edit>Field **N**ame			Enters or renames field name in List view
Edit>Pos**i**tion Selection			Moves field in Form view
Insert>**F**ield			Inserts a field in Form view
Edit>**F**ind			Locates record that matches instruction
Edit>**F**ind>**N**ext Record	F7		Locates next record in search
View>S**w**itch Hidden Records			Displays hidden records
View>Show **A**ll Records			Displays all records
T**o**ols>**C**reate New Query			Opens New Query dialog box
View>**Q**uery		🔲	Locates records meeting query criteria
T**o**ols>So**r**t Records			Rearranges records in order specified

LAB REVIEW

Matching

1. And _____ a. field that determines order in which records are sorted

2. F7 _____ b. descending order

3. ⇧Shift + F8 _____ c. file sorted on more than one sort field

4. sort field _____ d. logical operator used with query sentences

5. multilevel sort _____ e. locates all records matching specified condition

6. is equal to _____ f. can locate all records meeting more than one condition

7. Find _____ g. finds next match in Find

8. Z–A _____ h. comparison operator

9. Query _____ i. command to display records that do not meet query conditions

10. View>Switch Hidden Records _____ j. criteria select field command

DATABASE

Practice Exercises

1.   Ramona has created an employee database file of employees who work in her grocery store. Open the file GROCERY.WDB.

    a.   Edit the following records in List view:

Record	Field	Correction
3	First Name	Kevin
5	Address	90 E. Southern Ave.
10	City	Westwood
12	Emp #	8330
20	Last Name	Weston

    b.   Change the Date field name to Date Hired.

    c.   Use the Find command to locate Wendy Murphy's record. Change her last name to Henderson.

    d.   Enter a new record using your name in the First and Last Name fields and the current date in the Date Hired field. All other fields can be fictitious.

    e.   Sort the file by last and first name in ascending order.

    f.   Query the database to locate all records with a City of Elma or a Date Hired that is greater than or equal to 9/01/94.

    g.   Preview the query. Change the Page Setup to print the query output on one page with field names and record numbers. Print the query output. Display all records. Save the file.

2.   Kevin has created a customer database file for his mail order office supply business. Open the file OFFICE.WDB.

    a.   Format the zip code field to display leading zeros.

    b.   Use the Find command to locate each of the following records and edit the fields as shown:

Customer	Field	Correction
Lewis Camera	State	NM
The Sports Store	Street	2451 Southern Ave.
Up Word	Zip Code	83743

    c.   Enter your name as the customer name in a new record. Use your school address to complete the other fields.

    d.   Sort the file on the Customer Name field, in ascending order.

    e.   Query the database to locate all records with a state of CA or the city of your school.

    f.   Print the query output on one page with field names and record numbers, in List view.

    g.   Display all records. Save the file.

3.   James is the owner of the Gift Center. He has created a file to hold the store's inventory. You have been hired as inventory control manager and will use the database to create weekly summaries of the data. Open the file GIFTS.WDB.

a.   Edit the item descriptions that have irregular-case words and misspellings.

b.   Format the Retail Price and Discount Price fields to currency with two decimal places.

c.   Delete the following records in this order:

Record 17
Record 15
Record 3

d.   Use Find to locate the Yamaha Drum Machine record and change the price to $129.00 and the discount price to $100.00.

e.   Sort the file on Supplier and Description in ascending order.

f.   Create a query to locate all records with a discount price of $25.00 or more and $75.00 or less.

g.   Enter a title for the Query as a header. Enter your name and the current date in a footer. Print the query output.

h.   Display all records. Save the file.

4.   Wendy is the manager of the Travel Company, a small travel agency specializing in group tours. One of Wendy's responsibilities is to enter trips sold by the sales staff into the computer.

a.   Create a database file named TRAVEL to hold the trips sold information. Include the following fields: Emp #, Customer Name, Destination, Travel Date, and Return Date.

b.   Enter four records into the file using any of the following destinations: Hawaii, London, or Paris. Enter a fifth record using your name as the customer name.

c.   Adjust the size of the field widths in Form and List view appropriately.

d.   Sort the file in ascending order by Destination, Travel Date, and Return Date.

e.   Insert a new field in List view between the Customer Name and the Destination. Name the field Ticket #. Enter a six-digit ticket number for each of the records.

f.   In Form view, move the Ticket # field so it is displayed after the Customer Name field. Adjust the field size to 9.

g.   Using Form view, enter five more records into the file using any of the three possible destinations. Sort the records again using the same fields as in **d**.

h.   Query the database to locate all records with a destination of London or Paris. Display the Query output in List view.

DATABASE

i. Include a descriptive title in a header for the query, and your name and the date in a footer. Print the query on one page including record numbers and field names.

j. Display all records. Save the file.

5.   Create an inventory file for the Kids Express Toy Company. Add 15 records to the file. Adjust the field widths as necessary. Sort the table by one of the fields. Add two new records to the table. Enter your name and the current date in one of the fields. Print the file on one page, if possible.

11

Creating a Report

CASE STUDY

As you use the database, you have found that it is difficult to add records to the database using the default entry form. This is because it does not match the form the Personnel department gives each employee to fill out when hired. To make this process easier, you will create a customized data entry form.

In addition, the regional manager is impressed with the simple report you generated and has asked you to produce an employee payroll report. This report will be created on a weekly basis and will include the employees' names, titles, hourly pay rates, hours worked, and weekly pay organized by department. To do this you will use the Report view of the database tool to create a professional-appearing report.

Creating a Customized Form

Load Works and put your data disk in the appropriate drive for your system. Open the file EMPLOY4.WDB. If necessary, maximize the window. This file is the same as the one you created in Lab 10 except that it does not contain the record containing your personal data. The database is still sorted alphabetically by last name as it was when you saved the file at the end of the previous lab.

DATABASE

Adding new records to a database is a routine part of database maintenance. The input for the record is taken from the Employee Data Form that each employee fills out when hired. The form looks like this:

Personal Information

First Name:_____   Last Name:_____

Street Address:_____

City:_____   State:_____   Zip Code:_____

Sex:_____

For Personnel Use Only

Store #:_____   Employee #: _____   Hire Date:_____

Department:_____   Job Title:_____

Hourly Rate:_____   Hours:_____   Weekly Pay:_____

As you can see, the order of information in the Employee Data Form is different than the order in which the data is entered in the database file. To make the job of data entry easier, you decide to create a customized onscreen data entry form, reflecting the order of the paper form, to be used to enter the data into the file.

To modify the default form, switch to Form view.

Your screen should be similar to Figure 11-1.

Click 🖿 or press F9 .

FIGURE 11-1

default form layout

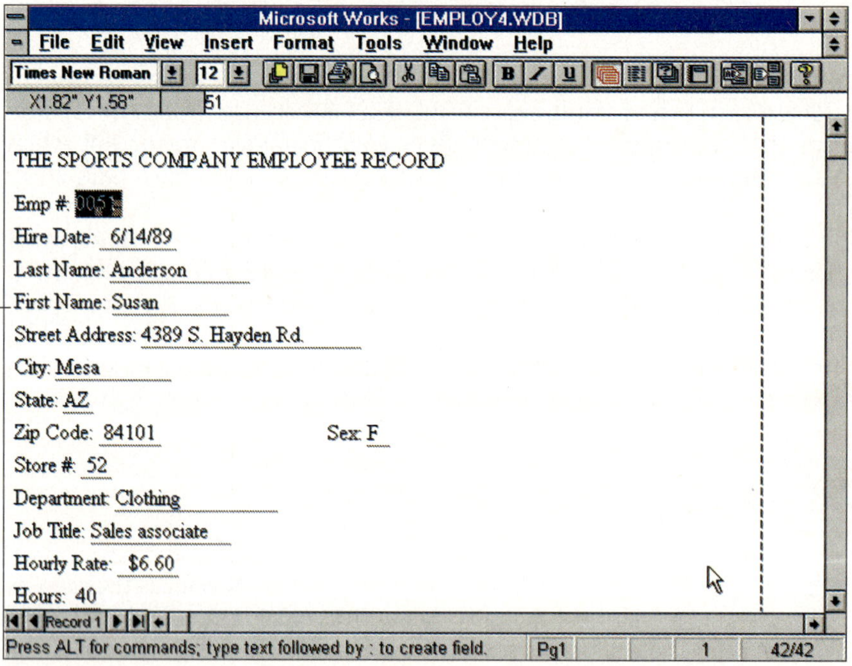

The default form layout displays the field names and field entry area as a column along the left margin. You can change the layout when you initially create the data entry form or at any later time. Just as you moved the Sex field in the form in Lab 10, you will move the fields on the form until they are located where they are in the handwritten Employee Data Form shown above.

When moving fields in Form view, you want to use the Snap to Grid command on the Format menu. This command uses an invisible grid that positions a field or label on the grid line, making it easier to line up entries on the form. Open the Format menu. If Snap to Grid is not marked, turn it on by selecting the command. Otherwise, close the menu without selecting the command.

The first field you will move is the Emp # field. Select the Emp # field.

You will begin by moving the Emp # field to the same line and to the right of the Store # field. When you move a field, use the X and Y coordinates in the formula bar for location reference to help you position the fields.

Move the Emp # field to the right of the Store # field at approximately the X2.92" Y3.58" position.

Your screen should be similar to Figure 11-2.

371
Creating a Customized Form

To select a field, click on it or use Tab or the arrow keys to move to it. Any part of the field can be highlighted.

To move a field, drag it or use the Position Selection command on the Edit menu.

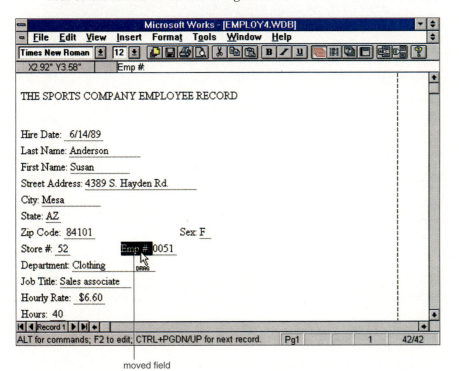

moved field

FIGURE 11-2

In a similar manner, move the other fields to the approximate positions shown below (refer to Figure 11-3).

Field	Position	
Hire Date	X 4.42"	Y 3.58"
Last Name	X 3.42"	Y 2.00"
First Name	X 1.33"	Y 2.00"
Street Address	X 1.33"	Y 2.25"
City	X 1.33"	Y 2.50"
State	X 2.92"	Y 2.50"
Zip Code	X 4.00"	Y 2.50"
Sex	X 1.33"	Y 2.75"
Job Title	X 4.00"	Y 3.83"
Hourly Rate	X 1.33"	Y 4.08"
Hours	X 2.92"	Y 4.08"
Weekly Pay	X 4.25"	Y 4.08"

DATABASE

Check the Y coordinates of all fields that have multiple fields on a line to ensure that they are the same.

Now that all the fields have been placed on the correct lines, you want to add the labels "Personal Information" and "For Personnel Use Only" to the form.

Enter the label "Personal Information" at position X 1.33" Y 1.67" approximately. Bold and italicize the label. Add a single-line border around it.

Enter the label "For Personnel Use Only" at position X 1.33" Y 3.25" approximately. Bold and italicize the label. Add a single-line border around it.

Your screen should be similar to Figure 11-3.

> The commands and toolbar buttons for bold, italics, and borders are the same as in the Spreadsheet tool.

FIGURE 11-3

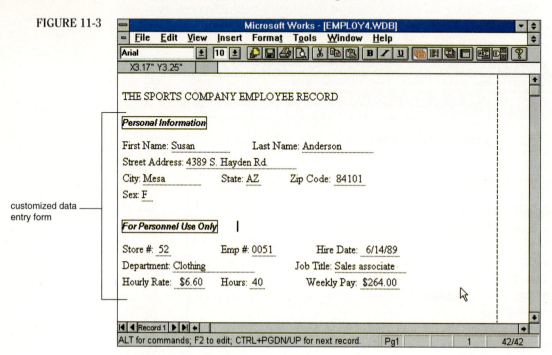

Finally, to use the form to enter your personal record,

Click: ▶| Bottom of Document

or

Press: Ctrl + End

Enter a record using your name in the First and Last Name fields and the information shown below in the fields specified. The data you enter for all the other fields can be fictitious.

Store #: **52**   Emp #: **9999**   Hire Date: **(current date)**
Department: **Operations**   Job Title: **Mgmt-trainee**
Hourly Rate: **8.25**   Hours: **40**

Using the form will make the job of entering new employee data much faster.

To sort the database again on Last and First Name,

Choose: Tools>Sort Records

The first and second sort fields are correct.

Choose: OK

Defining a Report Layout

Next you want to design the weekly payroll report. A **report** consists of introductory text such as a report title sorted groups of data, spacing between the groups, group subtotals, and report totals.

Works has a preset report form which will create a report automatically for you. Then you can customize the report specifically to meet your needs. You will create the report shown in Figure 11-4.

FIGURE 11-4

Employee Payroll Report
Week of May 15, 1995

First Name	Last Name	Job Title	Hourly Rate	Hours	Weekly Pay
Department	**Clothing**				
Susan	Anderson	Sales associate	$6.60	40	$264.00
Melody	Brooks	Stock clerk	$5.65	25	$141.25
William	Dunn	Supervisor	$8.65	20	$173.00
Michael	Granger	Sales associate	$6.25	20	$125.00
Meg	Ramage	Sales associate	$5.50	25	$137.50
Kimberly	Reynolds	Sales associate	$6.60	15	$99.00
Cory	Shearing	Sales associate	$6.45	35	$225.75
Jacob	Stinkemper	Sales associate	$6.25	25	$156.25
Blake	Thorp	Sales associate	$6.25	30	$187.50
Anthony	Williamson	Sales associate	$5.85	30	$175.50
Name	Student	Stock clerk	$5.75	40	$230.00
Total Department:			$6.35		$1,914.75
Department	**Operations**				
Scott	Briggs	Cashier	$6.60	30	$198.00
Kevin	Broeker	Head cashier	$6.75	30	$202.50
Todd	Cady	Cashier	$6.60	25	$165.00
Aaron	Davis	Cashier	$6.75	30	$202.50
Kurt	Ehmann	Supervisor	$8.65	15	$129.75
Jane	Fadaro	Custodian	$7.50	35	$262.50
Cindy	Fulton	Cashier	$5.85	40	$234.00
Jennifer	Little	Head cashier	$6.25	25	$156.25
William	Long	Cashier	$6.00	25	$150.00
Cody	McKay	Cashier	$5.85	30	$175.50
Jeffery	Rensmayer	Cashier	$6.45	30	$193.50
Kimberly	Robson	Custodian	$5.50	25	$137.50
Scott	Samuals	Cashier	$6.75	20	$135.00
Total Department:			$6.58		$2,342.00
Department	**Sports Equipment**				
Jose	Artis	Sales associate	$7.50	40	$300.00
Cara	Davis	Sales associate	$6.25	35	$218.75
Elizabeth	DeLuca	Sales associate	$6.60	15	$99.00
Nancy	Falk	Supervisor	$8.45	40	$338.00
Hart	Jessup	Sales associate	$5.85	20	$117.00
Damon	Lembi	Sales associate	$5.85	35	$204.75
Carman	Richards	Sales associate	$6.60	35	$231.00
Timothy	Spehr	Sales associate	$5.50	35	$192.50
Todd	Steverson	Sales associate	$5.85	25	$146.25
Total Department:			$6.49		$1,847.25
First Name	Last Name	Job Title	Hourly Rate	Hours	Weekly Pay
Department	**Warehouse**				
Drew	Bergstrom	Stock clerk	$5.50	35	$192.50
Jason	Bond	Shipping clerk	$5.95	15	$89.25
Patty	Davis	Shipping clerk	$7.00	15	$105.00
Scott	Davis	Stock clerk	$5.50	40	$220.00
Sarah	Fisher	Stock clerk	$5.50	35	$192.50
James	Kennedy	Supervisor	$8.85	35	$309.75
Kevin	Rawitzer	Stock clerk	$5.50	40	$220.00
Jill	Smalley	Shipping clerk	$6.25	40	$250.00
Brent	Smith	Stock clerk	$6.75	35	$236.25
Lucy	Toroyan	Stock clerk	$7.00	40	$280.00
Total Department:			$6.38		$2,095.25
Total:	COUNT: 43		AVG: $6.45		SUM: $8,199.25

To use the preset report form to create a report,

Choose: Tools>Create New Report

Your screen should be similar to Figure 11-5.

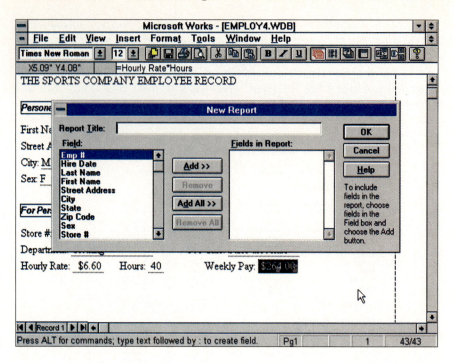

FIGURE 11-5

In the New Report dialog box, you specify the report title and fields to include in the report. The title of this report will be "Employee Payroll Report." In the Report Title text box,

Type: **Employee Payroll Report**

The Field list box displays all the database field names. To select only those fields to be displayed in the report,

Select: First Name
Choose: **A**dd >>

The Fields in Report list box displays the selected field, First Name.
     Continue to add the fields to the report by selecting the following fields in the same manner:

> The order in which fields are selected is the order in which they will appear in the report from left to right.

Last Name
Job Title
Hourly Rate
Hours
Weekly Pay

Your screen should be similar to Figure 11-6.

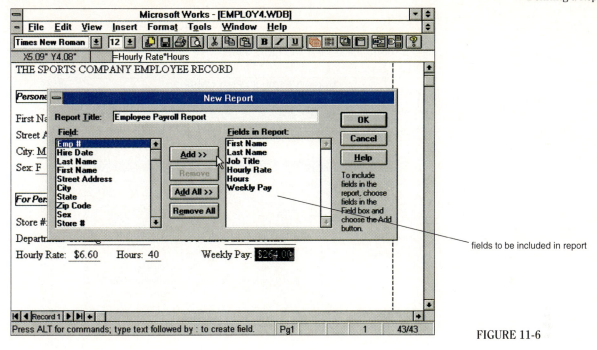

FIGURE 11-6

To continue defining the report,

Choose: OK

In the Report Statistics dialog box, you specify the statistics you want included in the report. You want the report to calculate the total number of employees, the average rate of pay, and the total weekly pay.

The Report Statistics dialog box lists the names of the fields you selected in the Fields in Report list box, and displays seven statistical functions in the Statistics option box. The functions perform the following calculations:

Statistic	Calculation
Sum	Total of group
Average	Average of group
Count	Number of items in group
Minimum	Smallest number in group
Maximum	Largest number in group
Standard Deviation	Standard deviation of group
Variance	Variance of group

The first statistic you want to include in the report will calculate the total number of records in the report. The Count Statistic will perform the calculation. First you select the field of data you want to calculate. To count the records using the Last Name field, from the Fields in Report list box,

Select: Last Name

To choose the Count Statistic,

Select: Count

Your screen should be similar to Figure 11-7.

FIGURE 11-7

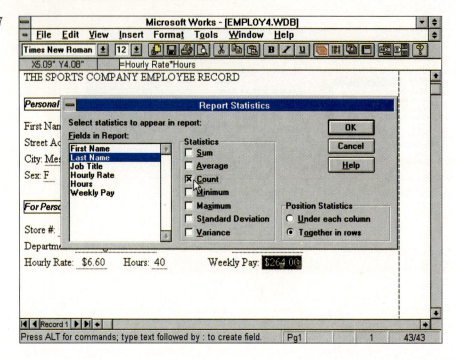

The second statistic you want the report to display will calculate the average hourly rate. To select the Hourly Rate field and the statistic to average this column of data,

Select: Hourly Rate
Select: Average

Although the Last Name field and Count Statistic were deselected, they are still remembered and will be calculated when the command is completed.

The final statistic will calculate the total weekly pay.

Select: Weekly Pay
Select: Sum

Next you need to indicate where you want to display the statistics. To display the statistics under the columns of data,

Choose: Under each column

To continue defining the report,

Choose: OK

Works displays an informational message box. To close the message box,

Choose: OK

Your screen should be similar to Figure 11-8.

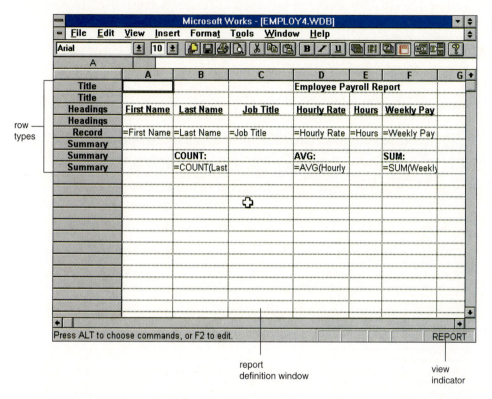

FIGURE 11-8

row types

report definition window

view indicator

The report definitions you specified are displayed in Report Definition view. In **Report Definition view** you can add to or modify the definitions that control the layout of the report. It is similar to a spreadsheet in that it consists of column letters along the top of the window. As in a spreadsheet, the intersection of a column and row creates a cell. The cell contents in each row determine what information appears in the report. The information can consist of explanatory text, data, or summary statistics.

The row labels identify the row types. The **row types** control the information displayed on each row of the report. They are:

Title   The first two lines of the report are the Title rows. They are used to enter report titles that appear on the first page of the report only.

Headings   The second two lines of the report are the Headings rows. Information in these rows appears at the beginning of each page of the report.

Record   This row prints one entry for each record in the report. It will print the actual data for each record.

Summary   The last three report lines are the Summary rows. They are used to display summary statistics for each column of data.

DATABASE

The row types print in a specific order that cannot be changed. However, you can have as many of each row type as you want.

The cells to the right of the row type labels control what information will be displayed in the report. The arrow keys and mouse are used to move around the report definition window just as you would use them to move around a spreadsheet window. The highlight should be positioned in column A of the first Title row. The title you entered is displayed in this row, formatted in bold. The second Title row is currently empty.

Press: ⬇ (2 times)

Your screen should be similar to Figure 11-9.

FIGURE 11-9

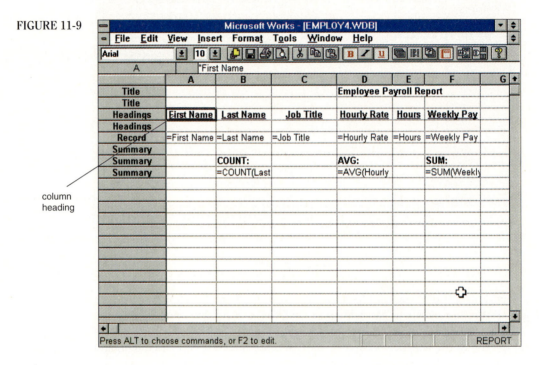

column heading

The highlight should be positioned in column A of the first Headings row. The cells in this row display the six field names as column headings in columns A through F. They are formatted to appear bold and underlined when printed.

The second Headings row is blank.

Press: ⬇ (2 times)

The highlight should be positioned in column A of the Record row. A Record row is printed for each record from the database. Each cell in this row contains a formula. A formula is used because each row contains different data. The formula in column A, =First Name, directs the program to enter the data from the First Name field in this column for each record.

Press: ⬇ (2 times)

The highlight should be positioned on the second Summary row. The Summary rows are used to display summary statistics for all records in the report. The second Summary row displays the labels COUNT, AVG, and SUM for three columns.

Press: ↓

Press: →

The formula "=Count(Last Name)" is displayed in the formula bar. This tells Works to count the number of records in the Last Name field of the report and display the calculated value at the end of the Last Name column of data. The formulas to average and sum the other two columns are displayed in their respective columns.

Viewing the Report

Now to view the report,

Choose: File>Print Preview

or

Click: 🔍 Print Preview

Your screen should be similar to Figure 11-10.

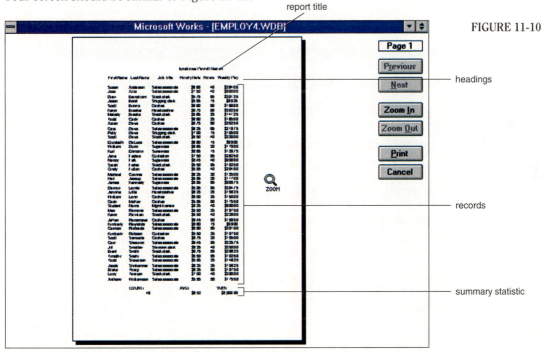

FIGURE 11-10

The report is displayed in the Preview window. The title is centered between the margins. The contents of the first field you selected appear in the leftmost column. The contents of the second field appear in the next column to the right, and so on. The records appear in alphabetical order, which is the order in which the database is sorted. Each field of data is displayed in a column below the column headings. You

> Your Preview window may be slightly different due to the selected printer.

DATABASE

want to improve the report by adding a report subtitle and subdividing the report into groups by department.

To return directly to the report definition window,

Choose: Cancel

Entering a Report Subtitle

The main title for this report is displayed in column D of the first Title row. The second title row is empty. You would like to enter a subtitle to display the time period the report covers. Entering information into Report Definition view is similar to entering information in a spreadsheet. If the information extends beyond the width of the cell, the entry will be fully displayed as long as the cells to the right are empty. As you type, the information is displayed in the formula bar.

To enter the subtitle,

Move to: column D of second Title row
Type: Week of [current date]
Press: ←Enter

Your screen should be similar to Figure 11-11.

FIGURE 11-11

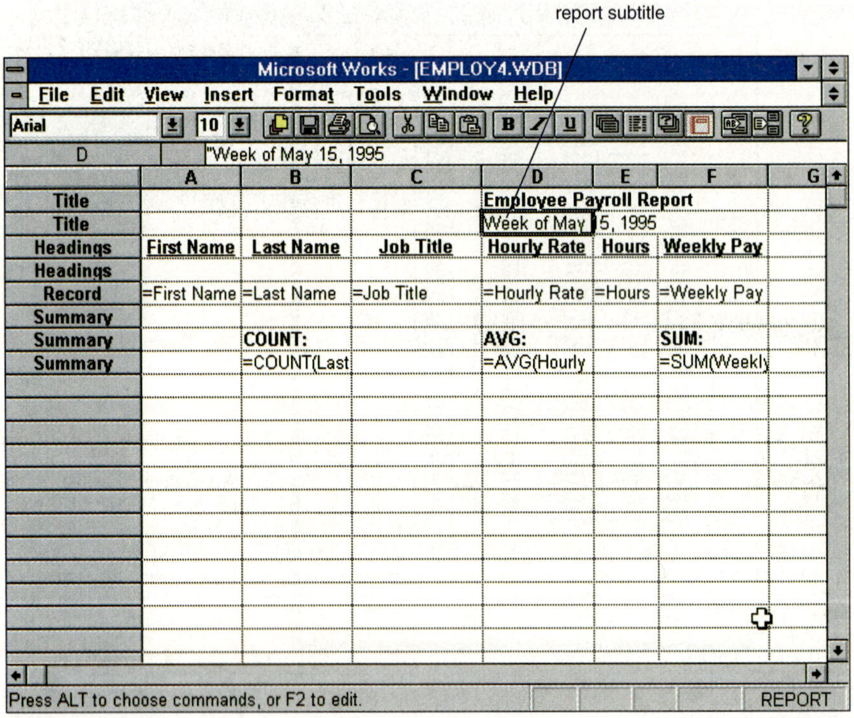

Both title lines are fully displayed in the Title rows. Your screen will display the date you entered.

Creating Subtotals

Now you want to divide the report into groups by department. To do this the Sort Records command on the Tools menu is used.

Choose: Tools>Sort Records

Your screen should be similar to Figure 11-12.

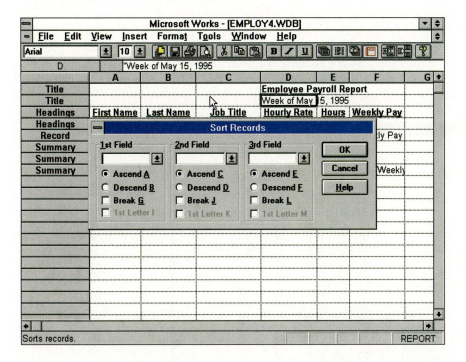

FIGURE 11-12

The Sort Records dialog box is displayed. This is very similar to the Sort dialog box you used in List view. You want the records grouped by department. From the 1st Field drop-down list box,

Select: Department

Since you want them organized in ascending alphabetical order, you do not need to change this setting. Two additional selections need to be made in the Sort Records dialog box. The Break check box allows you to separate a report into groups. If this box is not selected, Works sorts the data on the field specified but does not divide the records into groups. You want the report divided into groups with a blank line between them to be used as a summary row. To select the Break box for the first field,

Select: Break **G**

The 1st Letter check box is used when the sort field contains text and you want the break to occur whenever the first letter of the field changes, rather than breaking after each new word. In this case since the break will occur for each new word (department name), it is not necessary to select this box. To complete the command,

Choose: OK

After a few moments, the records are sorted and the Report Definition view displays a new row type, Summ Department.

Move to: column A of Summ Department row

Each cell in this row displays a formula that will calculate the statistics for each field in the group. Works automatically enters a formula to count the number of entries if the field contains text, and a formula to sum the entries if the field contains numbers. Three of the fields, Hourly Rate, Hours, and Weekly Pay, contain summary statistics that will sum the values in the field.

Preview the report to see how these changes have affected the layout. Your screen should be similar to Figure 11-13.

FIGURE 11-13

title and subtitle

data grouped by department

group statistics

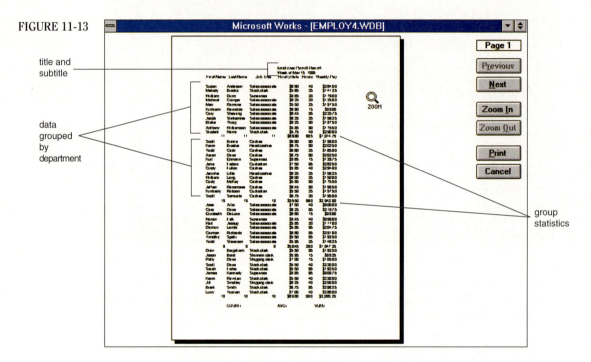

Zoom in on the report.

The report title and subtitle are displayed as the first two lines of the report. The column headings are immediately below the title. The records have been divided into groups according to department. However, it is impossible to know what department each group represents. A label identifying each group needs to be added to the report.

The numbers at the bottom of the columns in each group are the statistics calculated for that group. To return to Report view,

Choose: Cancel

Adding a Group Label

You need to add a row to the report to hold a label that will identify the groups of data. The highlight should still be on the Summ Department row. To enter the row and specify what type of row you want,

Choose: Insert>Row/Column>Row>OK

Your screen should be similar to Figure 11-14.

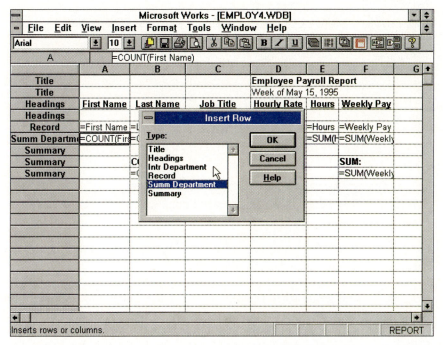

FIGURE 11-14

In the Insert Row dialog box, six row types are listed. Notice that one row type is called "Intr Department." Works automatically creates this row type whenever you create a group in a report. The field upon which the report is divided is displayed automatically following the row type label. The Intr Department row will insert a blank row before each group of data. The blank row can then be used to hold the descriptive group label information.

Choose: Intr Department>OK

The introductory department row is inserted into the report definition below the Headings rows. The type of row you select will determine where Works will enter the row on the report definition.

Next you need to enter a formula to direct Works to enter the name of the department for each group as the information to be displayed in this line of the report. To display the department name in column B,

Move to: column B of Intr Department row

Type: =Department

Press: ⏎Enter

Your screen should be similar to Figure 11-15.

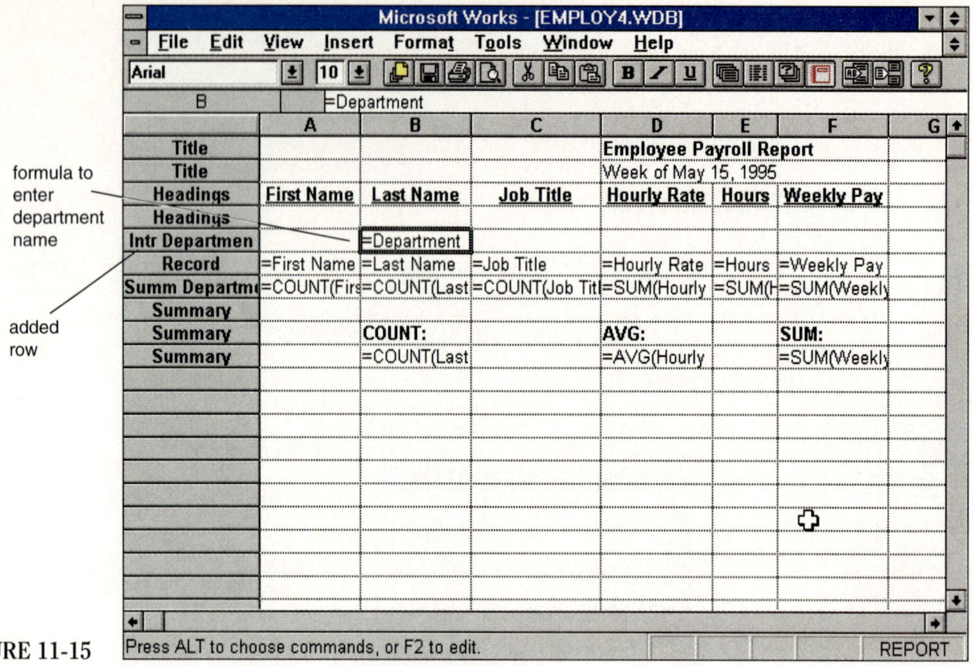

formula to enter department name

added row

	A	B	C	D	E	F	G
Title				Employee Payroll Report			
Title				Week of May 15, 1995			
Headings	First Name	Last Name	Job Title	Hourly Rate	Hours	Weekly Pay	
Headings							
Intr Departmen		=Department					
Record	=First Name	=Last Name	=Job Title	=Hourly Rate	=Hours	=Weekly Pay	
Summ Departm	=COUNT(Firs	=COUNT(Last	=COUNT(Job Titl	=SUM(Hourly	=SUM(H	=SUM(Weekly	
Summary							
Summary		COUNT:		AVG:		SUM:	
Summary		=COUNT(Last		=AVG(Hourly		=SUM(Weekly	

FIGURE 11-15

Press ALT to choose commands, or F2 to edit.   REPORT

Preview the change in the report. Above the Last Name column, the department name for the first group of data, Clothing, is displayed.

Zoom the window as necessary.

The second group label, Operations, is displayed after the summary statistics for the clothing group.

While looking at the report, you decide that the summary statistics for the First Name, Last Name, Job Title, and Hours fields do not add any important information to the report and you want to remove them. You also feel that a group statistic to average the Pay column would be more meaningful than the total currently displayed. Return to Report Definition view.

> Choose Cancel to return to Report Definition view.

Deleting and Editing Formulas

By default the department summary row calculated values for all the fields in the row. To delete the formulas from those fields that are not needed,

> Use ⇧Shift + → or drag to select in Report Definition view.

Select: columns A, B, and C of Summ Department row
Press: Delete

In a similar manner, delete the formula to sum the hours (column E).

To change the formula in the Hourly Rate field to average the numbers,

Move to: column D of Summ Department row
Choose: Insert>Field Summary>Hourly Rate>AVG>OK

Your screen should be similar to Figure 11-16.

new formula

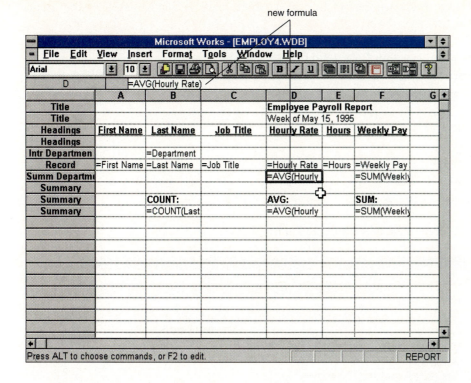

FIGURE 11-16

The First Name, Last Name, Job Title, and Hours fields no longer display formulas. The Hourly Rate field displays the formula to average the rate for the groups.

Preview the report.

Now that the report displays the required information, you want to improve the report's appearance. You want to add descriptive labels to identify the different parts of the report. You also want to format the department headings so that they are printed in bold. Finally, you want to insert several blank lines to separate the information in the report, adjust column widths, and center the report title.

Return to Report Definition view.

Adding Descriptive Labels

Because you created the report and specified the formulas, you know what the calculated group and report values mean. But someone else looking at the report would not know. The addition of descriptive labels will help clarify the meaning of the report. To add a descriptive label before the department group names,

Move to: column A of Intr Department row
Type: **Department:**
Press: ←Enter

You want the department group row to be printed in bold.

Select and bold the entries in columns A and B of the Intr Department row.

Next you want to add descriptive labels to clarify the statistics. They will be entered to the left side of the values. To enter a descriptive label for the group statistics,

Move to: column A of Summ Department row

Type: **Department Statistics:**

Press: ⟵Enter

To enter a label to identify the total report values,

Move to: column A of second Summary row

Type: **Total:**

Press: ⟵Enter

Your screen should be similar to Figure 11-17.

FIGURE 11-17

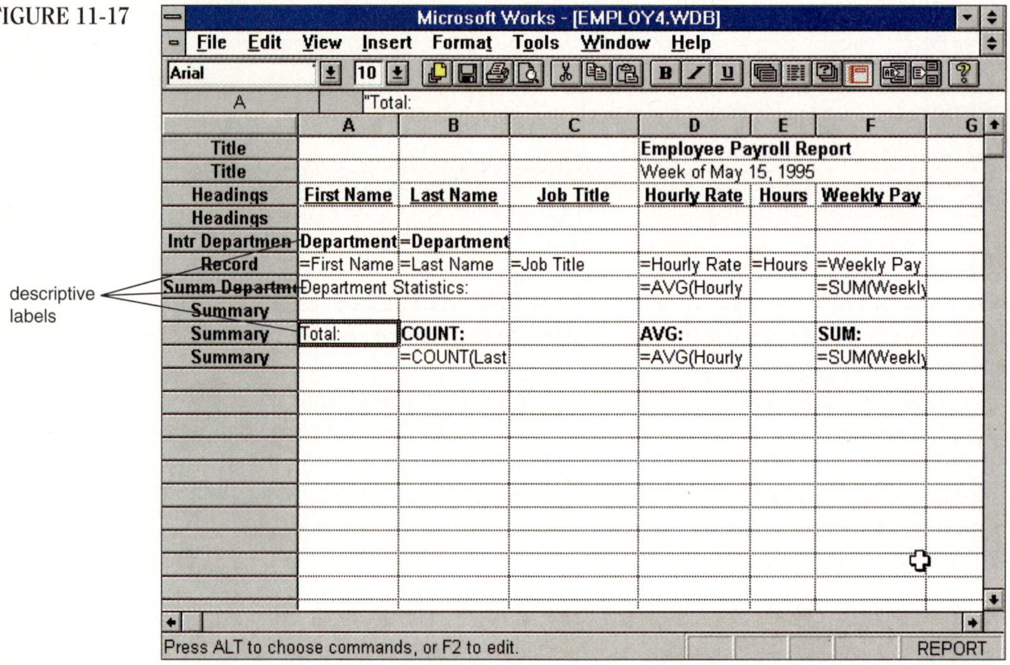

To see how these changes have affected the report layout, preview the report. Zoom in on the Preview window to see the labels clearly.

The descriptive labels greatly improve the meaning of the report, but they have made the report look very crowded. You will insert blank lines between categories to improve the readability of the report.

View the second page of the report.
Return to Report Definition view.

Inserting Blank Lines

You want the report title separated from the column headings by a blank line. To insert an additional row below the second title line,

Move to: first Headings row
Choose: Insert>Row/Column>Row>OK

In the Insert Row dialog box, you need to specify the type of row you want to insert. By default Works highlights the type of row that the highlight is positioned on. You want to insert another Headings row at this location.

Choose: OK

Your screen should be similar to Figure 11-18.

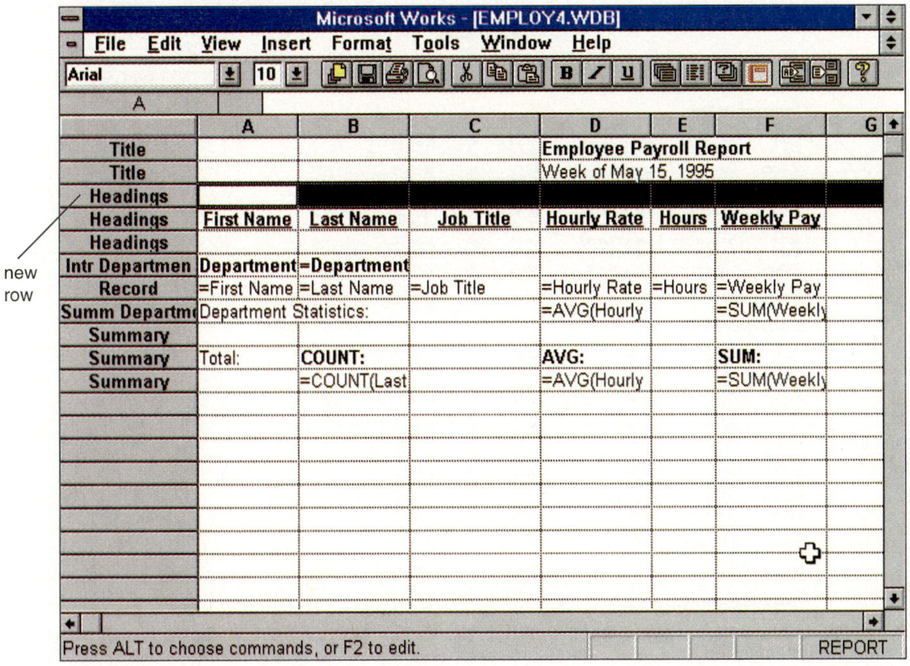

FIGURE 11-18

A blank row has been entered in the report definition window. Leaving the contents of this row blank will insert a blank row between the report title and the column headings.

To add space between the groups of data, you will add several more blank lines in the report. First, to insert a blank introductory department row between the group title and the first record of each group,

Move to: Record row
Choose: Insert>Row/Column>OK>Intr Department>OK

Next, to insert a blank row between the last record of each group and the department total,

Move to: Record row

Choose: Insert>Row/Column>OK>Summ Department>OK

Then to add another blank row to separate the group summary statistics from the group heading immediately below it,

Move to: first Summary row

Choose: Insert>Row/Column>OK>Summ Department>OK

Preview the report. Zoom the window.
Your screen should be similar to Figure 11-19.

FIGURE 11-19

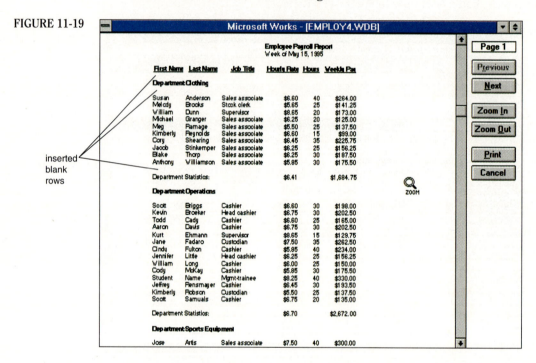

inserted
blank
rows

The blank lines separating the different categories make reading the report much easier.
After viewing the entire report, return to Report Definition view.

Increasing the Column Widths

You noticed that there is no space between the descriptive label "Department:" and each department name. You want to increase the width of the First and Last Name columns to insert space after the labels. The procedure is the same as changing the column width in Form or List view. To increase the width of the First Name and Last Name fields,

Select: columns A and B

Choose: Format>Column Width

Type: 13

Choose: OK

Changing the column width in Report view does not change the widths you set in Form and List views.

Preview the report. Zoom the window.
Your screen should be similar to Figure 11-20.

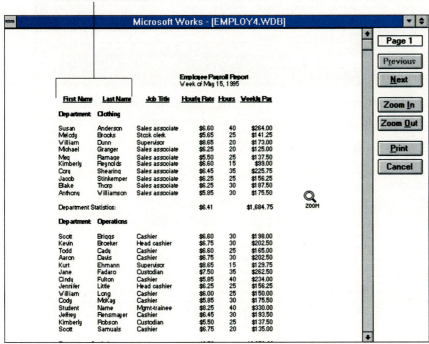

increased column widths

FIGURE 11-20

This change increases the readability of the data by adding more white space between the columns. You think the appearance could be further improved by centering the report title over the five columns of data.
Return to Report Definition view.

Enhancing the Report

Before centering the report title, you want to increase the point size and make the subtitle bold. Select and enlarge the title and subtitle in column D to 14pt. Bold the subtitle.
As you learned in the Spreadsheet tool, you can center data with the Center Across Selection command. The data to be centered must be in the first column of the row. You can move each title individually using the Cut command or you can cut both titles at the same time by selecting the two titles first.

You cannot drag to move a selection in Report Definition view.

DATABASE

Move the titles in column D of the first and second Title rows to column A in the same rows.

To center the selection,

Select: columns A through F in both Title rows

Choose: Forma**t**>**A**lignment>Center **a**cross selection>OK

Your screen should be similar to Figure 11-21.

titles centered across columns

FIGURE 11-21

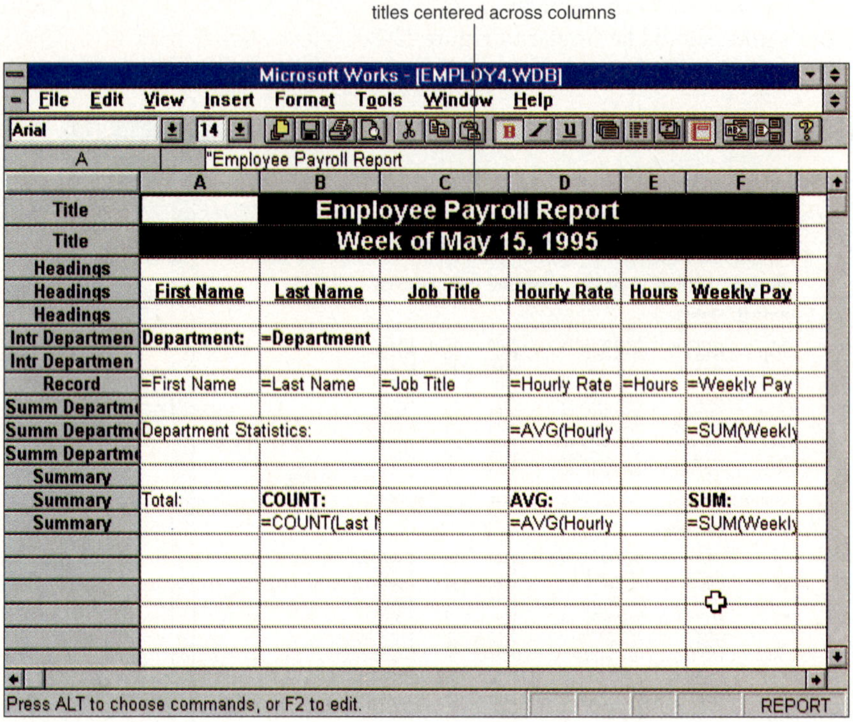

Now the report title is evenly centered over the report columns.

You would also like to left-align the First Name, Last Name, and Job Title column headings so they are aligned the same as the text in the columns. Left-align the First Name, Last Name, and Job Title headings.

Finally, you want to add a single line above each group statistic and a double line above each total report statistic. To add a single line above the Hourly Rate field average formula,

Move to: column D of the second Summ Department row

Choose: Forma**t**>**B**order>**T**op>OK

In the same row, enter a single line above the Weekly Pay total formula (column F).

Add a double line above the three report statistics in columns B, D, and F of the third Summary row.

Preview the report.

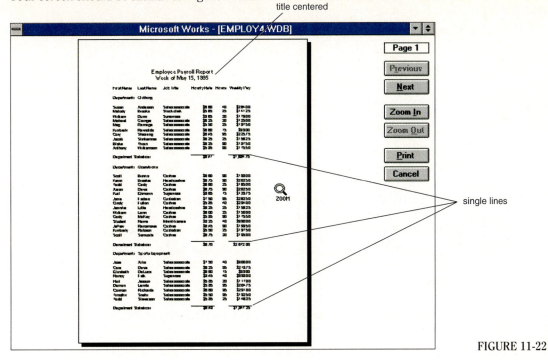

title centered

single lines

FIGURE 11-22

The first page of the report shows the title centered over the columns of data and the single lines above each group statistic. To view the second page of the report,

Choose: N̲ext

The total report statistics display double lines above the values. You are pleased with how the report looks and are ready to print a copy of it for the manager.

　　　Close the Preview window.

> If the first page of your report ends on a different line, this is because your selected printer affects the number of lines that can be printed on a page.

Naming the Report

Whenever a new report is created, Works automatically assigns it a default name of Report1. This is similar to how Works assigns names to charts in the Spreadsheet tool. Similarly you can assign a name to the report that is more descriptive of the information in the report. To rename the report,

Choose: T̲ools>N̲ame Report

In the Name text box,

Type: **Payroll**
Choose: **R̲ename**
Choose: **OK**

> A report name can have up to 15 characters.

DATABASE

If you have printer capability, to print a copy of the Payroll report,

Choose: File>Print>OK
or
Click: 🖨 Print

Switch to List view.

To return to the Emp # field of the first record,

Press: Ctrl + Home

Notice that the records are no longer in alphabetical order by last name. This is because when you sorted the report by department, the database was sorted in the same order. This is probably not how you want the database records to appear when the file is opened. To restore the original sort order of the database,

Choose: Tools>Sort Records

The first and second sort fields are the same as they were when you first sorted the database. To execute the sort,

Choose: OK

The records are sorted back in their original order. The report sort order is not affected.
   Save the file as PAYROLL. Exit Works or close the file if you are continuing to use Works.

> You cannot press F9 to switch to List view form Report Definition view.

Key Terms

report (373)
Report Definition view (377)
row type (377)
Title row (377)
Headings row (377)
Record row (377)
Summary row (377)

Command Summary

Command	Action
T**o**ols>Create **N**ew Report	Creates a new report
Insert>**R**ow/Column	Inserts a blank row or column of selected type
Insert>Field **S**ummary	Adds or changes group summary statistics in Report view
T**o**ols>N**a**me Report	Names report settings

LAB REVIEW

Matching

1. Sort Records _____
2. =COUNT _____
3. Record row _____
4. Name Report _____
5. =SUM _____
6. =AVG(Hourly Rate) _____
7. Title row _____
8. Summary row _____
9. Headings row _____
10. Insert>Row/Column _____

a. displays field name information printed on each page of report
b. Tools menu command used to change default name of a report
c. inserts a row or column
d. calculates average of Hourly Rate field
e. summary statistic that totals values in a field
f. displays statistics for each column of data
g. summary statistic that totals number of entries in a column
h. displays actual data for each record
i. Tools menu command to rearrange order of records
j. displays information printed on only first page of report

Practice Exercises

As you create the reports in the following practice exercises, preview the reports as needed.

1. As inventory control manager of the Gift Center, you would like to create some reports to display the information stored in the Gift Center database file. Open the file GIFTS.WDB, which you edited in Lab 10, Practice Exercise 3.

   a. Create a query that displays all the products supplied by supplier number 93 and that cost greater than $35.00.

   b. Print the query.

   c. Create a report in Report Definition view that displays the description, price, and discount price of all the gifts that cost less then $50.00 and are supplied by supplier number 89.

d.   Add appropriate titles, subtitles, and statistics. Print the report.

e.   Create a new report, grouped by supplier number, that displays the description and price of products that sell for more than $100.00.

f.   Add appropriate titles, subtitles, and statistics. Print the report.

g.   Name all of the queries and reports appropriately. Save the file.

2.   Your supervisor has asked you to create a report of all employees' salaries for annual review and possible raises. Open the database file TECHEMP.WDB.

a.   Create a customized data entry form by moving the fields on the default form. Add bolds, underlines, italics, and borders.

b.   Sort the file on the Last Name field. Format the Salary field to currency with 0 decimal places.

c.   Create a new report. Enter "Total Annual Salary" as the first line of the title. Enter your name as a subtitle line.

d.   Include the Last Name, First Name, Department, and Salary fields in the report.

e.   Sum the salary column.

f.   Remove the Department field column.

g.   Group the report by department. Add a group introductory row to display the department name and label. Bold the label and department. Add underlines above the group total salary values.

h.   Make any adjustments to spacing and placement of report titles as needed. Rename and print the report.

You have received a request from the Personnel department for a list of employees' dates of birth.

i.   Sort the file on Birthdate in ascending order.

j.   Create a new report. Enter "Employee Birthdates" as the first line of the title. Include the Last Name, First Name, Birthdate, and Year Started fields in the report. Do not include any statistics.

k.   Enter your name as a subtitle line. Make any adjustments to spacing and placement of report titles as needed. Rename and print the report. Save the file. Close the database file.

3.   Millie is the owner/operator of Millie's Rental and Supply company. She maintains records of the customer rentals using Works. Periodically she creates reports of the information in the database to track rental usage and customer charges. Open the database file EQUIP.WDB.

a.   Create a new report with "Equipment Charges" as the first line of the title.

b.   Include the fields Equipment #, Equipment Desc, and Total Due. Sum the Total Due column.

    c.   Change the report format to group on Job Number. Delete all group statistics except for the Total Due column. Add an introductory row to display the Job Number for each group and the descriptive label "Job Number." Bold the label.

    d.   Enter your name as a subtitle line. Insert blank rows and underlines as needed to improve the appearance of the report. Rename and print the report. Save and close the database file.

4.   Create a database of ten of your friends or family members showing the following fields: Last name, first name, address, city, state, zip code, and phone number. (*Hint:* The total width of a standard $8^{1}/_{2}$ by 11-inch sheet of paper is 80 characters, so determine field size accordingly.)

    a.   Sort the database file by last name.

    b.   Create a new report and enter an appropriate first line title.

    c.   Use the fields you created as column contents. Count the last name column.

    d.   Enter a subtitle that includes your name. Add spacing in the report as needed.

    e.   Save the report as NAME&ADD and print the report. Close the database file.

5.   Create database for a company of your choice. Include numeric data such as quantity, price, or salary in the file. Enter a minimum of 10 records in the file. Create a simple query using the database. Create a report that prints the records that are found with your query. Enter your name and the current date as a subtitle of the report.

12 Integrating Works Tools

CASE STUDY

The Regional Manager of The Sports Company is very pleased with your work and would like you to use Works to create a memo to the board of directors about recent sales trends. You have already created the memo using the Works Word Processor tool, but still need to insert a spreadsheet and chart of the sales information into the memo. Then you will send the memo to the board of directors' office using the Works Communications tool.

As a second project, you will modify the letter to new credit card holders. The regional manager has asked that the letter be made more personalized by including the customer's first name in the salutation and an inside address. You will create a form letter using Works to personalize each welcome letter.

Inserting Spreadsheet Data into a Word Processor Document

Load Works and put your data disk in the appropriate drive for your system.

To see the memo to the board of directors, open the word processor document BOARD.WPS. If necessary maximize the window.

Your screen should be similar to Figure 12-1.

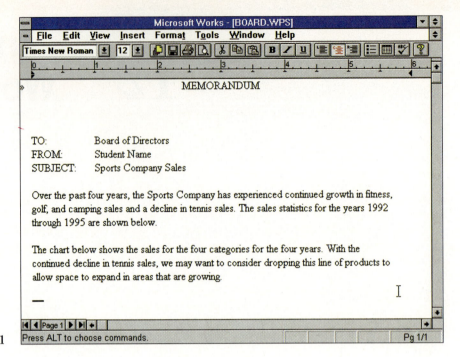

FIGURE 12-1

Replace Student Name following FROM: with your name.
    Below the first paragraph of the memo, you will enter the data from the spreadsheet CHARTS.WKS. Below the second paragraph, you will display a chart of The Sports Company sales.
    First you will insert the information from the spreadsheet file that you want displayed in the memo. The spreadsheet file you will use is CHARTS.WKS. This is the file you created at the end of Lab 8.
    Open the spreadsheet file CHARTS.WKS.

Note: If the spreadsheet file CHARTS.WKS. is not available, use the file LAB12.WKS.

    There are now two open files, BOARD.WPS and CHARTS.WKS. CHARTS is the active file and is displayed on the screen. BOARD is open but is not displayed. It is behind the CHARTS file.
    The highlight should be in cell A1. If it is not, move it there.
    To see both files at the same time,

Choose: Window>Tile

Your screen should be similar to Figure 12-2.

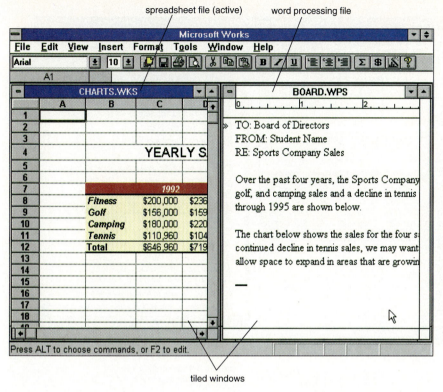

spreadsheet file (active)   word processing file

tiled windows

FIGURE 12-2

The two files are displayed side-by-side on the screen. CHARTS is the active file.

You want to copy the spreadsheet data into the memo. However, you do not want to include the 1996 projected sales data in column G.

Select cells B7 through F12.

Choose:	Edit>Copy
➤	Ctrl + C
Click:	Copy

Now you need to specify the location where you want the copied information displayed. To switch to the BOARD window and make it the active window,

Click:	anywhere in BOARD window
or	
Press:	Ctrl + F6

You want the spreadsheet data displayed below the first paragraph.

Move to:	blank line below first paragraph of memo

To paste the spreadsheet into the word processing file,

Choose:	Edit>Paste
➤	Ctrl + V
Click:	Paste

Select using ⬆Shift + directional keys or drag.

INTEGRATION

Your screen should be similar to Figure 12-3.

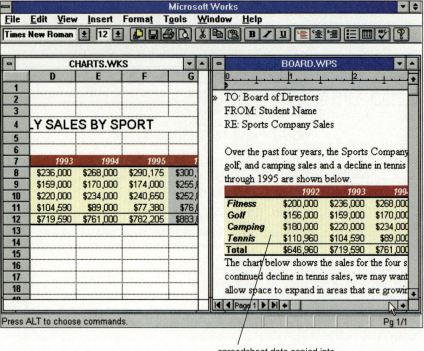

FIGURE 12-3

spreadsheet data copied into
word procesing document

The spreadsheet data has been copied into the word processor document. Maximize the window to fully display the memo.

Notice that the insertion point appears along the left edge of the spreadsheet data and it is the full height of the spreadsheet. This is because the spreadsheet is considered one object when placed in the word processor document.

You would like the spreadsheet to appear centered under the paragraph. To do this,

Choose: Format>Paragraph>Center>OK

or

Click: 🔲 Center

Because the spreadsheet is considered one object, the entire spreadsheet is centered between the margins.

Next you would like to add more blank space around the spreadsheet. Enter a blank line above and below the spreadsheet.

Your screen should be similar to Figure 12-4.

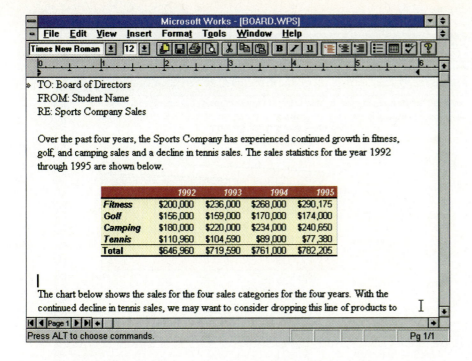

FIGURE 12-4

Inserting a Chart into a Word Processor File

Now you are ready to copy the area chart of the spreadsheet data into the memo. It will be displayed below the second paragraph.

Move to: blank line below second paragraph
Choose: Insert>Chart

The Insert Chart dialog box is displayed. The Spreadsheets list box displays the names of all open spreadsheet files. Since there is only one spreadsheet file open, the only name that is displayed is CHARTS.WKS. The spreadsheet file must be open in order to insert a chart into a word processor document.

Select: CHARTS.WKS

The file name is highlighted and the associated charts are displayed in the Charts list box. The chart you want to copy into the memo is AREA.

Select: AREA
Choose: OK

Scroll the window until the entire chart is displayed. Your screen should be similar to Figure 12-5.

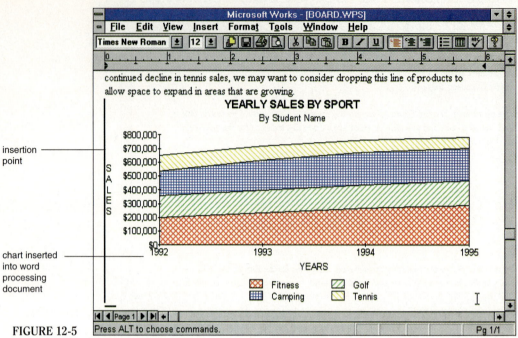

insertion point

chart inserted into word processing document

FIGURE 12-5

The area chart is displayed at the insertion point location in the word processor document. Works places the left and right edges of the chart even with the left and right margins of the word processor document. The program also determines the height of the chart automatically. These settings can be changed if you do not like how they appear.

To see how it will appear when printed, preview the memo.
Your screen should be similar to Figure 12-6.

FIGURE 12-6

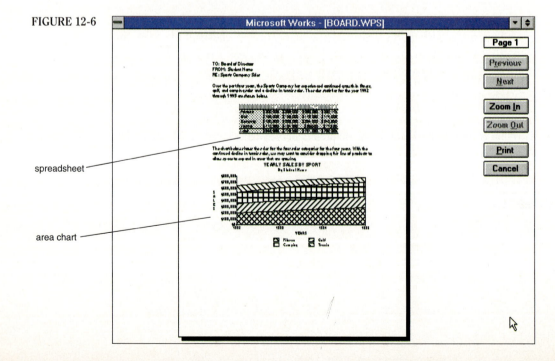

spreadsheet

area chart

Now that you can see the entire memo, you want to make several changes. First, you want to insert a blank line above the chart to separate it from the text. Second, you want to change the chart type from an area chart to a bar chart, which you feel will portray the information more precisely. Finally, you want to decrease the chart size.

Close the Preview window.

Insert a blank line between the second paragraph and the chart.

Next, to change the type of chart to a bar chart, you need to switch to the spreadsheet file and change the chart type.

Switch to the CHARTS.WKS window and view the area chart.

The area chart is displayed. To change this chart to the default bar chart,

Choose: Gallery>Bar

or

Click: 📊 Bar

Choose: OK

> To display the chart, choose
> Chart from the View menu
> and select AREA.

The chart changes to a bar chart. To improve the appearance of the chart, you will add patterns to the bars.

Use the Patterns and Colors command on the Format menu to add patterns of your choice to the four data series. To see the change in the memo, make the BOARD.WPS window active.

Your screen should be similar to Figure 12-7.

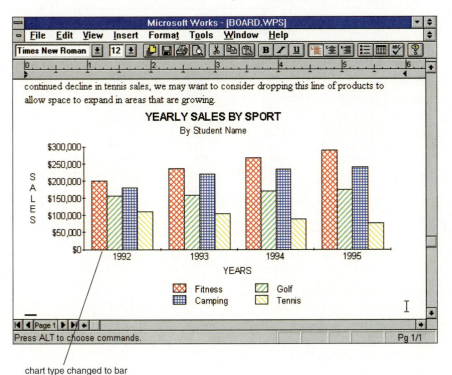

FIGURE 12-7

chart type changed to bar

Now the bar chart is displayed in the memo. This is because any changes you make in the inserted spreadsheet file will be automatically reflected in the word processor document. In addition, if you make any changes in the spreadsheet data that affect the chart, the changes will also be reflected in the chart displayed in the memo.

> To select the chart, click on it or move to the chart and press ⇧Shift + a directional key.

> You can also size the chart by dragging the handles.

Finally, you want to make the chart smaller. Once a chart is entered into a file, it can be moved or copied to another location or sized.

Select the chart. The chart is surrounded by a dotted border and eight handles. To size the chart,

Choose: Format>Picture/Object

In the Size tab box, set the width to 5 inches and the height to 3 inches.

Choose: OK

The chart is reduced to the specified size. To clear the selection,

Press: ⬅

Next, center the chart between the margins.
    Your screen should be similar to Figure 12-8.

FIGURE 12-8

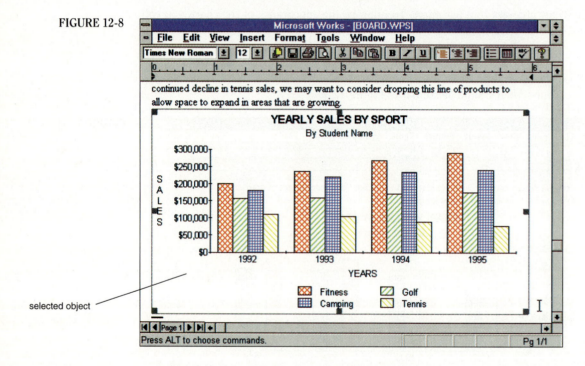

selected object

Preview and print the memo. Save the revised memo as BORDMEMO.

Note: Do not have the printer set to Draft quality. If you do, the chart will not print.

Save and close the CHARTS.WKS file.

Using the Communications Tool

Note: This section does not transmit data via modem and assumes that you do not have a modem connected to your computer.

Now you want to send the completed memo to the board of directors' office. You could send a hard copy using a fax machine, but the board of directors has asked that you send the completed report directly through their computer. This way the board office can save the incoming text as a file on their computer and incorporate the information in this report into the packet of information that is being created for the next board meeting.

The Sports Company board of directors' office is in another location, but they are able to connect directly between locations through their computers using a **modem**. A modem is a device that allows you to transmit data via telephone lines from one computer to another. By connecting to another computer, you can send and save text and files directly between computers.

You can also connect to another computer through a computer information service, such as CompuServe or Prodigy. These services usually require that you obtain an account with the service first. Then you have access to a variety of on-line services including travel, banking and shopping, and information sources such as personal computing forums, home, health, family, entertainment, and games. You can also send and receive mail, messages, reports, and memos to subscribers to the service in other locations.

When you connect with another computer or information service, you use a **communications file** to make the connection. Since the Sports Company frequently transmits information via modem to the board office, they already have created this file and named it BOARDCOM.WCM. All communications files have the extension .WCM. To open this file,

Choose: File>Open Existing File>BOARDCOM.WCM>OK

The Modem Setup dialog box may be displayed. If this dialog box is not displayed, skip the next two steps and continue with the discussion of the Connect dialog box. This dialog box is used to set the communications port on your computer. The **port** is the external connection device that links the computer to the telephone. Most computers have two communications ports, named COM1 and COM2. To have Works determine the port your modem is connected to,

Choose: Test

After a few moments, the Modem Test status box will display the port or the message "Could not find modem" if your system is not connected.

Choose: OK

The Connect dialog box appears asking if you want to connect to another computer. Normally if you were connected via modem, you would choose OK and Works would dial the number that is stored in the file and establish the link with the other computer. The other computer must be set to answer the incoming call. To not dial the number and work off-line,

Choose: Cancel

Your screen should be similar to Figure 12-9.

FIGURE 12-9

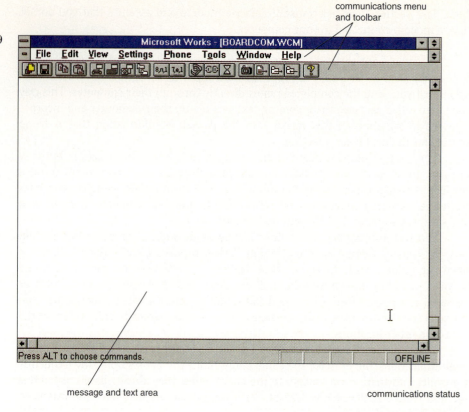

communications menu
and toolbar

message and text area

communications status

The communications window, menu, and toolbar are displayed. The window is blank. This area displays messages from your system to inform you of its progress as it dials and connects with the other computer. It will also display text as you type to communicate with another computer, or information as it is received. The status bar indictor shows that the communications session is off-line.

The communications file contains the telephone number to call to connect with the other computer or service, and establishes the settings that are required to match those of the other computer or computer service. These settings are saved in the file and are made by selecting options from the menu. To see the phone number setting,

Choose: Settings>Phone
or
Click: Phone Settings

Your screen should be similar to Figure 12-10.

Phone Settings button | access line number | pause | telephone number

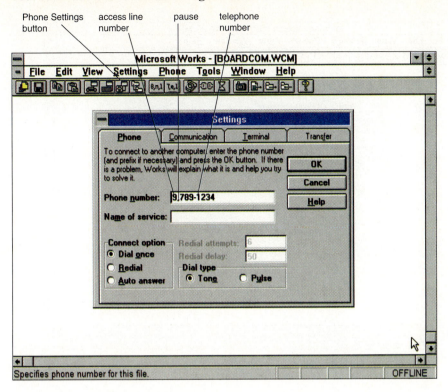

FIGURE 12-10

The Settings dialog box displays the phone number that was previously entered in this file to access the board of directors' computer. The "9" preceding the number is the access number that must be entered at The Sports Company in order to get an outside telephone line. The comma following the 9 tells the computer to pause before dialing the rest of the number. This gives the phone system enough time to access the line. You can have as many commas as needed to increase the length of the pause. The hyphens in the phone number are optional.

The Dial type option is set to Tone by default. If you had a rotary phone, you would need to choose the Pulse option. The other settings in the dialog box allow you to specify the number of times to redial if the line is busy and the seconds to delay before redialing.

To see the communications settings,

Choose: Communication

Your screen should be similar to Figure 12-11.

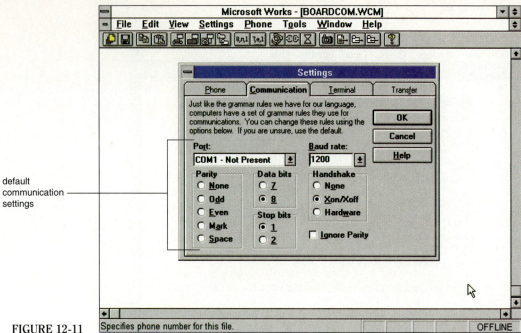

default
communication —
settings

FIGURE 12-11

The initial Works communication settings are designed to match those used by many information services. These settings would need to be changed to match the computer you are connecting to. For Help about these settings, from the dialog box,

Choose: Help

Read the Help information on the Communication commands. When you are done, close Help.

The initial settings and what they do are described below.

Type	Setting	Use
Port	COM1	Choose port your modem or cable is connected to. Reads "Available" if a modem is installed; "Not Present" if no modem is installed.
Baud Rate	1200	Choose highest transmission speed that both computers can accept.
Data Bits	8	Match other computer's setting.
Stop Bits	1	Match other computer's setting.
Parity	None	Allows communication regardless of other computer's setting.
Handshake	Xon/Xoff	Use when communicating via modem.

These settings are the default settings and match the requirements you need to communicate with the board of directors' computer.

Choose: Cancel

Although you cannot actually transmit the text, you will step through the procedure that would be used to send the memo to the board's office computer.

First you need to notify the board office that you plan to send information by computer, because the board office must prepare Works to receive the data. To do this they open their Sports Company communications file. This file contains the settings that match your computer settings. They also change the Phone setting to answer automatically. This stops the modem from dialing the phone number in the communications file. The sender can now place the call, and the board's computer will answer it and establish the connection.

Next you need to direct Works to connect with the other computer. This is done automatically for you when you first open the communications file and respond OK to the dialog box prompt to connect. If you do not do this, you can connect by choosing Easy Connect from the Phone menu. This command uses the settings in the communications file and tells Works to make the connection through the modem by dialing the telephone number, and to establish a link to the other computer.

Once you connect, the screen will display the commands Works sends to the computer and the message "CONNECT" to indicate that the link was made. If the message "BUSY" or "NO CARRIER" is displayed, Works was unable to connect. You could then choose Dial Again from the Phone menu to try to connect again.

Once a successful connection is made, you type a message to the receiving computer to confirm it is ready to receive the text. When you type in the communications window, Works sends the text you type to the other computer. The text is displayed on your screen as you type and on the receiver's screen. The receiver then types a message back indicating its system is ready to receive. This is just like carrying on a conversation.

If you were connecting to an information service, you would be prompted to enter your customer ID or password. Once access is approved, a menu of options appears to allow you to select the area of interest.

Besides transferring text by typing it, you can select and copy existing text from an open file or you can send an entire file. If you transfer text by copying it, it is displayed on both the sender's and receiver's screens as it is transferred. However, no formatting or special characters such as boldface are transferred. If you send the entire file, its formatting and special characters are transferred.

You want to send the memo by copying it from the BORDMEMO.WPS document.

Make the BORDMEMO.WPS window active.

To select the entire contents of the file,

Choose: Edit>Select All

The entire file should be highlighted. Then to copy the selected text,

Choose: Edit>Copy
➤   Ctrl + C
Click: 📋 Copy

Make the BOARDCOM.WCM window active.

To send the copied text,

Choose: Edit>Paste Text

INTEGRATION

A dialog box is displayed, indicating that you must be connected to send the text.

Choose: OK

You are returned to the BOARDCOM.WCM window.

If you were connected, the copied text would be displayed on your screen and automatically sent to the other computer. The receiving computer receives the text, displays it onscreen, and stores it in a temporary storage area called a **buffer**. The amount of text that can be received is controlled by the buffer size. Works provides three sizes of buffers: small (about 100 lines), medium (about 300 lines), and large (about 750 lines). If the buffer receives more text than it can hold, old text is deleted as new text is received.

As the receiver's screen fills, the text scrolls. You can scroll the contents of the text onscreen like any other document. To do this you must first pause communications using the Pause command on the Phone menu so that the computer will not accept any new information into the buffer. This command can only be used when you are connected. Then you can scroll the screen to see the text in the buffer and copy the text from the buffer to a file. Then you turn Pause off again to allow the computer to receive more text into the buffer.

As mentioned earlier, you can also send an entire file, such as an application file, a formatted text file, or any Works file. When you transfer a file, the receiving computer must set Works to receive the file using the Receive File command on the Tools menu. This command prompts for a file name to use to save the file to disk. The sending computer uses the Send File command on the Tools menu and selects the file name to send. Sending a file requires that you match the **protocol** used by the other computer. Protocol is a set of communications procedures used to transfer files between computers. The protocol settings are in the Settings menu.

Choose: Settings>Transfer
or
Click: 📇 Transfer Settings

Your screen should be similar to Figure 12-12.

Transfer Settings
button

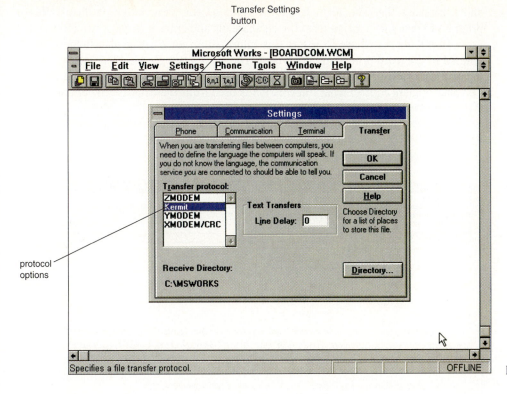

protocol
options

FIGURE 12-12

Choose Help for information about the protocols. Read the Help information. When you are done, close Help.

To cancel the dialog box,

Choose: Cancel

The transfer protocol you select depends upon the computer systems being used.

To quit a communications session, you disconnect. If you are using an information service, always log off according to the service's procedures so that the service does not charge you for the time it takes the other computer to recognize that you have disconnected. If you were connected to another computer, to disconnect you would choose Hang Up from the Phone menu. This command appears in the menu only when you are connected to another computer.

After disconnecting, you close the communications file.

Close the BOARDCOM.WCM file. If prompted to save changes, select No. Close the BORDMEMO.WPS file. If prompted to save changes, select No.

Creating a Form Letter

In the second project, you will create a form letter using the preferred credit card customer letter. A **form letter** is a standard letter sent to many different people that is personalized by adding information such as the recipient's name and address. You need to change the letter so that each letter includes the customer's first name in the salutation and his or her full name and address as the inside address.

INTEGRATION

A form letter requires the use of two files: a word processing form letter file and a database file. The form letter file contains the basic letter. It directs the program to take information from the database file and enter it in the form letter.

To tell Works where to insert this information, form letter placeholders are entered in the word processing document. The form letter placeholders identify the fields of data from the database to be inserted into the word processing document. The placeholders control what information is used from the database file and where it is entered in the document in the form letter file.

Open the word processor document CRDTLTR.WPS. If necessary, maximize the window.

Your screen should be similar to Figure 12-13.

FIGURE 12-13

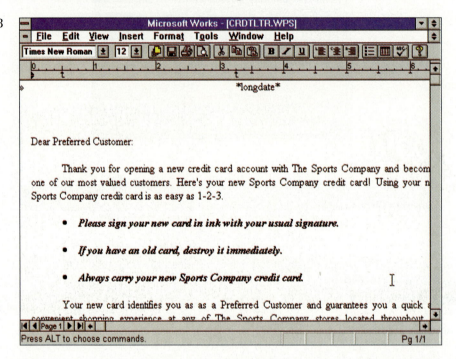

A letter very similar to the letter you saved at the end of Lab 4 should be displayed on your screen. The letter needs to be modified to allow entry of the name and address information for each customer from the preferred customer database file. The inside address will hold the following three lines of information:

> Title, First and Last Name
> Street Address
> City, State and Zip Code

The salutation will include the customer's first name.

Close the CRDTLTR.WPS file.

The database file CUSTOMER.WDB contains the name and address field information that will be used in the letter's inside address and salutation.

Open the database file CUSTOMER.WDB.

Your screen should be similar to Figure 12-14.

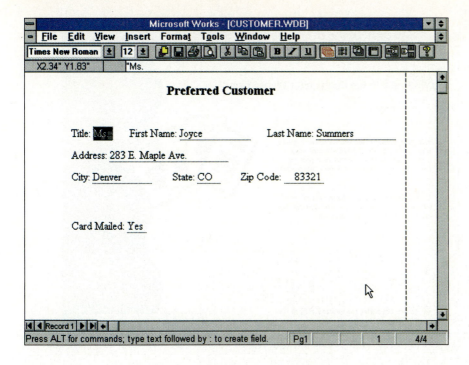

FIGURE 12-14

The Preferred Customer form is displayed, showing the fields of information for the first record. Notice the field Card Mailed. This field entry displays Yes when a credit card has been mailed and No when it has not been mailed.

To create a form letter, Works takes the field information from the database file and combines it with the word processing file. Form letter placeholders control what fields are used from the database file and where they are entered in the word processing file.

Enter your name and address (the address can be fictitious) as the fifth record in the database file. For the Card Mailed field data, enter No. Save and close the CUSTOMER.WDB file.

You will use a special feature in the Works program called the WorksWizards to help you create the form letter. WorksWizards are programs that lead you step-by-step through the procedures to help you perform some common tasks quickly.

> There are 12 WorksWizards.

Each WorksWizard is designed to ask questions about the procedure you want to perform, and then to carry out the task using the settings you specify. You will use the Form Letter WorksWizard to create the personalized preferred customer letter. From the Startup dialog box,

Choose: Use A WorksWizard>Form Letter>OK

INTEGRATION

Your screen should be similar to Figure 12-15.

FIGURE 12-15

The opening screen of the Form Letter WorksWizard is displayed. As the directions on the screen explain, you will answer a series of questions that will be used to design the form letter. You will read each screen and supply the requested information. After each screen you choose a button to move to the next screen.

Choose: Next >

This screen advises you that you must have a database and a letter file created before using the form letter WorksWizard. Because the default response is Yes and you have a database file already created, to continue using WorksWizard,

Choose: Next >

The screen asks you if you have a letter. Because you have a letter file already created and the default response is already set to Yes,

Choose: Next >

Next you are asked to open the letter file. From the list box,

Select: CRDTLTR.WPS
Choose: Open

The next screen asks you to open the database file. From the list box,

Select: CUSTOMER.WDB
Choose: Open

Your screen should be similar to Figure 12-16.

description of
form letter placeholders

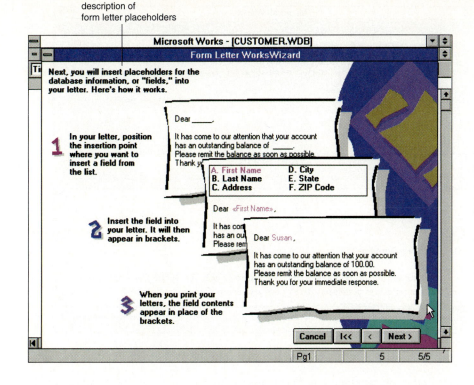

FIGURE 12-16

This screen describes how the placeholders are used in the letter. When you are done reading this screen,

Choose: Next >

This screen displays the field names from the database in the upper window and the letter file in the lower window. Notice that the insertion point is displayed in the letter window. To position the insertion point where the first field of the inside address will be placed,

Press: ↓ (3 times)

To use this screen to enter the first field, Title, you will hold down Ctrl and select the letter next to the field name you want to insert. To insert the Title field,

Press: Ctrl + A

Your screen should be similar to Figure 12-17.

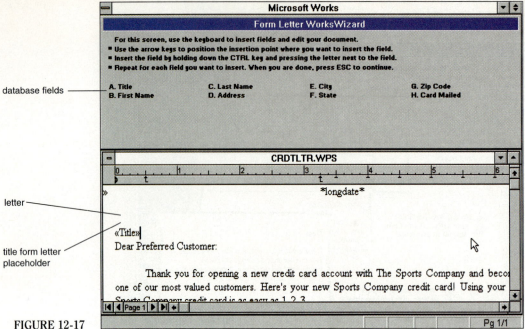

database fields ——

letter ——

title form letter
placeholder ——

FIGURE 12-17

A form letter placeholder has been entered in the letter at the location of the insertion point.

The next field that needs to be entered is the preferred customer's first name. To enter a blank space after the Title placeholder,

Press: Spacebar

To enter the First Name field placeholder,

Press: Ctrl + B

The third field of information on this line is the customer's last name. To enter this placeholder,

Press: Spacebar
Press: Ctrl + C

The next line of the inside address will contain the street address. To create and move to the next line,

Press: ←Enter

To enter the street address field placeholder,

Press: Ctrl + D

The third field placeholder is displayed in the credit card letter. The next line of the inside address will display three fields of data from the database file: city, state, and zip code.

Press: ⏎Enter

To enter the next field,

Press: Ctrl + E

To separate the City field from the next field,

Type: ,
Press: Spacebar

The State field will be entered on the same line as the City field.

Press: Ctrl + F

To separate the State field from the next field, Zip Code,

Press: Spacebar (2 times)
Press: Ctrl + G

To enter a blank line between the inside address and the salutation,

Press: ⏎Enter

Your screen should be similar to Figure 12-18.

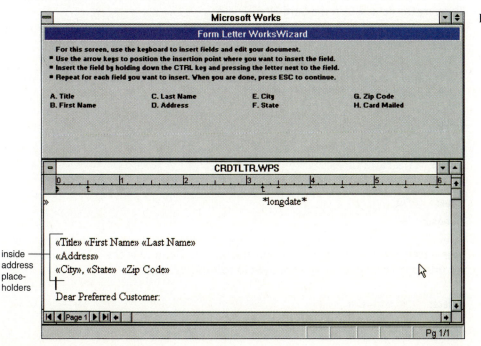

FIGURE 12-18

> If you have made an error, edit the placeholders just like any other text entry.

> You cannot move or select with the mouse in WorksWizard.

The inside address placeholders from the database file are now complete.

The last field of information that needs to be entered in the letter file is the preferred customer's first name in the salutation. First the words "Preferred Customer" need to be deleted.

Move to: "P" of "Preferred"

Delete the text "Preferred Customer" (do not include the :).

When the same field is used in two or more locations in the form letter file, the same placeholder name is used. To enter the first name in the salutation,

Press: Ctrl + B

The form letter placeholders have been entered in all appropriate locations to create an inside address and a salutation. The placeholders direct the program to enter the information for the field specified in the placeholder from the database file at the placeholder location in the form letter file. For example, the placeholder <<First Name>> directs the program to print the information for the preferred customer's first name from the database file at this location in the form letter. To continue,

Press: Esc

The form letter has been created. Now Works will ask you what records you want to print and in what order. You want to query the database to print letters for only those customers who have not yet received their new credit cards. To do this,

Select: Some
Choose: Next >

The next screen contains a list box that displays the fields in the selected database. To query the database on the Card Mailed field,

Select: Card Mailed

The comparison "is equal to" is acceptable for this query. To find the records that contain "No,"

Click: third text box
or
Press: Tab (2 times)

Type: No
Choose: Next >

This screen asks you if you want to sort the records. Because of the small number of records in the database, you do not need to sort the records.

Select: No sort, thanks
Choose: Next >

To exit WorksWizard,

Choose: Done

Your screen should be similar to Figure 12-19.

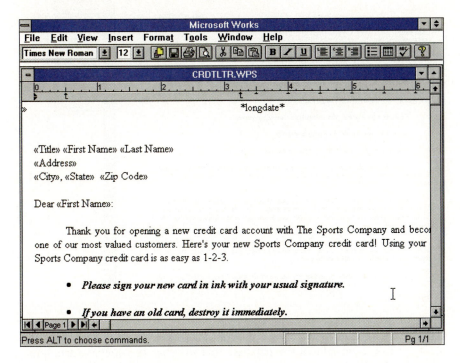

FIGURE 12-19

The form letter with placeholders is displayed again. Now you can edit the file like any other file. You can delete, copy, and move the placeholders if necessary. You can also enter placeholders directly into the word processing document using the Database Field command on the Insert menu. This command displays a dialog box of field names from which you select. The placeholder is entered at the location of the insertion point in the document.

Once all the placeholders that are needed in the form letter are correctly entered, the file should be saved.

Save the file as CUSTFORM.

To preview the form letters before printing them,

Choose: File>Print Preview

or

Click: 🔍 Print Preview

From the Choose Database dialog box, you need to specify the database file to be used in the creation of the form letter.

Select: CUSTOMER.WDB
Choose: OK

Zoom the window.

Your screen should be similar to Figure 12-20.

field contents
replace
placeholders

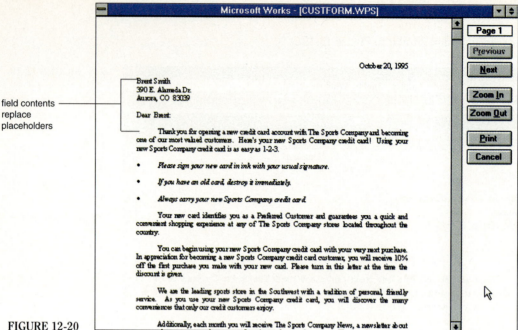

FIGURE 12-20

The first personalized form letter is displayed. The letter includes the name and address of the first customer in the database that matches the query instructions. Two records in the database matched the query instructions.

Choose Next to preview the second form letter, which contains your name and address information. The letters look good and you want to print them.

If necessary, prepare your printer to print.

Choose: Print

Now that the form letters have been completed for the two new preferred credit card holders, you need to change the Card Mailed field data for these records to Yes.

Switch to the CUSTOMER.WDB window. Change the Card Mailed field data in the two displayed records to Yes. Then display all records (View>Show All Records). Save the file. Close the file.

Now each time you need to send a new credit card, all you need to do is enter the data for the customer into the database file with the Card Mailed field as No. Then you need to create and apply the query. The query only needs to be created if another query was used since this query. Although the current query settings are saved with the database file, new query settings replace existing settings.

If necessary, to avoid creating the query again you can name the query using the Create New Query command as you learned in Lab 10, or you can use the Data Finder WorksWizard. Data Finder steps through the same query creation steps as in that section of the Form Letter WorksWizard.

To review, the steps in creating a customized form letter are:

1. Create the database file. It will contain the fields of data or information needed to complete the form letter.

2. Create the form letter file by entering placeholders in the document to tell Works where and what fields of information to use from the database file. You can use the Form Letter WorksWizard to enter placeholders and specify a query, or you can perform each step individually directly in the word processing and database files. Then save the form letter document file.

3. Apply the query to display only the records in the database file you want form letters printed for. Use the Print command to combine the form letter and database file to create a customized document for each displayed record in the database file.

Creating a Form Letter Template

Finally, you realize that you can use the same letter style with different information in the body for all letters sent to The Sports Company customers. Then you will not need to redesign the form letter layout each time. As with the Spreadsheet tool, any document you use over and over for similar tasks can be saved in a special template file. Works supplies many template files for use in the different tools, or you can create your own.

You want to delete the body of this document and save the form letter layout as a template. Then you can simply create the body using the template format. This will save having to enter form letter placeholders again.

Delete the body of the letter.

Then you will enter instructions for other users of the template file.

If necessary, insert several blank lines below the salutation.

To enter the instructions, on the second line below the salutation,

Type: **Replace the text in the body of this letter with the information you want. Save the new file using a new file name.**

Your screen should be similar to Figure 12-21.

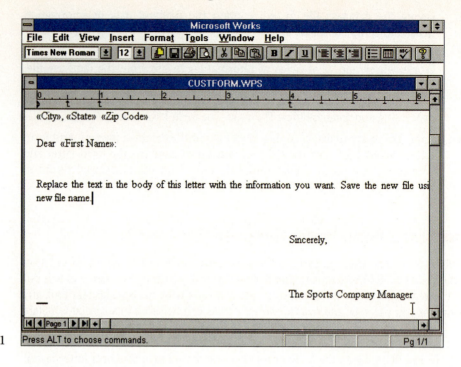

FIGURE 12-21

To save this file as a template,

Choose: File>Save As>Template

The Save As Template dialog box prompts you to enter the name for the template file.

> A template file name can be up to 18 characters long. It can also contain spaces.

Type: **FORM LETTER**
Choose: OK

Close the CUSTFORM file without saving the changes you made.
    You are returned to the Startup dialog box.

Choose: Cancel

Then to use the template file,

Choose: File>Templates

The Template Startup dialog box is used to select the template file you want to use. The template you created is a custom template. To open this category of templates, from the Choose a Template group drop-down list box,

Select: Custom

The Choose a Template list box displays the template name. since it is the only custom template file on your data disk, it is already selected. To open it,

Choose: OK

The template file is open. To use this file, you would enter the body of the letter and print the letter using the field data from the CUSTOMER database file (or any other database file that has the same field names). You can save the revised template document as a new document, or you can close it without saving it.

Enter your name on the line above The Sports Company Manager in the closing. Print a copy of the form letter template using the Print command. (Clear the Print Merger option in the Print dialog box.) Close the file without saving the changes you have made.

All template files supplied with Works can be used by selecting the template and following the instructions included in the file.

Exit Works.

Key Terms

modem (405)
communications file (405)
port (405)
buffer (410)
protocol (410)
form letter (411)

Command Summary

Command	Button	Action
Insert>**C**hart		Inserts a chart
Forma**t**>Pict**u**re/Object		Adjusts spacing and size of object
Settings>**P**hone	🖼	Displays phone number settings for communication between computers
Edit>**P**aste Text		Pastes text into a communication document
Settings>**T**ransfer	🖼	Displays protocol settings
Use A Wor**k**sWizard>Form Letter		Creates a personalized form letter

LAB REVIEW

Matching

1. <<City>>   ____   a. temporary memory storage area
2. form letter   ____   b. port address
3. Insert>Chart   ____   c. steps through common tasks
4. WorksWizard   ____   d. device used to send data through phone lines
5. modem   ____   e. example of database field data placeholder
6. COM1   ____   f. a standard letter sent to many people
7. buffer   ____   g. file extension for a communications file
8. template   ____   h. set of procedures used to transfer a file
9. protocol   ____   i. inserts a chart into a word processor file
10. WCM   ____   j. a master document used to create other documents

Practice Exercises

1. In this problem you will create a new word processing file. You will enter the text as directed and then you will copy a spreadsheet and chart from the file LAND.WKS, from Practice Exercise 2 in Lab 8, into the document.

   a. Enter the following text into a new word processing document:

      The leasing cost per acre for federal and private lands continues to increase every year. The following data shows the average cost of leasing both federal and private land for the years 1975 through 1990.

   b. Copy the spreadsheet LAND.WKS you created in Practice Exercise 2 in Lab 8 below this paragraph. Make any editing adjustments necessary. Separate the spreadsheet data from the text above and below it with two blank lines.

   c. Enter the following text below the spreadsheet data:

      The line chart below shows the change in the average cost of leasing federal and private lands from 1975 through 1990.

   d. Below this sentence, insert the line chart LANDLINE you created from the spreadsheet LAND.WKS. Size the chart appropriately. Adjust the spacing of the document so that it completely fills one page.

   e. Set the left and right margins to 1 inch. Add a header displaying your name and the current date.

   f. Save the word processor file as LAND.

   g. Preview and print the document. Close all open files.

2.   In this problem you will create a new word processor file. You will enter the text as directed in the problem and copy a spreadsheet and chart from the file CANDYBAR.WKS created in Lab 8, Practice Exercise 5.

   a.   Enter the following text into a new word processor document:

   Almost 40 percent of the United States market share for the candy industry is held by two companies, Hershey and Mars. The remaining 60 percent is held by other companies. The market shares for the 1994 candy industry are shown in the table below.

   b.   Copy the spreadsheet you created named CANDYBAR.WKS in Practice Exercise 5 of Lab 8 below this paragraph. Make any editing adjustments necessary. Separate the spreadsheet data from the text with two blank lines.

   c.   Enter the following text below the spreadsheet data:

   The pie chart below shows the percentage each company holds of the total market share.

   d.   Insert the pie chart CANDYPIE from the spreadsheet CANDYBAR below this sentence.

   e.   Add a header displaying your name and the current date.

   f.   Save the word processing file as CANDY.

   g.   Preview the document. Print the file. Close all files.

3.   In this problem you will create a form letter. You will enter the letter into a new word processor document and use the fields of information in the database file TECHEMP.WBD.

   a.   Open the database file TECHEMP.WBD. Add four appropriate fields to hold the employee address information. Add address information of your choice to all records whose starting date is before 1980 (use Find or Query to locate these records). Use your name in one of the records.

   b.   In a new word processing document enter the body of the letter and closing shown below:

   According to our records you have been an employee of the TechPower Distribution Company since [you will insert a date placeholder here]. We would like to confirm this date so that we can order anniversary gifts for the upcoming awards banquet. Please call the employment office at 555-2932 if this date is incorrect.
   Thank you very much for your prompt attention to this matter and we will see you at the banquet.

   Sincerely,

   [Your Name]

    c.   Save the word processing file as AWARDS.

    d.   Use the WorksWizard to create a form letter that includes the employees' names and addresses along with a salutation style that includes the first name. The letter is to be sent only to employees who started working before 1980.

    e.   Use the Insert Database field command to enter a placeholder for the Year Started field in the appropriate location in the letter.

    f.   Save the form letter as EMPLET. Preview the form letters. Print only the first form letter that matches the query condition. Close all open files.

4.   In this problem you will create a form letter. You will enter the letter into a new word processor document and use the fields of information in the database file NAME&ADD that you created in Practice Exercise 4 of Lab 11.

    a.   Enter a three-paragraph letter that can be sent to the people you entered in the NAME&ADD database in Lab 11. Make the letter specific to an upcoming event such as a workshop, company picnic, or retirement dinner. Save and close the document.

    b.   Use the WorksWizard to create a form letter that includes the name and address along with a salutation that includes the first name. The letter is to be sent to all people in the database.

    c.   Preview the form letter. Print the form letter that displays your name.

    d.   Save the form letter file as PERLETER. Close all files.

5.   Works includes many WorksWizards. They can all be used in a similar manner to the procedure demonstrated in this lab.

    a.   Open the WorksWizard to create a Home Inventory database.

    b.   Follow the instructions to create a Home Inventory that contains any or all of the available features. (*Note:* any item you select in the Add Field window will be entered on the database form.)

    c.   Enter eight records in the Home Inventory database.

    d.   Print the last record in Form view.

    e.   Save the database as HOMEINV. Close the file.

Works 3.0 for Windows

Glossary of Key Terms

absolute cell reference: In a formula, a cell address that includes a $ character before the column letter or row number or both, making the cell address remain the same (absolute) when copied.

active cell: The cell that is highlighted.

active field: The field containing the insertion point. It is the field that will be affected by your actions.

active pane: The pane that is affected by your next action.

active record: The record that is currently selected.

active window: The window you can work in. It is identified by a highlighted title bar, the cursor, and scroll bars.

alignment: The placement of a label within the cell space. A label can be left, centered, or right aligned.

area chart: Type of chart that emphasizes the sum of plotted values and separates each value (Y) series into distinct bands to show the differences among series.

argument: Specifies the data the function uses to perform the calculation.

arithmetic operators: Used in numeric formulas to calculate a value.

automatic recalculation: The recalculation of a formula in the spreadsheet whenever a value in a referenced cell in the formula changes.

bar chart: Displays data as a series of bars emphasising comparisons.

bold: Printed text that appears darker than surrounding text.

buffer: A temporary storage area in the computer's memory that stores text. Text transmitted via a modem.

bullet: A large dot or other symbol that is used to call attention to text.

category labels: Labels used to describe the X axis.

category series: The spreadsheet range that contains the category labels.

cell: The space created by the intersection of a vertical column and a horizontal row.

cell reference: The unique name of each cell, consisting of the column letter and row number.

chart: A visual representation of numeric data.

chart window: Second window created to display a chart.

circular reference: A formula in a cell that directly or indirectly references itself.

click: To press and release the mouse button without moving the mouse.

column: A vertical block of cells one cell wide in the spreadsheet.

column letters: The border of letters across the top of the spreadsheet area that identifies each column in the spreadsheet.

column width: The number of characters that the cells in a column can display.

combination chart: Chart that display bars and lines.

communications: A type of program that sends and receives information to and from another computer.

communications file: A file that accesses the communications tool of Works.

comparison operator: A symbol used in expressions that allows you to make comparisons. The > (greater than) and < (less than) symbols are examples of comparison operators.

context-sensitive: The ability of the Help system to display information about the current task or command you are performing.

copy: To duplicate the contents of a cell or cells in other worksheet cells.

cpi (characters per inch): The number of characters that fit in one inch.

current drive: The drive the program will access to open and save files.

criteria: A variety of conditions that help to locate groups of records.

data labels: Numbers that identify the exact values being plotted on a chart.

database: An organized collection of related information.

database window: Area beneath the database toolbars where values and labels are entered.

date entry: Numeric entries in a spreadsheet that are interpreted by Works as a date.

default: Settings automatically provided by Microsoft Works.

destination: The cell or cells into which the copied data is pasted.

dialog box: A window that displays the current command settings and from which you can select and change command options.

document window: A window that displays an open document file in the workspace.

double-click: To press the mouse button twice in rapid succession.

drag: To press and hold down the mouse button while moving the mouse pointer to a new location on the screen.

drag-and-drop: Feature that allows you to move selected text with the mouse without selecting Cut and Paste or Copy and Paste from the menu.

edit: To revise or correct text in a document.

end-of-file mark: The solid horizontal line below the last line in the document that marks the end of the document.

explode: To separate slightly a slice of a pie chart from the other slices in the pie.

field: A collection of related characters, such as a person's name.

field contents: The specific data contained in a field.

field entry: The information entered to complete each field of data.

field height: The number of lines needed to display the field entry.

field name: Title associated with each field in a database.

field width: The size of the column for a field in List view.

font: The different type sizes and styles that can be selected to improve the appearance of a document.

footer: Text that appears at the bottom of every page.

footnote: A note of reference in a document displayed at the bottom of the page where the reference occurs.

form: Displays field names and blank entry areas for entry of data into a database.

Form view: The database view that displays one record at a time in the window.

format: The display of numeric values in a spreadsheet.

formula: A mathematical expression that yields a numeric value based on the relationship between two or more cells in the spreadsheet.

formula bar: Line below the menu bar that displays the characters as you enter them into a spreadsheet.

freeze: To hold in place on the screen specified rows or columns or both when scrolling.

function: A built-in formula that performs a calculation automatically.

gridlines: Lines that extend horizontally or vertically across a chart.

handles: Small boxes surrounding a selected object.

header: Text that appears at the top of every page.

Headings row: Information in these rows appear at the beginning of each page of the report.

highlight: The dark border around a spreadsheet cell, indicating the active cell.

highlighting: Selecting text with the keyboard or mouse.

insertion point: The blinking vertical line that marks your location on the line.

integrated program: Software that combines two or more types of application programs. Works combines word processing, spreadsheet, database, and communication application programs.

italics: Printed text that appears slanted.

label: In Form view, any descriptive text that appears in every record.

landscape: Prints the document across the length of the page.

legend: A brief description of the chart symbols that represent the data ranges.

line chart: Displays data as a set of points along a line.

List view: The database view that displays multiple records at a time in the window.

logical operators: The operators And and Or used in database queries.

long entry: A text entry in a spreadsheet that extends beyond the width of the cell it is entered in.

manual page break: A page break that instructs Works to begin a new page regardless of the amount of text on the preceding page.

margins: The blank areas between the edges of the paper and the printed text.

maximize/restore button: Button on the right side of the title bar that alters the size of the current window.

menu bar: The second line of the Works application window. It displays the names of the menus that can be opened.

minimal recalculation: The recalculation of only the formulas in a spreadsheet that are affected by a change of data.

minimize button: Button on the right side of the title bar that reduces the size of the current window.

mixed cell reference: In a formula, cell address that is part absolute and part relative.

modem: A device that enables one computer to communicate directly with another computer using telephone lines.

monospaced: A font that uses the same amount of space for every character.

mouse pointer: A symbol on the screen that is controlled by the mouse and is used to select items on the screen.

multilevel sort: When a file is sorted on more than one sort field.

navigator buttons: Four buttons located at the left end of the horizontal scroll bar in the word processing document window that are used with a mouse to move to the next or previous page or the beginning or end of a document.

numeric entry: A spreadsheet entry that includes only the numbers 0 to 9, and any of the special characters, + - ( ) , . $ %.

option button: In a dialog box, round buttons in which a dot marks the selected option.

optional hyphen: A hyphen inserted by the program to make the right margin more even.

order of precedence: In a formula that contains more than one operator, the specific order in which Works performs the calculation.

page break symbol: The >> symbol displayed at the top of each page in a word processing document window.

page indicator: Displays the page number of the document on which the insertion point is located.

pane: The division of the window into two parts to allow viewing of separate areas of the document at the same time.

paragraph mark: A special character entered by the program whenever ⏎Enter is pressed.

personal dictionary: Dictionary you can create to hold words you use commonly but that are not included in the Houghton-Mifflin dictionary that is supplied with the program.

pie chart: A chart that compares parts to the whole. Each value in the data range is a slice of the pie (circle).

placeholder: A marker inserted by Works that instructs the program to insert text (for example, a date) in the selected format.

point: To move the mouse until the mouse pointer rests on what you want to point to on the screen.

pointing: Selecting a spreadsheet cell instead of typing the cell reference.

points: Measurement of type sizes. One point equals approximately 1/72 inch.

port: The connector between a computer and a modem.

portrait: Prints a document across the width of the page.

preselect: To select a spreadsheet range before choosing a command.

proportional: A font that varies the amount of horizontal space given to each character.

protocol: A set of communication procedures used to transfer files between computers.

query: A search command used in a database to find records that meet selected criteria.

query instructions: The conditions that instruct Works to locate the records specified in the query.

query sentence: The full sentence that queries use to sort data.

Query view: A blank version of a database form that is used to enter information.

range: A single cell or any rectangular group of adjoining cells in the spreadsheet.

range reference: One of the arguments required by a function. May include numbers, cell references, cell ranges, formulas, or a combination of these, each separated by a comma.

record: A group of related fields in a database.

record number: A number assigned by Works to each record in a database.

Record row: Prints one entry for each record in the report.

relative cell reference: A cell address in a formula that automatically adjusts to its new location in a spreadsheet when the formula is copied or moved.

report: A way of grouping database records.

Report Definition view: Specifies the database records to be included in a report.

resize handles: The squares surrounding an object when it is selected.

row: A horizontal block of cells one cell high in the spreadsheet.

row numbers: The border of numbers along the left side of the spreadsheet area that identifies each row in the spreadsheet.

row types: Control the information displayed on each row of a report.

ruler: The bar below the menu bar in the word processor document window that displays the line length, tables, indents, and margins.

scalable: A font that can be printed in nearly any point size.

scrolling: To move quickly line by line, screen by screen, or page by page through the document.

serial number: Numbers assigned to each day between January 1, 1900 and June 3, 2079.

shortcut key: A key or key combination that can be used for common commands instead of selecting the command from a menu.

soft space: A space automatically entered by Works to properly align the text on a single line.

sort field: Field used to arrange the records in a database.

source: The cell or cells containing the data to be copied.

spreadsheet: A type of program that arranges data and formulas in cells; used for financial planning, budgeting, and record keeping.

Spreadsheet window: Area used to display a spreadsheet.

stacked-bar chart: Displays data values as bars stacked upon one another.

status bar: The bottom line of the Works application window. It displays information specific to the tool you are using.

style: The attributes that can be associated with the typeface, such as bold and italics.

Summary row: Used to display summary statistics for each column of data in a report.

syntax: The structure or format for entering a function.

tab dialog box: Dialog box in which tab settings can be altered.

template: A prewritten blank document that is used repeatedly to enter data.

text entry: A spreadsheet entry that describes the spreadsheet's contents.

Thesaurus: Lists synonyms for a word in a word processing file and allows the replacement of the word with the synonym.

time entry: Numeric entries in a spreadsheet that are interpreted by Works as time.

title: In the spreadsheet tool, a descriptive label that identifies the contents of a chart or the X and Y axes.

title bar: The top line of a window, which displays the name of the window.

Title row: Used to enter the report title, which appears on the first page of the report only.

titles: Descriptive labels that identify a file or name a report.

toolbar: Provides mouse shortcuts for many commonly used commands.

tool: Complete word processing, spreadsheet, database, and communication software packages that are integrated in Works.

value series: A group of related data plotted on a chart.

what-if analysis: A technique used to evaluate the effects of changing certain values in the spreadsheet.

word processor: A type of program that allows for storage, editing, and manipulating of text data.

wordwrap: Feature that automatically determines when to begin the next line of text. The user does not press ⏎Enter at the end of a line unless it is the end of a paragraph or to insert a blank line.

workspace: Area of the screen where documents are displayed.

X-axis: The horizontal axis of a chart.

X and Y coordinates: The measurement of position (horizontal and vertical) in a database window.

Y-axis: The vertical axis of a chart.

Summary of Selected Works 3.0 for Windows Commands

Command	Shortcut	Button	Action
All Tools			
File>Create **N**ew File			Opens Startup dialog box
File>**O**pen Existing File			Opens an existing file
File>**W**orksWizard>Form Letter			Creates a personalized form letter
File>**C**lose			Closes file
File>**S**ave	Ctrl + S	🖫	Saves current file using same file name
File>Save **A**s			Saves file using new file name
File>Save **A**s>Temp**l**ate			Saves a file as a template
File>Page Setup			Changes printing options
File>Page Setup>**M**argins			Changes left, right, top, and bottom margins
File>Page Setup>**S**ource, Size, and Orientation>**L**andscape			Prints document sideways across the length of the page
File>Page Setup>**O**ther Options> Full page, **K**eep proportions			Sets document layout to a full page, keeping proportions
File>Print Pre**v**iew		🔍	Displays file as it will appear when printed
File>**P**rint	Ctrl + P	🖨	Prints file using selected printer
File>E**x**it Works			Exits Works
Edit>U**n**do Editing	Ctrl + Z		Reverses most recent editing or formatting changes
Edit>**R**edo Editing	Ctrl + Z		Reverses Undo
Edit>Cu**t**	Ctrl + X	✂	Cuts selected text and places it in Clipboard
Edit>**C**opy	Ctrl + C	📋	Copies selected text to Clipboard
Edit>**P**aste	Ctrl + V	📋	Pastes text from Clipboard
Edit>Cl**e**ar	Delete		Deletes contents of selected range
Edit>Select **A**ll	F8 (5 times)		Highlights all text
Edit>**F**ind			Locates record that matches instruction
Edit>Re**p**lace			Locates and replaces specified text or codes
Edit>**G**o To	F5		Moves to specified location
View>**Z**oom			Magnifies or shrinks display of text on screen
View>**H**eaders and Footers			Adds headers and footers
Insert>Page **B**reak			Inserts manual page break
Forma**t**>**F**ont and Style			Changes appearance of characters on printed page
Forma**t**>**F**ont and Style>**B**old	Ctrl + B	**B**	Changes selected text to bold
Forma**t**>**F**ont and Style>**I**talic	Ctrl + I	*I*	Changes selected text to italics
Forma**t**>**B**order			Adds borders to text

Command	Shortcut	Button	Action
Format>**B**order>**O**utline			Adds outline to selected text
Format>**B**order>**B**ottom			Adds border to bottom edge of selected range
T**o**ols>**S**pelling			Turns on Spelling Checker application
Window>**T**ile			Displays windows side-by-side
Window>**S**plit			Splits window into panes
Window>**#**<file name>	Ctrl + F6		Makes selected window active
Help>**S**earch for Help on			Searches for help on any command or feature

Word Processing Tool

Command	Shortcut	Button	Action
View>**P**age Layout			Displays document as it will appear when printed
View>Wra**p** for Window			Displays text so lines do not extend beyond window
View>**A**ll Characters			Displays special characters
View>**F**ootnotes			Displays/hides footnote pane
Insert>**S**pecial Character>Print lo**n**g date			Inserts placeholder for current date maintained by computer system
Insert>**S**pecial Character>**C**urrent Date			Inserts current date
Insert>**F**ootnote			Adds footnote to text
Insert>**C**hart			Inserts a chart
Insert>**W**ordArt			Displays text in a different shape
Insert>Draw**i**ng			Adds drawing to text
Format>**P**aragraph>**Q**uick Formats>**B**ulleted			Inserts bullets into document
Format>**P**aragraph>**I**ndents and Alignment			Changes indents and alignment of text
Left	Ctrl + L		Left-aligns selection
Center	Ctrl + E		Center-aligns selection
Right	Ctrl + R		Right-aligns selection
Justified	Ctrl + J		Aligns selection even with both left and right margins
Format>**P**aragraph>**Q**uickFormats>Han**g**ing Indent			Indents all lines of paragraph except first line
Format>**P**aragraph>Breaks and **S**pacing >Keep paragraph **w**ith next			Keeps related text together on a page
Format>**T**abs			Specifies alignment and position of tab stops
Format>**C**olumns			Displays text in columns
Format>Pict**u**re/Object			Adjusts spacing and size of an object
T**o**ols>**T**hesaurus			Turns on Thesaurus application
T**o**ols>**H**yphenation			Hyphenates text

Command	Shortcut	Button	Action
Spreadsheet Tool			
Edit>Fill Ri**gh**t			Copies selected cell contents to adjacent cells to right
Edit>F**i**ll Series			Automatically fills any number of cells with a series of numbers or dates
View>**C**hart			Displays a chart
View>**S**preadsheet			Returns to Spreadsheet view from Chart view
Insert>**R**ow/Column			Inserts a blank row or column
Insert>**F**unction>SUM	Ctrl + M	Σ	Totals all numbers in range reference
Forma**t**>**N**umber>**C**urrency		$	Displays numbers with dollar signs
Forma**t**>**N**umber>**P**ercent			Displays numbers followed by a % sign
Forma**t**>**N**umber>**D**ate			Displays number as date
Forma**t**>**A**lignment>**R**ight	Ctrl + R		Right-aligns selected cells
Forma**t**>**A**lignment>Center **a**cross selection			Centers cell contents across preselected cells
Forma**t**>**P**atterns and Colors			Changes color, pattern, and markers for specified value series
Forma**t**>AutoFor**m**at			Formats spreadsheet to one of 14 built-in table formats
Forma**t**>**S**et Print Area			Restricts area to print to selected area
Forma**t**>Freeze **T**itles			Freezes titles to top and left of active cell
Forma**t**>Column **W**idth			Changes width of columns
Forma**t**>Column **W**idth>**B**estFit			Changes width of columns so largest entry is displayed
T**o**ols>**C**reate New Chart			Creates a new chart from preselected range of data
T**o**ols>**N**ame Chart			Names current chart
Chart View			
File>Page Set**u**p>**O**ther Options> Full Page>Keep Proportions			Sets chart layout to a full page, keeping proportions
Edit>Select Title Te**x**t	Ctrl + T		Selects chart title
Edit>**S**eries			Adds value series to chart
Edit>**T**itles			Adds titles to chart
Edit>**D**ata Labels			Adds data labels to chart
View>Display as **P**rinted			Displays chart as it will appear when printed
Gallery>**A**rea			Changes chart type to area
Gallery>**B**ar			Changes chart type to bar
Gallery>**L**ine			Changes chart type to line
Gallery>**P**ie			Changes chart type to pie
Gallery>3-D P**i**e			Changes chart type to 3-D pie
Forma**t**>**P**atterns and Colors>**E**xplode Slice			Explodes selected data series slice
Forma**t**>**V**ertical [Y]Axis>Show **G**ridlines			Displays gridlines
Forma**t**>**M**ixed Line and Bar			Creates chart with lines and bars

Command	Shortcut	Button	Action
Database Tool			
Edit>Select Fiel**d**			Selects entire field
Edit>Field **N**ame			Enters or renames field name in List view
Edit>Posi**t**ion Selection			Moves field in Form view
View>**F**orm	F9	▥	Displays records in Form view
View>**L**ist	F9	▤	Displays records in List view
View>Query		▣	Locates records meeting query criteria
View>Show **A**ll Records			Displays all records
View>S**w**itch Hidden Records			Displays hidden records
Insert>**R**ecord/Field			Inserts record or field in List view
Insert>**D**elete Record/Field			Removes record or field in List view
Insert>**F**ield			Inserts field in List view
Insert>Field **S**ummary			Adds or changes group summary statistics
Forma**t**>**N**umber>**Le**ading Zeroes			Displays zeroes at beginning of numbers
Forma**t**>Field **W**idth			Changes width of fields
Forma**t**>Field **W**idth>**B**est Fit			Changes field width to size of largest entry
Forma**t**>Field Si**z**e			Changes field size
T**o**ols>So**r**t Records			Rearranges records in order specified
T**o**ols>**C**reate New Query			Opens Query dialog box
T**o**ols>N**a**me Report			Names report settings
T**o**ols>Create **N**ew Report			Creates a new report
Communications Tool			
Edit>**P**aste Text			Pastes text into a communication document
Settings>**P**hone		▦	Displays phone number settings
Settings>T**r**ansfer		▦	Displays protocol settings
Microsoft Draw			
File>**I**mport Picture			Opens an existing picture
File>E**x**it & Return to <filename>			Exits Draw